```
301.45    McWilliams,
M            North from Mexico
             OL00188240
  c 1
  Date Due
```

OC 27 70	MY 23 06		
JA 17 72			
JCarrie			
AP 18 72			
JGarcia			
MR 27			
OC 8 '74			
MY 6 75			
6-26-75 Valley			
DICKERS			
MY 22 '92			

BRODART Printed in U.S.A.

NORTH FROM MEXICO

North from Mexico

THE SPANISH-SPEAKING PEOPLE OF THE UNITED STATES

by

CAREY McWILLIAMS

With an Introduction to the
Greenwood Reprint Edition
by the Author

GREENWOOD PRESS, PUBLISHERS
NEW YORK   1968

Copyright, 1948, by Carey McWilliams

Reprinted with the permission of Carey McWilliams.

First Greenwood reprinting, 1968

LIBRARY OF CONGRESS catalogue card number: 68-28595

Printed in the United States of America

FOR IRIS. . . .

FOREWORD

Titles have always bothered me and never more so than in selecting a title for this book. My assignment was to tell the story of Spanish-speaking people in the United States; or, as Louis Adamic put it, "the story of those who came from Spain and Mexico." But how is one to characterize, in a phrase, a people so diverse in origin? An ethnic group has been defined as a people living competitively in relationship of superordination or subordination with respect to some other people or peoples within one state, country, or economic area. In this sense there can be no doubt that the Spanish-speaking constitute a clearly delineated ethnic group. But one must also recognize that there is no more heterogeneous ethnic group in the United States than the Spanish-speaking. Hence it is quite impossible to hit upon a phrase that aptly characterizes all the people now living in this country who by national origin, appearance, speech, or background might be called, and probably are called, "Mexican" or "Mexican-American."

Any phrase selected to characterize the Spanish-speaking will necessarily prove to be misleading, inaccurate, or possibly libelous. If there is a generally accepted usage it is to be found in the phrase "Spanish-speaking," but many people speak Spanish who cannot be identified with the Spanish-speaking group. Besides, the people who are generically Spanish-speaking are more Indian in racial origin, and perhaps in culture, than they are Spanish. "Latin-American" is vague and euphemistic; "Spanish-American" detracts from the importance of the Mexican and Indian heritage; while "Mexican-American" implies a certain condescension.

I was told that "Americans From Mexico" would be an appropriate title. But, strictly speaking, the Spanish-language minority did not come from Spain and Mexico; they were already very much a part of the landscape when the Anglo-Americans came to the Southwest. Basically the difficulty in nomenclature arises from the fact that the Spanish-speaking represent a fusion of Spanish, Mexican, and Indian heritages, both racially and culturally, and in every possible combination and mixture. The Spanish strain, as Mary Austin once observed, has chiefly served "to mollify temperamentally the aboriginal strain" and is therefore perhaps the least significant element in the heritage of the people. In the Southwest, the Spanish-speaking stand midway between the Indians and the Anglo-Americans, a people whose culture represents a fusion of Indian and non-Indian elements. While it is possible, of course, to distinguish between Indian-Spanish and Anglo-American elements in the culture of the Spanish-speaking, it is well-nigh impossible to label any one trait "Indian" or "Spanish" or "Mexican."

Since two or more ethnic groups constitute an ethnic system, one ethnic always implies the existence of another. In most portions of the Southwest, the term "Anglo" is used as a catchall expression to designate all persons who are neither Mexican nor Indian, while the term "Hispano" is used to designate the Spanish-speaking. In essence, therefore, the terms "Anglo" and "Hispano" are the heads and the tails of a single coin, a single ethnic system; each term has meaning only as the other is implied. The terms do not define homogeneous entities; they define a relationship. For the term "Anglo" is essentially as meaningless as the term "Hispano": it embraces all the elements in the population that are *not* Spanish-speaking. Thus a Jew is an "Anglo" in the Southwest and so is a Japanese or a Chinese. Erna Fergusson even tells of a Negro in Albuquerque who, in conversation with an Anglo-American, referred to "us Anglos."

The dichotomy implied in the terms "Anglo" and "Hispano," however, is real enough, no matter how vague either term may be as descriptive of the heterogeneous elements making up the two categories. The reality of this cleavage is to be found in the social history of the Southwest (much of which has been forgotten); and in the nature of the region. No matter how sharply the Spanish-speaking may differ among themselves over the question of nomenclature, the sense of cleavage from or opposition to the Anglos has always been an important factor in their lives and it is this feeling which gives cohesion to the group. The sense of group identity also arises from the fact that the Spanish-speaking have had a similar history and experience and have been influenced by a similar relationship to a sharply differentiated environment. "The race is not to the swift," wrote D. H. Lawrence, "but to those who sit still and let the waves go over them." Waves and still more waves have passed over the Spanish-speaking people, but they are still as firmly rooted in the Southwest as a forest of Joshua trees. In part, therefore, the difference between "Anglo" and "Hispano" relates to a difference in the degree of attachment to, and identification with, a most compulsive environment. The Spanish-speaking have an identification with the Southwest which can never be broken. They are not interlopers or immigrants but an indigenous people. As a consequence, they resent, and will always resent, any designation which implies a hyphenated relationship to their native environment and particularly so when this designation is applied by Anglo-American interlopers and immigrants. This sense of identification with the environment is most complex for it relates back to a memory of things Spanish. Mary Austin once suggested the real basis for this feeling when she said that the area of Spanish exploration north of the Rio Grande was substantially coterminous with the "cactus country": the Spanish travelled as far, but only as far, as the gypsy of the cactus family, the prickly-pear, had travelled. Did they stop where they did because the environment had ceased to be familiar? Whatever the reason, it is important to remember that geographically the Southwest is one with Mexico.

Obviously a title should characterize its subject; but just what, I asked, is the subject of this book? The people that constitute its subject are a product of their history, of the struggles and conflicts which have taken place in the Southwest. "Man is not himself only," as Mrs. Austin wrote, "not solely a variation of his racial type in the pattern of his immediate experience. He is all that he sees; all that flows to him from a thousand sources, half noted, or noted not at all except by some sense that lies too deep for naming." Hence the Southwest, as a sharply delineated region, is very much a part of the story of Spanish-speaking people in America. And so are the relationships which have emerged out of conflicts between Anglos and Hispanos in the region. But to emphasize these relationships or the region itself in the title would be to shift attention from the people, their origins and ordeals, their struggles and experiences.

And so, in the end, I was driven to the conclusion that the title would have to refer to a process, a movement, a point on the compass. For it is the direction in which the people have moved that has given unity to their lives; it is the point on the compass that has remained fixed and constant. The Spanish-speaking in the United States, whatever their origin, have moved "North from Mexico" and this is still the lodestar in their horizon. Whether born in Spain or Mexico, the ancestors of the present-day Spanish-speaking people of the Southwest came "North from Mexico" along the same trails from similar points of origin to similar destinations. Furthermore the phrase implies the extension of a way of life rather than a crossing or a jumping of barriers which, in this case, are non-existent. It also suggests a oneness of experience if not of blood or language or ancestry; a similar movement within a similar environment.

Invited to visit Santa Fe in 1883, Walt Whitman wrote to "Messrs. Griffin, Martínez and Prince and other gentlemen" that he must decline the invitation but would "say a few words off-hand." After first pointing out that the "states" showed too much of the British and German influence, he went on to say: "The seething materialistic and business vortices of the United States, in their present devouring relations, controlling and belittling everything else, are, in my opinion, but a vast and indispensable stage in the new world's development. . . . Character, literature, a society worthy the name, are yet to be establish'd. . . . To that composite American identity of the future," he concluded, "Spanish character will supply some of the most needed parts. No stock shows a grander historic retrospect—grander in religiousness and loyalty, or for patriotism, courage, decorum, gravity and honor." Three of these qualities are ineluctably apposite: "decorum" is one; "gravity" is another; "honor"—broadly construed—is the third. But, like so many of Whitman's catalogues, this one suggests rather than defines and to his roster of qualities one must add a belief in joy and happiness. As Haniel Long has said, "The Spaniard has known as little joy as anybody; but he bravely sees joy as an object of life, and speaks up for it." The charm of the Spanish-speaking people, in the borderlands, in Mexico, and in Spain, is that they have not been molded by modern industrialism; neither the want nor the caste bondage nor the deprivations which they have known has succeeded in destroying their sense of joyous living. They are a people, as Lorca said of the Spanish gypsies, "with their hearts in their heads—*gente con el corazón en la cabeza.*"

While that "composite American identity" is yet to be achieved in the Southwest, it is incontestably true that "Spanish character will supply some of the most needed parts." And it is also true that there is something about the Southwest, as Haniel Long has also said, that "gives to each type of human being more of its rightful chance to survive than is usual." Here identities change slowly; the spacing between peoples gives differences a chance to survive; and what survives has value for it has been severely tested. The naked earth shows through everything that grows in the Southwest and the desert light brings out, with distinctness, the unique character of plants and trees, of rocks and mountain ranges; things are seen sharply, distinctly, for what they are, as they were meant to be. Not only is the environment respectful of differences, but it preserves the unique qualities of the things, the institutions, the people that it permits to survive. The living qualities of "the Spanish character" that one can see in the region today have survived the test of time and can never be obliterated. Indelibly imprinted on the land, they are part of the cultural landscape of the Southwest.

CONTENTS

I. IN SPANISH SADDLEBAGS — 19
    1. The Spanish Prologue— 2. Footnote to the Prologue— 3. The Play-in-Prose— 4. The Climate of Spain

II. THE FANTASY HERITAGE — 35
    1. The Man on the White Horse— 2. The Birth of a Legend— 3. De Anza Doesn't Live Here Any More

III. THE FAN OF SETTLEMENT — 48
    1. "Sunshine, Silence, and Adobe"— 2. The Forgotten Link — 3. Lands of the Spanish-Speaking— 4. Mexico Is Not Europe— 5. The Border of the Borderlands

IV. HEART OF THE BORDERLANDS — 63
    1. A Lost World— 2. The People— 3. The Flowering of New Mexico— 4. After the Conquest

V. THE BROKEN BORDER — 81
    1. Pimeria Alta— 2. The *Tejanos*— 3. The *Californios*— 4. Lost Provinces

VI. "NOT COUNTING MEXICANS" — 98
    1. *Los Diablos Tejanos*— 2. Alas! the Alamo— 3. The Mexican-American War— 4. Slaves and Peons— 5. "Red Robber of the Rio Grande"— 6. "The Dead-Line of Sheriffs" — 7. The Salt War— 8. Open Season on Mexicans

VII. GRINGOS AND GREASERS — 115
    1. The Bloodless Conquest— 2. The Ghost of Father Martínez— 3. Disturbance in Socorro— 4. The Don System— 5. The Buffer State— 6. The Lynching of Juanita— 7. Birth of a Stereotype

VIII. THE HERITAGE OF THE SOUTHWEST — 133
    1. Mr. Marshall's *Chispa*— 2. Comstock's Mistake— 3. The Vermilion Cave— 4. Anglo-Saxon Law and Order— 5. Apaches and Copper— 6. Homage to the *Churro*— 7. *Los Pastores*— 8. From Gregorio de Villalobos— 9. "Ten Gallon Hats"— 10. Cortez Had a Brand— 11. A Drop of Water

IX.	THE BORDERLANDS ARE INVADED	162

1. Spanish Trails, American Rails— 2. Life in a Boxcar— 3. Cotton in Texas— 4. Cotton Moves West— 5. Vitamins and Mexicans— 6. Coyotes and Man-Snatchers— 7. *Los Betabeleros*— 8. In Midwest Industries— 9. The Balance Sheet

X.	THE SECOND DEFEAT	189

1. The Myth of Docility— 2. The Honeymoon Is Over— 3. The Gallup Incident— 4. In the Copper Mines— 5. *La Niña de Cabora*— 6. The Forty Blonde Babies— 7. The Battle of Cananea— 8. "The Wearers of the Red"

XI.	"THE MEXICAN PROBLEM"	206

1. The Structure of the Problem— 2. The Buffer Group— 3. The Conflict in Cultures— 4. The Pattern of Employment— 5. The *Colonia* Complex— 6. The Northern Settlements— 7. *Qué Maravilla!*

XII.	THE PATTERN OF VIOLENCE	227

1. The Case of Sleepy Lagoon— 2. Captain Ayres: Anthropologist— 3. Plotting a Riot— 4. The Origin of *Pachuquismo*

XIII.	BLOOD ON THE PAVEMENTS	244

1. The Taxicab Brigade— 2. Operation "Dixie"— 3. When the Devil is Sick . . .— 4. The Strange Case of the Silk Panties— 5. The Politics of Prejudice

XIV.	THE WAR YEARS	259

1. Joe Martínez and Company— 2. A Tear for José Davilla— 3. Across the Border— 4. *Los Braceros*— 5. The Counterpoint of Migration— 6. Good Neighbors and Band Music

XV.	AFTER A HUNDRED YEARS	275

1. A Beginning Is Made— 2. Grass-Roots Democracy— 3. The Westminster Case— 4. "Utilizable Cultural Residues"— 5. From De Anza to Juan López

XVI.	"ONE AND TOGETHER"	289

1. By Any Other Name— 2. Words That Fit— 3. Neighbors in Isolation— 4. Who Is Being Stubborn?— 5. The Indelible Imprint— 6. "The Sun Has Exploded"

ACKNOWLEDGMENTS	305
NOTES ON SOURCES	307
CHAPTER NOTES	309
INDEX	315

INTRODUCTION

Since *North from Mexico* was first published in 1950, there has been a new burst of interest in Mexican-Americans, which, in large part, has come about as a result of activities and developments for which they themselves are responsible. Historically, the Spanish-speaking have often complained that little is known about them (which is true) and that their problems have received little attention by the larger American public (which is also true). Dr. George Sanchez, a distinguished spokesman for the Spanish-speaking, once referred to them as "an orphan group, the least known, the least sponsored, and the least vocal large minority group in the nation." In the same vein, Representative Edward R. Roybal of California, himself of Mexican-American descent, has said that "the Mexican population of the Southwest... is little known on the East Coast and not much better understood in the Southwest itself." A Mexican-American was quoted in *Newsweek* as saying, "We're the best kept secret in America." But this is certainly no longer the case. Suddenly the nation has discovered Mexican-Americans. Witness the feature stories about them in *The Wall Street Journal* (May 3, 1966), *Newsweek* (May 23, 1966), *Time* (April 28, 1967), *U. S. News & World Report* (June 6, 1966), and other publications. In this introduction to the reprint edition, I have sought to summarize certain important developments since 1950 which account for this new burst of interest and concern.

Without attempting to fix an arbitrary date, it can be said that the Spanish-speaking began to develop a new political awareness and self-consciousness as a minority in the wake of World War II and, more noticeably, since the early 1950's, when the Negro civil rights movement began to emerge. The growing political maturity of Mexican-Americans, which became evident during World War II, was given a powerful impetus in the 1960 Presidential campaign in which *Viva Kennedy* clubs sprang up throughout the Southwest, with the aid and encouragement of the late President Kennedy. This was the first time that the Spanish-speaking vote had figured prominently in a Presidential election. It was this vote, enlarged by an active registration campaign, that probably saved Texas for the Kennedy-Johnson ticket. As a mark of recognition, President Kennedy appointed Raymond Telles, who had served as mayor of El Paso, as United States Ambassador to Costa Rica.

Other developments, at about the same time, helped set the stage for new efforts at self-advancement among the Spanish-speaking. The legislation under which Mexican farm labor had been imported by agreement between that country and the United States was finally permitted to expire in December, 1964. During the years of the labor importation, or *bracero*, program (1942-1964), resident Mexicans had carried on an active agitation against it on the ground that the imported workers constituted a form of unfair labor competition. Once the *bracero* program was terminated and the "wetback" influx had been checked, it became possible, in theory at least, to organize Mexican farm workers. Previously, the annual influx of imported farm workers and "wetbacks" had so thoroughly demoralized the labor market that any thought of organization was unrealistic. The fact that Mexican immigration was placed on a quota basis in 1965 also helped to stabilize the labor market. But there are still many "green card holders," those who live in Mexico but hold permits which make it possible for them to commute to jobs on the American side of the border.

On September 8, 1965, the eight-month-long "grape pickers strike" began in Delano, California, under the brilliant leadership of César Chávez, who, incidentally, had received some training in organizational techniques when he was associated with the Community Service Organization (see p. 279). In no small measure, the success of the strike was due to the manner in which Chávez converted it into a "strike of families" by basing the union structure on the strong Mexican family structure. The strike quickly became a national news story, extensively covered by all the media, and succeeded in winning the support of many church and civic organizations. The culmination of the strike was a long march from Delano to Sacramento—the state capital. The story of the strike, and the march, is told in an excellent pamphlet issued by the Farm Workers Press, entitled *Basta! La Historia de Nuestra Lucha* or *Enough! The Tale of Our Struggle*. A passage from the text, illustrated with superb photographs, reads as follows:

We are conscious of the historical significance of our Pilgrimage. It is clearly evident that our path travels through a valley well known to all Mexican farm workers. We know all of these towns of Delano, Fresno, Madera, Modesto, Stockton and Sacramento, because along this very same road, in this very same valley the Mexican race has sacrificed itself for the last hundred years.

At about the same time that the Delano grape pickers were marching into Sacramento, the Equal Rights Opportunity Commission decided to hold a public hearing in Albuquerque, New Mexico, on March 28, 1966. At this hearing, the entire Mexican-American delegation of fifty or sixty persons walked out in protest against the disinterested, condescending way in which the hearing was being conducted. This walkout has assumed great symbolic importance in the eyes of the "new breed" of Mexican-American leaders. To them it symbolizes the "coming of age," politically and socially, of the Spanish-speaking of the Southwest. They have referred to it as a "second El Grito," a reference to the famous *Grito de Dolores*—"the cry of Dolores"—with which Father Miguel Hidalgo y Costilla launched the revolt against Spain in Dolores, Mexico, on September 16, 1810. The Los Angeles delegates who had walked out of the Albuquerque hearing were honored, as heroes, at a banquet in Los Angeles on April 28, 1966, at which they wore tiny *huaraches* as proud symbols of their participation in the walkout. The walkout had wide repercussions throughout Spanish-speaking communities in the Southwest. Like the strike of the grape pickers at Delano, it was a sign that Mexicans had had "enough."

Then Mexican farm workers in Texas, under the leadership of Eugene Nelson, who had been identified earlier with the Delano activities (see *The Nation,* June 5, 1967, and also the article by Doug Adair, *The Nation,* December 11, 1967), called a strike on June 15, 1966, which, like the California strike, culminated in a long march from the Lower Rio Grande Valley to Corpus Christi and then on to the state capital. This dramatic 400-mile march terminated on September 4, 1966, when forty weary and sun-blackened Mexican farm workers marched into Austin shouting "Huelga!" or "Strike," and drew cheers from 8,000 enthusiastic supporters. "La Marcha," in Texas, is said to have awakened the conscience of the one and a half million Mexicans in that state as nothing has done in their history.

What these recent developments mean—the strikes in California and

Texas and the walkout at Albuquerque—is that the Mexican has resumed his never-entirely-abandoned struggle to achieve dignity, respect, and equality—or, in a word, full citizenship. To no small extent, these activities have been stimulated by, and patterned after, the kinds of marches and demonstrations that Negroes and their allies in the civil rights movement have organized.

Politically the Spanish-speaking vote, if it could ever be properly organized, would be of national significance. Accurate estimates are not possible, but there are probably six million Mexicans in the United States today and perhaps a total of nine or ten million Spanish-speaking, which would include 1.5 million Puerto Ricans in New York, a large Cuban contingent in Florida, quite a few Latin Americans, and, of course, some immigrants from Spain. There has been little contact or interchange between the other Spanish-speaking and the Mexicans of the Southwest, but such contacts are now being established. In estimating the future significance of the Spanish-speaking vote, it should be kept in mind that the young age brackets are heavily represented. Marvin Alisky, for example, estimates that by 1975 the Spanish-speaking may well total twenty million (*The Reporter,* February 9, 1967).

Even today the advances which Mexicans have made politically are quite impressive. Senator Joseph R. Montoya, of New Mexico, and Representatives Edward R. Roybal (30th Congressional District, California), Henry Gonzales (20th Congressional District, Texas), and Eligion De La Garza (15th Congressional District, Texas) serve in Congress. Four Mexican-Americans serve in the Arizona state legislature, one in Colorado, thirty-three in New Mexico, and ten in Texas. But not one Mexican serves in the California state legislature, although there are nearly two million Mexicans in the state—an indication of the extent to which the Spanish-speaking are still unrepresented. Mexicans also serve today on city councils and boards of education, and here and there, one will be found serving as a judge (Judge Cal Córdova of Maricopa County, Arizona) or county commissioner (Albert A. Pena, Jr., in Texas). Mexicans are making political gains all the time, and the White House no longer needs to be reminded that the Spanish-speaking have attained a new political maturity. By way of making amends for the Albuquerque hearing, President Johnson appointed Vicente Ximenes as the first American of Mexican descent to serve on the Equal Employment Opportunity Commission and, in White House ceremonies on June 9, 1967, released the report of a Cabinet committee entitled: "The Mexican American—A New Focus on Opportunity." On this same occasion, the President mentioned some of his recent Spanish-speaking appointments: Raul H. Castro, of Arizona, as Ambassador to El Salvador; Benigno C. Hernandez, of New Mexico, as Ambassador to Paraguay; followed by a long listing of Mexican-Americans recently appointed to various federal positions.

This growing political influence of the Spanish-speaking reflects new educational and economic gains and the rise of a new middle class. Among Mexican males in the Southwest today, some 29,229 are engaged in professional, technical, and similar work, either as employees or as self-employed persons: 3,761 as teachers in elementary and secondary schools, 404 in colleges and universities, 3,044 as engineers, 2,357 as designers and draftsmen, 2,140 as auditors and accountants, 1,866 as technicians, 1,291 as clergymen, 1,405 as musicians and music teachers, and, of course, quite a number as doctors, lawyers, and social workers. Not many Mexicans have yet achieved recognition as writers and artists, but there is a wealth of talent in the group that will some day—and fairly soon—burst forth on the national scene. Occupational differentiation is still restricted, but the spread of employment is increasing.

To measure the distance that must still be traveled, consider these facts: out of approximately 25,000 students at Berkeley (University of California), there are only 78 Mexican students—this is 1967—and at the University of California at Los Angeles, with an estimated enrollment of 26,000, there are only 70 Mexican-American students, about three in every thousand. This in a community that has close to a million Mexican residents! In 1966 there were more Negroes registered in state colleges in California than there were Mexicans, although there are more Mexicans living in the state than there are Negroes.

More impressive than statistics, though, is the quality of the new leadership that is emerging. In the past, leadership was in short supply. Too many Mexican-American leaders were of the "Uncle Tom" or "Tío Tomás" variety—the type who tried to improve their own lot by selling out the interests of the rank-and-file Mexicans they were supposed to represent. The Mexicans of the border have a phrase which describes this type: "El es un zero a la izquierda"—"He is a left-handed zero"—that is, a pompous flunky who is trying to act like a big shot. But these Uncle Toms are being rapidly succeeded today by young, honest, intelligent, progressive, well-educated types. Literally hundreds of these young men, in the twenty-five to thirty-five age category, have emerged as leaders. Many of them are college educated, with impressive war records, and they hold all manner of jobs—as social workers, in the antipoverty program, and in city, county, and state employment. They are articulate, bilingual, and thoroughly familiar with the background and the problems of the Spanish-speaking.

At Berkeley, for example, the young Mexican-American graduate students have formed a most interesting organization known as *Quinto Sol,* which has issued some excellent studies about the problems of the Spanish-speaking. And Ralph Guzman, son of a Mexican migrant worker, is today Assistant Director of the Mexican-American Study Project at the University of California at Los Angeles, which was set up in February, 1964, on the basis of a large grant received from the Ford Foundation. It has issued a series of studies about Mexican-Americans and has succeeded in focusing a great deal of attention on the problems of the Spanish-speaking. The new generation of Mexican "activists" has formed some impressive action organizations: MAPA, the Mexican-American Political Action organization; PUMA, Political Unity for Mexican-Americans; and PASO, Political Association of Spanish-Speaking Organizations.

One may conclude, therefore, and with confidence, that the Spanish-speaking are rapidly achieving a new political maturity. One does not need to worry overmuch at the moment about the "slowness" with which the Mexican is being "assimilated"; he is moving forward with a new vigor and confidence and with a new, strong sense of purpose and direction.

—Carey McWilliams
New York, 1968

*NORTH
FROM
MEXICO*

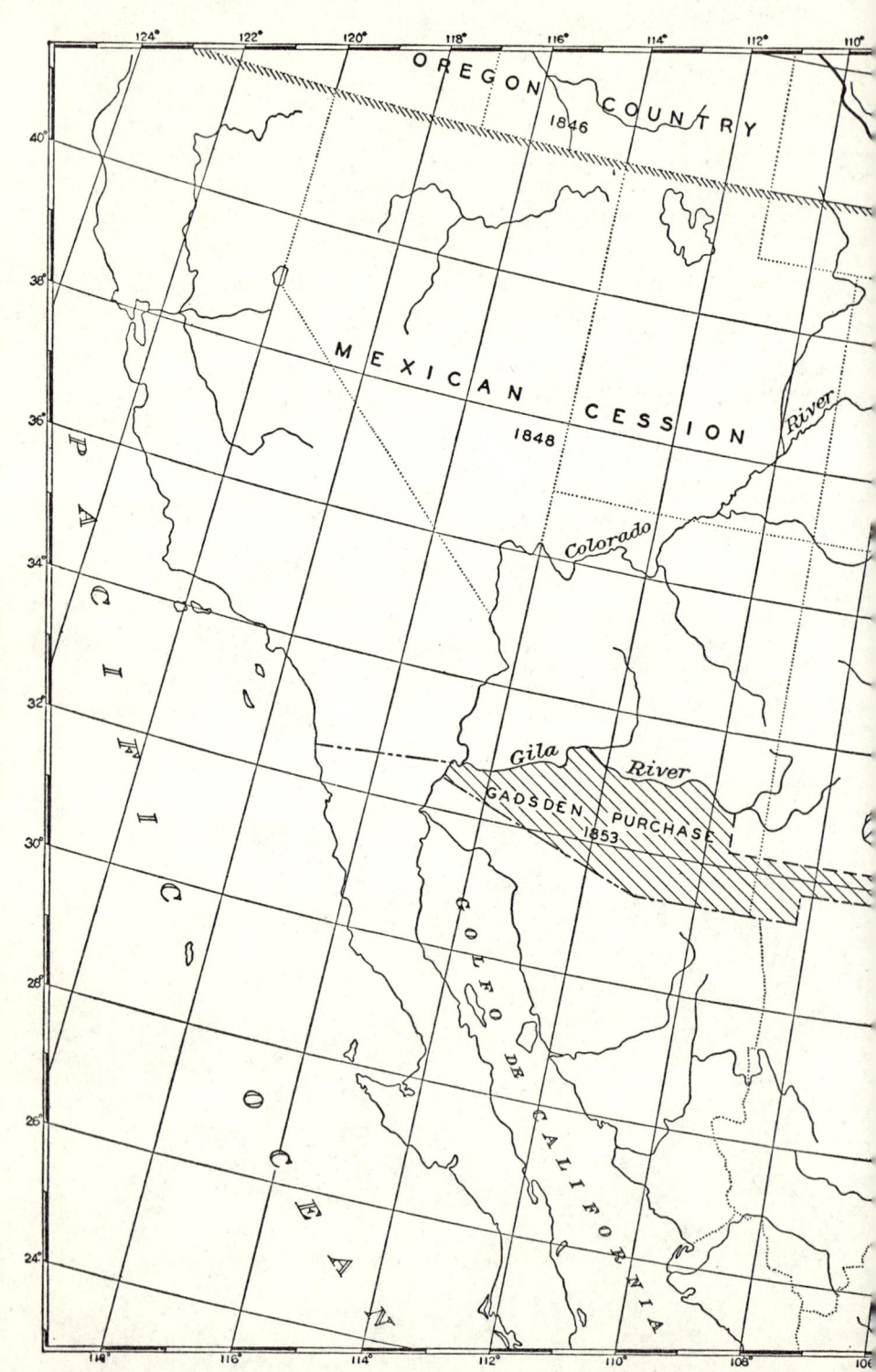

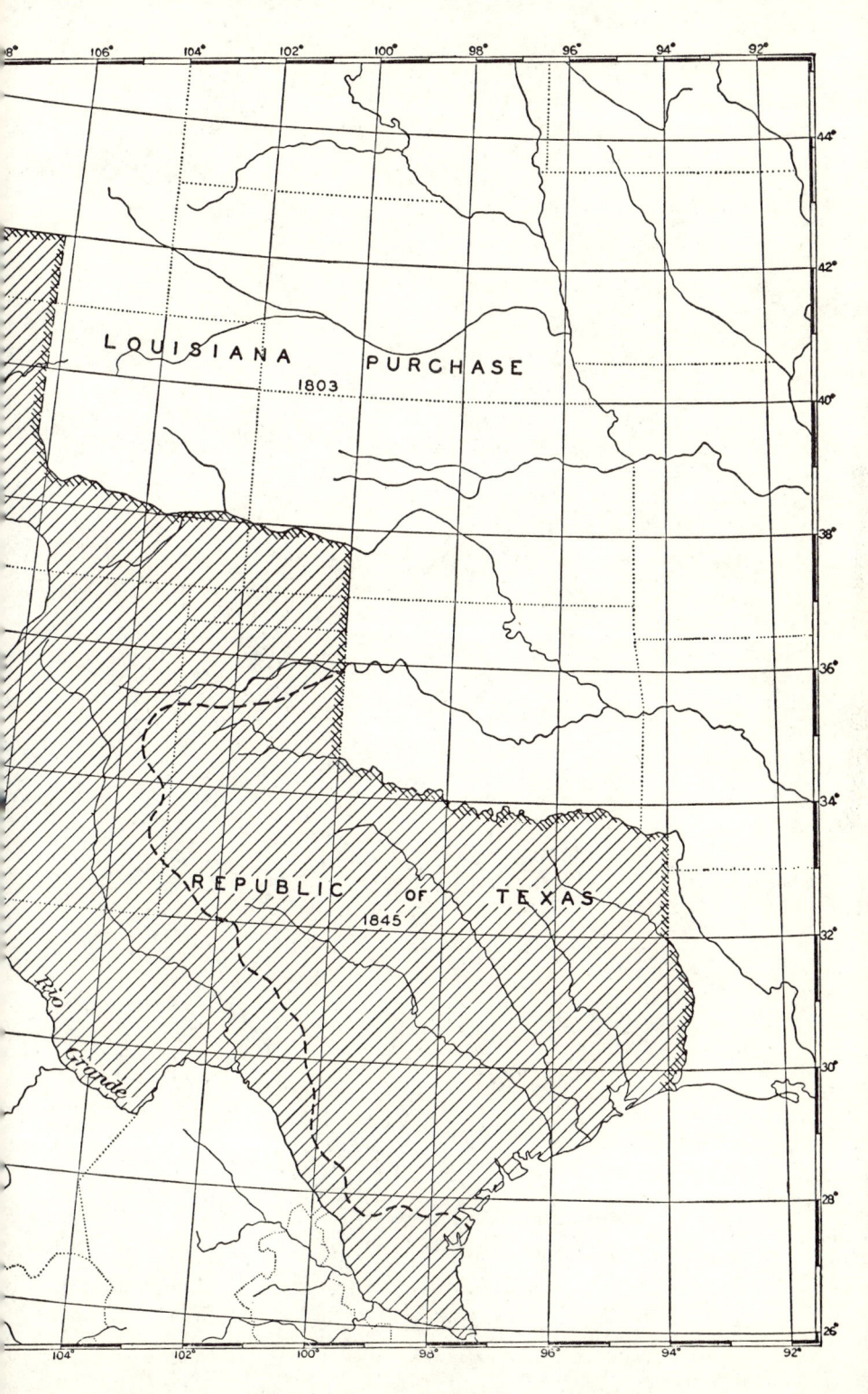

I

In Spanish Saddlebags

The Hispanic heritage of the Southwest has two parts: the Spanish and the Mexican-Indian. Originally one heritage, unified in time, they have long since been polarized. Carefully distinguished from the Mexican-Indian, the Spanish heritage is now enshrined throughout the Southwest. It has become the sacred or templar tradition of which the Mexican-Indian inheritance is the secular or profane counterpart. In a somewhat similar fashion, the Spanish part of the tradition has also been divided into two parts. The romantic-heroic side has been accepted and enshrined; the prosaic or mundane phase has been ignored and discredited.

While there are many explanations for this dichotomy in the tradition only one or two phases of the matter need be noted here. The eastern seaboard colonies were, of course, largely British in origin. Britain and Spain were mortal enemies. Hence the American colonists were predisposed to accept the Anglo-Saxon version of all things "Latin." That Spaniards could be prosaic realists was, of course, an idea that few Anglo-American historians were prepared to concede. Then, too, a considerable part of the territory of the United States was acquired by conquest from Mexico shortly after its liberation from Spain. In view of the antecedent hostility between Britain and Spain, it was quite natural that this conquest should be rationalized as a mere by-product of the innate superiority of the Anglo-Saxon. Nevertheless a niche had to be found for the Spanish part of the tradition—after all Spain had discovered America; so the romantic and heroic aspects of the tradition were artificially divorced from its prosaic accomplishments and preserved like a rusty suit of armor in a museum.

This tendency toward selective interpretation was abetted by a highly paradoxical aspect of Spanish influence in the New World. Although the Spaniards succeeded in transplanting their language, their religion, and many of their institutions in the Americas, they did so largely through the instrumentality of other groups. Spanish culture was superposed and inflicted on native peoples in the Americas; the Anglo-Saxon culture was carried over and preserved by immigrants. Not more than three hundred thousand Spaniards came to the Americas in the three colonial centuries and many of these, of course, came only for short periods and later returned. In the end the Spanish withdrew—from Florida, from Louisiana, and finally from Mexico itself. A retreating people may leave monuments and ruins but the reality of their experiences vanishes with the people, leaving only a faint memory, an easily erasable record. In such a sequence, it is only natural that the monuments and ruins should later acquire a piquant antiquarian interest and that the figures of the earlier scene should assume heroic proportions in the imagination of a later period.

In the territory that now makes up the United States, Spaniards have always been a negligible ethnic element. It is doubtful if more than fifty thousand Spanish-born persons have resided in the United States at any one period from 1820 to the present time. Spanish immigration, for this entire period, has probably not been in excess of 175,000. Thus things Spanish have been neglected or misunderstood in the absence of those familiar with the tradition and capable of interpreting the past in realistic terms. American school children have always known about La Fayette and of the aid which France furnished the colonies in the Revolutionary War; but few of them have ever been told that Spain also aided the colonies, that Spanish ports were open for the sale of prize-ships captured by American men-of-war, or that the Spanish governor of Louisiana furnished supplies of crucial importance to the American forces.

Then, too, the splendor and romance of the Spanish story has tended to obscure its prosaic realities. The Latins were the great discoverers and explorers: Columbus, Magellan, Balboa, Cortez, Coronado, De Soto; and many of them were grandees and nobles. Somehow they invited the romantic apotheosis, the heroic summation. Lifting the curtain on the New World, they enacted the prologue to the drama of its settlement. Prologues, by the nature of their function, are heroic, splendidly phrased, lofty in sentiment; but never really a part of the play. In the latter-day versions, the prologue has been retained but the play itself has been rewritten and embellished. One need never worry about the heroic side of the Spanish tradition being forgotten or neglected; the Spanish explorations in the Southwest will live forever, gleaming like fine Toledo blades in the history of the region.

1. The Spanish Prologue

From their base in the Indies,—"the nursery of Spanish culture in the Western Hemisphere,"—the Spaniards by 1525 had explored the entire shore line from Cape Breton to Cape Horn. Ponce de León had perished in Florida in quest of the fountain of youth. Lucas Vásquez de Ayllón had been lured to his death by the tall tales of Francisco Chichorana, a captured Indian, who had told the Spaniards of a race of Indians in the Carolinas with white skins and brown hair hanging from their heels, of domesticated deer, of pearls and precious stones, and of a giant named Datha who had a tail like a crocodile. . . .

After weeks of marching through the Florida everglades, fording rivers and wallowing through swamps up to their armpits, the survivors of Pánfilo de Narváez' ill-fated expedition of 1528 finally returned to the shore, where their ships had been left at anchor, only to find that the ships had vanished. Beating their crossbows into saws and their stirrups and spurs into nails, they made five boats of palmetto bark, saplings, and horsehair and set sail from Florida. Part of the expedition was lost at sea but one of the boats, containing Cabeza de Vaca, was shipwrecked on an island near Galveston.

Most of the survivors perished during the first winter among the Indians on the island and along the shore. To escape death, the resourceful De Vaca learned all that he could from the Indians: their language, their habits, and their lore. For nearly six years, he lived as a slave and medicine man among the various Indian tribes. Compelled to dig for edible roots along the shore, his fingers became so worn that "did a straw but touch them they would bleed." Journeying inland to exchange sea-snails, shells, and trinkets for food, De Vaca ever returned to the island, where Ovideo, one of his companions, was still confined. Eventually the two of them made their way to the mainland, naked, half-starved, armed only with bow and arrows and conch-shell knives. Deserted by the timid Ovideo, De Vaca finally came on Dorantes and Castillo, two members of the expedition, and with them the Christianized

Moor, Estevánico, sometimes called Estevan, "the Black Mexican."

Travelling with Indian tribes, the four men journeyed west of the Colorado "on the prickly pear plains." For a time they lived with the Arbadaos Indians who occupied the sand belt between the Nueces and the Rio Grande. Wherever they journeyed, it was De Vaca's fame as a medicine man that won food and protection for them. Convinced that direct passage to Mexico was impossible, the party started westward, crossed the Rio Grande west of the Pecos and followed it to a point near El Paso. Over all this distance, hordes of Indians travelled with them. "The Indians," wrote De Vaca, "ever accompanied us until they delivered us to others." From El Paso the party traversed the plains of Chihuahua and crossed the Sierra Madre Mountains to a town on the Rio Yaqui—somewhere near Sahuaripa, Sonora—where they were given six hundred "hearts of deer" and five arrows tipped with emeralds. Descending the Yaqui, they came upon a Spanish slave-hunting expedition on the Gulf of California and finally reached Mexico City on July 24, 1536.

Excited by the stories of De Vaca, the Viceroy Mendoza sent a preliminary expedition northward from Culiacán in 1539, consisting of Fray Marcos, the by-now-famous Estevan, and a small party of Indian servants and interpreters. No character in the Spanish prologue is quite as interesting as Estevan, the Arab Negro from Azemur, who, in the course of his wanderings with De Vaca, had acquired a knowledge of six Indian dialects and had learned the arts of the medicine man. "He really explored," writes Harvey Fergusson, "more of the Southwest and perhaps learned more about its people than any other man of his day." Being a slave, he knew how to dominate men. Once a mark of bondage, his black skin made him a strange and supernatural being to the Indians. Marching on foot, unarmed, without maps or charts, Fray Marcos and Estevan journeyed northward through Sonora. As they proceeded, Estevan marched ahead, several days in advance, planting crosses in the desert to mark the way. Up the Sonora Valley they went, through the valley of the San Pedro in Arizona, to the Zuñi villages of western New Mexico where, at long last, Estevan finally sighted in the distance Cibola, the first of the fabled seven cities of gold.

Among the polygamous Pima and Opata Indians, Estevan had been received like a strange and wonderful god. Bedecked with quantities of turquoise and feathers, carrying a gourd with tinkling bells, preceded by a large gray hunting dog, and followed by an entourage of enchanted Indian women, he sighted and perhaps entered the first of the Zuñi villages. From the Pima villages to Cibola, the number of attractive and brightly adorned Indian women who accompanied him had increased with every mile. It was probably this attraction he had for Indian women that brought about his death. For the Zuñi Indians were a sober, industrious tribe who greatly prized and honored their women. A year later the Zuñi chieftains told Coronado that they had murdered Estevan "because he had assaulted their women, whom the Indians love better than themselves." A strange figure of legend, this Estevan, who, born in Africa, wandered over most of the Southwest, the first European—really an African—to find the seven cities of gold.

Upon Fray Marcos' return to Mexico, the great expedition led by Francisco Vásquez de Coronado was organized in 1540. Journeying northward into the San Pedro Valley, Coronado skirted the Santa Catalina Mountains, crossed the Gila River, and proceeded to the Zuñi River and beyond to Hawikuh, one of the seven cities of gold, "a little, crowded village, looking as if it had been crumpled all together." Eastward the expedition came to the famous pueblo of Acoma, built on a flat-topped mountain three hundred and fifty feet in the air. It was at the village of Tiguex, above Albuquerque, that Coronado first heard, from an Indian whom the Spaniards named El Turco, of Golden Quivira on the Great Plains. Now that the seven cities of gold had turned out to be mud villages, Quivira became the goal of the expedition. Before leaving Tiguex, however, Coronado laid the foundation for most of the subsequent troubles of Spain in the borderlands by burning two hundred Indians at the stake—an "incident" which the Indians never forgot and for which they never forgave the Spaniards.

In search of Golden Quivira, Coronado continued his march eastward, entered the Great Plains of Texas, crossed the Arkansas River into Kansas, and finally reached the first of the Quivira villages near the vicinity of Great Bend. Annoyed to find that Golden Quivira was merely another collection of mud villages, Coronado had El Turco garrotted, set up a cross to mark the spot, and began the long march back to Mexico. When he finally presented himself before Mendoza, writes Bolton, he had brought with him nothing more precious than the gold-plated armor with which he had set out two years before.

A member of the Coronado expedition, Fray Juan de Padilla, returned alone to the Quivira villages where he was murdered by the Indians,—the first Christian martyr on American soil. It is said that his body is buried at Isleta, the pueblo below Albuquerque. "According to legend," writes Ruth Laughlin, "Padre Padilla rises in his coffin, hollowed out of a cottonwood log, every twenty years. Some say that his emaciated body is as dry as mummy and his brown gown crumbling . . . but when his coffin bursts the mud floor before the altar, it is the blessed omen of a good year."

On June 27, 1542—while Coronado was returning from the buffalo plains to Mexico—Juan Rodríguez Cabrillo set sail up the west coast of Mexico to find the fabled island of California, peopled by black women, "on the right hand of the Indies, very close to the Terrestrial Paradise." On the twenty-fifth of September, Cabrillo discovered the Bay of San Diego, where his ships rode at anchor off Point Loma for three days. Further north he came upon Santa Catalina and San Clemente Islands, entered the Bay of Santa Monica, or the Bay of Smokes, as he called it, and a few weeks later went ashore at San Buenaventura. With Viscaíno's discovery of the Bay of Monterey in 1602, one might well say that the prologue was concluded.

Between 1528 and 1602, a handful of Spaniards had explored the borderlands: from Galveston to San Diego; from Sonora to Santa Fe; from the west coast of Mexico to Monterey. If myth set them in motion, it was the Indians who lured them still further from their bases with tales of gold and silver, always seeking to draw them out of the Southwest. Where they had expected to find cities of gold, they found mud villages and uninhabited desert wastes. Something of this initial disappointment must have influenced their subsequent policy. For they neglected California from 1542 until the arrival of Fray Junípero Serra at San Diego in 1769; Texas was ignored for a century; and forty years elapsed before the settlement of New Mexico was undertaken.

The colonization of New Mexico,—"the first white colony in the trans-Mississippi West,"—was a by-product of the discovery of rich silver deposits at Zacatecas in 1548. It was a Zacatecas millionaire, Juan de Oñate, one of the four richest men in Mexico, who set forth in 1598 with eighty-three *carretas,* seven thousand head of stock, and four hundred soldiers to colonize New Mexico. Cabeza de Vaca had entered the borderlands from the southeast; Fray Marcos and Coronado from the southwest by way of Sonora; but De Oñate moved directly northward to El Paso and then up the Rio Grande to a point near Santa Fe. Poaching on the Pueblo Indians, the colonists managed to establish a series of settlements and by 1630 had founded some twenty-five missions. These initial settlements were extinguished in 1680, when the Indians revolted and drove the Spaniards from New Mexico in three days, killing four hundred of the settlers. Twelve years later, Diego de Vargas reconquered the province, made peace with the Pueblo Indians, and laid the foundations for settlements which survive to this day.

In northern Sonora and southern Arizona,—Pimeria Alta,—the work of settlement was begun in 1687 by the Jesuit, Father Eusebio Francisco Kino. Italian by birth, Bavarian by education, Spanish by consecration, Father Kino founded the mission of San Xavier del Bac—the most impressive monument that Spain left in the Southwest—on April 28, 1700. In twenty-four years of service on the border, Father Kino, "the padre on horseback," made over fifty important journeys of exploration and charted the Colorado from the mouth of the Gila to the Gulf of California. Based on these journeys, his map of the region was not improved upon for over a century.

It was from Tubac, in Arizona, that Juan Bautista de Anza set forth on his famous march across the California desert to San Gabriel in 1775. Returning to Tubac the next year, he led a second expedition from that point to the missions of Southern California and from there to Monterey and on to San Francisco. While De Anza was exploring the Bay of San Francisco, seeking a site for the presidio, the American colonists on the eastern seaboard, three thousand miles away, were celebrating the signing of the Declaration of Independence. This second expedition of De Anza's,—"the longest overland migration of a colony in North American history before the settlement of Oregon,"—has been rightly called the *Anabasis* of California history. Probably nothing in Xenophon's recital of the march of the ten thousand to the sea exceeds it in courage and endurance.

First and last, the Spaniards established twenty-one missions in California, spread like beads on a necklace at about one day's march apart, along the rim of the seacoast from San Diego to San Francisco; founded four presidial towns—San Diego, Santa Barbara, Monterey, and San Francisco; and two pueblos—San Jose (1777) and Los Angeles (1781). None of these settlements was more than a day's ride from the sea. While the Spanish penetrated the Central Valley, they established no colonies there (the Indians of the interior were quite unlike the docile coastal tribes). Although the Spanish founded some twenty-five missions in Texas, their principal and ultimately their only settlements between the Sabine and the Rio Grande were San Antonio (1718); Goliad or La Bahia; and Nacogdoches.

Thus the Spanish settlements in the borderlands really consisted of a firmly rooted colony in New Mexico; an easily held and fairly prosperous chain of missions in coastal California; and a number of feebly garrisoned, constantly imperiled settlements in Texas and Arizona.

While a dozen or more settlements were founded in Florida, largely as a protective flank for the silver of Mexico, the fate of these settlements was sealed when the British occupied Charleston in 1670. Reverting to Spanish rule in 1769, the Florida settlements were again outflanked when the United States negotiated the Louisiana Purchase. In 1821 the colonies were transferred to the United States, coincident with the liberation of Mexico from Spanish rule, and the Spaniards withdrew from the eastern seaboard.

2. Footnote to the Prologue

On April 16, 1605, Juan de Oñate chiselled a notation on Inscription Rock, located midway on the trail from Zuñi to Acoma. *"Pasó por acqui"* it read; "Passed by this way."

One of the earliest historical records within the present confines of the United States, the notation epitomizes the heroic side of the Spanish adventure in the borderlands. For many years the Spanish names on Inscription Rock were of no more interest to the Anglo-Americans than the monument itself. But toward the end of the nineteenth century, America discovered the Southwest and tourist hordes beat a trail to the monument to stare at the Indian hieroglyphics and the odd-sounding Spanish "names on a rock."

No sooner had the tourists begun to encircle Inscription Rock than a school of romantic American historians proceeded to elevate everything the Spanish had done in the Southwest to the level of high heroism and intense passion. In one sense the Spanish explorers fully merited this posthumous laudation for they were brave and courageous men,—tough, hard-bitten, and indomitable. But the saga that has grown out of their explorations is so inhumanly grandiose as to create a most misleading impression of their real accomplishments. Reading the admirable narratives which the Spanish left, one is today impressed with the prosaic, matter-of-fact manner in which they recounted their adventures. They were not nearly so impressed with their own heroism as were the American historians of a later date. What they consistently emphasized was their good luck, or as they put it, the grace of God.

That the scale of their achievement has somehow become askew can be easily demonstrated. Reading De Anza's report on the province of Sonora in 1777, one is struck by the small stage, the tiny settings, the miniature proportions of the drama. De Anza was not deploying "armies": he had exactly 502 soldiers at his disposal in all Pimeria Alta. Nor was he opposed by "armies" of Indians. In a great expanse of largely uninhabited territory, a handful of Spaniards,—tiny pinpricks on the desert,—were conducting a not-too-gory duel with a few widely scattered Indian tribes. At the heyday of Spanish expansion, one could have placed all the inhabitants of the borderlands, including the Indians, in a corner of the present-day County of Los Angeles. The Spanish prologue was a drama-in-miniature; the quality was heroic but the actors were puppet-like figures against an enormous backdrop.

Actually the famous marches and *entradas* were not quite as heroic or as difficult as they have been made out to be. Possessing an invincible superiority of weapons, the Spanish could march wherever they wanted to march; there was nothing to stop them. Trained and seasoned campaigners, they knew all the tricks of survival in an arid environment. Journeys that appear to us in retrospect as feats of incredible endurance were merely another day's march to them. Mexicans and Indians accompanied them wherever they went, often trudging on foot while they rode on horseback. During both the period of exploration and of settlement, Spanish casualties in the borderlands were negligible. While they were contained, within narrow limits, by warlike nomadic tribes, they fought few pitched battles. Had it not been for the Indians, neither their explorations nor their settlements would have been possible. Indian guides took them from one waterhole to the next, from one tribe to another; and wherever they settled they lived for years off the bounty of the Indian villagers. The key to Cabeza de Vaca's survival is simply that he was compelled to live with Indians and did so. Wherever they went, he went; whatever they did, he did.

The Spanish prologue should not, of course, be disparaged; but it cannot be understood or appreciated until it is first reduced to scale. In the fervid rhetoric of the historians, every move of these "soldiers of the Cross" was "magnificent," "heroic," and "epochal." Their achievements have been so inflated that they have lost much of their meaning and relevance. Once the record of achievement is looked at, not through a mist of romantic preoccupations, but as the Spaniards themselves saw their position and their achievements, then the facts fall into place and the scale assumes proper proportions. For the heroic side of the tradition, the part that is remembered and honored, was not the whole of the Spanish story in the Southwest. There was a play, a real drama, as well as a prologue. The prologue was written in heroic couplets; the play in prose. We know the prologue; it is the play that needs to be re-enacted.

3. The Play-in-Prose

From the conquest of Mexico to the end of Spanish rule, a corporal's guard of Spanish soldiers was able to march at will throughout Mexico, Central and South America, and the borderlands. A few hundred Spanish soldiers, officials, and priests seized, held, and ruled the province of California; for years on end the military might of the Spanish empire was represented in New Mexico by several companies of soldiers crudely armed. At the close of the period, there were not more than fifteen thousand Spaniards in the Americas,—less than one-third of one per cent of the population of New Spain. "Upon this slender basis," writes Ernest Gruening, "the conquering Hispanic minority superposed its political structure, religion, and language on the natives." What was the secret of this astonishing success?

The answer is twofold: horses and weapons. The Spaniards were superb horsemen: "the centaurs of the mesa." That they were horsemen enabled them to travel great distances and to wear armor. With neither armor nor horses, the Indians were simply no match for the Spaniards. Hence Cortez, with a few hundred men, could fight his way into Mexico City and hold it against unthinkable odds. "Superiority of weapons," writes F. S. Curtis, Jr., "made such exploits a possibility. . . . Against stone-tipped arrows and lances, obsidian daggers, stone-headed clubs, and the propelling force of the human arm alone, the Spanish opposed steel-tipped arrows and lances, steel swords and daggers, and the propelling force of gunpowder." As long as the Spanish possessed this superiority in arms and held exclusive possession of the horses which made their use possible, they could enact the role of conquistadores; and, for a time, they took every precaution to prevent the Indians from gaining possession of either.

The Spaniards themselves were well aware of the secret of their success. "The arrival which has been of greatest importance to the Spaniards of all those brought to the Indies," wrote the Jesuit, Bernabé Cobo, "is the horse; because with its aid they have been able to make so many and such notable conquests, and have discovered so many regions and have spread so far in so short a time through so many and extensive lands." When the Spanish began the conquest of the Americas, they had the best horses in Europe. Even before the Moors had brought them the famous "horses of the desert," they had developed fine breeds of their own. The American horse came almost entirely from the Spanish stock of New Mexico and Florida. One reads, for example, that Patrick Henry was in the habit of sending to the Pawnee country "for the best and most pure Spanish breed." The Apaches began to steal horses from the Spaniards as early as 1600; in fact, the Apache menace was as old as the first settlements in the borderlands (1). Contrary to Spanish policy elsewhere in the Americas, the New Mexico rancheros had been authorized in 1621 to use captive Indians as herders and to allow them to ride horses—a fateful mistake.

To the nomadic Indians of the borderlands, the coming of the horse was as important as the discovery of steam to the white man. "Mounted," writes Donald E. Worcester, "the Apaches presented a problem unlike any with which the Spaniards had previously been plagued. Whereas it was fairly simple to surround a pueblo and force the inhabitants to surrender, the Apaches had no homes or towns to be defended, and no large armies to be defeated." Spanish colonization in the Southwest proceeded, from the outset, under the cloud of Apache terror. The fifth century Europeans felt no greater fear of the Huns of Attila than the fear which the Apaches inspired in the Spaniards and the Pueblo Indians. Later the Indians began to barter captives for horses and to exchange horses, which they stole from the Spanish, for guns and powder which they got from the French.

While horses could carry the Spaniards into the Southwest, their system of colonization did not travel so well. Based on the presidio, the mission, and the hacienda,—the conquistadores to conquer; the priests to convert; and the *encomenderos* to exploit,—the system worked satisfactorily in the Central Mesa region of Mexico where sedentary Indians could be exploited. In the borderlands, however, the system quickly broke down, although it worked fairly well in New Mexico: the one province with a large population of sedentary Indians. Defeated in battle by the Spanish, the Pueblo Indians returned to their villages and tilled acres and accepted Spanish dominance; in effect, they were driven back by the nomadic tribes who functioned as policemen for the Spanish. But the nomads, having nothing to defend, could never be subdued. Although few in number, the heavily armed Spaniards could conquer wide territories but they could never consolidate their conquests nor could they win a decisive battle with the nomads. As a consequence, the Spanish were compelled to do what the Pueblo Indians had done centuries before: they concentrated their forces in a few well-chosen and easily defended positions. To these positions, however, they were pinned like butterflies on a screen.

The coastal Indians in California were sedentary but they did not live in villages; hence they had to be rounded up and brought to the missions. While some of the missions prospered, the Indians certainly did not; on the contrary, they died like flies. In Arizona and Texas, the Spaniards tried in vain to subdue the Apaches and the Comanches. Unworkable in the borderlands, the *encomienda* system was abandoned about 1720. Fifty years later the mission system had been virtually abandoned in Texas and Arizona and the secularization of the missions in California brought an end to the period of mission rule in 1834. "As the Spanish arms and civilization," writes Dr. George P. Garrison, "came in closer contact with the wild and fierce Apaches and Comanches of the north their progress became increasingly difficult and uncertain." Before many years had passed, it was brought to a kind of halt or stalemate. While their explorations "were wide enough for a schoolboy's dream, their grasp was too weak for permanence."

In locating settlements in the borderlands, the Spanish had pursued their time-honored policy of settling in areas occupied by sedentary Indians. Quite apart from the fact that their colonization scheme was premised upon the use of Indian labor, a sound instinct told them that where Indian settlements existed human life could be supported. Prior to their appearance in the Southwest, however, a great drama had been enacted of which they knew nothing and concerning which not too much is known today. It would seem, however, that the Pueblo Indians had for many years been fighting a losing battle against their hereditary enemies, the nomadic tribes. Driven out of the river bottoms and valleys, they had finally sought shelter in the nooks and crevices of the mountainous portions of the Southwest. Here, in cliff-dwellings, terraced adobes, and mountain villages, they were able to survive although in constant peril. As a result of protracted defensive warfare, their culture had begun to disintegrate and showed a marked decline in vigor at about the time the Spaniards arrived. In fact, it is altogether probable that the Spaniards rescued and to a degree revitalized the culture of the Pueblo Indians.

Unaware of this drama, the Spaniards passed by rich gold, silver, and copper deposits and marched through the fertile river bottoms of the south to plant their colonies in the narrow valleys of the Rio Arriba in northern New Mexico. It is important to note that the Spanish never occupied or settled more than a small portion of the province. Despite the great distances and the largely uninhabited terrain of New Mexico, the colonists were, paradoxically, more crowded than their contemporaries in the English colonies on the eastern seaboard. For the arid nature of the environment and the location of the Indian villages confined their settlements to the narrow strips of fertile land in the valleys of the north. Not knowing their problems, unaware of their predicament, the Anglo-Americans later jeered at their "mistakes" and derided their "failures." It was this failure to understand the nature of the situation which the Spanish faced that so largely accounts for the dismissal of their prosaic accomplishments as of slight importance.

4. The Climate of Spain

Despite the insurmountable obstacles which they encountered, the Spanish left an imprint on the borderlands which, as Bolton once said, "is still deep and clear." The names of three states in the region are Spanish in origin: California, Nevada, and Colorado. "Scores of rivers and mountains and hundreds of towns and cities," to quote Bolton again, "still bear the names of saints dear to the Spanish pioneers." From Los Angeles to San Antonio, the Spanish language is spoken today by upwards of two million people. Thousands of Indians living in the region speak Spanish in preference to English and profess the Catholic faith. The imprint of Spain is to be found in the land systems of the region; in the law of waters, of minerals, and of community property; and in many institutions now firmly planted in the Southwest. "It is to them and their followers and descendants," writes Dr. Frank C. Lockwood, "few though they were, and opposed as they were by harsh nature and hostile savages, that our Anglo-Saxon pioneers owed from the first a degree of exemption from such extremes of ignorance and crudity as most American pioneer settlers have experienced."

A major factor in the prosaic success of the Spanish in the Southwest consisted in the similarity of the climate and environment to that of Spain. Spain is the only European country with an arid or semi-arid environment. Over a period of thirty generations, the Spanish had acquired a profound knowledge of the nature and limitations of such an environment. The Spaniards knew and understood irrigated farming, for irrigation is necessary throughout the whole of the Spanish peninsula as it is throughout the Southwest. They had solved the problem of building without timber by the use of adobe, brick, and stone, a practice which proved of great value in the Southwest. In almost every respect, their institutions and culture were adapted to the environment which they found in the borderlands. "The scale was higher," writes Dr. Walter Prescott Webb, "but the difference was more of degree than of character or quality."

Everything that the Spanish brought to the Southwest was either driven or carried in saddlebags or *carretas*. But what they did bring was of enormous importance (I am speaking now merely of *things;* the question of institutions and cultural practices will be considered later). They brought the first cattle, horses, goats, pigs, cats, and barnyard fowls to the Southwest. At great effort they brought from Europe the first hoes, spades, grinding stones, clamps, plows, files, and pliers used in the region. The first wheels that turned on American soil were Spanish in origin. "There was no product contributed to the agriculture of America by the English," writes Harvey Bernstein (2), "which the Spanish had not planted earlier."

The list is a long one, indeed, including peaches, figs, oranges, apples, grapes, apricots, limes, pomegranates, pears, olives, and lemons. Over 260,000 orange trees were planted in the older mission groves of California by 1880. The vineyards that developed so rapidly in California after 1848 were planted in or near the original vineyards which the Spanish had laid out. Up to 1860, there was only one grape grown in California,—the Mission grape; but in that year the state's thirty million vines were producing upwards of seven million gallons of wine. The Spanish introduced raisin culture to California. The first wheat seeds brought to California came from Spain and were, on their arrival in 1770, already well-adapted to climatic and soil conditions not unlike those which existed in the state. The first wheat planted in Colorado was Spanish in origin and was known as "Sonora wheat." The grandfather of Don Amado Chaves brought the first alfalfa seed to New Mexico tied in a *manta*. The Spanish brought the important seed of the alfilaria or filaree to California as well as the first flax seeds. In 1806 the Spaniards introduced a cotton seed from Mexico that produced exceptionally large, wide, open bolls. Introduced by way of New Orleans, this seed spread rapidly throughout the Deep South.

While the area farmed by the Franciscans in California was not large, —perhaps not more than 10,000 acres,—the mission "gardens" provided a pre-view of the state's agriculture. "The fruits and nuts known to have been grown by the padres," writes Dr. Frank Adams, "included almost all those now produced in California, and some that have not succeeded commercially. There were pears, peaches, apples, almonds, plums, quinces, pomegranates, oranges, lemons, citrons, limes, dates, cherries, plantains, walnuts, grapes, olives, figs, strawberries and raspberries." Not only did the Franciscans demonstrate that all these crops could be produced in California, but some of the fruits now grown in the state have come directly from the mission gardens, notably the Mission grape, Mission fig, and Mission olive (4).

From the Spaniards, the Indians of the Southwest learned to hammer silver and copper; to work iron; and to use plows and hoes. From the Spanish the Navajo took over much of their present-day pastoral culture, including a knowledge of how to card and to weave wool. To this day, the Indians use Spanish terms to designate the colors used in their blankets: *morada subido, rosa baja, oro, amarillo, tostado, grano*. The Spanish introduced sugar cane to Louisiana and built the first sugar refinery in New Orleans in 1791. Spanish gardeners, farm laborers, blacksmiths, millwrights, and artisans brought a variety of skills to the Southwest. In fact it would take pages merely to list the things which the Spanish brought to the region that have long since been incorporated in its culture. Savants have written learned papers on what the introduction of the cat meant to the people of the New World (3).

What the Spaniards contributed to the Southwest, in addition to their language, religion, law, and institutions, were the seeds of things which were later of enormous importance. They were the trail blazers and seed planters. In most cases, the key to the success with which these seeds were transplanted is to be found in the similarity of the Southwest environment to that of Spain. The horses, sheep, cattle, and goats that the Spanish brought to the region, as well as the plants that they imported, were alike well adapted to the environment; and so were many of their cultural practices and institutions. That many of these seeds failed to reach full development and maturity under Spanish rule is due to a variety of factors: the intractable character of the plains and desert Indians; the dead weight of tradition; the highly centralized character of Spanish administration; the senseless restrictions imposed on initiative and innovation; the cheapness of Indian labor; and the feudal, caste-like social system which the Spanish also brought to the Southwest. That the Spanish failed to make the most of their opportunities, however, cannot detract from the importance of their prosaic accomplishments.

Still another key to the amazing success with which Spanish cultural influences were planted in the Southwest is to be found in the isolation of the borderlands. Isolated in time and space, the settlers were compelled to plant things firmly in the soil. What survived may later have appeared to be scrawny, crude, and misshapen; but it was unquestionably tough, well-adapted, and indigenous. While the form or model was often Spanish, the ultimate adaptation showed unmistakable Mexican and Indian influences. If the Spanish were the carriers of seeds and plows, Mexicans and Indians were the planters and plow hands. Beyond all doubt the culture of the Southwest, in 1848, was a trinity: a whole consisting of three intricately interwoven, interpenetrated, thoroughly fused elements. To attempt to unravel any single strand from this pattern and label it "Spanish" is, therefore, to do a serious injustice to the Mexicans and Indians through whom, and only through whom, Spanish cultural influences survived in the region. "I do not agree with all this talk about Coronado," Pablo Abeyta, the governor of the Isleta Pueblo, has said; "I don't know what they mean by Spanish culture. . . . The Spaniards got lost on the ocean and accidentally ran across the country." Whether by accident or otherwise, however, the prologue to the settlement of the borderlands is indubitably Spanish in origin (5).

II

The Fantasy Heritage

Long, long ago the borderlands were settled by Spanish grandees and caballeros, a gentle people, accustomed to the luxurious softness of fine clothes, to well-trained servants, to all the amenities of civilized European living. Inured to suffering, kindly mission *padres* overcame the hostility of Indians by their saintly example and the force of a spiritual ideal, much in the manner of a gentle spring rain driving the harsh winds of winter from the skies. Life was incomparably easy and indolent in those days. There was none of the rough struggle for existence that beset the Puritans in New England. The climate was so mild, the soil so fertile, that Indians merely cast seeds on the ground, letting them fall where chance deposited them, and relaxed in the shade of the nearest tree while a provident and kindly nature took over. Occasionally one of the fieldhands would interrupt his siesta long enough to open one eye and lazily watch the corn stalks shooting up in the golden light. . . .

In the evenings one or the other of the patios would witness the gathering of the Spanish dons from the ranchos. Here in the coolness of the evening air they would talk of the day's events, sipping gentle wines that revived memories of castles in Spain. While the men were thus pleasantly engaged, the women would continue their never-ending routine of tasks that kept the large households functioning smoothly. For the young people, it was a life of unrivalled enjoyment; racing their horses over the green-rolling hills and mustard fields of Southern California; dancing the *contradanzas* and *jotas* to the click of castanets. In the evening, the young ranchero strolled beneath the window of his love's boudoir. As the moon rose high over the Sierra Madres, he would sing the old love songs of Spain. . . . All in all, this life of Spain-away-from-Spain in the borderlands was very romantic, idyllic, very beautiful. . . .

Indeed, it's really a shame that it never existed.

Never existed? How can this be said when so much of the public life of Los Angeles is based on the assumption that it did? Why do churches in Los Angeles never hold bazaars? Why are they always called fiestas?

Why is a quarter acre and twenty chickens called a rancho? Why does a leading newspaper gossip columnist adopt the nom de plume of "La Duenna"? Why does the largest women's club, composed exclusively of Anglo-American women, hold an annual "gala Spanish fiesta program" in which the ladies appear in "full Spanish costume" to admire Señor Raoul de Ramirez' presentation of *The Bells of San Gabriel?* (1). And, lastly, why do so many restaurants, dance halls, swimming pools, and theaters exclude persons of Mexican descent?

Los Angeles is merely one of many cities in the borderlands which has fed itself on a false mythology for so long that it has become a well-fattened paradox. For example, the city boasts of the Spanish origin of its first settlers. Here are their names: Pablo Rodríguez, José Variegas, José Moreno, Felix Villavicencio, José de Lara, Antonio Mesa, Basilio Rosas, Alejandro Rosas, Antonio Navarro, and Manuel Camero. All "Spanish" names, all good "Spaniards" except—Pablo Rodríguez who was an Indian; José Variegas, first alcalde of the pueblo, also an Indian; José Moreno, a mulatto; Felix Villavicencio, a Spaniard married to an Indian; José de Lara, also married to an Indian; Antonio Mesa, who was a Negro; Basilio Rosas, an Indian married to a mulatto; Alejandro Rosas, an Indian married to an Indian; Antonio Navarro, a mestizo with a mulatto wife; and Manuel Camero, a mulatto. The twelfth settler is merely listed as "a Chino" and was probably of Chinese descent. Thus of the original settlers of Our City the Queen of the Angels, their wives included, two were Spaniards; one mestizo; two were Negroes; eight were mulattoes; and nine were Indians. None of this would really matter except that the churches in Los Angeles hold fiestas rather than bazaars and that Mexicans are still not accepted as a part of the community. When one examines how deeply this fantasy heritage has permeated the social and cultural life of the borderlands, the dichotomy begins to assume the proportions of a schizophrenic mania.

1. The Man on the White Horse

"Three hundred years," writes Tom Cameron in the Los Angeles *Times* of August 29, 1947, "vanished in an instant here in Santa Barbara today as the city and more than 100,000 guests plunged into a three-day round of pageants, parades, street dancing and impromptu entertainment. It is La *Fiesta*. Santa Barbara is a particularly bewitching señorita today. With glowing copa de oro flowers entwined in her raven tresses and with her gayest mantilla swirling above her tight-bodied, ruffled Spanish colonial gown, she is hostess to honored guests from near and far. It is a time when Santa Barbara gazes over her bare shoulders (*sic*) to a romantic, colorful era of leisurely uncomplicated living. . . ."

With one thousand beautiful, "gaily caparisoned" Palomino horses prancing and curveting along State Street—renamed for three days "Calle Estado"—the history of the region is dramatized in costly and elaborate floats. This year, 1947, the Kiwanis Club enters a float in honor of Juan Rodríguez Cabrillo; Rotary honors Sir Francis Drake; the Exchange Club pays homage to Sebastián Viscaíno. "A traditional wedding party of 1818 escorted by caballeros, canters along. It represents the wedding of Anita de la Guerra and Capt. Alfred Robinson." Following the *charros,* riders from San Gabriel and the Spanish grape carts drawn by donkeys with flower girls astride, come the Long Beach mounted police, the Del Rey Palomino Club, *Los Rancheros Visitadores* (headed by J. J. Mitchell of *Juan y Lolita Rancho*), and of course the Los Angeles sheriff's posse headed by Eugene Biscailuz, the sheriff, himself an "early Californian." The celebration comes to a finale with the presentation in the Santa Barbara Bowl of a pageant written by Charles E. Pressley entitled *Romantic California*—and very well titled it is.

"Spanish" food is served; "Spanish" music is played; "Spanish" costumes are worn. For this is the heritage, a fantasy heritage, in which the arbiters of the day are "Spaniards." The Mexicans—those who are proud to be called Mexican—have a name for these "Spaniards." They call them *"Californios"* or *"Californianos"* or, more often, *"renegados."* These are the people after whom streets are named in Los Angeles: Pico, Sepúlveda, Figueroa. It is they who are used by the Anglo-American community to reconcile its fantasy heritage with the contemporary scene. By a definition provided by the *Californios* themselves, one who achieves success in the borderlands is "Spanish"; one who doesn't is "Mexican."

This fantasy heritage makes for the most obvious ironies. Cinco de Mayo is one of the Mexican national holidays which Los Angeles, now a Good Neighbor, has begun to observe. It is celebrated by parades, fiestas, and barbecues; speeches by the mayor and the Mexican consul constitute the principal order of the day. Invariably the parade winds its way through Olvera Street and the Plaza—sections of the old Mexican town now kept in a state of partial repair for the tourist trade—to the City Hall. Leading the parade through the streets, riding majestically on a white horse, is a prominent "Mexican" actor. Strangely enough, this actor, a *Californio* three hundred and sixty-four days of the year, becomes a *"Mexicano"* on Cinco de Mayo. Elegantly attired in a ranchero costume, he sits proudly astride his silver-mounted saddle and jingles his silver spurs as he rides along. The moment he comes into sight, the crowds begin to applaud for he is well known to them through the unvarying stereotypic Mexican roles which he plays in the films. Moreover, they have seen him in exactly this same role, at the head of this or some similar parade, for fifteen years. Of late the applause is pretty thin and it may be that the audience is becoming a little weary of the old routine. A union organizer of Mexican descent once remarked to me: "If I see that white horse once more, I'm going to spit in its eye."

Following the man on the white horse will be other horsemen, few of them with any pretensions of Mexican descent but all similarly attired, mounted on splendid Palominos, horses worth their weight in gold, decorated with their weight in silver trappings. At one time there were men in Mexico who dressed in nearly this fashion. The full irony of the situation dawns when one realizes that the men who lead the parade are dressed like the same class whose downfall is being celebrated. The irony would be no greater if the *Angelenos* put on the brilliant red uniforms of British grenadiers when they paraded on the Fourth of July. For on Cinco de Mayo blood was shed to rid Mexico of grandee landowners who threatened to suck it dry. Here, in Los Angeles, the men who lead the parade symbolically represent the grandees while the Mexicans line the pavements.

These *Californios* are in no small part responsible for the fact that the Mexican population of Los Angeles,—the largest minority in the city,—is so completely deprived of meaningful civic representation. Since it is impolitic for any Los Angeles official to ignore the Mexican vote completely, care is taken that the roster of civic committees shall always include at least one name which is obviously Spanish or Mexican. If a quick glance is taken of the list of names appearing on the civic committees devoted to housing, juvenile delinquency, racial, and welfare problems, these same names constantly reappear.

THE FANTASY HERITAGE

It has only been of recent years that the *Californios* have been elevated to this anomalous and largely factitious status. There was a time when they scarcely existed in the eyes of the Anglo-Americans. When the Native Sons of the Golden West were asked, in the early 1900's, to submit a list of "the men who had grown up with Los Angeles," for a civic memorial, they included only Anglo-American names. When the first "pioneer society" was formed in Los Angeles in 1896, not a single Mexican or Spanish name appeared on the membership roster and the by-laws expressly provided that "persons born in this state are not eligible to membership." Ignored throughout this early period, the *Californios* promptly acquired a new and spurious status the moment it became necessary to use them to maintain the subordination of Mexican immigrants in the general scheme of things.

Today the typical *Californio* occupies, in most communities, a social position that might best be compared with that of the widow of a Confederate general in a small southern town. On all ceremonial occasions, the "native Californians" are trotted forth, in their faded finery, and exhibited as "worthy representatives of all that is finest in our Latin-American heritage." In appointing *Californios* to civic committees, most officials realize that they have achieved the dual purpose, first, of having a Mexican name on the roster for the sake of appearances, and, second, that the persons chosen will invariably act in the same manner as Anglo-Americans of equal social status. Thus the dichotomy which exists throughout the borderlands between what is "Spanish" and what is "Mexican" is a functional, not an ornamental, arrangement. Its function is to deprive the Mexicans of their heritage and to keep them in their place.

In community after community, the Anglo-Americans genuflect once a year before the relics of the Spanish past. Just as Tucson has its annual *La Fiesta de los Vaqueros* so nearly every city in the borderlands now has its annual Spanish Fiesta. It is during *La Fiesta* in Santa Barbara that the annual ride of the *Rancheros Visitadores* occurs. This particular revival is based on a practice of former years, when the rancheros made the rounds of the ranchos to pay a visit to each in turn. "In May, 1930," to quote from the Santa Barbara *Guide* (WPA), "some sixty-five riders assembled for the first cavalcade. Golden Palominos and proud Arabian thoroughbreds, carrying silver-mounted tack, brushed stirrups with shaggy mustangs from the range. Emerging from the heavy gray mist of a reluctant day, they cantered with casual grace down the old familiar trails of the Santa Ynez, to converge on Santa Barbara. . . . Here, amid the tolling of the bells, the tinkling of trappings, and the whinnying of horses, the brown-robed friars blessed them and bade them 'Vayan con Dios.' . . ." This was the first ride of the *Rancheros Visitadores* whose president, today, is Señor J. J. Mitchell. Since this auspicious beginning, the affair has steadily increased in pomp and circumstance. Nowadays it is invariably reported in the Southern California society columns as a major social event of the year. A careful scrutiny of the names of these fancily dressed *visitadores,*—these gaily costumed Rotarians,—reveals that Leo Carrillo, "the man on the white horse," is about the only rider whose name carries a faint echo of the past that is being celebrated so ostentatiously.

Numerous institutions have been founded in the borderlands to keep the fantasy heritage alive. First performed at Mission San Gabriel on April 29, 1912, John Steven McGroarty's "Mission Play" was presented at over 2,600 performances and was seen, according to its modest author, by over 2,500,000 people. The Padua Institute, located at the base of the Sierra Madre Mountains near Claremont, is another institution which works hard to keep the fantasy heritage alive. Here, in a beautiful setting, the lady from Des Moines can have lunch, see a Spanish or Mexican folk play, hear Mexican music, and purchase a "Mexican" gift from the Studio Gift Shop. The Padua Institute is dedicated to "keeping alive the romantic life and music of Old Mexico and Early California." Olvera Street, in the old Plaza section of Los Angeles, is still another attempt to institutionalize the false legend.

Harmless in many ways, these attempts to prettify the legend contrast most harshly with the actual behavior of the community toward persons of Mexican descent. To the younger generation of Mexicans, the fantasy heritage, and the institutions which keep it alive, are resented as still additional affronts to their dignity and sense of pride.

Try as they will, the Anglo-Americans cannot quite enter into the spirit of La Fiesta. Compliments are exchanged between the mayor and the consul-general and the usual remarks are made about Benito Juárez and Abraham Lincoln; but, somehow, the emptiness of the occasion echoes in the platitudes spoken. This meretricious quality is always apparent in the gauche efforts of the press to whip up some semblance of enthusiasm. "Vivas and olas filled the air. . . . Los Angeles yesterday donned the festive regalia of her Mexican heritage . . . Cinco de Mayo Festival On, Si, Si"—are excerpts from the Los Angeles *Times* of May 6, 1947. On the Sixteenth of September, 1947, a Miss Frances Anderson was selected as the reigning señorita in one Southern California town; while, in another, a Miss Virginia Thomas was selected. Both towns have a large Mexican population.

In an editorial commending a program to teach Spanish in the lower grades, the Los Angeles *Times* (August 29, 1944) in a fervor of *españolismo* wrote: "we have missed learning the homey, friendly gossip of the little people who have big hearts even if lean purses. We have missed much, señores . . . Viva Mexico! Viva el Español!"

2. The Birth of a Legend

Throughout the Southwest today the most striking aspect of Anglo-Hispano relations consists in this amazing dichotomy between the Spanish and the Mexican-Indian heritage. There is scarcely a public building constructed since the turn of the century, whether it be a library, a post office, or a courthouse, without murals depicting scenes in which Cabrillo, Serra, De Oñate, and Coronado played a part. Nowadays Juan Bautista de Anza could travel over the trail that he blazed from Tucson to San Jose and spend every night in a De Anza hotel. But there is scarcely a single community in the region in which the living side of this tradition has not been consciously repudiated.

"In spite of their willingness to borrow local color from neighboring Mexico," reads the Arizona *Guide* (WPA), "the Anglo-Saxons of Arizona have usually made a conscious effort to avoid the adoption of the more fundamental traditions and characteristics of the Mexican people. In general the Arizona-Mexicans have been segregated from the more fortunate Arizonians, both as strangers belonging to an alien race of conquered Indians, and as persons whose enforced status in the lowest economic levels make them seem less admirable than other people. They have consequently retained a firmer hold on their native customs and folklore than have other groups of foreigners less discriminated against." This same statement could be made of any state in the region. "When one sees the great sums spent to reconstruct the Spanish missions and other buildings of the Latin-American occupation," writes Jovita Gonzales de Mireles, "one cannot help but wonder at the inconsistency of things in general. If Anglo-Americans accept their art and culture, why have they not accepted the people?"

One reason, of course, is that the discovery of Spain-in-America has been of comparatively recent origin. Harry Carr, a veteran Los Angeles newspaperman, once remarked that when he came to live in the city as a youngster in the 'eighties, school children were taught nothing about the epochal adventures of Coronado, De Oñate, and De Anza. Once the Spanish past was resurrected, this early neglect was greatly overcompensated. Discovered as a tourist-promotion in the 1880's, the Spanish mission background in Southern California was inflated to mythical proportions. Originating in Los Angeles, the "landmarks" movement spread throughout the Southwest. Today community after community is busily resurrecting its "Spanish" ruins and, in a number of cases, master-plans have been adopted—as in St. Augustine in 1936; Monterey in 1939; and San Antonio in 1938—to rebuild whole communities along lines consonant with the original Spanish conception (2).

A second factor has to do with the amazingly heterogeneous character of the Spanish-speaking minority. "Biologically," writes Dr. George Sanchez, "they range over all the possible combinations of, first, their heterogeneous Spanish antecedents and, then, of the *mestizalje* resulting from the crossing of Spaniards and various indigenous peoples of Mexico and the Southwest. Historically, they are both old and new to this region—some came with Oñate in 1598, others with missionaries of the eighteenth century; some were a part of the gold rush of '49, others came to build railroads a few decades later; many came as contract-labor during World War I. Culturally, reflecting their varied biological and historical backgrounds, they are many peoples—the *californios,* the *hispanos,* the *mexico-tejanos,* and numerous other cultural personalities produced by the range of their antecedents and their environments, by their occupations, by their culture-contacts. These people, of whom only a minority are citizens of Mexico, are most often referred to as 'Mexicans.' Their mother tongue, their vernacular, is usually Spanish—though every conceivable variation of that tongue obtains, in terms of all phases of both quantity and quality. In fact, for some the home-language is English; for others a part-English, part-Spanish vernacular is the rule. These Spanish-Mexican Americans of the

THE FANTASY HERITAGE

Southwest, then, defy categorical classification as a group and no term or phrase adequately describes them."

The native-born Spanish-speaking elements resent any attempt to designate them in a manner that implies a "non-white" racial origin. Being called "Mexican" is resented, not on the basis of nationality, but on the assumption of racial difference. Because of the Anglo-American's attitude toward race, the first reaction of the New Mexican, as Dr. Arthur L. Campa has pointed out, "is to disassociate himself from anything that carries a Mexican implication." To do this, he must insist on his difference in origin. Thus he is of "pure Spanish blood," a direct descendant "of the Spanish conquerors," etc. Carried to its logical conclusion, this line of reasoning results in the deductions (a) that the New Mexican is not "Mexican"; and (b) that he has no Indian blood. "Being American citizens, the next step is to combine the concept of race with that of nationality and the hyphenated Spanish-American is the result. Such a term serves a triple purpose: it lifts from the New Mexican the opprobrium of being a Mexican; it makes him a member of the 'white' race, and expresses his American citizenship." But the difficulty with "Spanish-American," as Dr. Campa adds, is that, while it suits the New Mexican in the abstract, there is little in his appearance and origin that upholds the distinction he is trying so hard to make (3).

The differences between New Mexicans and Mexicans being regional distinctions occurring within a similar culture, the substitution of the name "Spanish" does not change the substance of traits that are undisputedly Mexican. "The 'Spanish' suppers," writes Dr. Campa, "given by clubs and church societies are in reality Mexican dishes to which no truly Spanish palate is accustomed. The 'Spanish' songs sung by school children and by radio performers in New Mexico are as Mexican as *tortillas de maíz, chicharrones de puerco, chile con carne,* and the *sopaipillas* at Christmas time."

To the Anglo-Americans of the borderlands, with their racial preoccupations, it is second nature to refer to the Spanish-speaking group as "Mexican"; whereas the *Californios,* the *Tejanos,* and the New Mexicans insist that they are "Spanish" or "Spanish-American." The trouble with all the terminology, as Dr. Campa puts it, is that it is based on logic and excludes the human factor. "The whole thing is characterized by anomalies which attempt to justify prejudices and defense mechanisms." Certainly the attitude of the *Californios*, the *Tejanos*, and the New Mexicans has been a factor in the cultivation of an absurd dichotomy between things Spanish and things Mexican.

3. DE ANZA DOESN'T LIVE HERE ANY MORE

Still another reason for the persistence of the fantasy heritage has been the negligible amount of immigration from Spain. The number of Spaniards in the United States, in or out of the borderlands, has always been so small that they have never been a factor in group competition. Hence it has always been possible to praise things Spanish without having to accept an embarrassingly large Spanish element. Despite the poverty of its population, Spain has always rigorously discouraged emigration. The number of Spanish-born in the United States was 22,108 in 1910; 49,535 in 1930; 109,407 in 1940 (half of whom were temporarily resident in this country)—0.3 per cent of the population. Furthermore, it is a safe assumption that most of the Spanish-born have always resided outside the Southwest.

In Florida and Louisiana a few colonies survived after the Spanish withdrew. For example, St. Bernard's Parish in Louisiana, named after Bernardo de Gálvez, once governor of the province under Spanish rule, is still made up of the descendants of some 1,500 Canary Islanders—"the Isleños" as they are called—who settled there in 1770.

In the Far West one can find a few colonies of Basque immigrants who came to this country by way of South America. Today some seven thousand Basques reside in the Boise, Idaho, area. They are, for the most part, descendants of immigrants who moved eastward from Jordan Valley in Oregon as the West Coast flocks began to be driven eastward for pasturage. Basques have been coming to California, in small numbers, for a hundred years. One reads that Yudarte, a Basque herdsman, once grazed hundreds of sheep in San Francisco between what is now Van Ness Avenue and the Presidio. Basque names like Duque, Echeverre, Mindiano, Hermasoillo, and Indiano are not uncommon in California. The Spanish Basques are to be found north of San Francisco, along the Sacramento River, and down the coast range; while the French Basques are concentrated around Fresno and Bakersfield. The Hotel Español and the Hotel De España in San Francisco have long been recognized as unofficial headquarters for the Basque sheepmen or *boscos*.

There are, also, a few colonies of Spanish-speaking Puerto Ricans in California, mostly in the East Bay area. Most of these immigrants came to California from Hawaii following the expiration of the labor-contracts under which they had been imported to the islands. Mingled with the Puerto Ricans are a few thousand Spaniards who managed to elude Spanish immigration inspectors by going to Gibraltar where they signed labor-contracts to work in the canefields of Hawaii. For the most part, however, Puerto Ricans are concentrated in the City of New York. Today it is estimated that Little Spain or Spanish Harlem has a population of about 350,000 Puerto Ricans. Most of the recent immigrants have come to New York in "bucket seat" planes at a fare of $72 from San Juan (4). To the number of Puerto Ricans one might add some 47,699 Filipinos, many of whom, of course, are Spanish-speaking. However none of these elements,—Spanish immigrants, Spanish Basques, Puerto Ricans or Spanish-speaking Filipinos,—figure at all in the Spanish-Mexican scheme of things in the Southwest.

In Florida there are perhaps 30,000 Spanish-speaking people: around 15,000 Cubans; 8,500 Spanish-born; and small settlements of several thousand each of Minorcans and Spaniards in St. Augustine and a few other towns. With the exception of those in St. Augustine, most of these people are fairly recent immigrants. The movement of Cubans to Florida began in 1868, when Vicente Martínez Ibor, a Spaniard who owned a large cigar factory in Havana, opened a factory in Key West. He was followed to Florida by other factory owners who sought to evade the import duty on cigars. The struggle for independence in Cuba was, also, an important factor in stimulating this exodus. With the cigar-owners came thousands of cigar-makers from Havana, Bejucal, San Antonio de los Baños, Guines, Santiago de las Vegas, and other small towns near Havana (5). When the cigar-makers first arrived, Tampa was "a wilderness settlement comprising some four blocks of houses." As the cigar-making industry expanded, several thousand Spanish cigar-makers joined the colony.

The Spanish-speaking colonies in Florida were, of course, "the cradle of Cuban Independence." At one time the headquarters of the Cuban revolutionary movement was located in Key West. It was here that José Martí, "the George Washington of Cuba," founded the

Partido Revolucionario Cubano in 1892. Originating in Florida, sympathy for Cuban independence spread throughout the nation. Just as there were Americans who took part in the movement which finally won independence for Cuba in 1902, so there were a few Cubans who fought with the colonists in the American Revolutionary War. Today small, scattered colonies of Cubans are to be found outside Florida, chiefly in New York, Philadelphia, New Orleans, and in Atlanta.

"Cuba," writes Manuel Pedro Gonzales, "more than any other Spanish American country, has contributed to the evolution of cultural relations between the two races. From 1823 to the present time she has been a kind of connecting link between the two cultures; she has played the double role of interpreter and propagandist of both cultures. For more than a century her most distinguished poets, writers, historians, and philosophers have endeavored to disseminate knowledge in the United States about Spanish America and her intellectual life; at the same time these men, who were far more familiar with the culture of the United States than their colleagues south of the Rio Grande, have tried to interpret and reveal to them through translations and critical studies the literary and scientific wealth of this country" (6).

Cuban cigar-makers founded the first trade-unions in the South. One of these organizations, *Los Caballeros del Trabajo* was a branch of the Knights of Labor; and, from 1886 to 1901, the dominant Tampa group was known as *La Resistencia*. In 1900, and again in 1910, the Spanish-speaking cigar-makers of Florida conducted militant strikes which were suppressed with great violence. They founded the cigar industry in Florida which in 1908 was valued at $17,175,000; some 10,500 employees of the industry were then receiving a weekly wage of $200,000.

Important as the Florida colonies have been they have had no relationship with Spanish-speaking settlements in the borderlands. And it is a rare case, indeed, when a Spanish immigrant has established any sort of contact with the Spanish-speaking people of the Southwest. Dr. Joaquín Ortega, of the University of New Mexico, born in Ronda, Spain, is one of the few individuals in whose career the two traditions are linked. From 1820 to 1940, the total Spanish immigration to the United States was about 175,000, three-fourths of which came after 1900. During the first World War, a large number of Spaniards worked in the shipyards but returned to Spain after the war. Most of the Spanish immigrant colonies are located outside the borderlands: in West Virginia;

Philadelphia; Cleveland; Newark; New York; and Tampa. There is, therefore, simply no relation between Spanish immigration and the Spanish-speaking minority in the Southwest.

Quite apart from these factors, there has long existed, as I have previously pointed out, a determination to subordinate the Spanish-speaking minority in the Southwest. One of the techniques used to effect this subordination has been to drive a wedge between the native-born and the foreign-born and to cultivate the former at the expense of the latter. To some extent, elements of the native-born have encouraged this strategy by seeking to differentiate themselves from the immigrants. By emphasizing the Spanish part of the tradition and consciously repudiating the Mexican-Indian side, it has been possible to rob the Spanish-speaking minority of a heritage which is rightfully theirs, rather in the same manner that Negroes have been robbed of their heritage. The constant operation of this strategy has made it difficult for the Spanish-speaking people to organize and it has retarded their advancement.

One of the first conditions to an improvement in Anglo-Hispano relations in the Southwest, therefore, is, as Dr. A. W. Bork has suggested, to give back to Indo-Hispano citizens the heritage of racial pride of which we have robbed them and to teach Anglo-Americans to respect and honor this heritage (7). The first step in this direction is to get rid of the fantasy heritage, the latter-day version of the Spanish prologue, which has so perniciously beclouded relations between Anglos and Hispanos in the borderlands. Once this veil of fantasy has been lifted, it should be possible for both groups to recognize the reality of cultural fusion in the Southwest. This reality is to be sought, first of all, in the nature of the region in which the great bulk of the Spanish-speaking people have always resided.

III

The Fan of Settlement

Starting in California, run a line from Santa Barbara along the base of the Tehachapi Mountains, around the rim of the San Bernardino Range, and then across the desert to the border of Arizona; draw the line through the center of Arizona; embrace all of New Mexico, including the San Luis Valley and portions of southeastern Colorado; then move down the eastern boundary of New Mexico to El Paso. From El Paso, pull the line diagonally to San Antonio and from San Antonio to Corpus Christi on the gulf. Between this line,—the northern border of the borderlands,—and the present Mexican-American border, reside upwards of eighty-five per cent of the Spanish-speaking people in the United States. Stated another way and with less exactness, the Spanish-speaking reside in a belt of territory about 150 miles in width, paralleling the border, and extending from Los Angeles to the Gulf of Mexico. This territory is the fan of Spanish-Mexican influence "north from Mexico" which spreads across the borderlands with the tip of the fan resting in New Mexico.

1. "Sunshine, Silence, and Adobe"

As one can see by glancing at a map, the fan of Spanish-speaking settlement embraces a subregion of the American Southwest. Topographically, it is a fairly distinct region-within-a-region: the basin and range country which extends from Los Angeles to the southern tip of the Great Plains, including the Lower Rio Grande Valley in Texas. By no means uniform in terrain, climate, and vegetation, it does have certain distinctive regional characteristics. The surface is made up of mountain ranges and basins; the climate is sub-humid, semi-arid, or arid; and the land itself is largely treeless. Many varieties of cactus are to be found throughout this region of glaring sunlight and intense heat. The amount of rainfall is slight and the rate of evaporation is extremely high. The principal rivers are the Colorado, the Gila, and the Rio Grande, none of which is navigable. Water is of prime importance throughout the area. The mountains tend to be bare and rugged, harshly sculptured, violently silhouetted, seamed with deep arroyos. Embracing the old Spanish borderlands, or Spanish highlands as they were sometimes called, this is the region, as Charles Fletcher Lummis once said, of "sunshine, silence, and adobe."

Historically, it is much the older part of the Southwest, being roughly coterminous with the original area of Spanish settlement. In settling the borderlands, the Spanish moved north from Mexico up the V-shaped central plateau: from the Mesa Central to the Mesa del Norte to the borderlands. The Florida and Louisiana settlements were detached from New Spain, based on parent colonies in the West Indies; the borderland settlements were integrally a part of Mexico. Between St. Augustine and Santa Fe, the Spanish made little impression within the present boundaries of the United States; but the borderlands carry the indelible imprint of Spain and Mexico to the present day. "Institutionally," write Messrs. Richardson and Rister (1),* "the basin and range country is a land of peculiar interest. Its northern boundary constitutes an institutional fault line that divides the Anglo-American Southwest, on the north, from the country to the south, where Spanish and north European institutions are mixed. In the more favored localities the natural environment afforded by the basin and range country is similar to that in Spain and Mexico over which the Spaniards passed in their northward advance." Settling the region when the Anglo-Americans were hardly aware of its existence, the Spanish planted their institutions so firmly "that the trace of the Spaniard and his Mexican successor can never be beaten out of the land."

Although geographically similar to Mexico, the borderlands were separated from the heart of Spanish settlement in Mexico by a belt of desert which served to isolate the borderland settlements in time and space. Just as the Pueblo Indians were isolated from Indians of a similarly high culture in central Mexico, so the Spanish settlers in the borderlands were isolated from the older and more populous Spanish settle-

* Reprinted by permission of the publisher, The Arthur H. Clark Company, from *The Greater Southwest* by Rupert N. Richardson and Carl C. Rister.

ments in Mexico. The borderlands were thus true borderlands in the dual sense that they extended as a wide belt between Anglo-Americans, on the north, and the Spanish Americans on the south and in the further sense that they were separated from their parent colonies in Mexico by the great wastes of desert in northern Sonora, Chihuahua, Coahuila, Nuevo Leon, and Tamaulipas.

The ban of desert terrain across northern Mexico always served as a more or less effective barrier to the extension of Spanish influence and control. There were no barriers of this sort, however, to the east or to the north; in fact the weight of geographical factors tilted the borderlands more toward the Anglo-American than toward the Spanish-American sphere. With the opening of the Santa Fe Trail in 1820, residents of New Mexico could trade with St. Louis more easily than with Chihuahua. Similarly the Spanish settlers in California could trade with Boston merchants, via the clipper ships, more easily than they could with points in Mexico by the overland routes.

While the weight of geographical factors ultimately severed the borderlands from Mexico, the fact that they were similar to and yet detached from Mexico is largely responsible for the persistence of Spanish cultural influences in the region. The similarity of environment accounts for the fact that Spanish institutions were readily adaptable to conditions in the borderlands and proved to be of lasting value. By the same token, however, the southwest was a new world for the Anglo-Americans, a world quite unlike that in which their institutions had been evolved. Learning to live in the borderlands was a novel experience for the Anglo-Americans and one that required a basic modification in their institutions and a slow adaptation of their imported cultural practices. In the ensuing competition, Spanish cultural traits showed a remarkable tenacity since they were better adapted to the environment and more firmly rooted in time.

Not feeling at home in a semi-arid environment, the Anglo-Americans were at first somewhat reluctant to settle in the Southwest. Had the region been more accessible and familiar, more fertile and inviting, every vestige of Spanish influence might have been quickly obliterated after 1848. But the isolation and aridity of the borderlands kept the Anglo-Americans out for a time and later limited their number in relation to the Spanish-speaking. Coincidental with the annexation of the Southwest, gold was discovered in California and the lure of gold pulled the tide of Anglo-American immigration through and beyond the borderlands. The discovery of gold in turn accounts for the fact that railroads did not penetrate the Southwest until the 1880's, so that the isolation of the region survived for twenty or thirty years after through rail service had been extended to the Pacific. The time-lag created by these factors naturally favored the survival of Spanish and Mexican influences.

Later, when the tide of Anglo-American immigration began, the arid nature of the environment imposed definite limitations on the number, the spacing, and the character of the settlements which they established. Thus, in some areas, Spanish-speaking people continued to outnumber English-speaking for many years. The Spanish-Mexican settlements, moreover, were located in more or less compact clusters, as a consequence, again, of the nature of the environment. The cluster-like pattern of these settlements made, of course, for cultural cohesiveness and permanence of influence.

2. The Forgotten Link

Under the terms of the Treaty of Guadalupe Hidalgo, executed on February 2, 1848, Mexico ceded to the United States a vast territory, including California, Arizona, New Mexico, and other large fragments, and also approved the prior annexation of Texas. The lands which Mexico ceded to the United States were greater in extent than Germany and France combined and represented one-half of the territory which Mexico possessed in 1821. All citizens of Mexico residing within the ceded domain were to become citizens of the United States if they failed to leave the territory within one year after ratification of the treaty. Only a few thousand Mexican nationals, perhaps not more than 1,500 or 2,000, took advantage of this provision; the rest became citizens-by-default. The treaty also provided specific guarantees for the property and political rights of the "native" population and attempted to safeguard their cultural autonomy, that is, they were given the right to retain their language, religion, and culture. No provisions were made, however, for the integration of the native peoples as a group, as a society. While the treaty contained a promise of early statehood, the promise was not redeemed, in the case of New Mexico and Arizona, until some sixty-four years after the treaty was ratified. The reluctance to grant statehood to New Mexico and Arizona, moreover, should be compared with the alacrity with which California and Nevada were admitted to the union. Obviously the reluctance to admit Arizona and New Mexico was based on "skepticism as to the advisability of granting full civil rights to a people largely illiterate and of an alien culture." The fact that statehood was so long delayed served to retard the "assimilation" of the native population and encouraged the survival of Spanish-Mexican cultural influences.

There was still another factor, however, which made for the survival of these same influences. When the Treaty of Guadalupe Hidalgo was signed, approximately 75,000 Spanish-speaking people were living in the Southwest: around 7,500 in California; a thousand or so in Arizona; 60,000 in New Mexico; and perhaps 5,000 in Texas. The great majority of these people were of mixed Spanish-Indian blood. But there were then living in the Southwest some other people who also passed under American sovereignty with the ratification of the treaty, namely, about 180,000 Indians, not including some 72,000 Indians in California. These Indians constitute the forgotten link in Anglo-Hispano cultural relations in the Southwest.

In 1848 the Indians of the Southwest, apart from the California Indians, could be divided into two broad categories: Pueblo and non-Pueblo; mesa-dwellers and desert-and-plains Indians. The Pueblo Indians were, of course, one of the few sedentary tribes of the New World. At the time the Spanish arrived, they were divided into four groups: the Pueblos along the Rio Grande; the Zuñi in western New Mexico; the Hopi in northwestern Arizona; and the Pima in southern Arizona. These four branches of the Pueblo tribe lived at peace with the Spaniards for many years, becoming closely identified with them in blood, language, and religion. In fact the Spanish settlements were superposed on the Pueblo Indian villages and never extended beyond the ambit of these villages. Although the four Pueblo groups differed in custom, language, and mythology, they had some traits in common: they lived in villages of stone or adobe dwellings; they were monogamistic; and they had practiced irrigated farming in the Southwest for centuries.

The nomadic Indians of the Southwest,—the "eastern" and "western" Apaches, the Utes, the Navajo, and the Comanches,—were of an entirely different breed. For untold centuries, they had preyed upon the Pueblo

THE FAN OF SETTLEMENT

Indians. For many years these nomadic and warlike Indians surrounded, bedeviled, and lived off the Spanish settlements just as they had always exploited the Pueblo villages. Never vanquished by the Spanish, they were the real masters of the Southwest in 1848; in fact the Spanish-speaking were everywhere on the defensive at the time of the Anglo-American conquest and actually occupied less territory than at any previous period.

From the earliest date, the nomadic Indians had prevented the Spanish from either expanding or consolidating their settlements in the borderlands. The Apaches were in full possession of the desert territory which separated the California and the Arizona settlements. Their destruction of the Spanish outpost at the junction of the Gila and Colorado rivers in 1780 broke the link between California and Arizona. So complete was this severance that the early-day Mexican residents of Tucson scarcely knew that such a country as California existed. The Apaches likewise held undisputed control of the territory separating the settlements in southern Arizona from those in New Mexico. As a matter of fact it was not until about 1880 that the United States finally succeeded in wresting control of this territory from the Apaches. Nor were the Spanish ever successful in attempting to open a through-line of communication between the New Mexico and the Texas settlements. Surrounded on three sides by nomadic Indians, the New Mexico colonists had great difficulty in maintaining the route between Santa Fe and Chihuahua. As late as 1848, the trail from San Antonio to Santa Fe ran south to Durango; from Durango to El Paso; and from El Paso to Santa Fe.

The resistance of the nomadic Indians retarded Anglo-American settlement of the Southwest for several decades and thereby threw a mantle of protection around Spanish cultural influences and institutions. From 1848 to 1887, the Anglo-Americans were so preoccupied with the Indians that they had little time left to devote to the settlement of the region or the exploitation of its resources. For many years the federal government was forced to maintain a series of military posts throughout the Southwest which provided important local markets for the native New Mexicans and gave them the first real protection against Apache raids that they had ever known. Both under Spanish and Mexican rule, the borderland settlements were separated from each other and from parent settlements in Mexico as much by Indian hostility as by the nature of the terrain. On the other hand, it was the nature of the terrain, as much as anything else, which enabled the nomadic Indians to hold out for so many years against Spaniards, Mexicans, and Anglo-Americans.

3. Lands of the Spanish-Speaking

The most graphic way to envisage Spanish settlement north of the Rio Grande is to imagine a fan thrust north from Mexico with its tip resting on Santa Fe. Gradually the fan unfolds—eastward to Texas, westward to California—with the ribs of the fan extending northward from the base in Mexico. Long a part of the social structure of the region immediately north of the present border, that fan-of-influence still rests on the land. Indigenous and indestructible, it is a basic aspect of the cultural landscape.

Today an undetermined number of Spanish-speaking people reside in the old Spanish borderlands. The first attempt to estimate the size of this population was made in the 1930 census. This census included in the category of "Mexican" all persons "born in Mexico or having parents born in Mexico who are not definitely white, Negro, Indian, or Japanese." Premised upon the assumption that the Mexican minority should be regarded as "a race," this category was obviously misleading and inexact. It overlooked the fact that portions of the Southwest had been a Spanish cultural province for several hundred years. For example, the census returned a figure of 59,340 "Mexicans" for New Mexico; but Dr. George Sanchez demonstrated, through a school census, that the figure should have been 202,709—an under-enumeration of 144,389. Similarly the census returned the number of Mexicans in Los Angeles as 97,116, when 385,000 would have been a more accurate estimate.

Nevertheless an analysis of the 1930 census does provide a substantially accurate picture of the distribution of "Mexicans" in the United States. The total figure given by the census was 1,422,533—the third largest "racial" group in the nation. Nine-tenths of the Mexican population was found in five states: Texas, California, Arizona, New Mexico, and Colorado. Texas had 683,681 or 48.1 per cent of all Mexicans living in the United States; California 368,013 or 25.9 per cent; Arizona, 114,173 or 8 per cent; New Mexico, 59,340 or 4.2 per cent (a grossly inaccurate figure); and Colorado had 57,676 or 4.1 per cent. Illinois returned 28,906—virtually all in Chicago; and Michigan 13,336—half of this number residing in Detroit. A language enumeration made in 1940, based on Spanish as the mother tongue, indicated that there were 1,861,400 Spanish-speaking people in the United States and that, of this number, 1,570,740 resided in Texas, California, Arizona, New Mexico, and Colorado. There is good reason to believe that the concentration of Mexicans in the Southwest is even more pronounced today than it was in 1930, since the Middle Western states furnished a relatively higher percentage of Mexican *repatriados* during the depression than did the states of the Southwest.

Inaccurate in other respects, the 1930 census may also be taken as a fairly reliable *immigration* census. In this census the Mexican population was divided into the following categories: first generation foreign-born immigrants 616,998 (43.4 per cent of the total); native-born of foreign-born or mixed parentage, 541,197 (38 per cent of the total)—in effect the second generation; and 264,338 or 18.6 per cent native-born of native-born parents. The first category is substantially accurate; the second is reasonably accurate; but the third is quite misleading. For in 1930 there were probably more Spanish-speaking people in this category in New Mexico than the census returned for the nation. Of this category,—"native Mexicans of native parentage,"—95.6 per cent were concentrated in the Southwest. The numbers so reported, and the percentage which they represented of the Mexican total for each state, were as follows: Texas, 146,806 or 21.5 per cent; Colorado, 32,956 or 51.1 per cent; California, 29,138 or 7.9 per cent; New Mexico, 25,586 or 43.1 per cent; and Arizona, 18,955 or 16.6 per cent. These figures are only accurate in the sense that they indicate that the "native-born of native-born parents" are most heavily concentrated in New Mexico, Colorado, and Texas.

The importance of the Spanish-speaking group in the Southwest may be shown in the proportion that this group constitutes of the total population in the key states: 26.2 per cent of the population in Arizona; 14 per cent of the population of New Mexico (this is the census figure; the actual percentage for New Mexico would be much closer to 40 per cent); 11.7 per cent in Texas; 7 per cent in California; and 6 per cent in Colorado. Ignoring the 1930 census, one can estimate the total Spanish-American population of the Southwestern states somewhat as follows:

Texas, 1,000,000; New Mexico, 250,000; Arizona, 120,000; California, 500,000; and Colorado around 90,000. These estimates are based on school censuses, local social studies, and similar sources. That two million is a conservative estimate may be shown by the fact that the National Resources Committee in 1938 placed the total for the United States at close to three million.

Not only is the Mexican population overwhelmingly concentrated in the Southwest, but it is highly concentrated within the belt of territory which I have previously described. This is merely another way of saying, of course, that the bulk of the Spanish-speaking people are concentrated within the boundaries of the old Spanish borderlands. In each of twenty-four counties extending from Santa Cruz in Arizona to Willacy in Texas, more than fifty per cent of the population is of Mexican origin. There is a tier of counties, predominantly Mexican, in southern Texas that is three-fourths as large in area as that of the New England states combined. Roughly speaking, there are ten counties in southern Texas in which so-called "Latin-Americans" constitute seventy per cent or more of the youngsters of school age; twenty-five counties in which they constitute from fifty to seventy-five per cent of the scholastics; and nineteen counties in which the percentage ranges from twenty-five to fifty per cent.

In New Mexico the Spanish-speaking element is highly concentrated in the Upper Valley of the Rio Grande,—the Rio Arriba section where the first colonies were planted. In each of fifteen out of thirty-one counties in the state, the Spanish-speaking comprise fifty per cent of the population and in each of seven counties they make up eighty per cent or more of the population. In Colorado, the native-born Spanish-speaking element is concentrated in the San Luis Valley and the southeastern corner of the state, while the immigrant element is to be found in Denver and the northern sugar-beet counties. In Arizona the bulk of the Mexicans reside in the southern tier of counties along the border.

Today as yesterday most of the Spanish-speaking residents of California are to be found in the southern counties. In 1920 these counties had seventy-eight per cent of the Mexican population and this proportion would be higher today than in 1920. Under Spanish rule, the missions in Southern California were more prosperous than those north of the Tehachapi Mountains and had a larger Indian-Mexican population. By the time of the American conquest, two political parties had developed in the state: the *arribeños* or *norteños* (the upper or northern people) and the *abajeños* or *sureños* (the lower or southern people). This same north-south division became more pronounced under American rule, for the discovery of gold brought thousands of immigrants into the northern counties but left the predominantly Spanish-speaking counties in the south in relative isolation for many years. Thirty years after the discovery of gold, Los Angeles was still a small Mexican town in which Spanish was spoken almost universally, with all official documents, including city ordinances, being published both in Spanish and in English.

Contrary to popular belief, the Mexican population in the Southwest is today predominantly an urban population. In 1930, for example, 723,428 "Mexicans"—fifty-one per cent of the total in the United States according to this census—resided in urban areas. The Mexican population in the United States is thus much more highly urbanized than the population of Mexico. In areas outside the Southwest, the Mexican population is overwhelmingly urban: eighty-five per cent of the seventy thousand-odd Mexicans in the Midwest reside in cities. Within the Southwest, the three largest Mexican urban centers are Los Angeles, around 385,000 (for the county area); El Paso, 58,291 (fifty-seven per cent of the population); and San Antonio, 82,373 or thirty-six per cent of the population. Next to Mexico City, Los Angeles has the largest Mexican urban population of any city in the world.

Social as well as physiographic factors have influenced the concentration of Spanish-speaking people in the old borderlands. The most pronounced discrimination against Mexicans has always existed, not in the predominantly Spanish-speaking or bilingual counties along the border, but in the areas further removed from the border. The existence of this invisible but highly effective social wall has kept both old-resident and immigrant Mexicans within the familiar, and, to some extent, more congenial social atmosphere of the old borderlands.

4. Mexico Is Not Europe

Since the tendency of Spanish-speaking people to concentrate in the Southwest appears to be permanent and cumulative, it is reasonable to assume that the small islands of Mexican settlement outside the region will soon be absorbed in the general population. Studies of these communities have shown that they are rapidly losing their distinctive Mexican characteristics. But the situation is quite different in the Southwest. Here the Spanish-Mexican influence cannot be "beaten out of the land." For the Mexican minority—actually a majority in some areas—occupies a unique relation to the land, the culture, and the institutions of the region. Like the Indians, the Mexicans were "here first." It is most misleading, therefore, to assume that they occupy a relation to the majority element which is like that, say, of Poles in Detroit or Italians in New York.

Most Americans have been taught to think of immigration as a process by which Europeans picked up bag and baggage and came "to these shores." From the immigrant's point of view, the Atlantic crossing was of the utmost psychological and sociological importance; it was a severance, a crossing, an abrupt transition. But Mexican immigrants have seldom ventured beyond the fan of Spanish influence in the borderlands. They have been drawn to the borderlands by a feeling of continuity, of gradual transition, of movement within the confines, the protective mantle, of a familiar environment. The river which many of them have forded to enter the United States has a Spanish name. Most of the cities and counties in which they have settled, and even the streets on which they live, have Spanish names. One can travel from Chihuahua to Santa Fe with scarcely any feeling of abrupt change in the physical environment. Migration from Mexico is deeply rooted in the past. It follows trails which are among the most ancient on the North American continent. Psychologically and culturally, Mexicans have never emigrated to the Southwest: they have returned. In many cases, they have returned for the second, third, fourth or fifth time. It is altogether possible that there are immigrants from Sonora now living in Los Angeles whose grandparents or great-grandparents once lived in the old pueblo or who, as Sonora miners, made the long trek to the goldfields. "The old Mexican centers and the old routes," as Semple noted, "have still the power to attract."

In migrating to the borderlands, Mexicans have not founded immigrant colonies so much as they have "moved in with their relatives." In fact their in-laws and relatives are scattered all along the route. One can travel from Sinaloa or Sonora to Los Angeles, or San Antonio, speaking Spanish the entire distance, moving continuously within the fan-spread of Spanish-Mexican culture, and living throughout the journey among Spanish-speaking people. Anglo-Americans emigrate to Mexico; but no Mexican is really an "immigrant" in the Southwest. The key to this distinction is to be found in the nature of the "border" which separates Mexico from the United States—one of the most unrealistic borders to be found in the Western Hemisphere.

5. The Border of the Borderlands

From Brownsville to San Diego, the present boundary between Mexico and the United States is approximately 2,000 miles in length. From Brownsville the border extends up the Rio Grande to El Paso; proceeds westward from El Paso across some of the most rugged and desolate terrain in America; skirts the Gulf of California; and then extends westward to the Pacific. Not too much was known about this long stretch of territory when the Treaty of Guadalupe Hidalgo was signed in 1848. The negotiators did fairly well in fixing the line from Brownsville to El Paso—they simply followed the Rio Grande. But at El Paso they got lost, for a subsequent survey revealed that the line described in the treaty had been made with reference to a map which proved to be inaccurate.

Once this discovery was made, Texas threatened New Mexico; New Mexico threatened Texas; both threatened Mexico; and Mexico sent troops to the border. For a moment or more it looked as though the Mexican-American War of 1846 would be resumed. To escape from this impasse, the United States sent James Gadsden to Mexico City to negotiate a new acquisition. By the use of high-pressure methods already painfully familiar to the Mexicans, Gadsden managed to secure for us another bite of Mexican territory—45,532 square miles in size. The original line—that defined by the treaty—would have followed the Gila River in Arizona. By the time Gadsden arrived in Mexico, however, we had become interested in the possibility of a rail line along the southern route to the coast. Hence the line that Gadsden finally accepted ran south of the Gila and just managed—by pure accident—to include in the United States, by a mile or more, some of the most important copper-mining properties in the world.

As finally fixed, the border was a border of the borderlands rather than a national boundary based on economic and ethnic factors. Economically, the line made very little sense. By including Guaymas in the Mexican zone—the Mexican negotiators tried their best to force Guaymas on Mr. Gadsden—the interior basin was deprived of what might have become an extremely important seaport and the naturally advantageous and long-established commerce between Sonora and Arizona was disrupted. This circumstance has given rise to various ambitious schemes, originating in Arizona, for the purchase of Lower California. The present border also left the whole question of water rights—a matter of vital importance—suspended in midair. From 1848 to the present time, Mexico and the United States have been at loggerheads over the water rights of the Colorado and Rio Grande rivers. From the point of view of the borderlands, the boundary should have been pushed further south so as to have included within the United States Lower California, the port of Guaymas, and all lands lying within the watershed of the Colorado and Rio Grande river systems. "The Rio Grande," wrote Ellen Churchill Semple in *American History and Its Geographic Conditions* (1903), "is anything but a satisfactory boundary between the United States and Mexico. Dry for many months of the year, it bears no semblance of a barrier. . . . The political frontier line which is run along a river is an artificial one, for every drainage system forms an unbroken whole."

It should be noted, also, that the Mexican population living north of the border is, even today, somewhat larger than the Mexican population in the border states of northern Mexico. At various periods, this circumstance has filled the Anglo-Americans with fear and apprehension and has made for troubled relations between Mexico and the United States. As between Mexico and the United States, the movement of population has been consistently northward: into the northern Mexican border states and from there into the borderlands. The reverse movement, that is, of Anglo-Americans into Mexico, has always been negligible. Ethnographically, therefore, the border might well have followed the northern line of the old borderlands from Santa Barbara eastward, as traced in the first paragraph of this chapter.

Due to the isolation of the region, the border for many years was merely a line on a map. The Border Patrol of the Immigration Service was not established until 1924. As late as 1911, a few Mounted Watchmen, as they were called, patrolled this two-thousand-mile-stretch of territory most of which was desolate and sparsely populated. Prior to 1924 the border could be crossed, in either direction, at almost any point from Brownsville to San Diego, with the greatest of ease. While the border was at least visible along the Rio Grande, it was by no means permanent. For the river has constantly changed its channel; islands formerly in Mexico have passed over to the American side; and new islands have been formed.

From El Paso to Brownsville, the Rio Grande does not separate people: it draws them together. Along the river, as along the entire border, the towns are twins, and Siamese twins, in some cases, for many of them have interconnecting communications. Below El Paso, Ysleta is linked with Sargossa, San Elizario with Loma Colorado, Del Rio with Villa Acuña, Eagle Pass with Reimosa, Brownsville with Matamoros. El Paso and Juárez are, of course, essentially one community. Throughout south Texas, back from the border, most of the towns are twins: an American town and a Mexican town being joined together. Speaking of the residents of El Paso and Juárez, Walter Prescott Webb has said that "the river instead of separating them, rescued them from the desert and bound them together; all depended upon it both for domestic purposes and for irrigation of their meager crops; across its muddy channel the Mexicans intermarried, celebrated the same festivals, observed the same religious rites, rejoiced in the same feast days, and shared their sympathies, passions, and prejudices."

Westward from El Paso, the desert mines along the border draw people together much as the Rio Grande does from El Paso to Brownsville. Here, again, the towns are twins, sometimes having a similar name: Douglas, Arizona, and Agua Prieta, Mexico; Naco, Arizona, and Naco, Sonora; Nogales, Arizona, and Nogales, Mexico; Calexico, USA, and Mexicali, Mexico. Prior to the time when the government required sixty feet of "free space" along certain sections of the border, the border-towns not only overlapped but the mythical line ran through particular stores, buildings, and saloons. Many stories are told, for example, of the old Brickwood store in Nogales, the counter of which was right on the line. For years the proprietor evaded the tax systems of both countries by stepping to one side or the other of the counter in making sales. Wanted by Mexican authorities lined up outside an adobe house in Nogales, an Arizona cowboy once escaped by sawing a hole in the rear wall and stepping out on American soil.

Unreal in every sense, the Mexican-American border has greatly influenced relations between the two countries and has profoundly affected Anglo-Hispano relations throughout the Southwest. In summarizing the issues which have disturbed Mexican-American relations through the years, J. Fred Rippy has given top priority to the unreality of the border. Between Mexico and the United States, he writes, "there have been no natural barriers, the two nations being separated by an imaginary line, a barbed-wire fence, an easily forded river, an undergrowth of mesquite or chaparral. Citizens of both nations have passed back and forth with little difficulty or interruption, or have settled in neighboring states amidst natural surroundings which have not repelled them by their unfamiliar aspects. Bandits, filibusters, and Indians have raided freely back and forth. Smugglers have often plied their trade with ease and security. Robbers of stock sometimes have been able to operate on a large and profitable scale. Political insurgents and refugees have often sought and found safety across the international line" (2).

In short, the old Spanish borderlands were well named. The dictionary definition of "borderland" is the land lying along the frontier of two adjacent countries; but, in this case, the borderland runs along only one side of the frontier and that side is in the United States. I have often speculated on what form relations between the United States and Mexico might have assumed if there had been no Spanish-speaking people or settlements within the borderlands. Had this been the case, the chances are that more formality and less friction might have prevailed. But, in the long run, the distance between the two countries might have been greater; the sense of separation more pronounced. While relatives who live in widely separated communities may quarrel less than those who live on the same street or in the same house, it is doubtful if much real affection or understanding ever develops between them.

Anglos and Hispanos have fought and quarrelled along the border as only close relatives can quarrel; but they have not faced each other across a fixed boundary with the sullen and undying enmity that the Germans and the French have faced each other across the Rhine. Borderlands unite as well as separate; they make for fusion rather than total acceptance or rejection. Differences tend to shade off in such a complex manner that soon various combinations of the two major types have appeared and with the emergence of these intermediate types the two antithetical elements have been inextricably bound together. There is no stronger bond between Mexico and the United States today than the living and organic union of the two cultures which exists in the borderlands. The process by which this union has been effected can never be reversed for it is a product of the similarity, the oneness, of the environment.

IV

Heart of the Borderlands

"The most cohesive Hispanic population in the United States," writes Dr. Joaquín Ortega, "the one most faithful to a long and uninterrupted tradition of identification with the soil is to be found in New Mexico." The New Mexico settlements are, of course, among the oldest in the United States. Founded in 1609, Santa Fe is the oldest capital in the nation and, next to Florida, New Mexico is the oldest "state." Over a period of a hundred years, from 1846 to 1946, the population of Santa Fe only increased from 6,000 to 20,325—old roots, slow growth. Like the dwarf evergreens on the surrounding hills, however, these roots have acquired a remarkable strength and sturdiness.

1. A Lost World

In isolation, a people identified itself with its environment.
DR. GEORGE SANCHEZ

Isolation is the key to the New Mexico cultural complex. "The deepest penetration of civilized man in North America," New Mexico was a lonely outpost of Spanish settlement for three hundred years,—isolated from Mexico, California, Texas, and Arizona; isolated by deserts, mountain ranges, and hostile Indian tribes. It would be difficult, in fact, to imagine an isolation more nearly complete than that which encompassed New Mexico from 1598 to 1820. For its isolation was multiple and compound: geographic isolation bred social and cultural isolation; isolated in space, New Mexico was also in time. Primitive means of transportation and the lack of navigable streams extended distances a thousandfold. It took the New Mexicans five months to make the 1,200-mile round-trip, along the Turquoise Trail, from Santa Fe to Chihuahua. On the west, the north, and the east, the settlements were hemmed in by warlike nomadic tribes whose presence in these areas isolated New Mexico more effectively than distance or the lack of natural communications.

To appreciate the degree of isolation, it should be noted that the Spaniards settled only a small portion of New Mexico. The early settlements were all in the Upper Sonoran life-zone in which agricultural possibilities were narrowly limited but where the Spanish did find a limited source of wood, fairly good forage, and a dependable water supply. Ever-mindful of the fact that fully half the men who came to the New World died of hunger in the first thirty years, the Spaniards in New Mexico followed the age-old device of conquerors: they made the conquered work for them and support them. Hence they settled near the Pueblo Indian villages. Down to the summer of 1608, they had failed to make a crop and were entirely dependent upon the resources of the Indian villages.

Later, when small outposts were established along the streams of the Upper Rio Grande Valley, the new settlements were often as shut off from each other and from the major towns as the towns were from the nearest settlements in Mexico. The north-central part of New Mexico is rugged and mountainous and communication between the villages has always been difficult. Many of the villages in this area are severely isolated to this day. In the Upper Rio Puerco Valley, it still takes the villagers of Guadalupe two hours, under favorable conditions, to make the twelve-mile trip to Cabezon. Since the irrigable lands were few and far between, the settlements were non-contiguous and small in size. Hidden in mountain valleys, many of these settlements were tiny worlds-to-themselves. The coming of the railroad had little effect on the mountain villages some of which can only be reached today by barely passable roads. At the present time, eighty per cent of the Spanish-speaking people of New Mexico live in villages of less than one thousand population. Automobiles, radios, and telephones are still rare items in many villages and studies made as late as 1940 have shown that eighty-five per cent of the villages in the more inaccessible areas receive virtually no mail.

Since the imported cultural pattern heavily stressed traditional values, it is not surprising that a homogeneous culture should have developed in an isolation so severe or that this culture should have shown such a sturdy resistance to change. Protected from outside or alien influences, the culture became highly integrated and relatively static. "Custom ruled with a blinding force" and innovation was suspect. Over the years the people themselves became genetically homogeneous. In many respects, as John Russell has pointed out, the "people are alike physically and in behavior. Born in the same region, they came from parents alike in race, and in physical type. Although there has been considerable intermarriage with the Indian tribes at present the descendants seem to have taken on characteristics which differentiate them from the Indians. They learn the same language and have similar cultural forms. Thus, they think alike, talk alike, differing only as individuals, but more alike in their social behavior than different."

With many of the villages being settled by a few families—in some cases by a single family—there naturally has been much marriage among blood relatives. Intermarriage and social isolation have made for an extremely cohesive family unit. To be born into a community is to inherit an identification with it that is never forgotten. With satisfactory companionship being found within the enlarged family group, individuals were seldom attracted outside the village in which they were born. Being largely self-sufficient, there was little specialization of function or division of labor. Much of the work was performed on a communal basis and the villages were generally of such a size that little outside help was necessary in the performance of routine tasks. Thus most contacts were limited to a single, uniform culture type. Many of the mountain villages have never known anything but poverty so that poverty itself has become an isolating factor in their lives. "Poverty," as Dr. Paul Walter has said, "is part of their cultural inheritance."

The religion of the villager has also been a factor making for social isolation since it has always been a central, unifying, cohesive force in their culture. Jealous of their loyalties, it has deeply penetrated every aspect of their existence and has been a powerful shield against intrusive alien influences. The color of its pageantry, the mystery of its rituals, and the dramatic character of its ceremonies have always been potent attractions to lonely settlers in a forgotten world. Under the circumstances, its value as pure entertainment has been, perhaps, the principal explanation of its survival and dominant influence. In most instances, also, the priests were the only educated or learned men in the province, a circumstance that naturally gave added weight to their edicts and pronouncements.

The practices of the Inquisition were not unknown in New Mexico. "Independence of thought or action," writes Dr. Carolyn Zeleny, "brought heavy punishments." In the isolation of New Mexico, the power of the Church was greatly magnified, for there was no escape from its rulings. The Church was also an enormous economic burden on the people. Its fees, tithes, and other exactions were truly exorbitant in a society in which money was always scarce. Superior both to the military and to the administrative bureaucracy, the Church was the dominant institutional influence in the lives of the people. The skeins of its influence were woven, from the earliest date, into the social fabric of the province.

The institutions of the family and the Church were, in turn, closely interlocked with the patron-peon relationship. Based on tradition and authority, each institution supplemented the other and made for social isolation. By tradition, leadership rested in the priest, the patron, and the head of the family. Being institutional rather than personal, leadership tended to be non-competitive. In the mountain villages today, the *viejo* or "old man" and the *vieja* or "old woman" are consulted on all matters of importance and their decision is usually final. Similarly the patron and the local *jefe politico* still retain much of their traditional authority. At nearly every point of contact, the insulated character of the culture re-enforced institutional authority. "Peonage," wrote Josiah Gregg, "acts with terrible severity upon the unfortunate poor, whose condition is but little better, if not worse indeed than that of the slaves of the south." And peonage could no more be avoided than the power of the Church, for the nomadic Indians were the most efficient constabulary that despotic authority could desire. No prison was ever guarded more effectively than the Utes, the Apaches, and the Comanches "guarded" New Mexico.

"Indian warfare," writes R. E. Twitchell, "sapped the very life-blood of the intrepid settlers for more than two hundred and fifty years." Generations were born with a mortal fear of Indians and lived and died with this fear uppermost in their minds. The hatred of the Apaches for the New Mexicans and of the latter for the former reached a point of ferocity beyond which it is impossible to go. The Indians were still making devastating raids on the New Mexico settlements in the 1860's and in 1879 alone over a hundred expeditions were sent out against the Apaches. Between 1861 and 1870, the federal government spent $40,000,000 and lost one thousand lives in its duel with these same Apaches.

Contemptuously referring to the New Mexicans as their "shepherds," the nomadic Indians harried the settlements on all sides; prevented the establishment of communications with other outposts in the borderlands; restricted the area of settlement; drained off the energy and wealth of the settlers and robbed them of incentives as well as goods and livestock. Rarely attacking a hacienda, the Navajo relentlessly pursued the poor New Mexican villagers and drove the peons "under the shadow of the great houses." Indeed, most of the other factors mentioned in this section pale into insignificance when compared with the influence of Indians in the production of an inbred, isolated, homogeneous culture in New Mexico.

2. The People

Today there are approximately 250,000 Spanish-speaking people in New Mexico most of whom are native-born of native-born parents, grandparents, and great-grandparents. With little latter-day immigration from Mexico, the population is indigenous to the region. The number of Spaniards was never large and for many years they were outnumbered by the Pueblo Indians in the ratio of ten to one. Dr. Zeleny puts the number of Spaniards at 2,400 in 1680 and around 3,479 in 1750. In fact it was not until about 1800 that the Spanish-Mexican group achieved a numerical ascendancy over the Pueblo Indians.

"In every frontier Spanish colony," writes Bolton, "the soldiery was to a large extent made up of castes,—meztisos, coyotes, and mulattoes— and New Mexico was no exception to the rule." Tlascalan Indians accompanied De Oñate as well as a number of Mexico-Indians who served as muleteers, packers, camp attendants, herdsmen, and drivers. While the Spanish soldiers and colonists were supposed to live apart from the Indian pueblos, the rule was never enforced. According to Gregg, an entire Indian village often abandoned its seclusion and became identified with the conquerors. Most of the hybrid population, however, developed out of the traffic in Indian slaves. "Indian women," to quote Bolton, "were required for household service, with resulting scandals." The practice of taking Indian captives, moreover, had a long history in New Mexico. As late as 1866, an Indian agent complained of the "pernicious system of slavery."

Over the years, therefore, the amount of Spanish blood declined in direct relation to the increase in population. By 1822 the population had increased to forty-two thousand but only a small portion of this total could be regarded as Spanish in ancestry. In the preceding quarter-century, the Pueblo Indian population had remained nearly stationary while the number of mixed-bloods had rapidly increased. It is quite obvious, therefore, that the present Spanish-speaking population is of a very mixed racial origin with the Spanish strain being the least important element in the mixture. For example, Gregg estimated the number of creoles or Spaniards at one thousand in 1846 by comparison with sixty thousand mixed-breeds. In the Rio Arriba section the Indian strain was more pronounced, of course, than in the Rio Abajo, where the large landed estates were located.

From an early date the population of New Mexico was divided into two major classes: *ricos* and *pobres,* the rich and the poor. To some extent, the division marked a caste as well as a class differentiation, for the *ricos* were "lighter," more "Spanish," than the *pobres*. Holding the reins of social, economic, and political power—the beneficiaries of the large land grants—the *ricos* were a law unto themselves. Constituting one-fiftieth of the population, they owned all that was worth owning and were autocrats in every sense of the word. Theirs were the great estates and the vast herds of sheep in the Rio Abajo section. The soldiers, artisans, and peasant farmers were allotted small family and community grants in the Rio Arriba and worked, often as peons, on the large estates. Always quite rigid, the barriers between the two groups became more effective as the lower classes mixed their blood with the Indians. From the founding of the colony until 1846, writes Haniel Long, the *ricos* grew richer, the *pobres* poorer, and "the priests lazier and more avaricious." The Navajo preyed on the rich, who in turn preyed on the poor, "and the poor could prey on nobody." Harried by Indians, the poor were driven to the rich for protection; protection implied peonage; and from peonage there was no escape.

In one sense, however, even the *ricos* lived in a state of bondage. For them everything was cheap and nothing quite so cheap as labor. They had hardly more incentive for progress and activity than the poor. In such a society there was really little need for literacy and most of the population, of course, was illiterate. There were no schools or newspapers and few books. The government was highly personalized in character and absolutist, so that little competition for place or power could take place. Don Pedro Pino was the first native-born New Mexican to visit Spain and his visit took place in 1810. While a few of the *ricos* sent their sons and daughters to St. Louis and other Missouri Valley points for their education, the *ricos* were certainly not an educated class. There was no tradition of self-government or, as Blackmar said, "no rights which arose out of the situation." An appointed governor appointed the provincial officials, and much the same arrangement prevailed under territorial rule. The New Mexicans took no part in the movement by which Mexico achieved its independence and only once, in 1837, was the province stirred by a revolution. Throughout the period of Mexican rule, the province was corruptly and despotically "bossed" by one man, Manuel Armijo.

In this intellectually airless world, the *ricos* developed a life of their own. Sociability, within the class, was a necessity born of isolation. The families, large in size and ruled in patriarchal style, saw much of one another. Built as fortresses against the Navajo, the great low houses of the *ricos,* shaded by cottonwood trees, were scattered along the highway near the river within easy travelling distance. There was little furniture in the homes, for a lack of tools and cabinetmakers had forced the colonists to adjust to a rather primitive existence. Chairs, bedsteads, and tables were rare items and, in eating, the *ricos* squatted on the beaten-earth floors *"a l'Indienne."* Walls three and four feet in thickness enclosed a courtyard or patio, behind which was still another square used as a quarter for the slaves and peons and a place for carts and wagons. "Each great house," writes Harvey Fergusson, "reproduced the isolation which beset the colony as a whole."

The New Mexicans knew little of the mechanical arts and much of what they made was rough and unfinished in character. Sawmills were unknown; there was little mining; and agricultural implements were largely limited to the hoe and wooden plow. Nor were they an agricultural people. Such agriculture as they developed rested solidly on Pueblo Indian foundations, with the principal crops being such Indian staples as corn and beans. "Of fruits," writes Twitchell, "there were practically none." Wheat was cut by hand with a scythe and threshed by turning livestock loose in a compound. In the mountain villages, grain was ground between large pumice stones run by primitive water wheels, some of which are still in use. Essentially a pastoral people, the New Mexicans showed great skill and enterprise in the management of their herds. Like their counterparts in California, the *ricos* were superb horsemen.

Of commerce there was very little, for the economy of the province was a *cambalache* or barter economy. To the annual fair at Taos, the New Mexicans brought horses, mules, knives, hatchets, and trinkets which they traded to the Indians for captive children and the skins of deer and buffalo. In the Chihuahua markets, a handsome price was paid, in barter terms, for the few luxury items which could be imported. Once partially free of colonial restrictions, the New Mexicans did conduct a considerable commerce with the Indians on the eastern plains and deep in the Utah basin. The two annual fairs; a trip to the salt mines; the buffalo-hunting expeditions in the fall; and the Indian campaigns made up the principal items in the routinized existence of the *ricos*.

As a class, the *ricos* have largely vanished. According to Erna Fergusson, there are not more than a dozen of the old families left. Not one of the great houses has been preserved. In disappearing, the *ricos* even failed to leave much in the way of memoirs, records, letters, or memorials: "the only form of life in the Southwest," writes Haniel Long, "that has left no ruins."

The mission system, as it was known in California, never existed in New Mexico. "There were no mission estates," wrote Bancroft; "no temporalities managed by padres." Each pueblo had a church, where the padres preached, taught, and said mass; but the Indians were left in their villages with the padres being essentially parish priests or curates. Prior to Bishop Lamy's arrival in 1851, the New Mexico priests were indescribably corrupt, lazy, and avaricious. Most of them had numerous wives and a vast collection of children whose paternity was hardly a secret and not much of a scandal. While they did try to throw a mantle of protection around the Pueblo Indians, they lacked the enterprise of the Franciscans in the heyday of the mission system in California.

The real settlers of New Mexico were the villagers, whose descendants still inhabit such fabulous mountain villages as Cundiyo, Cordova, Truchas, Trampas, Chamisal, and Penasco. Most of these villages were established as part of a series of outer defenses against the Indians. Here the soldier-settler was given a small grant in payment for his services in manning a lonely outpost against the Indians. Many of the mountain villages were based on community or family grants. Often the irrigable lands were granted in individual ownership with the grazing lands and wooded portions being held in common. In addition to tending their small acres, the villagers herded sheep, hauled wood, campaigned against the Indians, and drove the large herds and the carts to the market fairs. They milled their own grain; wove their own cloth; made their own tools, cooking utensils, household goods, and furnishings; and built their own adobe homes. Probably as much of their inheritance is Indian as Spanish: Spanish their language—a baroque sixteenth century Spanish—and their religion; but Indian their knowledge of hunting, farming, and the ways of the land. Their attitude toward land tenure, for example, is quite similar to that of the Indians. These are the real peasants, the *paisanos,* the men of the country. And it is through them that Spanish-Mexican influences have survived in New Mexico.

No new currents of life moved in this remote colony of Spain for nearly three hundred years. Education had little meaning in a society in which there was literally nothing to learn. Competition and change, initiative and innovation were, for similar reasons, mostly non-existent. The life of any today was the same as the most remote yesterday that anyone could remember; and tasks were performed as they had always been performed. Aside from the Indian influence, the society was, in Haniel Long's phrase, "a huge room in the Southwest hermetically sealed so far as any vital touch went with the life they had left behind in Mexico and Spain." Over the mystery of the slow growth of New Mexico, writes Ross Calvin, "there really is very little mystery after all": poverty and isolation explain whatever was mysterious.

3. The Flowering of New Mexico

Such terms as "isolation" and "poverty," however, must be qualified as applied to the Spanish settlements in New Mexico. Poverty is always relative to historical and social circumstances. If the New Mexicans were poor, their poverty originally had little meaning and was hardly "poverty" as we understand the term today. For if money was scarce, there was little to purchase. Isolated the settlements never were in any complete sense, for the Pueblo, the Navajo, and the other Indians colored the pattern of the culture from the earliest date. As the settlements became more firmly established, more of the energy of the people began to flow into ornament, design, and decoration. The best that they achieved may have been unsophisticated and naive, and somewhat primitive, but it was certainly not lacking in grace and fine feeling. In the relative isolation of the province, a folk culture developed which, in the period from the opening of the Santa Fe Trail to 1846, achieved a brilliant, if brief, flowering.

In any number of crafts, the New Mexicans achieved real artistic distinction. In the so-called "Rio Grande" silverwork, fashioned into dinner services, candlesticks, household ornaments, and picture frames; in the elaborate wrought-iron designs; in the tinwork with which the *pobres* sought to imitate the silver ornaments of the *ricos;* in the woodcarving on the old cupboards or *trasteros,* chests, chairs, doorways, and the lintels, corbels, and posts; in all types of elegant needlework; and in the beautiful weaving which centered in the village of Chimayo, the New Mexicans made a contribution to the colonial crafts as interesting and as distinctive as that which developed on the eastern seaboard. Filigree work, in silver and gold, was another highly developed craft. Images of saints were painted upon small panels of wood (*santos de retablos*) and carved from wood (*bultos* or *vueltos*). Some of the *santeros,* or saint-makers, were indeed extraordinary workmen. Considering the limited number and crude character of the tools available, much of this craftwork was amazingly fine in design and execution. What emerged in the way of arts and crafts was, as Frank Applegate has pointed out, Indian in feeling, Spanish in plan. Creating from memory, working with crude tools, improvising materials, the New Mexicans were consistently under a heavy debt to the Indians who, in turn, borrowed freely from them. Rediscovered after 1918, the Spanish-Colonial arts and crafts have since enjoyed a great vogue.

It is significant that saint-making and weaving,—two of the most highly developed arts in New Mexico,—reached their peak in the period from 1830 to 1835. This would seem to indicate that the stimulus of trade and the new wealth that came with trade had momentarily opened up new markets for the arts and crafts. Since 1890, writes Ruth Laughlin, there has been a decreasing demand for wooden *santos,* although a few of the *santeros* still practice their craft. Spinning, dyeing, and needlework are lost arts; furniture-making largely ceased with the appearance of the Anglo-Americans; while the main arts to survive are those of weaving and working in tin, iron, gold and silver (1).

Since the Indian influence was much stronger in New Mexico than elsewhere in the borderlands what emerged there in the way of architectural forms is both more interesting and more usable than what currently passes for "Spanish" or "Spanish-Colonial" in Texas, Arizona, and California. To the use of adobe, the Spanish brought the practice of molded and sun-dried bricks to replace the puddling system which the Indians had previously used. To the adobe house, also, the Spaniards added doors, windows, stairs, fireplaces, and flues. Rescued from a threatened oblivion by the Santa Fe renaissance which began about 1910, this Pueblo-Spanish house, as improved and adapted by Anglo-Americans, is a most attractive form, simple, sturdy, well-adapted to the environment.

In California nearly everything that passes architecturally by the name of "Spanish" stems from the rash of Spanish-Colonial stucco-and-red-tile construction that swept the region after the San Diego World Fair of 1910. It is primarily the Indian influence, the influence that made for adaptability, that is lacking in this ostentatious pseudo-Spanish architecture. While the Spanish missions of the Southwest have great historic interest and some slight merit as structures, they quickly became a deplorable architectural influence throughout the region. "More architectural crimes," wrote Irving Gill, the California architect, "have been committed in the name of the missions than in any other unless it be the Grecian Temple." Nevertheless in domestic architecture, and to some extent in public buildings, the Southwest has benefited from the adaptation of Indian-Spanish forms and usages.

The folk tradition of the New Mexicans is, of course, rich and varied. Dr. Arthur L. Campa has made amazing collections of the folk songs and poetry,—the *décimas, corridos,* and *versos,*—of the Spanish-speaking and Dr. Aurelio M. Espiñosa has accumulated a library of the richest folk materials,—folk tales, riddles, proverbs, myths, and children's games. Some of the folklore current in New Mexico has long since been forgotten in Spain. Much of this traditional Spanish folklore was brought to New Mexico by settlers who had first lived for some years in Mexico. This circumstance is said to account for the fact that, in all the New Mexico folk materials, there is scarcely a mention of a king or queen or royal family. Generally speaking, the oral side of the tradition has been losing ground rapidly in New Mexico since 1910 and much of the authentic folk quality has been lost (2).

In many respects, the arts, crafts, and folk culture of the New Mexicans is strikingly similar, in type, to the folk culture of the "mountain people" of the Southern states. Both represent curious survivals in the New World of Old World cultural traits and archaic modes of speech and expression. "A Castilian of the year 1525," writes Mencken, "would understand a New Mexican far more readily than he would a Spaniard," just as an Englishman of 1630 would understand a Kentucky mountaineer more easily than he would a resident of Louisville. Like all survivals of this kind, the folk culture of New Mexico seems doomed to extinction. Only a few of the crafts remain alive; tradition, custom, and folk expression are rapidly losing their indigenous quality; and archaicisms in speech are vanishing. In central New Mexico, where the Anglo-American influence is most pronounced, Dr. Campa notes that "the whole manner of living is fast becoming Americanized, in some cases to the point where Spanish is no longer spoken in the home." Where the language vanishes, the traditions and customs are soon forgotten.

On the other hand, in southern New Mexico, near the border, Spanish has the vitality of a language that is living and active. This is the area of true bilingualism in New Mexico. For in northern New Mexico, English is spoken with a heavy accent just as in central New Mexico, Spanish is spoken with an English accent. What appears to be happening in New Mexico, particularly in the southern part of the state, is that encrusted Spanish traits, long preserved in isolation, are being replaced with traits more clearly Mexican in character. In effect the flowering of the older culture ceased when its social and economic underpinnings began to disintegrate under the impact of the Anglo-American invasion.

4. After the Conquest

Motivated by a lust for conquest, Spanish colonization in the Americas was imposed from above. By comparison with the English, a large part of the Spanish expeditions were made up of the nobility and gentry, elements that loomed large in Spanish life. Since Spain had very little in the way of a middle class, middle-class elements were hardly represented at all in the expeditions that came to the New World. Few lower-class Spaniards settled in Mexico, South America, or in the borderlands. The nobles came to win fame and to replenish their fortunes, not to settle; and no succeeding waves of immigration fortified or revivified the culture which their conquests had succeeded in imposing on the native peoples.

The absence of a Spanish-speaking middle class was one of the factors that complicated Anglo-Hispano relations in the borderlands. A large part of the Anglo-American influx to the borderlands after 1846 was made up of middle-class elements in the sense that they were neither very rich nor extremely poor. In the borderlands, these elements did not find their Hispanic "opposite numbers." What they found, in Harvey Fergusson's phrase, was "a small feudal aristocracy and an illiterate half-savage proletariat." The absence of local self-government and the presence of a population that was seven-eighths illiterate in 1850, predisposed the Anglo-Americans to form an extremely negative opinion of the Mexican lower classes who constituted nine-tenths of the population. If a larger middle-class element had existed, the adjustment between the two cultures might have been facilitated and the amount of intermarriage might have been greater. The subordinate status of the *pobres* in relation to the *ricos,* and their poverty, served to set them apart in a category that, in Anglo-American eyes, was roughly comparable to that of the Indians.

By comparison with the *pobres,* the *ricos* made the transition to American rule with comparative ease. Some had travelled in the states and spoke the English language. Others were related to the newcomers by marriage. Becoming rich from the commerce which developed after the opening of the Santa Fe Trail, many looked with favor upon closer ties with the Anglo-Americans. Twitchell reports, for example, that the wives and daughters of the *ricos* had begun to acquire elements of the language, style of dress, and mannerisms of the Anglo-American world prior to the conquest. With the arrival of American women in the province, this process was greatly accelerated. In 1866 Colonel J. F. Meline noted that the *rebozo* had almost disappeared in Santa Fe and that hoop skirts, on sale in the stores, were being widely used. The costume of the caballero had begun to disappear in the 1830's, with the serape and sombrero being the last to vanish.

Geographically segregated from the Anglo-Americans, who moved into the south-central part of the state, the villagers were at first not greatly affected by the transition. In fact some improvement could be noted. New markets were opened; the Indian raids were eventually eliminated; and the railroads brought opportunities for jobs as construction workers, section hands, and maintenance employees. Up to 1880, there was little Anglo-Hispano competition for land or resources; but, with new markets, land values began to rise and the Spanish-speaking element began to feel, at a dozen different points, the pressure of Anglo-American competition. For a time commercial cattle-raising assumed something like bonanza proportions in New Mexico. The number of cattle increased from 160,000 in 1880 to one million head in 1900. Competition for grazing lands became keen, with control of "waterholes" being used by wily Anglo-Americans as a means of acquiring ownership of the available range lands. A similar expansion took place in commercial sheep-raising. The Hispanos also began to feel the competition of dry-land farming which the Anglo-Americans introduced to the eastern portions of the state. Later, with the passage of the Reclamation Act in 1902, competition for agricultural lands became intense.

The consequences of these changes, so disastrous in human terms, did not become fully apparent until the middle 1920's. In the end, the Hispanos were caught up in the meshes of Anglo-American banking, finance, and legal intrigue. Prior to the conquest, there had been no land tax in New Mexico; but, with Anglo rule, came taxes, litigation over land titles, mortgages, and the other incidents of a monetary economy. However, the process by which Hispanos were entangled in the cash system was much slower in New Mexico than in Texas or in California. The debacle that engulfed the Spanish-speaking in California in the first decade after 1848 did not become fully apparent in New Mexico until seventy years after the conquest.

In New Mexico, land grants had been loosely defined, with boundaries often being fixed by reference to trees, rocks, and mountain peaks. Under Spanish and Mexican rule, this vagueness of boundaries had caused little trouble or confusion; for use and occupancy, rather than ownership, were the important considerations. Under American law, the filing of a claim based on a Mexican or Spanish grant automatically prevented the land from being considered a part of the public domain until the validity of the grant was determined; in the meantime, however, the lands could be grazed. As a consequence, of course, all sorts of bogus claims were filed. George W. Julian, appointed surveyor-general by President Cleveland, contended that gross frauds had been committed through the machinations of Anglo-Americans in close alliance with a few large Spanish-American landowners. While Twitchell refers to Julian as a "mountebank," his charges were certainly not groundless, for Blackmar, some years later, also referred to "the wily intrigues" by which Anglo-Americans were exploiting the confusion in land titles.

Many of the villagers neglected to bring their papers into court and often had lost evidences of title. Most of them lacked funds to defend titles; or, if they retained an Anglo-American lawyer, a large part of the land went in payment of court costs and fees. The confusion became so great that in 1891 a Court of Private Land Claims was established to pass upon the land grants in New Mexico. Needless to say, the members of this court were all Anglo-Americans; and, as nearly as I can determine, there was not a single Spanish-American lawyer in the territory. Litigation over land titles was highly technical and involved; cases dragged on in the courts for years; and, in the general process of settling titles, control of resources shifted to the Anglo-Americans.

Erna Fergusson has given a graphic description of one of numerous processes by which Anglo-Americans encroached upon the property rights of the Spanish-speaking people after 1846. Under Spanish law, the children inherited in equal shares, always with a small frontage on the stream or river. Consequently, even a small grant might in time have a hundred owners, each possessing a small strip of land running back from the river or "mother ditch" to the hills, while the grazing lands were held in common by all the heirs. Then some far-seeing Anglo-American stockman would purchase one of the individually owned parcels and claim an unlimited right to use the commonly owned grazing lands. In this way, she writes, "some men so achieved the use of millions of acres" for grazing purposes. Later the Anglo-American owner would induce the Spanish-Americans to petition for a division of the grant. In the end, title to the grazing lands had passed to the Anglo-American and the Spanish-Americans were left with their small irrigable plots and a portion of the proceeds from the sale of the commonly held lands.

In many cases, the Spanish-Americans could not pay land taxes of $1.50 an acre, or more, levied against grazing lands. Anglo-Americans would then buy up the lands at tax sales and promptly have the land tax reduced to thirty or forty cents an acre. Often the villagers would be permitted, for a time, to continue grazing their small flocks on the range; but the pinch came with the appearance of ever-larger commercial flocks which monopolized the range. Over-grazing of the range, by large-scale commercial sheep-raisers, destroyed the cover of vegetation, ushering in a period of floods and soil erosion. In literally hundreds of cases, one can see this process at work in New Mexico. The Anton Chico grant near El Cerrito, embracing 275,000 acres, was confirmed in 1860. By 1926 the grant had become chronically tax-delinquent. As more and more land was sold to pay taxes, the grant was reduced to 85,000 acres by 1939, of which 22,000 acres were under lease. Seven hundred families were, by 1939, dependent on the remaining portions of the grant.

For a time the Hispanos were able to eke out an existence by part-time supplemental labor: in the mines, on the railroads, and as migratory agricultural workers. By 1920 approximately 12,500 New Mexicans were leaving the state every year for seasonal work. But, with the depression, this number declined to 2,500. During the depression years from sixty to seventy per cent of the villagers were on relief. It was around 1926, in fact, that a real "crisis" developed in the village economy of New Mexico. A few facts tell the story: in 1930, New Mexico, with a death rate of 13.8, had almost 3 deaths more per 1,000 population than the national average; the counties with the highest death rates were uniformly those where the Spanish-speaking people constituted more than fifty per cent of the population (in Mora County almost eighty per cent of the deaths were reported as occurring from *unknown* causes!); the counties with the largest Spanish-speaking population were the poorest counties—the higher the percentage of Spanish-speaking people the lower the per capita assessed valuation (in 1933, eighty-five per cent of the taxpayers in the Spanish-speaking counties were assessed for less than $100). Compared with a national rate of 57 deaths per 1,000 live births, New Mexico had a rate of 118—the highest in the nation. In 1940 New Mexico reported 26,488 residents, twenty-five years of age or over, who had not completed one year of schooling (3).

As this crisis developed, a change began to occur in Anglo-Hispano relations. For it was about this time that such terms as "Spanish-speaking," "Spanish-American," and "Spanish-Colonial" came into use to designate the native New Mexicans. "Mexicans," writes Erna Fergusson, "was the term universally applied to them within the memory of most of us. Suddenly, nobody knows just when or why, it became politic to use the hybrid-term, 'Spanish-American.'" In general, this change coincided with a similar change in nomenclature in south Texas, where the term "Latin-American" began to be used about 1927. Writing in 1931, Ruth Laughlin said that it had only been "within the last generation" that the Spanish-speaking element in New Mexico had "rebelled at being called Mexicans and spoke of themselves as Spanish-Americans," thereby reversing a usage which had been quite common for nearly a century. Mary Austin, concurring, said that the change dated from the first World War. While the change in usage is related to the large influx of Mexican immigrants—the native New Mexicans sought to distinguish themselves from the immigrants—its emergence also marks a growing self-consciousness on the part of the Spanish-speaking and a desire, on their part, to escape from a subordinate status.

By 1918 or 1920, the first "school generation" had begun to reach maturity in New Mexico (the public school system dates from 1890); and the first World War had broken, at numerous points, the insularity of the state. During World War I, wrote Natalie Curtis Burlin, "the whole Southwest found itself abruptly seized by the collar and jerked out of its isolation." By 1918, also, a middle-class business element had begun to emerge in New Mexico (4); and, as elsewhere in the borderlands, prejudice has been most keenly resented by the emerging middle class. Having always been called "Spanish," the *rico* element had experienced little discrimination or prejudice; while the poorer classes, being segregated by poverty and geographic location, had partially adjusted to a bicultural relationship. But the middle-class elements, small in number, lacked the social prominence to win exemption from discrimination and, at the same time, sought to distinguish themselves from the "Mexican" lower class.

While the two upper-class groups have always hobnobbed together, exchanging compliments and courtesies and genuflecting before the "Spanish" monuments of the past, the respective middle-class elements have not gotten along so well together. Most of the service clubs in New Mexico—notably those in Albuquerque—systematically exclude Spanish-Americans and the Junior Service League of Albuquerque some years ago refused the application of Senator Dennis Chavez' daughter. The fraternities and sororities at the University of New Mexico draw a sharp line against Hispano students; and a rigid taboo excludes these students from much of the social life of the campus. Carolyn Zeleny, who observed the campus life for two years, reports that the Spanish-speaking students do not, as a rule, attend school dances and that "an unwritten code does not permit an Anglo girl to date an Hispano boy."

New Mexico occupies a uniquely important position in the pattern of American culture. Protected by geographic, social, and cultural isolation, the Spanish-speaking element was given a sufficient margin of time in which to make the transition from Hispano to Anglo rule so that much of their cultural heritage has been preserved. The time-lag made possible the preservation of important elements of the culture through a process of slow adaptation. The semi-arid character of the environment will continue to serve, as it has in the past, as a mantle for the protection of the Spanish-speaking people. The average density of population in New Mexico today is five persons per square mile, about one-ninth the density for the United States as a whole. One hundred years after the American conquest, the population of the state is only slightly in excess of five hundred thousand, and the Spanish-speaking element comprises fifty per cent of this total. The Hispano element is too numerous, therefore, in relation to the Anglos, to be absorbed piecemeal and Hispano cultural influences are now too deeply impressed upon the land to be easily obliterated.

Both in New Mexico and in Arizona, the Indian population should be regarded, in some respects, as part of the Hispanic element; for they are similar in racial background, language, and religion. Infant mortality rates are falling for both groups while their birth rates remain among the highest in the nation. Add the Indian population to the Spanish-speaking total, and it becomes quite apparent that Spanish-Indian-Mexican elements have a long life expectancy in the Southwest. New Mexico is the anchor for these elements: the rock upon which Spanish culture rests today.

V

The Broken Border

The Spanish scheme for colonizing the borderlands called for a strong central colony in New Mexico, the establishment of widely separated outposts in California, Arizona, and Texas, and, eventually, the linking of these settlements into a broad band across the northern part of New Spain. The central colony of New Mexico was finally anchored, after great effort, but more than a hundred years passed before the colonization of the three outlying provinces could be undertaken. While these salients were ultimately established, the colonies were never consolidated. During their existence as Spanish outposts, they went their separate and different ways, with little intercommunication or exchange; each with its own pattern, its own special problems.

The failure of Spain to consolidate the borderland outposts has had important latter-day consequences. For the Spanish-speaking of the borderlands remain, to some extent, separate and disparate groups, sharing a common heritage but never having known the experience of functioning together. Spanish-speaking people in California know little of the experience of their compatriots in New Mexico; and those in New Mexico are unacquainted with conditions in Arizona and Texas. No effective liason has ever existed between these groups; their experiences have run parallel but have never merged. For the border was broken, the links were never forged.

1. Pimeria Alta

The Mission Nuestra Señora de los Dolores in Sonora was the "mother mission" for the settlements in southern Arizona. From this base, Father Kino established a chain of missions along the upper waters of the San Miguel, Altar, Santa Cruz, and San Pedro rivers: Guevavi (founded in

1692), Tumacacori, San Xavier del Bac. The discovery of huge silver nuggets just south of the present border in the Altar Valley, near a place which the Indians called Arizonac, encouraged the Spaniards, for a time, to make something of the southern Arizona settlements. During this spurt of activity, the missions in southern Arizona, or Pimeria Alta as it was called, enjoyed a brief period of prosperity and expansion. But they were virtually extinguished in 1751 when the Pima and Papago Indians joined in a general uprising. At this time, there were no Spanish garrisons north of Fronteras in northern Sonora and Pimeria Alta was almost wholly unprotected.

In the following year, a garrison was established at Tubac in the Santa Cruz Valley and some of the priests, soldiers, and settlers returned. But the Apaches, who had been raiding the Sonora missions for a century, prevented any effective recolonization. In a report on the state of the province in 1777, De Anza pointed out that fifteen years of incessant Apache raiding had depopulated the settlements; that the mines, haciendas, and missions, if not ruined by these attacks, had been abandoned for fear of them. In a decade devoted to counteroffensives against the elusive Apache, the Spanish had managed to kill only 276 Indians. At this rate it was apparent that the Arizona settlements were doomed to failure.

Always a lightly garrisoned province, the Sonora-Arizona frontier was exposed to renewed Apache attacks when the government withdrew its troops during the struggle for Mexican independence. Taking advantage of this opportunity, the Apaches laid waste to the entire province: mines were abandoned; haciendas were deserted; and any stock that the Apaches failed to kill roamed wild along the border. In the wake of this disaster, the discovery of gold in California induced thousands of Sonorans to desert their Apache-ridden land. Not more than three hundred Mexicans were left in Arizona by 1856 and most of these were huddled in abject terror in the walled town of Tucson. But, within a few years, the population of Tubac and Tucson increased to 1,500 or 2,000, as some of the ex-soldiers returned to their *milpas* and the miners drifted back from the goldfields. For a brief time, the orchards of Tumacacori blossomed once again and the attractive fields and gardens which Father Kino had laid out near the missions came back into cultivation.

With the commencement of the American Civil War, however, the government withdrew the troops which it had stationed along the border. Once again the Apaches made a bloody havoc of every ranch-house, village, and mining camp in the region of the Santa Cruz. From 1861 to 1871, the famous Apache chief, Cochise, ravaged the entire area from the Gila River far into Sonora and eastward to the Mimbres River in New Mexico. "Throughout Sonora," wrote Sylvester Mowry, "the Apaches gradually extirpated every trace of civilization and roamed uninterrupted and unmolested, sole possessors of what was once a thriving and populous Spanish province" (1). J. Ross Browne, who visited both sides of the border in the 'seventies, reported that the mines had been abandoned; that the stock had been driven from the ranches; and that the Mexicans who remained in the province were apathetic, ridden by despair and a feeling of utter helplessness.

While there had once been a few great estates and haciendas in southern Arizona, the territory was miserably poor and indescribably primitive in 1848. For over a hundred years, Arizona had been beset with calamities and misfortunes. It was the orphan, the pauper of the Spanish provinces. Too remote to participate in the trade which developed in New Mexico after the opening of the Santa Fe Trail, it was also too far removed from California to feel the leavening effects of the clipper ship trade. Its missions never attained the prosperity or stability of those in California; in short the settlement of the province was abortive. The Mexicans who were living in southern Arizona at the time of the American conquest were a miserable, landless, bewildered people, living in mortal fear of the Apaches. Twenty years after the conquest, Mowry estimated the Mexican population of Arizona at approximately two thousand, all of whom were *pobres* for the rich had long since vanished.

The first Anglo-American settlers to arrive in Arizona were mostly from the states of the late Confederacy. Perhaps because of this circumstance, they lost little time in making Arizona "a white buffer state" between the Spanish-speaking people of New Mexico and those of Sonora. Granted separate territorial status in 1863, Arizona thereafter resisted a long series of proposals to admit it, along with New Mexico, as one state to the union. Since the colonization of Arizona had never been effective, the Spanish-speaking people of the state lacked foundations on which to build. Until the copper mines, the railroads, and the large reclamation projects began to attract Mexican immigrants, Indians remained a more important influence in Arizona than the Spanish-speaking.

2. THE *Tejanos*

While a few missions were established in eastern Texas in 1716, they were soon abandoned and the principal settlements remained those at San Antonio, a combination presidio-mission-and-pueblo; Goliad or La Bahia; and Nacogdoches. Exposed to Indian raids on all sides, none of these settlements prospered. The great rolling plains, stretching in all directions, made it impossible for the Spaniards to subdue the Comanches, who showed a marked disinclination to be enrolled as neophytes in the missions. Between 1722 and 1744, the Spanish spent three million pesos in an effort to colonize Texas but the number of colonists was less at the end than at the beginning of the period. By 1791 most of the Indians had fled from the missions and the few who remained were dispersed some years later.

Poorly organized, feebly garrisoned, chronically neglected, the Texas settlements were swiftly engulfed in the tide of Anglo-American invasion. According to Bancroft, there were not more than 5,000 Mexicans in Texas in 1836: about 2,000 at San Antonio; 1,400 at La Bahia; and perhaps 500 at Nacogdoches. If one is to believe contemporary accounts, these Mexicans were a sorry lot: backward, illiterate, impoverished. The former Mexican soldiers, in particular, were a most bedraggled crew: "the lowest type of humanity that could be picked up," according to Dr. George P. Garrison. Even the civilians were a source of considerable embarrassment to the Mexican officials who inspected the province. By the 1870's those who remained in the old settlements were completely submerged, surviving only as a "picturesque" element in the population: tamale venders, chili venders, peddlers of sweets (*nueces dulces*).

The historians all agree, however, that quite a different situation prevailed along the border. Beginning in 1748, the rancheros of Santander (Tamaulipas) had been encouraged to settle along the Rio Grande in an effort to build a line of defense against the Indians. Most of these settlers came from such Mexican communities as Guerrero, Camargo, and Miero. Over a period of some years a few towns began to appear on the Texas side of the river: Dolores in 1761; Rio Grande City in 1757; Roma in 1767. Once Mexico had achieved its independence, the government parcelled out most of the land lying between the Rio Grande and the Nueces in the form of large grants to favorites of the new regime and the movement of settlers into the region became more rapid.

Due to the troubled state of affairs which prevailed during the decade of the Texas Republic, most of the Anglo-Americans settled north and east of the Nueces and this pattern prevailed for some years after the conquest. During this interregnum, however, Mexicans continued to cross the river and to settle between the Rio Grande and the Nueces. From 8,500 residents in 1850, the population of the border counties increased to 50,000 in 1880 and then to 100,000 in 1910. A large part of this increase was made up, of course, of immigrants from Mexico. The early Anglo-American settlers in the border counties were principally large cattle-operators (all of the land originally embraced in Mexican grants in Kleberg County became part of the famous King Ranch); and cattle-raising did not attract a large English-speaking population. As a consequence, sixty per cent of the property-owners in Starr, Zapata, and Cameron counties, as late as 1930, were descendants of the original Mexican grantees.

In the Lower Rio Grande Valley a way of life developed that was quite similar to that which had prevailed in early California. Here was to be found the same patriarchal set-up in which a few large Mexican landowners lived an idle and lordly existence based on a system of peonage, vestiges of which still survive in the region. The peons were Mexican-Indian, being really more Indian than Mexican; while the landowners and vaqueros were mestizo. The peon was always in debt; in fact, he usually inherited the debts of his father. Landowners sold high-priced goods on credit to their peons, often refusing them permission to make purchases in the towns. Paid six reales a day (twelve cents in American money), the peon was not permitted to cultivate land, even to supply his own table needs; and his ownership of stock was limited to a few chickens, pigs, and goats. Throughout the lower valley, the peons lived in one-room thatched-roofed dirt-floor *jacales,* with a *portal* or arbor made of dry corn stalks from which the inevitable *olla* and its gourd, used as a dipper, were suspended. Closely resembling the California pattern, Mexican ranch life in Texas survived well into the present century.

Taking great pride in their Mexican culture, the landowners encouraged their families to keep the old customs and traditions alive and ruled their establishments like feudal lords. Their square, flat-roofed homes, usually made of stone, were often furnished with luxurious items purchased in Matamoros and Laredo. Here, as elsewhere in the borderlands, the kitchen was built around a huge fireplace and the oven was located in the yard. Since the border *ricos* consciously sought to retain their Mexican culture, the children were sent to private or parochial schools along the border or in Mexico. One of these schools, *El Colegio Altamiro,* founded in 1897, is still in existence. As more and more Mexicans came to the border counties, they were "Mexicanized," not Americanized; for they had few contacts, at the outset, with the Anglo-Americans. Many of the border towns, such as Eagle Pass, developed as Spanish-speaking communities, with street signs and store names in Spanish. "The people are Texans," wrote Lee C. Harby, "but do not speak English and have kept their blood, language, and manners" (2).

The *Tejanos,* like the New Mexicans, took little part in the Mexican independence movement and had no tradition of self-government. Manhood suffrage was, of course, unknown. The lack of democratic traditions, the system of peonage, and the persistence of the patron-peon relation, combined to produce a type of political boss-ism similar to that which prevailed for so many years in New Mexico. The Anglo-American cattle-barons naturally assumed the prerogatives of the Mexican *ricos* and were accepted by the *peones* as patrons and protectors. Jim Wells, after whom one of the southern counties is named, is said to have bossed the border counties from 1880 until his death in 1920. Property-owners not only "voted their Mexicans," but, when occasion demanded, brought droves of Mexicans from across the border, held them under guard in corrals and stockades, and voted them, too, on election day. Nor were all the bosses Anglo-Americans: Don Manuel Gerra was the undisputed political boss of Starr County until his death in 1915.

As in California, many marriages took place, at an early date, between Anglo-American men and Mexican women in the border counties. Such names as Lacaze, Laborde, Lefargue, Decker, Marx, Bloch, Monroe, Nix, Stuard, and Ellert, according to Jovita Gonzales, represent families which claim the Spanish language as their own and boast of their Spanish blood. "The descendants of the Americans who married Mexican wives in the 1800's," she writes, "are more Mexicanized than the Mexicans." Some of these marriages, it is interesting to note, were a by-product of the Mexican-American War. One of the early settlers in Rio Grande City, Henry Clay Davis, was a Kentuckian who returned to south Texas after the war to marry a Mexican-American.

Retarded by a hundred years of border warfare, the economic development of the Lower Rio Grande Valley did not get under way until the completion of the St. Louis-Brownsville-Mexican rail line in 1904. Thus for more than a hundred years the *Tejanos* lived a life apart, cultivating their own customs and traditions. Even after 1848 they knew very little about what was going on in the United States and cared less. When they travelled, they went to Mexico. If they attended school, they were instructed in the Spanish language; if they read a newspaper, it was printed in Spanish. Like their compatriots in the mountain villages of New Mexico, they were hardly conscious of a change in citizenship. The moment the economic development of the region was undertaken, however, this feeling of indifference was soon dissipated.

After the turn of the century, the economic development of the lower valley enabled the peons and *jornaleros* to profit by the change in rule. Never wholly escaping from a kind of peonage, they nevertheless managed to evade the more obvious forms of control. Those who got jobs in the citrus groves and on the truck farms began to purchase small lots in the towns and to acquire a measure of independence.

The position of the landowners, on the other hand, began to deteriorate with the economic transformation of the region. The *ricos* were extremely annoyed to see Anglo-Americans come into the valley and, with the aid of farm machinery and the extension of irrigation systems, reclaim lands which they had long regarded as of little agricultural value. Nor was it long before the Mexican-American middle class, which had emerged in the valley, became intensely dissatisfied with the new dispensation. "The friendly feeling which had slowly developed between the old American and Mexican families," writes Miss Gonzales, "has been replaced by a feeling of hate, distrust, and jealousy on the part of the Mexicans." By the middle 'twenties, the word "white," used to distinguish Anglo-Americans, affected the *Tejanos* "like a red flag to a bull."

South Texas was one of the first areas in the borderlands to develop a Mexican-American middle class. The retarded economic development of the region kept the Anglo-American element at a minimum prior to 1900, thereby giving the *Tejanos* a margin of time in which to develop a middle class of their own. The need for a middle class, moreover, was much greater in the border counties than in the remote mountain villages of New Mexico, where the possibilities of producing a surplus for trade were far less favorable. The emergence of a Mexican-American middle class in Texas has had an important effect on Anglo-Hispano relations.

On August 24, 1927, these middle-class elements formed the League of Latin-American Citizens at a meeting in Harlingen. The formation of the "Lulacs," as they are called, has been described as "the first attempt on the part of Mexican-Americans to organize themselves for the purpose of giving voice to their aspirations and needs as citizens of the United States" (3). From Harlingen the Lulac movement has spread to the other Texas towns but the nature of the "broken border" has minimized its influence in New Mexico and Arizona, California and Colorado. True to its origins, it has remained largely a middle-class organization.

3. The *Californios*

The Spanish-speaking settlements in California differed in a number of respects from those in the rest of the borderlands. Unlike the other borderland settlements, California was both a sea *and* land frontier. The California missions, particularly those in the southern counties, were well administered (from the Spanish point of view) and became quite prosperous. When the first secularization decrees were issued in 1834, the lands and holdings of the missions were valued at $78,000,000. Mission San Gabriel, for example, operated seventeen large ranchos, worked 3,000 Indians, and owned 105,000 head of cattle, 20,000 horses, and 40,000 sheep. While the Spaniards had a great deal of trouble with the Indians of the Central Valley, they encountered little opposition from the coastal tribes. Furthermore, California was inherently a richer province than the other borderland settlements, with a milder climate and a great superiority in natural resources. For these and other reasons the character of the people of California, as Blackmar wrote, "differed from that of every other Spanish province. Owing to its isolated position, there was but little communication with the remainder of the Spanish dominion, and there sprang up an independent spirit not observed elsewhere in the

Spanish Americas" (4). Revolutions were a matter of more or less normal occurrence in California.

The population of California, however, was divided by the same sharp class and status lines. At the top of the hierarchy were the Spanish Franciscans, the Spanish officials, and the Spanish officers of the troops garrisoned in the province. Included in this category were some soldiers and non-commissioned officers who did not rate the distinction of being *soldados distinguidos* but were nonetheless a cut above the average in the borderlands. Some of the most prominent families in California,— the Castros, Picos, Bandinis, Alvarados, Ortegas, and Noriegas,—belonged in this category. While there were some distinguished families in the province, the number having "pure Spanish blood" has been grossly exaggerated. "A very small percentage," wrote Charles Dwight Willard, "were pure-blooded Spaniards, although few were ready to admit they were anything else." Most of these *gente de razón* families, like the *ricos* of New Mexico, were related by marriage and constituted a kind of ruling-class elite.

After the opening of the clipper trade, a few of the homes in the presidial towns had an atmosphere reminiscent of the social graces, refinement, and elegance of the Old World. But most of the *gente de razón* lived the same rough, semi-primitive existence as their counterparts in New Mexico. Always outnumbered by the lower classes in the ratio of ten to one, the number of *gente de razón* families was never large. Included in the first generation were some well-educated, capable, energetic individuals; but they were certainly a minority element. Accustomed to indolence and denied an opportunity for education, the second generation was demoralized by the ubiquitous use of cheap Indian labor. The inefficiency of this element was unmatched in Spanish America.

Below the *gente de razón* were the Mexicans: soldiers, artisans, colonists, the *cholos* of the province. Recruited from among the riffraff of Sonora and Sinaloa, they were certainly a nondescript lot. "Presidial society looked down upon these rustic villagers," writes Dr. John W. Caughey, "and the missionaries regarded them askance, as being likely to corrupt the neophytes." * In the towns and on the ranches, the Mexicans were sharply set apart from the *gente de razón*. Largely illiterate, speaking a different dialect, they thought of themselves as Mexicans, not as

---

* Reprinted by permission of Prentice-Hall, Inc. from *California* by John Walton Caughey. Copyright, 1940, by Prentice-Hall, Inc.

Spaniards. Marriage between the Mexicans and the *gente de razón* elements was, of course, unthinkable. Seldom, if ever, did the Mexicans rise to positions of prominence. Unlike New Mexico, there were no small-farming villages in California so that the state never produced a class of independent, self-sufficient *paisanos*.

In many respects, the social structure of Spanish California resembled that of the Deep South: the *gente de razón* were the plantation-owners; the Indians were the slaves; and the Mexicans were the California equivalent of "poor white trash." These sharply differentiated groups reflected a division of labor which had become traditional. The Mexicans were the artisans, vaqueros, and major-domos of the ranchos; the craftsmen and *pobladores* of the pueblos. The *gente de razón* held all the government positions, made up the officer class of the military, and controlled the great ranchos. While showing a lively interest in cattle and horses (the care of which they feared to entrust to the Indians), they were never interested in farming so that the agriculture of the province remained largely undeveloped and primitive. At the base of the pyramid were the Indians, upon whose unpaid labor the entire economy was based.

To these elements must be added, however, a unique strain made up of the American, British, Scottish, German, and French adventurers who had infiltrated the province prior to 1846. There were only a hundred or so of these adventurers but they played a role of crucial importance at the time of the conquest. With scarcely a single exception, these curiously assorted characters had married daughters of the *gente de razón* after first joining the Catholic Church and accepting Mexican citizenship. Once related to the "best families" by marriage, they became eligible for land grants and were permitted to engage in trade. Embracing the daughters of the land, they also made a pretense of embracing its customs, adopting the prevailing style of dress and Hispanizing their surnames. At the time of the conquest, of course, they went over to the American side en masse and, in many cases, induced their in-laws to collaborate with those who were directing the American invasion.

No matter what his social status was—doctor, trader, sailor, or smuggler—the ultramontane adventurer had little difficulty in joining the *gente de razón,* provided he joined the Catholic Church and became a citizen of Mexico. As long as California remained isolated from the rest of the country, these interlopers were quite willing to pose as *hijo del país;* but with the influx of Anglo-American women they quickly discarded their Spanish trappings, and often their Spanish wives, and reverted to type. Conversely, those settlers—and there were a few—who married Indian women never achieved the status of *gente de razón.* To the same point, an early-day resident of Los Angeles once remarked that he had never known "of a Spaniard or Mexican of this section marrying an American wife." With the break-up of the ranchos, the intermarriage and limited cultural fusion of this earlier period came to an abrupt cessation.

Essentially the difference between California and New Mexico, as Spanish provinces, was that the former was the home of the cattle ranch, the latter of the sheep ranch. In New Mexico, the *pastores* were permitted to have their own subsistence farms and to graze a few sheep along with those of their patron; but all economic activity in California was centralized, first in the missions, and later in the rancho establishments. The opening of the clipper trade with Boston gave, of course, a great impetus to cattle-raising. The more money there was to be made in cattle, the greater became the clamor to secularize the missions. Once the missions were secularized, the number of range cattle soared to new heights.

Between 1830 and 1846, the period of secularization, eight million acres of land in California passed into the ownership of less than eight hundred grantees. Many of these ranchos were baronial in extent, with cattle grazing "on a thousand hills." With the discovery of gold, the price of cattle promptly soared from $2 and $4 a head to $20 and $50 and the cattle ranches and vineyards of Southern California became immensely profitable. Of short duration, this soaring prosperity had disastrous consequences for the ranchero class.

The moment herds of cattle began to be driven overland to the mines, the price of California cattle quickly dropped. Soon great herds of beef cattle were being raised and pastured in the San Joaquin Valley and few cattle buyers bothered to make the long trip south of the Tehachapi to purchase scrawny Spanish steers from the rancheros. During two years of ruinous drought, in 1862 and 1864, nearly three million cattle perished in the "cow counties" of Southern California and nearly five-sixths of the land was reported tax-delinquent. Forty per cent of the land held in Mexican grants was sold to meet the costs and expenses involved in confirming land titles after the conquest. The Rancho de los Alamitos, consisting of 265,000 acres, was sold for delinquent taxes of $152—one of many similar cases. Interest rates of five per cent compounded monthly were not uncommon. The Rancho Santa Gertrudes, worth a million dollars, was forfeited for non-payment of a $5,000 debt. So general was the debacle that by 1891 not more than thirty *gente de razón* families in the northern part of the state had managed to preserve even a semblance of their former prestige and power.

In Southern California, however, the *gente de razón* retained a measure of their former power and influence for some years after the conquest. Here they were concentrated in sufficient number so that they remained an important political factor through the 1880's. In most elections, from 1849 to 1880, the newcomers were pitted against the Spanish-speaking. "Down to the end of the 1870's," writes Owen O'Neil, "local politics in Southern California were complicated by a natural tendency to diverge on racial lines. Vast and complex family connections would make it impossible to trace these cleavages by any process so simple as noting Spanish names, but they were a real and potent factor which became more evident after 1865, when so many of the old Californians, once magnates of the land, were being crowded to the wall by economic misfortune." Among the first representatives of Santa Barbara County in the state legislature were such individuals as Pablo de la Guerra, Antonio María de la Guerra, Romauldo Pacheco (later lieutenant-governor), and J. Y. Cota. An Estudillo and a Coronel became state treasurers and, in Los Angeles, a member of the Sepúlveda family was elected to the bench. As late as 1870, native Californians outnumbered Anglo-Americans in Santa Barbara, owned more than a third of the property, and occupied most of the political positions; but, by the end of the decade, the native element was almost entirely eclipsed.

Unlike New Mexico, California was engulfed by a tidal wave of Anglo-American immigration after 1848. While the northern counties received the bulk of this immigration at the outset, the tide shifted to Southern California in the 1880's. "This overwhelming horde of new arrivals," wrote Willard, "took possession of the land and proceeded to make things over to their own taste." The Spanish-Mexican appearance of the Southern California towns changed overnight. As much as anything else, this transition was symbolized by the rapid disappearance of the adobes. "Death and emigration," wrote J. P. Widney in 1886, "are removing them [the Californians] from the land. . . . They no longer have unnumbered horses to ride and vast herds of sheep, from which one for a meal would never be missed. Their broad acres now, with few exceptions, belong to the acquisitive American. . . . Grinding poverty has bred recklessness and moroseness."

If this process of change bore heavily upon the *gente de razón,* it had a simply crushing effect upon the Mexicans. One after another the economic functions for which they had been trained were taken from them. The Mexicans were excellent and well-trained vaqueros but this function disappeared with the collapse of the ranchero regime. The rapid rise of the sheep industry after 1860 momentarily provided employment as herders and shearers; but the period of bonanza sheep-raising soon came to an end. The Mexican then reappears in the local annals as a farm worker and livery-stable hand. Long before the livery stables disappeared, however, the Chinese began to displace the Mexicans as farm workers. Visiting Southern California in 1888, Edward Robert noted that the "houses of the Spanish-speaking people are being taken over by the Chinese, who have invaded the adobe cottages." Anglo-Americans infiltrated New Mexico; they engulfed California. The difference in impact was also a function of the size of the Spanish-speaking element in the two states: 60,000 in New Mexico, 7,500 in California. In California, moreover, there was no buffer group to stand between the Spanish-speaking and the Anglo-Americans in the manner that ten thousand well-settled Pueblo Indians stood between Anglos and Hispanos in New Mexico.

With the eclipse of the Spanish-speaking element after 1880, few visible evidences of Spanish culture could be noted in California. Some Spanish words had been incorporated into the speech and important elements of Spanish-Mexican jurisprudence had been woven into the legal fabric of the state. A considerable amount of Spanish-Mexican blood flowed in the veins of local residents with such names as Travis, Kraemer, Reeves, Locke, and Rowlands. Most of the Spanish street names had been Anglicized, although few of the place-names were changed. At the turn of the century it appeared—in fact it was generally assumed—that the Mexican influence had been thoroughly exorcized.

But what had really happened was that the "old life,"—the Mexican life,—of the province had retreated "along the coastal plains that reach from Los Angeles to Acapulco." Just as the Spanish-speaking had retreated from the northern counties to the southern, so they later withdrew, to some extent, to Mexico. But the number of Spanish-speaking residents in Southern California was at all times sufficient to keep vestiges of the earlier life and culture alive. Later, in the period from 1900 to 1920, these surviving elements of the old life were renewed and revived by a great influx of Mexican immigrants and the long-dormant conflict of cultures entered upon a new phase.

4. Lost Provinces

In two parts of the borderlands, southern Colorado and western Texas, the Spanish settlements which existed were even more severely isolated than those in New Mexico. These were the real "lost provinces." Although both De Vargas and De Anza had explored southern Colorado, the first permanent colony was not established in the Costilla Valley until 1849. The town of San Luis, founded in 1851, is said to be the oldest settlement in the state. Most of the Colorado colonists came from New Mexico, many of them from Taos, which was, in a sense, the parent colony. The Colorado settlements had been planned as a series of listening posts by means of which New Mexico might be forewarned of Indian raids. To induce the colonists to settle in these lonely outposts, the provincial government had made small land grants to individuals and to families.

The first settlers in southern Colorado lived in crudely built *jacales* which were later replaced with adobe structures. The form of settlement, both in Colorado and west Texas, was the plaza: a series of flat-roofed adobe houses joined together in the form of a square or rectangle with an opening at each end or on the sides. In effect, the plaza was a form of walled village inhabited by a number of families. The enclosed patio frequently served as a corral or stockade into which the stock were driven at night. The thick exterior walls, without doors or windows, had an extension around the roof, called the *pretil*, which was used as a barricade. Since no glass was available, the windows on the patio side were covered with a parchment or *pergamino,* made from sheepskin. Doors were ponderous affairs without hinges or locks and the floors were of beaten earth. The well-to-do lived in single-family dwellings, called *plazuelas,* located at some distance from the plaza.

Farming and stock-raising activities were limited in Colorado by the incessant danger of Indian raids. As late as 1854 there were only two guns to be found in Costilla, one an old musket; and for years the principal weapons were bows and arrows. Everything the colonists possessed was

THE BROKEN BORDER

home made: their brooms and utensils; their household furnishings; their clothing; their agricultural implements. Long after the Indian menace had been eliminated, the thick walls of the patio served to enclose the lives of the people; to set them apart in a world by themselves. In much the same way, the self-sufficient character of their economy made it possible for them to carry over into the present many elements of their Spanish culture. Walled off by mountain ranges, the San Luis Valley has always had stronger economic and cultural ties with New Mexico than with the rest of Colorado. Never having attracted a large number of Anglo-American settlers, it remains predominantly Spanish-speaking (about fifty-eight thousand Spanish-speaking people live in southern and southeastern Colorado today).

If possible more isolated and landlocked than the mountain villages of New Mexico, a folk culture has survived in the San Luis Valley, some phases of which stem directly from the Middle Ages. Olibama López, a native of the region, has given the following vivid description of what happened, a few years ago, when one of the communities re-enacted the entire story of the capture, trial, and crucifixion of Christ:

> On Wednesday evening a group representing soldiers and Jews led by the armored centurion, riding a spirited horse and flanked by two *lacayos* or lackeys, to the accompaniment of martial music produced by a fife and drum, went forth to capture "Christ." The latter was represented by the Image of Christ that belonged to the church, and the priest acted as the voice. The capture occurred in the *cementerio* of the church, a large patio where the dead were buried during the first years of settlement. The Image was carried in a procession; then it was brought back to the church.
>
> On Thursday morning the story of the capture and trial was read at church. On Friday afternoon, after a procession through the village, in which several men dragged an enormous cross, the Image was crucified in church. A group of *piteros*—fifers—played a dirge, a plaintive melody that penetrated the very hearts of the listeners, and made the scene they had just witnessed very real to them. On Friday night, after the last mass, occurred the *tinieblas,* representing the darkness that fell over the earth as Christ expired. . . . The church was left in darkness except for several candles burning behind a heavy curtain where the *rezadores*— men who prayed,—were stationed. Before the prayers began, one of the *rezadores* would say in a loud voice, *salgan, vivos y difuntes, que aquí estamos todos juntos*—come forth ye dead and living for we are all here

together. No sooner had he said this, than chains were dragged across the floor, the *matracas* were rattled, and the *pitos* were blown behind the curtain. This represented the earthquake and the opening of the graves which occurred as Christ died. . . . After the *tinieblas,* the Christ was taken from the cross and laid in a coffin. A *bachillero*—a talkative fellow —was left to guard it all night, though the soldiers returned every hour to see that the body was still there.

Here in the Spanish-speaking towns and villages the children still play dozens of Spanish games: *la pelota, las cazulejas, pitarilla, el canute, el coyotito, la ponsona, la cabra.* In former times, the villagers were visited once a year by travelling troupes of *maromeros* or tumblers from Taos, each with its *payaso* or clown. Old folk songs, such as *"La Cautiva Marcelina,"* and *"El Vaquero Nicolás,"* are still popular. Each village has its *poeta,* or poet, adept at composing *coplas* for all occasions. While Mexico and Spain are "foreign" countries to most of the residents, they are addicted to a kind of *españolismo*: a complacent self-satisfaction with everything Spanish.

While the San Luis Valley is made up principally of small agricultural holdings, it has had, in times past, one or two princely estates. Casimiro Barela, after whom the town of Barela is named, served Las Animas County in the state legislature for forty years (1876 to 1916). His home at Rivera, near Barela, was patterned after the large Mexican hacienda and maintained by a retinue of servants. The owner of important properties in Mexico and a coffee plantation in Brazil, Barela was the "boss" of the region during most of his lifetime. In the southern part of the state, also, is the famous Trinchera Ranch, once part of the 1,038,000-acre Sangre de Cristo grant.

For years New Mexican *ciboleros* or buffalo-hunters had roamed the famous *El Llano Estacado,* or Staked Plains of the Panhandle, hunting buffalo with the lance. Crews in huge cumbersome wooden-wheeled *carretas* followed the *ciboleros* to skin the animals and strip the meat, hanging it out to dry in the sun. This dried meat the Mexicans called *charqui* which, on the tongue of the Anglo-Americans, became "jerky." The routes of the *ciboleros* were marked by buffalo skulls; hence the name "Staked Plains." Moving down the Canadian from Las Vegas to a point near the present town of Canyon, the *ciboleros* had various points of rendevous along the river.

Out of this buffalo-hunting came the trade with the Comanches, with the *comanchero* gradually replacing the *cibolero*. To the plains, the *comanchero* brought merchandise which was traded to the Comanches at the old rendevous points along the river: Las Tecovas, Las Linguas ("The Tongues," so named because many languages were spoken there), and other points. The *comanchero* trade was long a source of great friction between Anglos and Hispanos in the Southwest, for the Anglos charged, and with some truth, that the stock which the Comanches offered in exchange for New Mexico merchandise was contraband stolen from Texas ranches. Eventually the Anglo-American buffalo-hunters drove the Mexican *ciboleros* and *comancheros* from the plains but as late as 1875 one José Taffola was found, with a full caravan of merchandise, roaming the plains in search of Comanches who had failed to keep a rendezvous.

At an early date, perhaps as early as 1830, a few New Mexico families, principally from Taos, began to settle in plazas along the Canadian River. The famous early-day town of Tascosa, from *atascosa* ("boggy"), was an outgrowth of such a settlement. In 1876 Casimero Romero moved into the region with a huge caravan of fourteen prairie schooners to be followed, the next year, by a number of other families from New Mexico. Down the river the plazas bore the names of the various families: Trujillo, Valdez, Ortega, Chávez, Romero, Sandoval, Domingo, Callinas, Joaquín, Ventura, Montoya. For over fifty years, these Mexican families were about the only settlers in the region, living in their low, flat-roofed stone plazas, grazing their sheep on the plains. Later, when large Anglo-American cattle interests invaded the Panhandle, the Mexicans retreated to New Mexico. "Two of the large ranch outfits," writes the historian of Tascosa, "set about moving the Mexican plaza residents as soon as they had completed their fences" (5). The last survivor of the old Mexican life in the Panhandle, one Sandoval by name, died near the turn of the century.

VI

"Not Counting Mexicans"

When asked how many notches he had on his gun, King Fisher, the famous Texas gunman, once replied: "Thirty-seven—not counting Mexicans." This casual phrase, with its drawling understatement, epitomizes a large chapter in Anglo-Hispano relations in the Southwest. People fail to count the non-essential, the things and persons that exist only on sufferance; whose life tenure is easily revocable. The notion that Mexicans are interlopers who are never to be counted in any reckoning dies but slowly in the Southwest. To this day Mexicans do not figure in the social calculations of those who rule the border states. As I write these lines, the Mexican consul-general in Los Angeles has just entered a vigorous protest against the insulting behavior of custom inspectors at the municipal airport.

A majority of the present-day residents of the Southwest are not familiar with the malignant conflict of cultures which has raged in the borderlands for more than a century. Blinded by cultural myths, they have failed to correlate the major events in a pattern of conflict which has prevailed from Brownsville to Los Angeles since 1846. Once this correlation is made, it becomes quite apparent that the Mexican-American War was merely an incident in a conflict which arose some years before and survived long after the Treaty of Guadalupe Hidalgo. It is only within the framework of this age-old conflict that it is possible to understand the pattern of Anglo-Hispano cultural relations in the Southwest today. In summarizing the history of this conflict, one necessarily starts with Texas, for there the first blood was shed.

1. Los Diablos Tejanos

In Texas the Spanish-Mexican settlements were directly in the path of Anglo-American expansion. Unlike the rest of the borderlands, Texas was not separated from the centers of Anglo-American population by mountain ranges and desert wastes; geographically it invited invasion. In a series of belts or strips, its rich, alluvial plains stretched from the plateaus to the gulf. The rivers that marked these belts could be crossed, at all seasons, at almost any point, without much trouble. On the other hand, between the most southerly settlements in Texas and those in Mexico, there was, as Dr. Samuel Harman Lowrie has pointed out, "a great expanse of semi-arid land which at that time served as a more or less natural, though temporary barrier to the effective extension of Mexican influence and control." Texas was 1,200 miles removed from its capital, Mexico City.

By 1834 the Anglo-Americans outnumbered the Mexicans in Texas: thirty thousand to five thousand. Most of the Mexicans were concentrated in the old Spanish towns or along the border, while the Anglo-Americans were to be found on the farms and ranches. Mexican townspeople had few opportunities for acculturation for they saw very little of the Anglo-Americans. From the outset, moreover, relations between the two peoples were clouded by the fear of war. The Anglo-Americans bore the brunt of Mexico's hostile distrust of the United States and were, in turn, encouraged to take an unfriendly attitude toward the natives by the unconcealed, aggressive designs of the jingoes in Washington.

As might have been expected, each group formed a highly unfavorable initial impression of the other. To the early American settlers, the Mexicans were lazy, shiftless, jealous, cowardly, bigoted, superstitious, backward, and immoral. To the Mexicans, on the other hand, the Texans were "*los diablos Tejanos*": arrogant, overbearing, aggressive, conniving, rude, unreliable, and dishonest. The first Mexican ambassador to the United States had complained in 1882 of the "haughtiness of these republicans who will not allow themselves to look upon us as equals but merely as inferiors." Still another Mexican official had charged that the Americans in Texas considered themselves "superior to the rest of mankind, and look upon their republic as the only establishment upon earth founded upon a grand and solid basis." Full of brag, bluster, and spread-eagle chauvinism, the Americans of the 1800's were hardly the most tactful ambassadors of goodwill. The truth of the matter is that the border residents were not a credit to either group.

Under the most favorable circumstances, a reconciliation of the two cultures would have been difficult. The language barrier was, of course, a constant source of misunderstanding; neither group could communicate, for all practical purposes, with the other. The Mexicans knew almost nothing of local self-government, while the Americans, it was said, travelled with "their political constitutions in their pockets" and were forever "demanding their rights." Although tolerant of peonage, the Mexicans were strongly opposed to slavery. The Anglo-Americans, most of whom were from the Southern states, were vigorously pro-slavery. The Anglo-Americans were Protestants; the Mexicans were Catholic. Speaking of a Mexican, a Protestant missionary is said to have remarked: "He was a Catholic, but clean and honest." Both groups lacked familiarity with the existing Mexican laws, for there was no settled government in Texas. Anglo-Americans found it extremely difficult to respect the laws of Mexico in the absence of law-interpreting and law-enforcing agencies. Thus it was, as Dr. Lowrie writes, that "cultural differences gave rise to misconceptions and misunderstandings, misunderstandings to distrust, distrust to antagonism, and antagonism on a very considerable number of points made open conflict inevitable."

The first Anglo-Americans literally fought their way into Texas. While most of these early filibustering expeditions were defeated, they succeeded in laying waste to the country east and north of San Antonio. Both Mexicans and Americans were killed by these invading private armies. No sooner had the Mexicans driven out the filibusters, than the Comanches raided the entire stretch of country between the Nueces and the Rio Grande. According to one observer, the whole region was "depopulated, great numbers of stock were driven off, and the people took refuge in the towns on the Rio Grande." Preoccupied with revolutionary events in Spain and Mexico, the government could give little attention to the Texas settlements. After 1821, however, a measure of protection was provided against the devastating raids of the Comanches and many of the settlers moved back across the Rio Grande.

2. Alas! the Alamo

With the Texas Revolution came the embittering memories, for the Texans, of the slaughter of Anglo-Americans at the Alamo and Goliad; and, for the Mexicans, of the humiliating rout and massacre at San Jacinto. Prior bitternesses were now intensified a thousandfold. "Towards the Mexicans remaining within the limits of the Republic," writes Dr. Garrison, "the feeling of the Texans was scarcely better than towards the Indians." Memories dating from this period still poison relationships between Anglos and Hispanos in Texas. Some years ago a district judge told of how, as a child, he had heard an old man give an eye-witness account of the slaughter at the Alamo. "I never see a Mexican," he confessed, "without thinking of that." José Vasconcellos, the well-known Mexican educator and philosopher, tells in his autobiography of how these same memories poisoned his boyhood in Eagle Pass. After the Texas Revolution, as Erna Fergusson has pointed out, "Texans could not get it out of their heads that their manifest destiny was to kill Mexicans and take over Mexico."

Throughout the decade of the Texas Republic (1836–1846), the shooting war continued in "the Spanish country" south of the Nueces. Murder was matched by murder; raids by Texans were countered by raids from Mexico. Since a peace treaty was never negotiated, no boundaries could be fixed. Texas claimed to the Rio Grande, while Mexico insisted that its boundary rested on the Nueces. In the bloody zone between the two rivers an uninterrupted guerrilla warfare continued throughout the life of the Texas Republic. In 1839 General Don Antonio Canales launched a revolution on Texas soil against Santa Anna and raised the banner of the Republic of Rio Grande. Of the 600 men who rallied to his standard, 180 were Texans. Awakening to the fact that Texans were using his insurrection as a cover for an attack on Mexico, General Canales finally surrendered but not until his troops had fought several engagements along the border. At the head of a raiding party of five hundred men, General Vásquez captured San Antonio in 1842 and held it for two days. These are but two of many similar episodes that occurred during the hectic life of the new republic.

Throughout the period of this border warfare, the Texas-Mexicans were caught between opposing forces. "When the Americans have gone there," explained a delegate at the Texas constitutional convention, "they have preyed upon the Mexicans; they have been necessarily compelled by force or otherwise to give up such property as they had. So vice versa, when the Mexicans have come in, they have been necessarily compelled to furnish them the means of support. . . . Since 1837 they [the Texas-Mexicans] have been preyed upon by their own countrymen as well as by ours." The Texans constantly suspected the Mexicans of inciting the

Indians against them and every Indian raid provoked retaliation against the *Tejanos*. The Mexicans naturally regarded the Texas Revolution as American-inspired and the prelude to the conquest of Mexico.

However all Mexicans were not equally affected by this complex warfare. A sizable number of the upper-class settlers quickly became identified with the Texans. These Texanized Mexicans or "the good Mexicans" were called *Tejanos* and were invariably of the *rico* class. Two of the fifty signers of the Texas Declaration of Independence were native Mexicans and a third, born in Mexico, became the first vice-president of the republic. At a later date, Captain Refugio Benavides commanded a company of Texas-Mexicans which operated along the border against Mexican raiders and marauders.

3. The Mexican-American War

Provoked by the annexation of Texas in 1846, the Mexican-American War represented the culmination of three decades of cultural conflict in Texas. To the Mexicans, every incident in Texas from the filibustering raids to the Revolution of 1836 was regarded, in retrospect, as part of a deliberately planned scheme of conquest. To the Anglo-Americans, the war was "inevitable" having been provoked, in their eyes, by the stupidity and backwardness of the Mexican officials. Not only did Mexico forfeit an empire to the United States, but, ironically, none of the signers of the Treaty of Guadalupe Hidalgo realized that, nine days before the treaty was signed, gold had been discovered in California. That they had unknowingly ceded to the United States territories unbelievably rich in gold and silver—the hope of finding which had lured Coronado and De Oñate into the Southwest—must have added to the Mexicans' sense of bitterness and defeat.

Furthermore the way in which the United States fought the Mexican-American War added greatly to the heritage of hatred. A large part of our invading army was made up of volunteers who, by all accounts, were a disgrace to the American flag. General Winfield Scott readily admitted that they had "committed atrocities to make Heaven weep and every American of Christian morals blush for his country. Murder, robbery and rape of mothers and daughters in the presence of tied-up males of the families have been common all along the Rio Grande." Lieutenant

George C. Meade, of later Civil War fame, said that the volunteers were "driving husbands out of houses and raping their wives. . . . They will fight as gallantly as any men, but they are a set of Goths and Vandals without discipline, making us a terror to innocent people."

How bitterly these outrages were resented is shown by a passage which Lloyd Lewis has culled from one of the Mexican newspapers of the period: "the horde of banditti, of drunkards, of fornicators . . . vandals vomited from hell, monsters who bid defiance to the laws of nature . . . shameless, daring, ignorant, ragged, bad-smelling, long-bearded men with hats turned up at the brim, thirsty with the desire to appropriate our riches and our beautiful damsels." The year 1844 had seen the rise of a Native American Party in the states and much anti-Catholic feeling found expression during the war. Mexicans charged that the volunteers had desecrated their churches, "sleeping in the niches devoted to the sacred dead . . . drinking out of holy vessels." Two hundred and fifty American troops, mostly of Catholic background, deserted and joined the Mexican army to form the San Patricio battalion. The barbarous manner in which eighty of these deserters were executed in San Angel, a suburb of Mexico City, was long cited by the Mexicans as further proof of Yankee cruelty.

Nothing was more galling to the Mexican officials who negotiated the treaty than the fact that they were compelled to assign, as it were, a large number of their countrymen to the Yankees. With great bitterness they protested that it was "not permissible to sell, as a flock of sheep, those deserving Mexicans." For many years after 1846, the Spanish-Americans left in the United States were known in Mexico as "our brothers who were sold." As late as 1943 maps were still used in Mexican schools which designated the old Spanish borderlands as "territory temporarily in the hands of the United States." It is to the great credit of the Mexican negotiators that the treaty contained the most explicit guarantees to protect the rights of these people, provisions for which they were more deeply concerned than they were over boundaries or indemnities. It should never be forgotten that, with the exception of the Indians, Mexicans are the only minority in the United States who were annexed by conquest; the only minority, Indians again excepted, whose rights were specifically safeguarded by treaty provision.

Just as the end of the Texas Revolution did not terminate hostilities in Texas, so the Treaty of Guadalupe Hidalgo failed to bring peace to the borderlands. Under the terms of the treaty, it became the obligation of the United States to police 180,000 Indians living in the territories which we acquired from Mexico. This obligation the United States failed to discharge for many years. Taking advantage of the confusion which prevailed, the Indians launched fierce raids on both Anglo and Hispano settlements, conducted marauding expeditions deep in Mexican territory, and cunningly exploited the hatred that had been engendered between Anglo and Hispano. The Anglos promptly attributed these raids to Mexican duplicity and instigation; the Hispanos as promptly charged them up to the malice or carelessness of the Americans. Hard-pressed on all sides, the Indians had come to live off the plunder seized in these raids which, with the confusion and demoralization which prevailed in Mexico, were conducted on a larger scale than ever before. It was not until about 1880 that the United States finally managed to bring the Indians of the Southwest under close police surveillance.

Nor were Indians the only troublemakers in the post-war decades. Between 1848 and 1853, various American filibustering expeditions violated Mexican territory in Sonora, Lower California, and at various points along the border. When word of the discovery of gold reached the Eastern states, swarms of emigrant gold-seekers passed along the southern routes to California, often travelling in Mexican territory without passports, and not infrequently helping themselves to Mexican food and livestock en route.

In 1850 José M. Carvajal organized a revolution in Mexico, sponsored by American merchants, which aimed at converting the State of Tamaulipas into the Sierra Madre Republic. Carvajal was a Texan by birth who had been educated in Kentucky and Virginia. Backed by Richard King and Mifflin Kennedy, two of the great cattle-barons of south Texas, the Carvajal revolution was supported by bands of armed Texans who crossed the Rio Grande. The American ambassador reported that these raids, in which as many as five hundred Texans participated, had "awakened a feeling of intense prejudice against everything connected with American interest."

The fateful strip of territory between the Nueces and the Rio Grande once again became the home of numerous outlaw bands who preyed indiscriminately upon both Mexican and American settlers. In the face of these staggering blows,—filibustering expeditions, Indian raids, revolution, war, and constant guerrilla fighting,—the Mexicans in Texas constantly retreated and their retreat, of course, gave rise to the notion that their conquerors were pursuing a mandate of destiny. Major Emery, writing in 1859, said that the "white race" was "exterminating or crushing out the inferior race"; and an American soldier wrote home that "the Mexican, like the poor Indian, is doomed to retire before the more enterprising Anglo-Americans."

4. SLAVES AND PEONS

As early as 1839 fairly large numbers of Negro slaves had escaped from their Texas owners by crossing the Rio Grande and a sizable colony of ex-slaves had sprung up in Matamoros. During the Civil War, the Texans suspected that native Mexicans were implicated in the flight of fugitive slaves, an accusation that found circumstantial confirmation in the known opposition of Mexicans to slavery (Mexico had sought to insert a provision in the treaty barring slavery forever from the territory ceded to the United States). "The possession of slaves in Western Texas," wrote Colonel Ford, "was rendered insecure owing to the contiguity of Mexico, and to the efforts of the Mexicans to induce them to run away. They assisted them in every way they could."

To some extent, the movement of Negro slaves across the border was matched by the flight of Mexican peons into Texas. According to Dr. Paul S. Taylor, some 2,812 servants with families numbering an additional 2,572 persons, escaped to Texas from Nuevo Leon and Coahuila in the period from 1848 to 1873. The loss in unpaid debts, which the flight of these peons represented, was estimated by the Mexican government to be in excess of $400,000.

In 1856 a Negro insurrectionary plot was uncovered in Colorado County. According to the Texans, the Negroes had planned to rebel, kill their masters, and, with the aid of native Mexicans, fight their way across the border. Without exception every Mexican in the county was "implicated" and over two hundred slaves were arrested and punished (two were whipped to death). Mexicans were ordered to leave Matagorda and Colorado counties immediately and in Uvalde they were forbidden to travel the roads without passes. "Anti-Mexican sentiment," writes Dr. Taylor, "based on the belief that the peons imperilled the institution of slavery, broke out in meetings which in Austin, Gonzales, and other towns, passed resolutions protesting against their employment. At Goliad the resolution declared that 'the continuance of the greaser or peon Mexicans as citizens among us is an intolerable nuisance and a grievance which calls loudly for redress.'" As always, the circumstance that Mexicans were concentrated in the strip of territory immediately north of the border aroused the most dire forebodings.

The Negro insurrection was quickly followed by the Cart War which broke out in 1857. Prior to this time, Mexican ox-cart freighters had been hauling—between San Antonio and the coast and from San Antonio to Chihuahua—an annual cargo of goods and merchandise valued at several million dollars. The Cart War involved a systematic campaign on the part of Anglo-Americans to force Mexican freighters out of this lucrative business. For over a year, organized bands of Texans preyed on the Mexican freight trains, killing the drivers, stealing the merchandise, and generally disrupting the traffic. So tense did the situation become, with the Mexican ambassador filing one vigorous protest after the other, that federal troops were finally dispatched to protect the cartmen.

5. "Red Robber of the Rio Grande"

In the wake of the Cart War came the highly significant Cortina episode. Juan Nepomuceno Cortina,—"the red robber of the Rio Grande,"—was born near Brownsville. A blocky, powerfully built, red-bearded Mexican, Cortina came from a prominent and well-to-do family. Like so many Mexicans in Texas, he was a magnificent horseman. The Cortina War, which was to last a decade, started on July 13, 1859, when a deputy sheriff arrested a Mexican who had been a servant of the Cortina family. Contending that the arrest was merely another example of gringo arrogance, Cortina shot the deputy and freed the prisoner. On the morning of September twenty-eighth, Brownsville awoke to the cry of *"Viva Cortina! Viva Mexico! Maten los Gringos!"* as Cortina, at the head of an armed force, swept into the town, killed five Americans, released the *pelado* culprits from the jail, and plundered stores and shops. By 1860 Cortina had laid waste to the country from Brownsville to Rio Grande City—a distance of a hundred and fifty miles—and inland as far as Arroyo Colorado. Fifteen Americans and eighty "friendly" Mexicans were killed in these raids, while Cortina is said to have lost a hundred or more of his men.

For fifteen years, Cortina was the scourge of the Lower Rio Grande Valley, defying capture, constantly eluding his pursuers. At one point in the Cortina War, Captain McNelly of the Texas Rangers crossed the Rio Grande, in defiance of orders, and gave Cortina's forces a severe defeat in a pitched battle at Las Cuevas. Incensed by these continued raids, the Texans burned the homes of all Mexicans suspected of being implicated or of giving aid and comfort to Cortina's forces. On his part, Cortina terrorized the Mexican residents and made short shrift of those suspected of being informers. This continued terror naturally silenced the Mexicans—a circumstance which only confirmed the Texans' belief in their innate duplicity and treacherousness.

A real expert in border warfare, Cortina hoisted the Mexican flag in Texas, and, so it was said, often raised the American flag in Mexico. Both Texas Rangers and Mexican troops from Matamoros on more than one occasion met defeat at his hands. Although he was a bandit and a cattle-thief, there was unquestionably something of the Robin Hood about Cortina. He had become a desperado, so he said, because the Anglo-Americans had tried "to blacken, depreciate, and load with insults" the Mexican residents of Texas. In one of numerous manifestoes, he pointed out that "a multitude of lawyers" in Texas sought to rob the Mexicans of their lands. In particular, he charged that one Adolph Glavecke, a deputy sheriff, acting in collusion with certain lawyers, had spread terror among the Mexicans, threatening to hang them and to burn their homes unless they abandoned the country. "Our personal enemies," he said, "shall not possess our lands until they have fattened it with their gore." Major Heintzelman, on the border at the time, stated that after the Brownsville raid Cortina was a great hero in the eyes of the people. "He had defeated the gringo and his position was impregnable. He had the Mexican flag flying in his camp and numbers were flocking to his standard. He was the champion of his race—the man who would right the wrongs of the Mexicans and drive the hated Americans to the Nueces."

While some Mexicans undoubtedly sympathized with Cortina and gave him aid, it is also a matter of record that others, at great personal peril, joined in the fight to defeat him. Despite this fact, however, the Anglo-Texans believed that every Mexican along the border was in league with Cortina and would, if given a chance, "murder every white inhabitant." At the request of the American government, Díaz finally brought the Cortina War to a close in 1873 by making Cortina his prisoner; but, as Walter Prescott Webb has written, "the evil consequences lived on."

6. "The Dead-Line of Sheriffs"

In the period from the close of the Civil War to 1880, there was nothing resembling "law and order" in the territory between the Nueces and the Rio Grande where friction between Anglo and Hispano was intense and continuous. In this strip of territory resided about eighty per cent of the Mexicans then living in Texas. For fifty years after 1846, this territory was known as "the dead-line of sheriffs." American officials refused to provide Catholic bishops safe conduct through the area and even the Texas Rangers hesitated to enter it.

Neglected during the Civil War, great herds of cattle roamed wild in the brush country and plundering expeditions crossed and recrossed the border as cattle-stealing became an accepted business. To complicate matters, Mexico had established a narrow strip of territory on its side of the Rio Grande in which goods could be sold free of custom charges and duties. The existence of this "free zone" was an open invitation to smuggling and greatly annoyed American merchants in the Texas towns. From 1871 to 1875 the whole border was aflame with a type of lawlessness and violence even worse than open warfare. Historians have despaired of listing the murders committed by both sides and have never succeeded in counting the number of raids. On dozens of occasions, American troops were sent on expeditions into Mexico; nor were Mexicans much more respectful of American sovereignty.

On May 8, 1874, a band of Mexican outlaws murdered four Anglo-Texans at Penascal; and, earlier, Albert Garza, a Mexican cattle-thief, raided far and wide in Texas. "Ghastly murders," writes Dr. Taylor, "and shootings of Mexicans, each attributed, probably often correctly, to the other race, became not infrequent occurrences."* General Ord

---

* Reprinted from *An American-Mexican Frontier* by Paul S. Taylor by permission of The University of North Carolina Press. Copyright, 1934, by The University of North Carolina Press.

reported that the raids were so frequent that the whole territory was entirely in the possession of cattle-raiders and bandits and that it was utterly impossible to "execute the laws at all." Formerly Mexicans had borne the brunt of frontier lawlessness but, after 1870, the tide was somewhat reversed, and it was the Anglo-Texans who were on the receiving end. The raids culminated in March, 1875, when a band of 150 Mexicans crossed the border near Eagle Pass and raided as far east as Corpus Christi.

For this daring raid, the retaliation of the Texans was swift, violent, and indiscriminate. Bands of Texans raided Mexican settlements, burning houses, shooting Mexicans, spreading terror throughout south Texas. Large parties of mounted, well-armed men, wrote N. A. Jennings, "committed the most brutal outrages, murdering peaceful Mexican farmers and stockmen who had lived all their lives in Texas." The adjutant-general of Texas, who can hardly be accused of pro-Mexican bias, reported that parties of Anglo-Americans had "banded together with the object of stopping the killing of cattle for their hides, but have themselves committed the greater crimes of murder and arson." Merchants in Corpus Christi began to complain that "every good Mexican is afraid to navigate the roads on horseback or with carts, and the business in these parts has commenced turning into another channel, where less risk is found."

The temper of the feeling, on both sides, is indicated in a report of General Steele in 1875 in which he said that "there is a considerable Texas element in the country bordering on the Nueces that think the killing of a Mexican no crime" and a collection of "Mexican thieves and cut-throats who . . . think the killing of a Texan something to be proud of." Reminiscing about the period, in 1929, a Texan told Dr. Taylor that "Mexicans despised us, and we hated the Mexicans like a human hates a rattlesnake." Throughout this period, there were elements in Texas who were deliberately fomenting disorder and violence in the hope that the United States would take another slice of Mexican territory; and it is a matter of record that in 1876 President Hayes toyed with the idea of provoking a war with Mexico to divert attention from the shady deal by which he had robbed Tilden of the presidency (1).

For this period as a whole, there is simply no telling, as J. Frank Dobie has said, "how many Mexicans bit the dust." Naturally robbery and theft went hand in hand with physical violence. "There is a disposition," as one witness testified before a congressional committee in 1875, "on the part of some Americans, which crops out every once in a while, not to respect the property rights of Mexicans living southwest of the Nueces River." The "beef packeries" on the American side of the Rio Grande often winked when Texas cattlemen brought in large herds of cattle clearly marked with Mexican brands. It was during this period, writes Garrison, that "large bodies of land that now have enormous value were then secured [from Mexican settlers], sometimes legally and sometimes illegally, for almost nothing." On the other hand, Mexican cattle-thieves, in raiding Texas herds, laughingly said that they had come to collect *"las vacas de tata"* or "grandfather's cattle." One of the last large-scale raids was that organized by Catarina Garza in 1892 whose raid on the Norias Ranch is celebrated in a famous *corrido* (2).

"Not only were the Mexicans bamboozled by the political factions," writes Walter Prescott Webb, "but they were victimized by the law. One law applied to them and another, far less rigorous, to the political leaders and to the prominent Americans. The Mexicans suffered not only in their persons but in their property. The old landowning Mexican families found their titles in jeopardy and if they did not lose in the courts, they lost to their American lawyers. The humble Mexican doubted a government that would not protect their person and the higher classes distrusted one that would not safeguard their property." In an official investigation in 1878, the American consul in Matamoros testified that the authorities were never interested when a Mexican was killed in Brownsville; but, if a "white man" was molested in any way, "there is generally a great fuss made about it by those not of Mexican origin." As late as 1879 the Anglo residents of Crio Canyon posted an order commanding all Mexicans to leave the area within three days. "In passing through Bee county," said Senator Dwyer, "we heard of a Mexican, a quiet citizen, who had been brutally murdered a few days before our arrival, by several Americans because the Mexican would not go and play the fiddle for them."

7. THE SALT WAR

In 1877 there were about twelve thousand people living along the Rio Grande at El Paso, all but eighty of whom were Mexicans. The Mexicans, writes Dr. Webb, "felt that Texas was by right still a part of

Mexico" for El Paso had been "Mexican" for nearly three hundred years. After the Mexican-American War, a few Anglo-Americans appeared on the scene, monopolizing the government positions and showing a general tendency to take over. About a hundred miles east of El Paso was a salt mine which the Mexicans had discovered in 1862. By general consensus the Mexican residents of El Paso had been accorded the privilege of digging salt at the mine, without charge, for their personal needs. An ambitious American acquired control of the salt mine, by a series of devious manoeuvres, and announced that henceforth it would be operated as a private monopoly. Outraged by this action and inflamed by the demagoguery of Father Borajo, a local priest, a mob of El Pasoans seized the city on October 10, 1877, killed three Anglos and committed property damage that ran into thousands of dollars. In the process of restoring "law and order," the usual retaliations were committed with a number of Mexicans being killed and several more being lynched. As might have been expected, "bitter hatreds were sown" as a consequence of the short-lived Salt War.

From the inception of the Díaz regime, a degree of quiet prevailed along the border until the outbreak of the Mexican Revolution in 1910. But, even during this period, incidents were constantly occurring. When a Ranger shot and killed Ramón de la Cerda of the King Ranch in 1902, a general resentment against the Rangers flared up all along the border. Annoyed by this protest, a Ranger proceeded to whip a Mexican boy with a quirt and, shortly afterwards, Albert de la Cerda, a brother of the slain man, was shot by the Rangers. Incidents of this kind, with which the record is studded, served to keep the old antagonisms alive.

8. Open Season on Mexicans

From 1908 to 1925, the whole border was aflame, once again, as revolution engulfed Mexico. No one knows how many American and Mexican civilians were killed along the border in these years but the estimates, according to Dr. Webb, range from five hundred to five thousand. As war approached in Europe, the Texans inevitably suspected the Mexicans of being in league with the Germans. "There is a fear constantly stored away in the back of the El Pasoan mind," wrote Tracy Hammond Lewis, "that these Mexicans will take it into their heads to have an especially-appointed uprising at the expense of the Americans" (3).

Fearful of the revolution, Mexican cattle-owners drove tens of thousands of cattle across the border to cash in on wartime beef prices in the United States. Once the ranges were deserted, the feed became, of course, very good on the Mexican side. Raiders then crossed the border, rounded up thousands of American-owned cattle, pastured them in Mexico, and later sold them to one or another of the various factions fighting in Mexico. As a consequence, property losses ran into the hundreds of thousands of dollars. From Brownsville to Calexico, raiders crossed and recrossed the border, exploiting the confusion which prevailed on both sides of the line. On March 9, 1916, Francisco Villa spread terror up and down the border with his raid on Columbus, New Mexico; and, before much time had passed, the Pershing expedition was deep in Mexican territory. Over two thousand postcards a day were sold in El Paso depicting "Mexican atrocities" while American troops marched through the streets singing:

> "It's a long, long way to capture Villa;
> It's a long way to go;
> It's a long way across the border
> Where the dirty greasers grow."

In this bloody seventeen-year period, hundreds of innocent civilians were killed. "Americans," writes Ernest Gruening, "continued to be killed by the vengeful Villistas, at times for no other reason than that they were 'gringos.' Mexicans likewise were killed in Texas chiefly because they were 'greasers.'" In an article in *World's Work,* George Marvin reported that "the killing of Mexicans . . . through the border in these last four years is almost incredible. . . . Some rangers have degenerated into common man-killers. There is no penalty for killing, for no jury along the border would ever convict a white man for shooting a Mexican. . . . Reading over the Secret Service records makes you feel almost as though there were an open game season on Mexicans along the border."

Carranza, in a well-documented report, charged that 114 Mexicans had been murdered on the American side and a number of American officials acknowledged the accuracy of the charge. A formal protest filed by the Mexican ambassador in 1912 complained of the mistreatment of Mexicans in California and Texas and listed any number of lynchings and murders. On November 11, 1922, a Mexican, Elías Zarate, was lynched in Weslaco, Texas. Zarate had been arrested after a fist fight with an American and the Mexican consul had warned the authorities of the danger of mob violence. In its issue of July 12, 1922, *The Nation* documented a series of cases, all occurring in Texas, in which Mexicans had been brutally assaulted; in some cases, murdered. Following an old-established pattern, the authorities in Breckenridge, Texas, warned all Mexicans to depart overnight. The lawlessness became so widespread that Secretary of State Hughes had to warn the governor of Texas that some action would have to be taken to protect Mexicans. In an editorial of November 18, 1922, the New York *Times* said that "the killing of Mexicans without provocation is so common as to pass almost unnoticed"—nearly a hundred years after the signing of the Treaty of Guadalupe Hidalgo.

Much of the lawlessness against Mexicans in Texas had an official or semi-official status, for the Texas Rangers had become a kind of "black-and-tan" constabulary bent on terrorizing the Mexican population. Jovita Gonzáles quotes a local historian to the effect that the Rangers had executed, without due process of law, between one hundred and three hundred Mexican residents of the border counties. "The Rangers," wrote Tracy Hammond Lewis, "are only cold-blooded where the Mexicans are concerned, and this solely because they have learned it is the one manner in which they can be properly handled." J. T. Canales, a Mexican-American member of the Texas legislature from Brownsville, filed formal charges against the Rangers over the mistreatment of *Tejanos* and there must have been some merit to these charges for the number of Rangers was shortly reduced and, some years later, the organization was disbanded.

This eruption of violence against persons of Mexican descent had important international repercussions. For example, Carranza at first refused to permit Mexico to join the League of Nations on the ground that the Covenant of the League did not insure racial equality. Nothing so much infuriated the influential anti-Yankee Latin-American publicist Manuel Ugarte as the conditions which he had observed along the border. "From the very frontier," he wrote, "the irreconcilable opposition between the two communities presents itself vividly and obviously. The Anglo-Saxon, hard, haughty, and utilitarian, infatuated with his success and his muscular strength, improvises towns, dominates nature, imposes everywhere the impress of his activity and ambition; and, like the Romans in their palmy days, has as his auxiliaries and servants the subject races,—Indians, Chinese, Africans,—who gather up the crumbs of the feast in return for discharging their subaltern tasks. As opposed to him, the Mexican . . . continues in his easy-going customs and accepts the fruits of the earth" (4).

The general attitude of Latin-Americans was reflected in an editorial of May 15, 1922, in *Heraldo,* published in Mexico City:

> It is thoroughly irritating that while in our country American citizens enjoy ample guarantees and when anything happens to them it is settled by the United States consuls, in that country, on the other hand, Mexicans are still being killed without any effort by the American authorities to punish the murderers. . . . Up to the present time, not a single person has been electrocuted for killing a Mexican, no matter how brutally or basely he might have perpetrated the crime.

Viewing this record in retrospect, one can thoroughly appreciate the comments, without sharing the conclusions, of F. L. Olmstead (5):

> . . . between our South American and the Mexican there is an unconquerable antagonism of character, which will prevent any condition of order where the two come together. . . . The mingled Puritanism and brigandism, which distinguishes the vulgar mind of the South, peculiarly unfits it to harmoniously associate with the bigoted, childish, and passionate Mexicans. They are considered to be heathen; not acknowledged as "white folks." Inevitably they are dealt with insolently and unjustly. . . . Guaranteed by the treaty of Guadalupe Hidalgo, equal rights with all other citizens of the United States and of Texas, the whole native population of county after county has been driven, by the formal proceedings of substantial planters, from its homes, and forbidden, on pain of no less punishment than instant death, to return to the vicinity of the plantations.

VII

Gringos and Greasers

In the Southwest, Anglos have always been "gringos" to the Hispanos while Hispanos have been "greasers" to the Anglos. The two terms pretty accurately reflect the measure of mutual esteem which has prevailed. For many years the origin of the word "gringo" was traced to a song,—"*Green Grow the Rushes, O!*"—, which the Yankees sang in 1846 when they marched into Mexico. Actually "gringo" is to be found in all Spanish dictionaries. Defined as a corruption of *griego* or "Greek," it is said to be a nickname applied to foreigners. *Hablar en gringo* is to talk gibberish; much as Americans would say, "It's all Greek to me." In popular Southwestern usage prior to the conquest, "gringo" referred to any foreigner who spoke Spanish with an accent and was first recorded in the New English Dictionary in 1884 (1). It should be noted that the term, as used by Mexicans, is less insulting in its implications than "greaser."

The origin of "greaser" has been variously explained. It is said that a Mexican once maintained a small shop at the crest of Raton Pass where the ox-carts and wagons of the Santa Fe Trail were greased before they made the descent to the New Mexico plateau; hence a Mexican was literally a "greaser." In California the term has been traced to the days of the hide-and-tallow trade and is said to have first been applied by American sailors to the Indians and Mexicans who loaded the greasy, tick-ridden hides on the clipper ships. It is also said to have had some relation to sheep-shearing. The term was certainly well known in early California for Harris Newmark tells of the lynching of an Anglo in Los Angeles in 1854 who objected most strenuously to being shuffled off "by a lot of greasers" (2). The term is defined by Vizetelly as "Mexican; an opprobrious term," and a note states that it is "California slang for a mixed race of Mexicans and Indians" with Bret Harte's "Carquinez Wood" being cited as authority for this usage. The definition to be found in the Century Dictionary is: "a *native* Mexican or *native* Spanish-American, originally applied contemptuously by the Americans of the Southwestern United States to Mexicans" (emphasis added). In any case, gringo and greaser it has always been and it is in reference to the hostility and opposition which these terms imply that the pattern of Anglo-Hispano relations outside Texas will be discussed in this chapter.

1. The Bloodless Conquest

The conflict between greasers and gringos never assumed the proportions in New Mexico that so long prevailed in Texas. Being off the main path of Anglo-American expansion, New Mexico grew very slowly. At the time of the conquest the population of the territory was 61,525 which was made up almost entirely of Spanish-speaking people. From this figure the population increased to 87,034 in 1860 (79,249 native-born); and then to 91,784 in 1870 (83,175 native-born). Hence the population of the state remained ninety per cent Spanish-speaking during the first two decades after the conquest. In fact it has only been of fairly recent date that the Anglo-Americans have achieved a slight numerical ascendancy. Furthermore the two groups have always been geographically segregated in New Mexico, with the Spanish-speaking element concentrated in the north-central part of the state and the Anglo-Americans in the larger towns and in the southern and eastern areas. Distance has made for a formality and civility the absence of which is most conspicuous in Texas.

The Anglo-American immigration to New Mexico was of an entirely different character, in quality as well as quantity, from the immigration that so quickly engulfed the Spanish-speaking in Texas and California. Only a hundred or so Anglo-Americans had settled in New Mexico prior to 1846 and most of these had married into prominent "native" families. During the height of the commerce on the Santa Fe Trail, not more than 150 Anglo-Americans entered the province each year and most of these visitors departed as soon as their wares had been sold. After the conquest, the first Anglo-American settlers were federal officers, followed by territorial officials, lawyers, and merchants. Since there was never a large influx of farm families, active competition for resources was kept at a minimum until about 1880. The economic conquest of Texas and California was achieved by the Anglo-Americans overnight and by the use of superior force; in New Mexico the process was indirect and subtle and took the form of a gradual assertion of dominance through manipulation rather than by outright expropriation.

At the outset there was less opposition to the Anglo-Americans in New Mexico than in Texas for neither the *pobres* nor the Indians felt much loyalty to Mexico. Twitchell described their allegiance to Mexico as "not overly strong," while Bancroft said that it was "only nominal." Nor were the *ricos* united in opposition to the Americans. Those who had profited by the commerce which developed with the opening of the Santa Fe Trail saw in American rule the hope of expanding markets and better communications. The resistance of those who opposed the conquest, moreover, was frustrated by the treachery of their leader, Governor Manuel Armijo, who is said to have presented New Mexico to the American agent, James W. Magoffin, for a handsome consideration. Under the terms of the Treaty of Guadalupe Hidalgo, Mexican residents were given one year in which to leave the borderlands; those who remained automatically became citizens of the United States. According to Bancroft, not more than 1,200 residents of New Mexico left the province during the year of grace.

There was still another reason for the lack of opposition to the conquest in New Mexico. In 1841 the Republic of Texas had sent an expedition of 270 soldiers to seize New Mexico. Intercepted by the New Mexicans, the invading army was defeated in battle and its leaders were sent as prisoners of war to Mexico City. By way of retaliation, the Texans began to raid the Santa Fe caravans with such regularity that all commerce was suspended for one year (1843). George Kendall's famous account of the Texas expedition, emphasizing the cruelty of the captors, has been called the *Uncle Tom's Cabin* of the Mexican-American War. This initial clash was merely the first of a long series of incidents which served to create and maintain a traditional antipathy between Texans and New Mexicans. The antipathy was so keen in 1846 that the New Mexicans were inclined to look upon the arrival of American troops as a measure of protection against further encroachments on the part of the Texans.

2. The Ghost of Father Martínez

Although the pattern of antecedent conflict was lacking in New Mexico, the conquest was not entirely bloodless. Shortly after the arrival of federal troops in the province, the New Mexicans organized a revolt in the course of which the first American civil governor, Charles Bent, was assassinated. A most interesting New Mexican is said to have played a major role in organizing the brief revolt. Born in Abiquiu, educated in Durango, Father José Antonio Martínez had been named curate of Taos in 1830. A man of great energy and outstanding ability, Father Martínez was the undisputed boss of Taos. The owner of several ranches and a flour mill, he published the first newspaper printed in New Mexico, *El Crepúsculo*—"*The Dawn.*" Something of a freethinker, he denounced heavy tithes and church fees; founded the first schools in the province; and served as a member of the provincial assembly. In line with the prevailing moral standards of the New Mexican curates, Father Martínez had several wives and his progeny were numerous. Many of his offspring still live in Taos and are rightly proud of their paternity. A shrewd man, Father Martínez once observed that a republic was a burro on which lawyers jog along much better than priests. In the opinion of Erna Fergusson, Martínez still ranks as perhaps "the outstanding New Mexican."

Although the historians have been unable to define the precise responsibility of Father Martínez for the ill-fated revolt of 1846, they are agreed that he was one of the principal organizers of the revolt whose nominal leader was a peon, one Pablo Montoya. Shortly after the assassination of Governor Bent, federal troops arrived at Taos under Colonel Price and laid seige to the old church in which the rebels had barricaded themselves. About 150 New Mexicans were killed in this engagement; some twenty-five or thirty prisoners were shot down by firing squads; and many of those who surrendered were publicly flogged. Colonel Price's troops are said to have been so drunk at the time that the Taos engagement was more of a massacre than a battle.

In the restoration of order Kit Carson, who, like Governor Bent, had married a Spanish-American, played a leading role, as did Domiciano Vigil, a native New Mexican of the *rico* class who became acting governor. While the revolt was quickly suppressed, it left a heritage of ill-will and bitterness which survived for many years. George F. Ruxton, the English traveller, reported that he had "found over all New Mexico the most bitter feeling and the most determined hostility against the Americans who . . . by their bullying and overbearing demeanor toward them [the natives] have in great measure been the cause of this hatred."

With the arrival of Bishop Lamy in 1851, Father Martínez was suspended as a priest and later denied communion, all as part of Lamy's general effort to reform the worldly, pleasure-loving curates of New Mexico. Despite these retaliatory measures, however, Father Martínez continued to preside in his church until his death in 1867 at the age of seventy-four.

Some years later, still another priest emerged as a leader of the native-born New Mexicans and achieved, for a time, considerable power and influence. This priest, Father Gallegos, was excommunicated by Bishop Lamy for concubinage. Perhaps because they were Mexican-born, both Father Martínez and Father Gallegos were close to the people, sharing their feelings and sentiments. The leadership which they provided for the native peoples is supposed to have had a marked influence on Catholic policy. Since Father Gallegos was excommunicated, the Church has been careful to select French, German and Belgian priests for service in New Mexico.

3. Disturbance in Socorro

While the Taos revolt was, as Harvey Fergusson has written, "the last battle on the Rio Grande between the old order and the new," a number of later incidents indicate that the conflict continued in other forms. Francisco Perea, one of the *ricos,* once ran for office on a platform which opposed the building of the rail lines. "We don't want you damned Yankees in the country," he said; "we can't compete with you; you will drive us out." And, at a place called Cow Creek Hill, a pitched battle was fought in 1880 between railroad construction workers and local Spanish-speaking residents (3). With the railroads, of course, came the cattlemen. In the 1880's a number of Texas cowboys began to drive their herds, and occasionally their neighbors' herds, into the region around Socorro, north of El Paso on the Rio Grande. They were men, wrote William French, "who lost no opportunity of displaying their hatred of Mexicans. To them all Mexicans were 'greasers' and unfit associates for the white man" (4). A few brave words about Davy Crockett and the Alamo were all that was needed to work these men into a Mexican-killing mood.

When the Texans began to invade Socorro, shooting up the town and terrorizing the natives, many of the Mexicans abandoned their homes and ranches and crossed the border into Mexico. In the town of Dona Ana alone some sixty New Mexican families moved out when the Texans moved in. John R. Bartlett, of the United States Border Commission, reported that "immediately preceding and after the war with Mexico, the Mexican population was greatly annoyed by the encroachments of the Americans and by their determined efforts to despoil them of their landed property. This was done by the latter either settling among them or in some instances forcibly occupying their dwellings and cultivated spots." The murder of Manuel Otero by Texas cowboys at Estancia Springs was merely one of many similar incidents of the period (5). Control of the rich pasture lands of western New Mexico and eastern Arizona was the prize for which Anglos and Hispanos contended along the lower Rio Grande in New Mexico.

Out of this conflict emerged one of the present-day folk heroes of New Mexico,—Elfego Baca. A native New Mexican, Baca greatly resented the arrogance of the Texans and volunteered to serve as a deputy sheriff. When the Texans went on their next shooting spree, he proceeded to arrest a Texas cowboy. Once word reached the ranches that the unheard-of had happened—that a "Mexican" had actually arrested a "Texan"—the cowboys came trooping in for the kill. In the meantime, however, Baca had lodged his prisoner in the jail and had carefully barricaded himself in an adobe. When the dust of battle finally subsided, after a night and a day of blazing guns, Baca still held possession of the adobe. A truce was then negotiated and the Texans gathered up their dead and wounded and departed from Socorro. Once Baca had demonstrated that New Mexicans could shoot as accurately as Texans, the encroachment of Texas folkways in New Mexico came to a dead-halt.

In the Panhandle of Texas still another Mexican folk hero emerged: Sostenes l'Archevêque, who was born in Santa Fe, of a French father and a Mexican-Indian mother. After his father was shot down by Anglo-Americans in the little town of Sapello in eastern New Mexico, the young man lost little time in acquiring twenty-three "gringo" notches on his gun—two more notches than were to be found on the gun of Billy the Kid. In the Panhandle, however, Sostenes over-reached himself. After killing and robbing an Anglo-American sheepman, as part of his bitter vendetta, he was lured into a trap by his own people. It was said that his executioners felt that they must avenge his crime in order to prevent wholesale retaliations. If this was their motive, then the sacrifice of Sostenes was needless, for the reprisals were swift and cruel. For a week or more, Texas cowboys ran wild in Tascosa, shooting up the Mexican plazas, killing several innocent Mexicans, and lynching those suspected of complicity in the murder of the sheepman. It was largely as a result of these reprisals that the Mexicans retreated from the Panhandle to New Mexico.

4. THE DON SYSTEM

Confronted by an overwhelming Spanish-speaking majority whose property and political rights were guaranteed by the Treaty of Guadalupe Hidalgo, the Anglo-Americans were forced to proceed by stealth and indirection in their campaign to acquire control of New Mexico. They had, however, one great advantage: control of the territorial government and the courts through the appointive power. When one compares the celerity with which California and Nevada were admitted to the union with the prolonged struggle for statehood in New Mexico, it is readily apparent that forces were at work, both within and without the state, to delay admission *until* an Anglo-American majority had been established. "The mass of the people are Mexicans," as Thaddeus Stevens explained to his colleagues in Congress, "a hybrid race of Spanish and Indian origin, ignorant, degraded, demoralized and priest-ridden." One of the leaders in the fight to extend the franchise to the Negro freedmen in the South, Stevens showed little interest in democracy in New Mexico. Whatever the motive, the federal government ruled New Mexico for sixty-three years as a dependent province.

Even under the forms of territorial government, however, it was necessary for the Anglo-Americans to cultivate the *ricos* through whom they could control the Spanish-speaking majority. Jealous of their power, the *ricos* used the patron-peon relationship to develop what came to be called "the don system" of politics in which the *haciendado* was said to have voted his sheep as well as his peons. For years the phrase "New Mexico politics" was synonymous with political corruption. The corruption had little to do with the character of the people: it was a function of the political system. Most of the governors and other territorial officials were, of course, Anglo-Americans; but the territorial legislature was dominated by Hispanos from its establishment until about the time New Mexico was finally granted statehood in 1912. Throughout its history, the territorial legislature was made up of members who belonged to, or were controlled by, some twenty prominent families of the *rico* class. Thus to control the legislature and the territorial delegate in Congress, it was necessary for the Anglo-Americans to work through and to ally themselves with the *rico* class.

Out of this alliance there developed what was called "the Santa Fe Ring,"—a small, compact group of Anglo-American bankers, lawyers, merchants, and politicians who dominated the territory through their ties with the *ricos* who in turn controlled the votes of the Spanish-speaking. "The professional connections made by them," writes Twitchell, "with the representative families of the Rio Abajo and Rio Arriba in guarding their interests in the matter of Spanish and Mexican land grants enabled them to maintain what seemed to be an invincible position in the control of all matters of business or of a political character." It was the members of this "ring" who manipulated the Indian Bureau; controlled the allocation of contracts to supply the army posts; dictated territorial appointments; and exercised a great influence over the courts.

On at least two occasions, however, the neat alliance between the Santa Fe Ring and the *ricos* was seriously challenged. As a boy, Colonel J. Francisco Chaves had been told by his father, a member of the *rico* class, that "the heretics are going to overrun the country. Go and learn their language and come back prepared to defend your people." From New Mexico, young Chaves was sent to school, first in St. Louis, and then to New York, where he graduated from the College of Physicians and Surgeons. During the Civil War, he was one of a number of native-born New Mexicans who fought with the Union Army. Returning to New Mexico in 1867, he ran for the post of territorial delegate in Congress against an Anglo-American and was finally seated after a bitter campaign which had resulted in a contested election. In 1869 he was re-elected as delegate, following another heated and bitterly fought campaign. Then, with the election of 1871, came the "Mesilla Riots" in which nine men were killed and forty or fifty were wounded. Most of the casualties were Spanish-speaking supporters of Colonel Chaves, who was defeated. These were state-wide campaigns with the Anglos and their *rico* allies being lined up against the Spanish-speaking lower classes.

Following his defeat, Colonel Chaves served for twelve years as president of the territorial state senate. Here, again, he waged an unrelenting campaign against Anglo-American boss-ism and opposed the alliance which existed between the Santa Fe Ring and the *ricos*. Later, as the first superintendent of public instruction in New Mexico, he put up a gallant although unsuccessful fight to bring about an adequate allocation of federal funds for the schools of the territory. In 1904 Colonel Chaves was murdered "under the most mysterious circumstances." "The charge was made," writes Twitchell, "that it was political assassination involving men of great prominence in Santa Fe and elsewhere."

On the death of Colonel Chaves, leadership of the Spanish-speaking element passed to Octaviano A. Larrazolo, the first person born in Mexico to serve as governor of an American state. It was largely as a result of his effective leadership that the New Mexico constitution incorporated the guarantees of the Treaty of Guadalupe Hidalgo safeguarding the rights of Spanish-speaking residents. "Whether for good or evil," writes one historian, "it is because of the impress of his day that the cleavage between the descendants of the Spanish conquerors and colonists and those who came from other states continues to be felt in political life, and is felt even in business, in the professions, and in social activities." From that day to this the demand by the Spanish-American group for at least one-half of the candidates on the tickets of the two major parties has been a *sine qua non* in every state campaign. Larrazolo was the second Spanish-speaking governor of New Mexico (Ezequiel de Baca, the first, was elected in 1916), and the first Spanish-speaking New Mexican to serve in the United States Senate.

The careers of Colonel Chaves and Larrazolo serve to indicate that beneath an apparently calm surface much ethnic ill-feeling has long existed in New Mexico. When Bronson Cutting reversed the usual pattern of New Mexico politics by espousing the cause, not of the *ricos,* but of the Spanish-speaking majority, the Santa Fe Ring suffered its first serious defeat. The undisputed boss of New Mexico politics, Cutting was regarded by most Anglo-Americans as a renegade, a traitor to his "race" and class. The first Anglo-American politician to champion the cause of the Spanish-speaking element in the Southwest, Cutting is still revered in New Mexico. The following that he developed with such tact and skill is today represented in the United States Senate by Dennis Chavez, a native-born New Mexican.

Throughout the borderlands Mexican-Americans are still struggling, often in a most confused and inchoate way, to overthrow a dual dominance: an Anglo-American hegemony imposed through the instrumentality of a quisling-like, upper-class "Spanish" element. "The poverty and social condition of the lower classes," wrote Twitchell, "the system of peonage which prevailed, and above all the attitude of the upper or official class displayed and maintained toward those of their own people whom they regarded in every way as servitors, may well be said to account for social infirmities, encouraging and patronizing which it may safely be said was always some foreigner who was a more or less active partner in the enterprise."

While conflict between Anglos and Hispanos is less evident in New Mexico than elsewhere in the borderlands, it has long existed and, of late years, has become more pronounced. It is often masked by religious issues, as in the consistent opposition of the Catholic Church to the work of Protestant missions and in the opposition of Protestant groups to the employment of nuns and Catholic brothers as teachers in the public schools. One can even detect an ethnic cleavage within the Catholic Church. For the larger communities usually have one church for the English-speaking; another for the Spanish-speaking. From the earliest times, the Protestant sects have separated Spanish-Americans from the Anglos in their churches, schools, and other institutions. Most of the larger towns are divided into an "Old Town" and a "New Town," or an Anglo and Hispano section, with the high school being customarily located in the "new" or Anglo community. The cleavage is most apparent and the group-consciousness of the Spanish-speaking is most pronounced in the areas which have received the heaviest Anglo-American influx.

"The participation of Spanish-American people in the social life of the Anglos," writes Carolyn Zeleny, "is even more restricted than that of Anglos in Spanish-American society. During two years residence in an Anglo-dominated city, the writer never met a Spanish-American at a social gathering." Originally most of the mixed marriages were between Anglo men and Spanish-speaking women of the *rico* class; but nowadays mixed marriages among the working class are not uncommon as shown by the disconcertingly large number of Carmencita O'Briens and Juan O'Rourkes to be found in the schools of the larger towns. While the mores preclude an open discussion of prejudice—both groups being most reluctant to discuss it—there can be no doubt that prejudice serves as a mechanism by which the rise of Spanish-Americans to positions threatening the advantaged place of the Anglo-Americans is retarded if not prevented (6).

5. The Buffer State

In Arizona relations between Anglos and Hispanos at the outset were, as Dr. Frank C. Lockwood has observed, "on the most friendly terms; neither race scorned the other." Other long-time residents of Arizona, such as John C. Vosburg, have also commented on the surprising amount of "good will that existed between Americans and Mexicans" who were united, in the pioneer phase, by a mutual fear of the Apaches. In the local annals, one reads of many marriages between Anglo men and Spanish-speaking women. Such well-known "pioneer" residents of Tucson as L. J. F. Jaeger, Samuel Hughes, Hiram S. Stevens, Solomon Warner, Peter H. Brady, Fritz Contzen, and William S. Curry, all married "Spanish" ladies.

It was not long, however, before elements of conflict developed. The rich mining "strikes" around Tombstone in the late 'eighties, and the campaigns against the Apaches, created a lively demand for beef cattle at fancy prices. As this demand mounted, so-called "Texas cowboys," more often Texas outlaws, began to raid Mexican ranches along the border. One "outfit" alone is said to have harbored more than three hundred outlaws in the San Pedro and Sulphur Springs valleys. The business of the "outfits," of course, was to raid Mexican ranches and to drive off the herds which the Mexicans attempted to get through to the mines and army posts. The celebrated Clanton "gang" participated in these raids, often killing, as Paul I. Wellman has written, "a dozen or so Mexicans in a negligent way" (7). W. M. Breakenridge, author of a spirited history of Tombstone, once said that the hatred of the Texans "was so bitter that they had no compunction about stealing from Mexicans or shooting them and robbing them whenever they got an opportunity." Later the situation was somewhat reversed and the Mexicans began to do most of the killing and raiding.

Throughout the Southwest, the conflict between gringo and greaser often masked a conflict between cattle and sheep interests. "The two callings," writes Mr. Wellman, "fostered the mutual distrust and dislike which the races held for each other." Wherever sheep were driven, Mexicans came with them; wherever cattle went, Texans were to be found. Hence the hatred of cattlemen for sheepmen was, in most cases, a hatred of Anglos for Hispanos. During the period that this warfare prevailed, Mexican sheepherders were murdered in every Western state. Teofilo Trujillo, of Taos, who pioneered sheep-raising in southern Colorado, was clubbed to death by "cowboys" in 1884. In the same raid, his home was burned and his herds were driven from the range. Cowboys employed by the Chiricahua Cattle Company rode into the sheep camp of Don Pedro Montano in Arizona one morning in 1889 and murdered three Mexican sheepherders in cold blood. Nearly every sheep-raising section in the West has a record of one or more such "incidents."

Having completed its line to Casa Grande, the Southern Pacific Company discharged some 1,500 Mexican workers in the summer of 1879, most of whom, instead of returning to Mexico, decided to settle in Phoenix. Since Phoenix was a new Anglo-American town, the influx of this number of unemployed Mexican workers was immediately resented and feeling between "greaser" and "gringo" soon reached the boiling point. One day a drunken Mexican, brandishing a sabre, dashed on horseback through the streets of Phoenix shouting Cortina's famous war cry: *"Maten los Gringos!"* By way of additional provocation, the unemployed Mexican workers gathered in a park where they listened to harangues by their spokesmen against the railroad and the Anglo-Americans. In the meantime, leaders of the Anglo-American elements quietly assembled a lynch mob. Apparently reluctant to launch a frontal attack on the Mexicans, the mob took two Anglo prisoners from the jail, escorted them to the park, and there lynched them in the presence of the Mexicans. After the lynching, a spokesman for the Anglos made a speech in which he warned that a similar fate might await some of the

Mexicans if the meeting was not immediately dispersed. Needless to say, the warning was heeded.

Like Texas and California, Arizona has a long record of Mexican lynchings. One Mariano Tisnado was lynched in Phoenix on July 3, 1873; Leonardo Cordoba, Clement López, and Jesús Saguaripa were lynched in Tucson on August fourth of the same year, with a coroner's jury defending the lynchings. Still another Mexican was lynched in Bisbee, a stronghold of anti-Mexican sentiment, on August 11, 1882. So firmly were the Anglo-Americans entrenched in power that, in the 1890's, one reads of the enactment of ordinances outlawing Mexican fiestas in Arizona. There is also a record of a number of Mexican lynchings in Colorado (8).

6. The Lynching of Juanita

Mexican miners from Sonora were among the first emigrants to arrive in California after the discovery of gold. Staking out important claims in the "southern" mines—those in Calaveras, Tuolumne, Mariposa, and Stanislaus counties—they had made remarkable progress before the stream of Anglo-American migration had reached California. Even before the arrival of the Sonorans, several hundred Chilean and Peruvian miners had reached the goldfields by the summer of 1848. Settled by Spanish-speaking miners, the towns of Sonora and Hornitos quickly became populous, world-famous mining camps. The first Anglo-American mining settlements were in the "central" and "northern" districts, along the American, Feather, Bear, and Yuba rivers. It was not long, however, before the Anglo-Americans began to invade the southern mines.

"The Mexicans," writes Walter Noble Burns, "who poured into California during the gold rush, were still inflamed with the anti-American prejudices engendered during the Mexican War. Their attitude towards Americans was hostile from the first and, in return, the Americans regarded them as secret enemies and treated them with frank contempt." One of the first acts of the California legislature was the adoption of a foreign-miners' license tax which was aimed specifically at eliminating the competition of Mexican miners. Shortly after this act was passed, a mob of two thousand American miners descended on Sonora, "firing at every Mexican in sight." The camp was burned to the ground and a hundred or more Mexicans were rounded up and driven into a corral or stockade. During the week that the rioting lasted, scores of Mexicans were lynched and murdered. In the wake of the riots, most of the Mexicans abandoned their claims and fled to the Spanish-speaking counties in the southern part of the state. One of these former miners, Joaquín Murieta, became the leader of a famous band of Mexican outlaws.

A year later, on July 5, 1851, a mob of American miners in Downieville lynched a Mexican woman who was three months pregnant. During the excitement of the previous day's Fourth of July celebration, a drunken miner had broken into a shack in which the Mexican woman, whose name was Juanita, was living with a man who may or may not have been her husband. "In keeping with the characteristics of her race (*sic*)," writes Owen Cochran Coy (9), "Juanita had a quick passion." When the miner returned the next day, some say to apologize, a dispute arose which ended with the fatal stabbing of the miner. Stephen J. Field, later a justice of the United States Supreme Court, made an eloquent plea to the miners to spare the life of Juanita. The miners heard him out and then proceeded with the lynching. With incomparable courage, Juanita adjusted the rope with her own hands, smilingly bade the miners *"adiós,"* and swung from the scaffold.

The first person to be lynched in California was a Mexican and vast research would be required to arrive at an estimate of the number of Mexican lynchings between 1849 and 1890. In the mining camps, every crime or reported crime was promptly blamed on some Mexican and lynching was the accepted penalty for crimes in which Mexicans were involved. "We can see only indirectly," wrote Josiah Royce, "through the furious and confused reports of the Americans themselves, how much of organized and coarse brutality these Mexicans suffered from the miners' meetings." As violence mounted throughout the mining camps, the Mexicans took refuge in the "cow counties" of Southern California where, in canyon and foothill hideouts, they licked their wounds and plotted their revenge.

The *gente de razón* enjoyed, of course, immunity from the violence which raged in the mining districts. Ties of marriage and bonds of commerce brought them quickly into the American camp. During the first years of the conquest, the Americans were at some pains to distinguish between "native Californians," meaning *gente de razón*, and "Mexicans," meaning "greasers" and *cholos*. For it was generally recognized that the *gente de razón*, if properly cultivated, could be of major importance in consolidating American rule in California. When the first constitutional convention was called, seven out of forty-eight delegates were "native Californians." Needless to say, the *cholos* were not represented. But by 1876 Walter M. Fisher, the English journalist, could report that "the meanest runaway English sailor, escaped Sydney convict, or American rowdy, despised without distinction the bluest blood of Castile, and the half-breeds descended from the Mexican garrison soldiers, habitually designating all who spoke Spanish by the offensive name 'greasers' for whom remains only the rust and the dust of a lost power" (10).

The ease and swiftness of the victory over Mexico and the conquest of California had bred in the Americans a measureless contempt for all things Mexican. This feeling naturally found violent expression in California for there was really no government in the state from 1846 to 1850. The miners who made up the major element in the Anglo-American population were a tough and hard-bitten lot. Indeed the circumstances were unique for here a large body of restless, adventuresome, single men had been suddenly catapulted into a foreign land, with the excitement of gold in the air, and with no government of any sort to curb their predilection for violence and direct action. "Nowhere else," wrote Josiah Royce, "were Americans more affected than here, in our lives and conduct, by the feeling that we stood in the position of conquerors in a new land . . . nowhere else were we driven so hastily to improvize a government for a large body of strangers." It is not surprising, therefore, that the manners and actions of the first Anglo-American immigrants to reach the state after 1848 produced a silent bitterness among the Californians which was to last for many years.

Crimes of violence had been almost unknown in California prior to the conquest. "Perfect security for the person prevailed in California," wrote the South American, Don José Arnaz, of his stay in the province in the years from 1840 to 1843. But, after the conquest, the lower classes became extremely disaffected and their unrest often assumed a covert or "criminal" design. It was after 1846, wrote the historian J. M. Guinn, "that a strange metamorphosis took place in the character of the lower classes of the native Californians. . . . Before the conquest by the Americans they were a peaceful and contented people. There were no organized bands of outlaws among them. . . . The Americans not only took possession of their country and its government, but in many cases despoiled them of their ancestral acres and their personal property. Injustice rankles, and they were often treated by the rougher American elements as aliens and intruders, who had no right in the land of their birth."

Such, in general, is the origin of the much discussed "Mexican banditry" of the period. In the 'fifties, the country between Los Angeles and Fort Miller in the San Joaquin Valley was infested with "Californian and Mexican outlaws" who raided the herds of cattle being driven north to the mines and looted the mining settlements. Two companies of rangers were recruited in Southern California to fight off the raids. Typical of the attitudes of the bandits was the statement of Tiburcio Vásquez, a native Californian, who was executed in 1852. "A spirit of hatred and revenge," he said, "took possession of me. I had numerous fights in defense of what I believed to be my rights and those of my countrymen. I believed we were being unjustly deprived of the social rights that belonged to us."

The local county histories contain many references to the activities of these bold and daring outlaws: Vásquez, Joaquín Murieta, Louis Bulvia, Antonio Moreno, Procopio, Soto, Manuel García, Juan Flores, Pancho Daniel, and many others. Not a few of these men had fought on the side of Mexico in the war of 1846. Called *El Patrio,*—"The Native,"— by the Mexicans, Joaquín Murieta boasted that he could muster two thousand men. Many of the outlaw bands, in fact, contained a hundred or more men and were well organized for guerrilla fighting. "The racial loyalty of the Californians," to quote from one local history, "not to mention the entanglements of family relationships with the outlaws, plus a tacit policy of non-interference among the old American population, resulted in a negligent tolerance of these evils which within five years after 1849 swept the local situation entirely out of hand."

Mexican banditry gave a color of justification to the practice of lynching Mexicans which soon degenerated from a form of vigilante punishment for crime to an outdoor sport in Southern California. In 1857, four Mexicans were lynched in El Monte; eleven in Los Angeles. Throughout the 1860's the lynching of Mexicans was such a common occurrence in Los Angeles that the newspapers scarcely bothered to report the details. Horace Bell, who was himself once indicted for killing a Mexican, describes any number of murders and lynchings, in which the victims were Mexicans, in his memoirs: *Reminiscences of a Ranger* and *On the Old West Coast*. The last reported lynching of a Mexican occurred in August, 1892, when one Francisco Torres was lynched in Santa Ana. A homicide a day was reported in Los Angeles in 1854, with most of the victims being Mexicans and Indians. The previous year California had more murders than the rest of the states combined and Los Angeles had more than occurred elsewhere in California. The subordination of Mexicans in the social structure of California cannot be understood apart from this early-day pattern of violence and intimidation.

7. Birth of a Stereotype

From Brownsville to Los Angeles, the first impressions which the Anglo-Americans formed of the "native" element were highly unfavorable. Accurate and fair-minded observers like Josiah Gregg in New Mexico, Richard Henry Dana in California, and Frederick Law Olmstead in Texas, all drew essentially the same picture of the "idle, thriftless natives" by contrast with the charm of the *ricos* and the splendor of their *bailes*. The poverty and backwardness of the people were consistently stressed without any accompanying explanation of the factors—notably the isolation—which had produced such a "degraded" population. The puritanism of many of the Anglo-American observers was shocked by the "half-naked children" and the "immodesty" of the native women who dressed without benefit of underwear, petticoats, bustles, bodices, or long sleeves. More than one of these observers told, with unconcealed horror, of having seen native women step out of their red skirts and skimpy *camisas* and go bathing in the streams or of having seen women who drank, gambled, and smoked cigarettes.

In these early impressions, carefully embalmed, one can find the outline of the present-day stereotype of the Mexican. "The greater part of them," wrote Marmaduke, "are the most miserable, wretched poor creatures that I have ever seen, poor, petty, thieving, gambling, bullbaiting. . . ." Essentially this same impression was formed by a wide variety of observers: men and women; officers, miners, surveyors, trappers, mountainmen, sea captains, and journalists. Passed along to those who were about to leave for the borderlands, repeated by all observers, these same stereotyped impressions were given national currency during the Mexican-American War and the patriotic sanction long continued. It was only natural, as Twitchell explained, that the Missourians who came to New Mexico over the Santa Fe Trail should have carried home "unfavorable comments upon the character of the people when it was notorious that in the capital itself [Santa Fe] only the children of the *dueños* or *ricos* had any opportunity whatever to receive even the most rudimentary schooling. . . . A country without courts, officially bankrupt, and notoriously corrupt in its executive, certainly created anything but a favorable impression upon the minds of the Santa Fe traders." The trouble was that the tales told by the traders "became the basis of American opinion of Mexican character in toto; a most unfortunate conclusion in its moulding of public opinion of a people who were not themselves properly chargeable with the racial delinquencies so glibly commented upon by the 'strangers within the gates.' "

Above all it is important to remember that Mexicans are a "conquered" people in the Southwest, a people whose culture has been under incessant attack for many years and whose character and achievements, as a people, have been consistently disparaged. Apart from physical violence, conquered and conqueror have continued to be competitors for land and jobs and power, parties to a constant economic conflict which has found expression in litigation, dispossessions, hotly contested elections, and the mutual disparagement which inevitably accompanies a situation of this kind. Throughout this struggle, the Anglo-Americans have possessed every advantage: in numbers and wealth, arms and machines. Having been subjected, first to a brutal physical attack, and then to a long process of economic attrition, it is not surprising that so many Mexicans should show evidences of the spiritual defeatism which so often arises when a cultural minority is annexed to an alien culture and way of life. More is involved, in situations of this kind, than the defeat of individual ambitions, for the victims also suffer from the defeat of their culture and of the society of which they are a part.

VIII

The Heritage of the Southwest

Unlike the Middle West, there were no rich, fertile valleys in the Spanish borderlands; no plains which invited the plow; no lakes well stocked with fish; no rivers to be used for navigation or harnessed for power; no forests to provide lumber and fuel. The few areas capable of cultivation required irrigation in a land where water was scarce. Learning to survive in this region was a harsh and difficult undertaking. Resources had to be carefully husbanded; communications were hard to establish and difficult to maintain; and isolation magnified every aspect of the problem of settlement.

Yet the Spaniards, in a triangular relationship with Mexicans and Indians, succeeded in laying the foundations for the present-day economic structure of the region. Anglo-Americans in the Southwest have been the beneficiaries of three hundred years of experimentation, adaptation, and innovation. If one thinks of the Southwest in terms of mines, sheep, and cattle, and irrigated farming, then it is readily apparent that the underpinnings of the economy are of Spanish origin.

1. Mr. Marshall's *Chispa*

The lure of gold and silver was, of course, a prime motivation for Spanish explorations in the New World. In the Americas, the ancient mining culture of Spain was fused with elements of Aztec metallurgy to form, what was for the period, an advanced mining technology. Mining is still the most important, as it is the oldest, industry in Mexico. Mexico had its "gold rush" at Zacatecas in 1548, three hundred years before the discovery of gold in California. Out of this experience, the Spaniards and Mexicans had learned a great deal about placer and quartz mining and had made of prospecting a fine art.

Although the Spanish had sought gold and silver with the sword and spear, rather than with pick and shovel, they were the first to discover gold in California. On March 9, 1842, Francisco López, a Mexican herdsman, discovered gold in Santa Feliciana Canyon forty miles from Los Angeles. For a decade prior to James W. Marshall's famous discovery, Mexicans had worked various "diggings" along the coast range between Los Angeles and Santa Cruz and had found gold in paying quantities. There is no mystery whatever about why they failed to make the big discoveries in California, for the gold of California, as Dr. Rodman W. Paul has pointed out, "was secreted in the interior of the province: precisely the region that the Spanish race had not colonized." *

In one of the most famous and popular scenes in California history, Marshall is supposed to have rushed into Fort Sutter with a nugget in his hand shouting, "Gold! Gold!" Actually, Marshall did not say that he had discovered gold; nor did he use the word "gold" or "nugget." What he said was that he had discovered a *chispa,* which is Spanish for "bright speck" or "spangle." That he should have used this term is some indication of how widely Spanish mining practices, and the Spanish mining vocabulary, had permeated California prior to 1848. The importance of Mexican metallurgy in the Southwest, however, rests on foundations more secure than such circumstantial details.

When American mining engineers began to explore the Arizona-Sonora frontier after the Gadsden Purchase, they discovered a long history of prior mining operations in the region. Literally hundreds of mines had been worked by Mexicans in Sonora subsequent to the discovery of the famous *bolas de plata* at Arizonac in 1763. But most of these mines had been abandoned when Mexican troops were withdrawn from the frontier during the struggle for independence. In the face of incessant Apache raids, most of the equipment had been stored in the tunnels of the mines and the pits were closed in, with the thought of a later re-opening once order had been restored. But the confused situation created by the Mexican-American War, the Gadsden Purchase, and the American Civil War had resulted in even more extensive raids by the Apaches.

In their hatred of everything American, the Mexicans had mutilated

---

* Reprinted by permission of the publishers from Rodman Wilson Paul—*California Gold: The Beginning of Mining in the Far West.* Cambridge, Mass.: Harvard University Press, 1947.

boundary markers and continued to regard Arizona as legitimately a part of Sonora. Instead of reopening the mines, the *gambussinos,* or professional prospectors, then became freebooters who raided abandoned properties on the American side of the border and carried off equipment to Mexico which was used to smelt ores stolen from American properties.

These Sonora *gambussinos* were among the first outsiders to receive word of the discovery of gold in California. In fact they were first attracted to California by the secularization of the missions. "They came flocking in," wrote Hugo Reid, "to assist in the general destruction, lending a hand to kill cattle on shares, which practice, when at last prohibited by government orders, they continued on their private account." By midsummer of 1848 some five thousand Sonorans had left for the goldfields. Small bands travelled to California from points as distant as Sinaloa, Chihuahua, and Durango. Starting from Tubac, they followed the old De Anza trail to Yuma, crossed the Colorado, and then came to Los Angeles by way of San Gorgonio Pass.

In California the Sonorans were treated with great contempt. Wearing cotton shirts, white pantaloons, sandals, and huge sombreros, they were known as *calzonaires blancos* or "white breeches." In small groups of fifty and a hundred, they started out in the early spring from Mexico, worked in the southern mines in the summer, and returned south in the fall. Not infrequently, their families came along, riding the pack mules and burros. Between 1848 and 1850, ten thousand Sonorans passed through Los Angeles each spring and the processions continued for several years. Katherine M. Bell said that she had seen hundreds of Sonorans in Santa Barbara in 1849 on their way to the mines. Camped in caravans of ten, twenty, and thirty families on the outskirts of the town, they made merry with much singing and dancing to the music of "violins, guitars, and flutes."

The mining camps in the southern district—in Calaveras, Tuolumne, Mariposa, Stanislaus, and San Joaquin counties—were largely made up of Spanish-speaking people: Sonorans, Mexicans from Southern California, Chileans, and Peruvians. The town of Sonora, named after the Sonora miners, was the center of the southern district. As large as Stockton, it was described as being "far ahead of it for gold, gals, music, gambling, and spreeing." A visitor of 1861 said of Hornitos, still another Mexican mining camp in the district, that "the town is certainly of Spanish origin and . . . there seems to be an omnipresent struggle between the Mexican and American element. . . . This rivalry is visible in everything. . . . Even the very signs seem to fight it out, or compromise. The stage house is the 'Progresso Restaurant'; the bakery is a 'panadería'; the hotels invite both in Spanish and English. . . . In the plaza Brother Jonathan, however, has it pretty much all to himself, and manifest destiny will, undoubtedly, prevail in the end."

True to this prediction, Brother Jonathan had driven the Mexicans from the southern mines by the late 'sixties; but, before doing so, he had first appropriated their traditional mining lore. "The average American in 1848," writes Dr. Paul, "was 'handy' with a considerable number of trades and occupations, but mining was not one of them." There had been of course some placer mining in the Carolinas and Georgia prior to 1848 but, by and large, the Anglo-Americans were not a mining people. On the other hand, the Sonorans were experienced miners,—the heirs to the great mining tradition of the Spanish people (1).

It was the Sonorans who first introduced the *batea,* a flat-bottomed pan or bowl with gently sloping sides, which was widely used in early creek-bed or placer mining in California. The southern mines were so-called "dry diggings," that is, there was a general shortage of water, except in the rainy season, to wash the dirt from the gold. Mexicans introduced the first successful extractive technique used in the dry diggings. "It was their custom," writes Paul, "to dry the mixed gold and sand in the sunlight, or over the fire, then to separate the two by blowing upon the dry sands or by tossing them up in the air as one would wheat and chaff." Known as the "dry-wash" method, this technique was widely used in the southern mines and had an important bearing on the rapid exploitation of mineral wealth in California. In 1850 the *Alta California* remarked that "American energy and assiduity, and Mexican skill and experience have together developed the riches of the Southern Placer." Up to 1860, Mexicans were a majority in perhaps all of the counties in the southern mines; but, by the end of the decade, they had largely disappeared. Even before they had been driven from the district, however, the importance of their contribution to mining technology was widely recognized in California as witness this item from the Stockton *Times:*

> The Mexican is of the utmost service in the Southern mines. We ask those who have had actual experience in mining operations in this country,

whether the American, with all his impatience of control, his impetuous temperament, his ambitious yearning, will ever be content to deny himself the pleasures of civilized life in the states, and for the sake of from four to eight dollars per day, be content to develop the resources of the dry diggings of the country.*

2. Comstock's Mistake

Most of the gold produced in California from 1848 to 1860 was obtained by working surface placers. As the miners worked up the streams and rivers, however, they soon discovered the ledges or deposits from which the gold had come. Once these deposits were located, the period of quartz mining began. If the Anglo-Americans were novices in placer mining, they knew literally nothing of quartz mining. "The first quartz miners in California," wrote J. Ross Browne, "were Mexicans, who knew how gold-bearing rocks were reduced in their native country" (2). Thus the Morgan Hill mine in Calaveras County, one of the first quartz mines in California, was originally operated by Mexican labor. From this one mine alone over $2,000,000 in gold was taken in 1850.

The first quartz ores in California were so rich in gold that the Mexicans treated them by hand mortars, but it was not long before they introduced the *arrastre* (more often spelled *"arrastra"*) or "Chili mill." In building an *arrastra,* the Mexicans constructed a circular stone pavement in the center of which stood a post. To an arm extending out from the post a mule was hitched, or, in some cases, the *arrastra* was operated by a water wheel. The mule dragged a heavy piece of granite around the post which pulverized the quartz on the pavement. Once the quartz was pulverized, the gold or silver was then amalgamated by the use of quicksilver. Primitive as it was, the *arrastra* could be built on the spot, required no manufactured or imported parts, and was simple to operate. Quartz mining might have been retarded for many years in the West had it not been for the Mexicans' familiarity with the *arrastra,* its use and construction.

In the middle 'fifties, Ignacio Paredes, a miner from Alamos in Sonora, discovered some valuable ores in Nevada which he tried to work,

* On the role that Mexicans played in the development of gold and silver mining in the West, including the inauguration of pack-trains which supplied the mining camps, see *The Gold Rushes* by W. P. Murrell (1941), pp. 98, 102, 104, 137, 140, 156, 191.

first by the use of the *batea,* and, later, by the dry-wash method, but without success. Some years later, Comstock, prospecting in the same area, kept complaining about "base metals" and "blue stuff" that made it difficult for him to isolate the gold. At this time, Comstock was convinced that he had discovered a gold mine. One day a Mexican miner happened along when Comstock and his partner were rocking gold with a *batea.* Noticing the heavy stone with bluish cast, he became very excited and started shouting, *"Mucha plata! Mucha plata!"* It was only then that Comstock realized that he had discovered one of the richest silver mines in the world.

Dan De Quille, one of the most accurate of observers, reported that "the business of working silver-mines was then new to our people, and at first they depended much on what was told them by the Mexican silver-miners who flocked to the country." These miners, he wrote, "were in great demand" and much of what was subsequently learned about quartz mining was based on their experience and knowledge. The *arrastra* made possible the early development of the Comstock Lode; at one time, some sixty *arrastras* were in operation at the mine. "The Spaniard of old and his Mexican successor," wrote the Arizona historian, James H. McClintock, "were the best prospectors and the closest judges of ore ever known . . . the first American mining followed the pathways made by the Spanish" (3). J. Ross Browne, who prepared the first official report on the mineral resources of California, pointed out that "by far the larger portion of the work-people in the California mines are Mexicans who are found to be more adventurous than Cornishmen, and willing oftentimes to undertake jobs which the latter have abandoned."

Quite apart from many technical mining expressions in Spanish which passed into American mining law and the vocabulary of American miners, dozens of Spanish-Mexican mining terms found wide popular acceptance in the West. *Bonanza* or rich ore is one such expression; *borrasco* or barren rock is another. Such terms as *placer, xacal* (slack), and *escoria* (slag) are merely a few of many terms that might be cited. In *The Big Bonanza,* Dan De Quille devoted three pages to a glossary of Mexican mining terms in general use in the Washoe territory. Appropriation of these terms was a necessity since there were, of course, no equivalent expressions in Anglo-American speech.

3. THE VERMILION CAVE

In 1557 Bartolomé de Medina, a miner at Pachuca, Mexico, revolutionized mining technique by the invention of the *patio* process for separating silver from ore by the use of quicksilver. Thereafter quicksilver became an essential material in quartz mining. Immediately upon the discovery of the *patio* process, the Spanish reserved the quicksilver monopoly for the famous Almadén mine in Spain by prohibiting quicksilver mining in the Americas. By monopolizing the supply of quicksilver, they hoped to control all mining in the Americas. Most of the quicksilver used in Mexico, Central, and South America, in fact, was imported from the Almadén mine. "This fiat," writes Gruening, "destroyed a potential industry and greatly hampered an existing one."

In the mountains about twelve miles from San Jose, California, was a cave which contained a bright vermilion clay. For many years, Indians had visited the cave, dabbing their faces with its clay. As early as 1824 two Mexicans, Antonio Sunol and Louis Chaboya, had tried to extract silver from the clay but had failed to do so. In 1845 the Mexican government sent Captain Andrés Castillero, a young cavalry officer, on a military mission to Fort Sutter. When Castillero, who had been trained in metallurgy, heard about the famous vermilion cave from a priest at the San Jose mission, his interest was immediately aroused. Putting some of the cinnabar clay in his gun, he found that drops of quicksilver gathered in the gun-barrel after the gun was fired. On returning to Mexico City he filed a claim on the property but the intervention of the Mexican-American War forced him to assign the claim to a British company. This mine,—the famous New Almaden,—was the first important quicksilver mine to be discovered in the Western Hemisphere.

It was the discovery of the New Almaden that unlocked the gold and silver resources of California and the West. The timing of the discovery and the location of the mine were nothing short of providential. Small quantities of quicksilver were produced late in 1848 and, two years later, the mine was in heavy production. The New Almaden, moreover, was conveniently located with reference to the California mining districts. Prior to its discovery, quicksilver, a monopoly product, had sold on the world market for $99.45 per flask; but once the New Almaden was in production the price fell to $47.83. J. Ross Browne once said that the discovery of gold and silver in California would have meant very little had it not been for the simultaneous discovery of the New Almaden which, as late as 1918, was still producing one million flasks of quicksilver a year.

Not only was the New Almaden discovered by a Mexican, but it was developed by Mexican labor. J. Ross Browne said that five-eighths of the 1,973 miners employed at the property in 1865 were Mexicans. "The laborers," said another visitor, "are all Mexicans and have generally served a sort of apprenticeship in the silver mines of Spanish-America" (4). Living in a town on the hill near the mine, the Mexicans were divided into two categories: the actual miners or *barreteros;* and the ore-carriers or *tanateros*. Starting from the pit of the mine, the ore-carriers would fill a large sack or pannier made of hide with two hundred pounds of ore and then ascend the *escalera* or ladder-like circular path to the surface. Open at the top, the pannier was flung over the shoulder and supported by a strap passing over the shoulders and around the forehead. Ore-carriers made from twenty to thirty trips a day up the *escalera* for all the ore was carried to the surface by hand. The *escalera* was narrow, slippery, and lighted only by a few flickering torches. Visitors told of seeing the *tanateros,* dressed in pantaloons rolled tight above the knees, and calico shirts, hurrying up the *escalera* with "straining nerves and quivering muscles."

In the *patio* near the mine, where the ores were reduced, Americans were employed at wages of from $5 to $7 a day; but the miners and ore-carriers received a wage of from $2 to $3 a day. "In the early years," writes Dr. Paul, "the Mexicans tended to form a special element in the labor supply, paid at a lower rate than Americans and Europeans." Living in straw-thatched huts on the hill, the Mexicans were a carefree lot, "spending their money on the visiting señoritas from San Jose," and celebrating their *días de fiesta* by sending for girls, *guitarristas,* and wine. It is also interesting to note that the British and American owners of this fabulously rich mine sent their engineers to Spain to study the processes used in quicksilver production, and later entered into a cartel with the owners of the Almadén to control the world market.

4. Anglo-Saxon Law and Order

Prior to the discovery of gold in California there had been so little American mining that the Anglo-Saxon common law had virtually no mining-law precedents. Precedents were never more badly needed than in California, for most of the miners were trespassers on the public domain. With no mining law on the statute books and with no precedents for guidance, the federal government was powerless to bring order out of the chaos that prevailed. Faced with this situation, the miners were forced to develop their own codes and rules which were the only "law" on the subject of mines and mining in effect in the United States from 1848 to 1866. Later these codes, which form the basis of the present-day "law of mines," were carried by California miners throughout the West. Wherever these miners travelled, they also carried the knowledge and experience which they had acquired in California.

In the history books, the famous miners' codes are invariably cited as another illustration of "the extraordinary capacity of the Anglo-American for self-government" (5). Bearing in mind that it was the discovery of gold in California that gave birth to a distinctive American mining law—there having been no general mining law in force in the United States prior to 1848—just how was it that these inexperienced Anglo-American miners were able to develop, in such a brief period, a comprehensive system of mining rules and regulations and a law of mines? The Spanish-speaking miners of California had been trained, of course, under the mining ordinances of Spanish America which represented a complete body of mining law tested by experience.

"The miners of California," writes the legal historian, Halleck, "generally adopted, as being the best suited to their peculiar wants, the main principles of the mining laws of Spain and Mexico, by which the right of property in mines is made to depend upon discovery and development," principles that are still cited as being pre-eminently Anglo-Saxon in origin. Yale, the outstanding authority on the American law of mines, writes that "most of the rules and customs constituting the codes are easily recognizable by those familiar with the Mexican ordinances. . . . In the earlier days of the placer diggings in California, the large influx of miners from the western coast of Mexico and from South America, necessarily dictated the system of work to the Americans, who were almost entirely inexperienced with this branch of industry. . . . The Spanish-American system which had grown up under the practical workings of the mining ordinances of New Spain, was the foundation of the rules and customs adopted." Although this information has been common knowledge among lawyers for fifty years, there are California historians who still write eloquent chapters in praise of the Anglo-American miner's "capacity for self-government."

Under the Spanish law, possession of minerals in the subsoil was reserved to the crown. From 1836 to 1883, the State of Texas received five per cent of the gross receipts from all mineral concessions, which was used to establish a system of public schools. For this happy prevision, the Texans are indebted to the Spanish law of *regalia*. When Texas adopted the Anglo-Saxon common law in 1840, the only Spanish statute specifically retained was this doctrine of mineral rights.

5. APACHES AND COPPER

In the year 1800 a Spanish colonel, José Carrasco, guided by an Apache Indian discovered the famous Santa Rita silver and copper mine in western New Mexico. A native of Rio Tinto, Carrasco quickly identified the ores of the Santa Rita, for he remembered the appearance of copper ores from his youth. While the nearest smelter was four hundred miles from the mine, poverty had decreed that the peon population of Mexico should have a copper coinage. For many years, Santa Rita ores were carried by pack-trains to smelters in Mexico and sold for 65¢ a pound. As early as 1804, the Santa Rita was being operated on a fairly large scale with over six hundred employees living in the community which had grown up about the property. Incidentally, one of the watchtowers built by the Spanish still stands at the mine. The Santa Rita is, perhaps, the most famous mine in Western America for it was here that the techniques of copper-mining were first developed in the Southwest.

The Heintzelman mine, thirty miles from Tubac, with its attractive farms and orchards, had also been worked at an early date. Some eight hundred Mexican miners were employed in 1859 at the mine which was then producing $100,000 in silver a year. Along with the Santa Rita and many other mines, the Heintzelman property was abandoned during the Apache raids. At one time, the Arizona Mining Company at Tubac found itself besieged on one side by the Apaches and on the other by a band of enraged Sonorans. Engine boilers weighing six thousand pounds, which had been laboriously freighted in from Lavaca, Texas, a distance of 1,200 miles, were abandoned in 1861 when the owners were forced to move out.

Mexican miners from Sonora were employed, from the earliest date, at both the Santa Rita and Heintzelman mines. The prevailing wage of from fifty cents to a dollar a day was paid, according to Mowry, "in large part in merchandise sold at large profits." Since bullion was too clumsy to handle, wages were paid in company-issued *boletas* or paper bills with the denominations indicated by the figures of animals,—pigs, roosters, cows, and horses. "The only difference between peonage and Negro slavery," wrote Will H. Robinson, "was that a peon miner could not be sold from one master to another" (6). Visiting the reopened Santa Rita on pay-day, J. Ross Browne reported that "under every tree sits a group of thriftless vagabonds, conspicuous for their dirty skins and many-colored sarapes, shuffling the inevitable pack of cards or casting their fortunes of greasy 'hobos' upon capricious hazards of fortune. The earnings of the month are soon disposed of. The women and children are left dependent upon new advances from the store-houses; the workingmen are stupefied by mescal and many nights of debauch, and when all is over, the fandangos at an end, and the monte tables packed up, every miner is bankrupt."

A curious and accidental by-product of the final "pacification" of the Apaches in Arizona was the discovery of important new copper deposits by cavalry officers. The famous Bisbee mines were discovered around 1875 by cavalrymen in hot pursuit of Apaches. The development of these new properties was largely based upon the early experimental techniques which had been evolved at the Santa Rita mine and at various mines in Sonora. When Henry Lesinsky began to develop the rich copper deposits at Clifton in 1872, one reads that he went to Juárez to employ Mexican laborers who were "considered very skillful smelter men." These miners constructed the first furnaces to smelt copper ores in Arizona which were "of the Mexican type, built of adobe," and fired by charcoal made from mesquite (7). The adobe furnace had a capacity of about two tons of ore per day and its fire was sustained by hand bellows. Mexican miners, using burros, packed the crude ores from the mountains to the smelters. The smelted ore was then packed by ox and mule teams, operated by Mexicans, to Kansas City. Don Antonio, foreman of the Clifton mine, rode throughout Sonora recruiting Mexicans to work in the copper mines.

Western mining developed, of course, by a series of "waves": first gold, then silver, and finally copper. At first only the high-grade copper ores—those that ranged from five to twenty per cent copper—were exploited; but a new process was perfected around 1892 for smelting the low-grade ores (the disseminated or porphyry ores). The smelting of these ores involved an enormous capital outlay and brought about a rapid consolidation in ownership. Simultaneously new processes were developed for extracting ores in the underground mines. One of these techniques was the "cave-in" system whereby a whole section of earth would be caved in by a single blast. This system greatly increased the amount of ore that could be produced in a day, but the system was—and still is—extremely dangerous. Experienced miners often refused to work in underground mines where it was used; but Mexican immigrants, excluded from the skilled miner category, were compelled to work in these mines. In this way a rift developed, which has not yet been healed, between Mexican and non-Mexican labor in the copper mines.

Between 1858 and 1940 the Arizona mines produced three billion dollars' worth of metal. Copper production increased from 800,000 pounds in 1874 to 830,628,411 pounds in 1929. It was the vast expansion in the electrical industry which enabled copper, "the red metal," to dethrone its "white rival," silver. One might say, therefore, that Mexican miners in the copper mines of Arizona, Utah, and Nevada, have played an important role in making possible the illumination of America by electricity. The census of 1930 listed 16,668 Mexicans engaged in the extraction of minerals: 3,880 as "coal-miners," principally in Colorado and New Mexico; and 12,623 "other operators," mostly in the copper mines of the Southwest.

6. Homage to the *Churro*

Although Coronado brought the first sheep to the Southwest, the herds that were to constitute the basis of the pastoral economy of New Mexico came north in the famous *entrada* of Juan de Oñate in 1598. The raising of sheep is pre-eminently a frontier enterprise. Sheep helped to make the Spanish explorations possible for they were the mobile, marching food supply of the conquistadores. According to Messrs. Towne and Wentworth (8), sheep were an indispensable item in equipping every Spanish expedition to the north. From the founding of New Mexico until the Civil War, sheep fed, clothed, and supported the colonists. The only important source of cash income in the colony, sheep also served as a kind of currency. "Sheep," writes Winifred Kupper (9), "were the real conquerors of the Southwest."

In 1598 Spain had one of the oldest sheep cultures in the Western world. Its breeds were principally of two types: the beautiful, aristocratic *merinos* with their fine wool; and the ugly "scrubs" or *churros* long relegated to the periphery of the Spanish sheep culture. It was the scrub or *churro,* however, that the Spanish brought to the Southwest: a small, lean, ugly sheep whose wool was coarse and light in weight, seldom averaging more than a pound or a pound and a half at a shearing. But during a long period of adaptation to the semi-arid environment of Spain it had learned to hunt food and shelter, to make long marches, to survive in all sorts of weather, and to protect its lambs from wild animals. Its very "scrubbiness" made it ideally adapted to conditions in the Southwest.

The Spanish also brought to New Mexico their traditional sheep culture. Without this knowledge, based on six hundred years' experience under somewhat similar conditions, the value of the *churro* might have been negligible. There is no doubt whatever that "sheep husbandry in the United States," to quote Wentworth and Towne, "owes more to Spain than to any other nation on earth." Long prior to 1598, the Spanish had developed an extensive lore about sheep and had evolved elaborate institutions to protect and to further the sheep industry.

In Spain sheep were marched from the lowlands to the highlands and back from the highlands to the lowlands. The privilege of marching sheep in this manner had given rise to the *trashumante* system under which the rights and privileges of sheepmen were minutely regulated, defined, and safeguarded. To make this system function, an ancient organization of sheepmen had been effected known as the "Honorable Assembly of the Mesta," which has its almost precise counterpart today in the various "sheepmen's associations" in the Southwest. In Spain the various "sheep walks" were carefully laid out and defined; and what sheepmen could and could not do, on these marches, was also fixed by custom and ordinance. A somewhat similar system is in use today in the Southwest.

In short, Anglo-American sheepmen in the Southwest took over and adapted an already functioning and time-tested pattern of sheep-raising. About all they did was to enlarge the grazing areas by bringing the nomadic Indians under military control (a victory largely made possible by the introduction of the Colt revolver) and improve the breed of sheep. Apart from these contributions, they simply took over the customs, practices, institutions, personnel, and organization of an existing industry. The system of Spanish and Mexican land grants, based on larger units of land than were to be found in a non-arid environment, made possible the expansion of an industry which involved an extensive use of land resources. Similarly the practice of assigning fixed grazing rights to particular owners was Spanish in origin. Even the breeding of a heavy wool-bearing sheep came about as a result of crossing two Spanish types. For about 1820 some fine Spanish *merino* sheep were first brought to the eastern seaboard. These sheep reached the Southwest about 1876, with the general westward movement, and were then crossed with the *churro* to produce a new type ideally adjusted to the environment.

Under the Spanish system, sheep-raising was based upon a traditional social structure and a well-defined division of labor. At the base of the pyramid was the *pastor* or shepherd who was usually assigned a flock of about two thousand sheep. Over each two or three *pastores* was a *vaquero* or mounted rider. Supervising the *vaqueros* was a *caporal* or range boss and over the *caporal* was the major-domo or superintendent. Ultimate authority rested, of course, in the owner or *patrón*. In general, this system of organization was taken over in toto by the Anglo-Americans and still prevails on the large sheep ranches of the Southwest. Between the eastern seaboard and the boundaries of the Southwest, sheep-raising was, and still is, an avocation or side-line business. Once the center of the industry had shifted to the Southwest, which was around 1870, sheep-raising became a specialized business, conducted on a large scale, by men whose sole vocation was sheep-raising. This was the Spanish system and its excellent adaptation to conditions in the Southwest is shown by the phenomenal increase in the wool clip: from 32,000 pounds in 1850, to 493,000 pounds in 1860, to 4,000,000 pounds in 1880.

New Mexico was "the ovine nursery of the nation" whose herds provided the foundation stock for the entire West. The *Californios* had never looked with particular favor on sheep-raising; in fact there were only about seventeen thousand sheep in the province in 1850. But, with the discovery of gold, large herds were driven overland from New Mexico to the mines. It is estimated that, between 1850 and 1860, more than five hundred thousand sheep were driven from New Mexico to California. Here, again, the marching qualities of the *churro* were of considerable importance. From these drives came the herds that were soon grazing in the foothills and valleys of California. It was also in California that the *churro* was crossed with the *merino* to produce the present range stock of the Western states. From California large herds were then driven eastward to the Rocky Mountain states and the new and improved breeds made their way back to New Mexico. During the 'seventies and 'eighties, large herds were driven eastward every season, grazing as they marched, to the terminal points on the rail lines from which they were then shipped to Middle Western markets. In the process of making these "drives," such states as Idaho, Utah, Colorado, Wyoming, Nevada, Arizona, and Montana were stocked with sheep.

Once this development had taken place, American wool production soared from five million pounds in 1862 to twenty-two million pounds in 1880. Increased wool production in the West meant, of course, increased factory employment in the East. The development of the sheep industry also stimulated another Western industry in which Mexicans have played a key role. For with the establishment of the first Western sugar-beet factories, the modern era of lamb-feeding came into its own. One reason for the rapid growth of the sugar-beet industry in the West was the fact that sheep could be fed and fattened on the by-products of sugar-beet production. Thus one industry neatly supplemented the other.

It was the Spaniards, of course, who taught the Indians of the Southwest to weave with wool. From 1800 to 1850 many Navajo women were employed in weaving in New Mexico and these women carried back to the tribes the skills which they had learned. From the Spaniards and Mexicans, also, the Navajo inherited the *churro* sheep. That they are today largely a pastoral people is to be traced to this early cultural borrowing. In the development of the art of weaving, however, the Spanish borrowed designs and dyes from the Indians. According to Ruth Laughlin, the Spanish brought only two dyes to New Mexico; the rest were all developed from native dyes used by the Indians. Blankets were long an important item in the barter economy of New Mexico. When trade was opened with Los Angeles by way of the Spanish Trail, one reads that New Mexico blankets were exchanged on the Coast for California horses. Blankets were also a principal item in the barter-markets of Taos and Chihuahua.

7. Los Pastores

Throughout the Southwest, the term "Mexican sheepherder" is proverbial. In the folklore of the region the solitary, superstitious, patient Mexican sheepherder is supposed to be as witless and moronic as the sheep he herds. But Mexican herdsmen are the carriers of a great tradition and it has been their skill and knowledge which has sustained the sheep industry in the West. Full of incredible lore, they can read the signs of changing weather at a glance; they know the habits of predatory animals; their knowledge of range vegetation is unrivalled; and there is little about the care of sheep that is unknown to them. In the early journals, one reads of how they trained sheep dogs by suckling pups on ewes so that the dog would learn to follow the sheep while they grazed, and return them at night to the corral. Above all, these *pastores* know how to graze a flock, guiding their movements without driving them, so that the sheep travel slowly and graze contentedly as they travel.

Living on coarse meal, goat's milk, kid's flesh and peppers, New Mexico *pastores* have tramped over most of the West in all sorts of weather and under the most difficult conditions. Until the 1890's, sheepherding was a hazardous occupation in New Mexico. One reads of Apache raids that netted five thousand sheep and of a raid in 1850 in which forty-seven thousand sheep were stolen. The most famous New Mexico Indian fighters were sheepmen. Colonel Manuel Chavez, and his *pastores,* fought the Indians for fifty years. Nor were Indians the only hazard. In California the herdsmen lived in mortal terror of bears and slept at night on raised platforms, called *tepestras,* which were built on poles eight, ten, and twelve feet above the ground.

The isolation of the shepherds was even greater than that of the other colonists in New Mexico. Something of the present-day brooding, introspective quality of the Spanish-speaking people of New Mexico can probably be traced to this experience. The notion that sheepherders are a weird lot, often driven crazy by loneliness, may be unfounded; but they are certainly the most taciturn of men. To guard against the hazards of loneliness a state law in New Mexico requires that sheepherders must be employed in pairs. Carrying their giant jews'-harps, called *bijuelas,* the *pastores* sang folk songs on the ranges of New Mexico which were of great antiquity when Columbus discovered America. No one knows the precise origin of the ancient folk play, *Los Pastores,* which has been produced in New Mexico for as long as the colony has existed. Some of the most beautiful New Mexico folk songs are, of course, the songs of the *pastores* (10).

Lieutenant J. H. Simpson, who travelled west in 1849, reported that the first New Mexican he sighted was "a swarthy, copper-colored young Mexican, of eighteen or twenty years of age, most miserably clad, driving the sheep before him. The morning air was keen and cold, and as he, with brimless straw hat on, a forlorn blanket about his shoulders, and pantaloons which were only an apology for such, hugged his only wrapper, his steps slow and measured, I thought he looked the very personification of patience and resignation." Whether it was the scrawny character of the sheep or the appearance of the herdsman, somehow the combination of being both a sheepherder and a Mexican came to be synonymous, to most Anglo-Americans, with the lowest possible status.

From the 1860's, bands of New Mexican sheep-shearers, each with its *capitán,* made the great circle of the shearing pens from Texas to California to the Northwest and throughout the Rocky Mountain states. "I remember the Mexican sheep shearers galloping up," wrote Sarah E. Blanchard of her childhood on a ranch near Santa Paula, "and it was a time of thrilling excitement. Usually an old woman accompanied them to make tortillas and to provide them with Mexican delicacies. They were paid by ticket, so much for each fleece, and at night they gambled with these around the camp fires." Not infrequently a few Chinese sheep-shearers accompanied these bands. "The shearers would come in," wrote Sarah Bixby Smith, "a gay band of Mexicans on prancing horses, decked with wonderful silver-trimmed bridles made of rawhide or braided horsehair, and saddles with high horns, sweeping stirrups, and wide expanse of beautiful tooled leather. The men themselves were dressed in black broadcloth, ruffled white shirts, high-heeled boots, and high-crowned, wide sombreros which were trimmed with silver-braided bands, and held securely in place by a cord under the nose. They would come in, fifty or sixty strong, stake out their *caballos,* put away their finery, and appear in brown overalls, red bandanas on their heads, and live and work on the ranch [in Southern California] for more than a month, so many were the sheep to be sheared." Shearers were the migratory aristocrats of the industry. They were never herdsmen, for the shearing of sheep was an exclusive vocation. Paid a wage of from five to eight cents a fleece, New Mexicans monopolized sheep-shearing until around 1890 or 1900 when the first power-driven shearing machines were introduced in California.

"The New Mexicans," wrote Twitchell, "were essentially a pastoral people." Lummis once said that sheep were "the one available utilization of New Mexico" where society was divided into two classes: those who owned sheep and those who tended sheep. Today it is said in New Mexico that those who own sheep are Spanish-Americans; those who herd them are Mexicans. From the earliest date, the great herds of New Mexico were owned by a handful of *ricos*. According to the New Mexico *Guide* (WPA), a few large operators still own seventy-five per cent of the sheep. The Spanish governor, Bartolomé Baca, once owned two million sheep and employed 2,700 men. "El Guero" Chávez, the first governor under Mexican rule, owned a million head and Don José Leandro Perea of Bernalillo had herds of more than 250,000. In 1880 three-fourths of the sheep of New Mexico were owned by about twenty families, sixteen of whom were families native to New Mexico. Sylvestre Mirabal, who owned 250,000 acres of grazing lands at the time of his death some years ago, was descended from a family that had raised sheep in New Mexico since 1600.

The dependence of *pastor* on *patrón* was complete and absolute. The *patrón* protected the *pastor* against the Indians and before the law. In the 1890's New Mexico *pastores* were paid a wage of from $5 to $8 per month, board included; and as late as 1940 the wage was only $35 a month. Many of the *pastores* were bound to their *patrones* by debts inherited from their fathers; even after peonage was abolished, the *partido* system by which herds were "farmed out" on shares, functioned as a thinly disguised form of peonage. "The social effects of a system of economy," writes John Russell, "wherein four-fifths of the white male population were employees of a handful of landlords have left their stamp on present-day New Mexico." Long after 1846, all the *patrón* needed to do was to say the word and his *pastores* would vote, as a group, for any candidate he recommended. "The most paternalistic form of government in the world," writes Miss Kupper, "is a flock with a sheepherder as dictator" and the relationship between the herder and the flock is essentially that between the *patrón* and his *pastores*.

For several hundred years, thousands of New Mexico sheep were driven to points as far removed as Veracruz, Guadalajara, and Mexico

City, principally for sale at the mines. After Mexico won its independence, the annual sheep drives to Chihuahua became immensely profitable and between 1839 and 1850 about two hundred thousand sheep were driven south every year. For these drives, the *ricos* would purchase the small herds of the *paisanos* who were, of course, unable to drive their sheep to market. Profits of from three hundred to four hundred per cent were occasionally made on these annual drives to Mexico. With the discovery of gold in California, sheep sold for $16 a head and the drives to the West Coast took the place of the drives to Mexico. Little of this bonanza wealth ever found its way into the pockets of the *pastores*.

8. FROM GREGORIO DE VILLALOBOS

The cattle industry began in the mesquitals along the Rio Bravo.

J. FRANK DOBIE

By a curious cultural transmutation, Anglo-Americans have long claimed credit for the origin and development of the cattle industry. No folk hero in American life has enjoyed anything like the popularity of the American cowboy. Each week millions of Americans see "Western" films and their sons and daughters will probably line up at the box-office years hence to see cowboys ride, rope, and shoot on the screen. Yet with the exception of the capital provided to expand the industry, there seems to have been nothing the American rancher or cowboy contributed to the development of cattle-raising in the Southwest.

One Gregorio de Villalobos is supposed to have shipped the first cattle to the New World. From this initial shipment to the West Indies came the stock later used to establish the great herds in Mexico and from these herds, in turn, came the cattle that Coronado drove to the Southwest. Like the lowly *churros,* the cattle that the Spanish brought to the New World were not much to look at. Light-bodied, long-legged, thin, with elongated heads and muzzles, their wide-spreading horns often measured five feet from tip to tip. "The general carriage of a Spanish cow," wrote one early-day historian, "is like that of a wild animal: she is quick, uneasy, restless, frequently on the lookout for danger, snuffing the air, moving with a high and elastic trot, and excited at the sight of a man, particularly if afoot, when she will often attack him." Such was the parent stock of the American range-cattle industry. Dating from the latter part of the eighteenth century, the cattle industry had its real beginnings in California and Texas.

When the *San Carlos* anchored in San Diego Bay on April 30, 1769, as part of the Serra expedition, some six or seven head of cattle were taken ashore: supposedly the first cattle to appear in California. Somewhat later, small herds were driven overland to California by Rivera and De Anza. So rapidly did cattle multiply in the province that the mission fathers and rancheros could count a million head by the end of the century. In fact cattle came to be regarded as a major nuisance in California. People afoot were forever dodging behind trees or jumping into ditches to escape from the wild charges of Spanish steers, regarded as more dangerous than grizzly bears. Anyone could start a herd in California, for there was no limit to the available pasture. Beef in California, like mutton in New Mexico, became a principal staple in the diet; and the hides, worked up into rawhide, were used for manifold purposes. At the Mission San José, a hundred cattle were butchered every Saturday. Cattle horns topped the fences around the wheat fields and the hides of cattle, drying in the sun, were to be seen at all seasons of the year.

With the first shipments to South American ports (1810) and the opening of the hide-and-tallow trade with Boston (1822), markets were finally found for the great surplus of cattle in California. The clipper ships, described by Dana as floating department stores, brought merchandise to exchange for the hides and tallow and a flourishing trade developed. Between 1800 and 1848 over five million hides were exported from California. It so happened, also, that the opening of the hide-and-tallow trade coincided with the beginning of the Mexican regime and the secularization of the missions. Under the impetus of this trade, the mission estates were carved up into great ranchos and stocked with cattle often plundered from the missions. By 1860 some three million were grazing on the great unfenced pastures of California. The cattle industry in California, however, had reached its zenith and had begun to decline at about the time that Texas became the cattle nursery of the nation.

Large herds were to be found in Texas at an early date but incessant Indian raids kept the industry from developing as rapidly as it did in

California. In the chaotic period which followed the Texas rebellion, thousands of cattle roamed wild in the brush country between the Nueces and the Rio Grande. From an estimate of 100,000 in 1830, the number of cattle in the state increased to 382,733 in 1846. Four-fifths or more of this total was made up of so-called "Spanish cattle," for about the only cattle the Anglo-American settlers brought to Texas were a few milch cows. From these wild herds, the *cimarrones* of the brush country, came the cattle later driven to the rail terminal points in Kansas for shipment to the stockyards of Kansas City and Chicago and which were used, still later, to stock the ranges of Colorado, Wyoming, and Montana. While the Anglo-Americans may claim credit for the remarkable expansion of the cattle industry and for the conditions which made this expansion possible, the industry is indisputably Spanish in origin.

9. "Ten Gallon Hats"

It was the coming together, as J. Frank Dobie puts it, not in blood but in place and occupation, of the Anglo-American, the Spanish owner, and the Mexican *vaquero* that produced the Texas cowboy—"a blend, a type, new to the world." The word "cowboy" was unknown prior to 1836. "Cowboy" is the literal American equivalent of *vaquero* which is derived, of course, from *vaca* or "cow." Everything that served to characterize the American cowboy as a type was taken over from the Mexican *vaquero*: utensils and language, methods and equipment. The Spanish brought the horned saddle, to be distinguished from the English "muley" saddle, to the Southwest. Long before they came to the borderlands, the Spanish had taken this saddle over from the Moors. Along the Rio Grande, Mexican *vaqueros* made saddle stocks from the soft wood of the giant prickly pear and used a flat-topped silver horn as "big around as a soup plate." The saddle of the cowboy was merely an adaptation of this Spanish saddle. From the *vaquero*, the American cowboy took over, and adapted in his own way, the Spanish horned saddle, bridle, bit, and spur. From the *vaquero*, also, he got his lasso or lariat, cinch, halter, *mecate* or horsehair rope, "chaps" or *chaparejos*, "taps" or stirrup tips (*tapaderas*), the chin-strap for his hat (*barboquejo*), the feedbag for his horse (*morral*) and his rope halter or *bosal*. Even his famous "ten gallon hat" comes from a mistranslation of a phrase in a Spanish-

Mexican *corrido "su sombrero galoneado"* which referred to a festooned or "gallooned" sombrero (11).

"The very language of the range," writes Mr. Dobie, "is Spanish." Such terms as bronco (from *mesteño*), mesquite, chaparral, reata, grama, huisache, retama, remuda, cavyard from the Spanish *caballada*, lariat from *la reata,* outfit or *corrida,* lasso from *lazo,* buckaroo, burro, *cinchas,* latigo, quirt (from *cuerda*), stampede (from *estampida*), hondo or hondoo for loop, calaboose (from *calabozo*), vamoose, mesa, canyon, barranca (bluff), rodeo, corral, sombrero, loco, all these, and many more, are Spanish-Mexican in origin. From the Spanish-American War, the cowboys of the Southwest brought back the word "hoosegow," or lock-up from the Spanish *juzgado.* In the borderlands, a **ranchero** (ranch) was an estate where cattle were raised; while an estate where crops were raised was a *hacienda.* Among the cowboys with whom I consorted as a youngster in Colorado, nothing was resented more keenly than the suggestion that they worked on a "farm." The words "farm" and "farmer" were anathema; they were "cowboys" who worked on a "ranch."

The Mexican ranchero loved and understood horses and often had more horses about than he had cattle. Some of the ranches in Texas had as many as a thousand head of horses and these herds, and the wild horses of the range, made the horse market in San Antonio the greatest of its kind in the world. A *manada* was a unit of horses on the range: one stallion for each twenty-five mares. The bell-mare in the herd was the *remudera.* The cowboy expression "wind-broken" is from the Spanish. The technique of horse-breaking as practiced by the American cowboy was based directly on the technique of the *domador* or professional Mexican horsebreaker (12).

No language in the world is so rich in hairsplitting terms to distinguish the exact color markings and characteristics of a horse as the "sagebrush" Spanish of the Southwest. The following and many similar terms are really Southwest slang, with the Spanish words being given, by long local usage, a meaning of their own: *Alazán tostado,* a chestnut sorrel; *andaluz,* a yellow horse with blond mane and tail; *azulero,* a dark blue roan; *barroso,* a smudgy dun-colored horse; *canelo,* a blue-red roan; *cebruno,* a dark brown; *grullo,* a bluish gray; *moro,* almost blue; *tordillo,* iron-gray; *palomino,* a cream-colored horse; *roano* or *ruano,* shortened to "roan," a dapple-colored horse. A "pinto" is, of course, a painted, a piebald horse. An *estrello* is a horse with a star on its forehead; a *cuatralbo* is a horse with four white feet; a *potro* is an unbroken horse (13).

The American cowboy's elaborate lore about the rope and roping techniques was acquired directly from the Mexican *vaquero*. Roping by the forefeet was based on the *mangana* technique; while to rope by the hind feet or "to peal" was a feat also learned from the Mexicans. The Mexican expression *dale vuelta,* meaning to twist a rope about the horn of the saddle, became first "dolly welter" and, later, simply "dolly" on the Anglo-American tongue. The Mexican was an artist with knife and rope both of which he used as weapons. It was only when the Texans got the Colt revolver, about 1838, according to Dr. Webb, that they "became a terror to the Mexicans and all enemies." At a rodeo in Tucson on May 31, 1939, one José Romero, a Mexican *vaquero,* roped a full-grown golden eagle from horseback. It is also quite probable that the famous American cowboy songs are based on the *corridos* of the *vaquero.*

The great King and Kennedy ranches in Texas still rely upon Mexican vaqueros. The semi-feudal organization of these ranches, in fact, is directly patterned after the organization of the large *ranchería*. The managers are, nowadays, Anglo-Americans; but the "hands" are Mexican—the *vaqueros,* the *caporales* or foremen, the *pasteros* or pasturetenders, and the *jinetes* or horsebreakers. "The proudest men I ever saw," is the way George Sessions Perry describes them. They still love goat-meat or *cabra* and brew the tea of the *ceniza* or sage. Spanish-speaking to a man, they sing the old *corridos* about the bordertowns, the great cattle drives, the stampedes, and the song of the *caballo fragado* or broken-down horse. Voting pretty largely as their "boss" tells them, the hands on the King ranch still refer to themselves as *Kineños.*

10. Cortez Had a Brand

Long prior to the appearance of the Anglo-American stockman, the Mexicans had a fully developed system of brands and brand registrations. Their brands were of three types: the *fierro* or iron; the *señal* or ear-mark; and the *venta* or sale brand. Like much of the Spanish lore about cattle and horses, brands came to Spain with the Moors. Mexican brands are of great antiquity, some of them being based on the Moorish *rúbricas,*—signs used first as a signet or signature and later added as a flourish when the writers learned to spell their names. Many Mexican brands were also copied from Indian pictographs and from symbols of the sun, the moon, and the stars. The brand used by Cortez,—three Christian crosses—, is said to have been the first brand used in the Americas. "There were brand books in Spain," writes Dane Coolidge, "hundreds of years ago." The Spanish had a system of registering brands which was in use in Mexico as early as 1545. When a horse or cow was sold, the old brand was "vented,"—stamped on the shoulder,—as a bill of sale; and the new brand was burned below this marking. The American law of brands and the various brand registration systems in use today are based directly on these ancient Spanish-Mexican usages.

Once a year in California the rancheros held a general roundup or *rodeo* which was presided over by one or more *Jueces del Campo* or Judges of the Plain. These judges settled all disputes over ownership and saw to it that calves were branded with the right brand. "In West Texas, New Mexico, Colorado, and northward," wrote Charles Howard Shinn, "wherever great cattle ranges are found today, the stockmen, in their round-ups, still follow the ancient Spanish plan; not knowing it is a heritage from a race they despise, they choose 'cattle judges' to settle disputes and uphold their decisions as final."

The well-organized and powerful cattlemen's associations of the West today are based upon the Spanish institution of the *alcaldes de la mesta*. When Austin drew up his code for the first colony in Texas, the Mexican officials added only two articles: one governing the registration of brands and the other having to do with *cimarrones* or wild cattle. As with the sheep industry, all the Anglo-Americans did was to provide capital for expansion, drive the Indians from the range, and improve the breed of cattle. The same can also be said of horses, goats, and mules. The mule industry of Missouri—once a thriving industry—was Spanish-Mexican in origin. Spanish range laws had an influence even in the Southeastern coastal part of the United States. Many Southern fence laws, range laws, and toll systems in use today are said to have grown out of customs and practices which the Spanish brought from the West Indies.

11. A Drop of Water

Just as Anglo-American settlers knew little about mining, sheep, or cattle, so they were almost wholly unfamiliar with irrigated farming. In fact there was little in Anglo-Saxon law or institutions that was applicable in the semi-arid environment of the Southwest. The Anglo-Saxon common law, with its doctrine of riparian rights, had been formed in Great Britain where water was not a problem. On the other hand, the Spanish civil law was based on a recognition of the shortage of water and the need for irrigation. The Moors had brought many of their irrigation practices and water-saving institutions to Spain in the tenth century. The similarity in environment made it possible for the Spaniards to carry over into the borderlands practices and institutions which had arisen out of the need for irrigation on the Spanish Peninsula.

The oldest irrigation systems now in use in the United States are to be found in the Rio Grande Valley in New Mexico. Here the Spanish were irrigating the bottom lands around Las Cruces when the *Mayflower* arrived at Plymouth. The Pueblo Indians were irrigating between fifteen thousand and twenty-five thousand acres in the valley when the Spaniards first appeared on the scene. Indeed there are evidences that the Indian irrigation systems of the Southwest are more than nine hundred years old. The Spaniards naturally had a lively interest in and respect for the accomplishments of Indians in the field of irrigation and noted, in their early journals and records, how closely Indian practices resembled those with which they were familiar. While the New Mexico colonists were familiar with irrigation, it is also apparent that they learned a great deal from the Pueblo Indians (14).

Irrigation is an art. To prevent wastage of precious water, soils have to be carefully prepared and levelled; and the question of when to irrigate, and to what extent, are matters learned only from long experience. "There are some arts," writes Edith Nicoll Ellison, "of which a man becomes master in the course of three hundred years or so. Levelling land is one, irrigation is another. In both these arts the Mexican is at his best. . . . With his big hoe and inherited lore, the Mexican is a valuable person" (15). It was from the Mexican and the Indian that the Anglo-Americans learned how to irrigate (16).

After carefully levelling the land, the Mexicans blocked out their fields in squares, the sides of which were just high enough to hold the water. When one block was *soaked*—not flooded—a hole was made in the side wall of earth and the water was permitted to flow into the next square. This manner of irrigating is still known in the Southwest as "the Mexican system." The first irrigation systems in Texas, Colorado, New Mexico, Arizona, and California were Mexican-Spanish in origin, if the Indian experience is excepted. It was only after the Anglo-Americans had learned to irrigate, after the Mexican-Indian manner, that they became successful irrigation farmers.

Irrigation has always been a communal enterprise. In New Mexico, the diversion dams, laterals and canals were always regarded, and are still regarded, as common property. Every spring the villagers elect a *mayordomo* who has charge of directing work on the irrigation system. A survey made by the government in 1891 revealed that in New Mexico no one was allowed to take waters from the main irrigation ditch unless he had either personally or by proxy performed the tasks assigned to him by the *mayordomo*. All work of this kind was performed by the villagers together, as a joint enterprise. The village type of agricultural settlement in both New Mexico and Utah is in part a consequence of the necessity of communal controls in irrigated farming.

The pueblo of Los Angeles, at an early date, appointed a *zanjero* to keep the main ditch or *zanja* in repair and the office was continued for many years after the American conquest. The word of the *zanjero* was supreme in all matters relating to water and took precedence over that of the alcalde, the priest, and the military commander. The *zanjero* was authorized, if necessary, to impose corvées of labor upon the population and to utilize every resource of the community to preserve the water supply. Many of these practices have a striking similarity with those of the Moors and such Spanish words as *acequia, zanja,* and *zanjero* are said to be Arabic in origin (17). To the borderlands, also, the Spanish brought a very considerable lore about water wells, both of the hand-drawn and water-wheel variety, and of the technique of drilling wells. Above all the Spanish colonists had an inherited social sense of the importance of water which they transmitted wherever colonies were founded.

The attempt of the Anglo-Americans to apply the doctrine of riparian rights in the arid Southwest resulted in years of conflict and litigation and retarded the development of the region. In the end most of the states were forced to repudiate the doctrine or to modify it in many important respects. The only state that had little trouble with irrigation law was New Mexico, where water rights were regulated by immemorial custom. At the present time, most of the Western states have adopted the Arid Region Doctrine, or, as it is sometimes called, the Doctrine of Appropriation. In developing this doctrine, Anglo-American jurists were no doubt influenced by the law of waters in Mexico. Under Mexican law, the government was vested with ownership of all rights in rivers and streams but could grant the *use* of waters to private owners. This use could be conferred on both riparian and non-riparian properties but it was customarily conferred subject to certain conditions and limitations so as to insure the maximum utilization of a limited water supply. While Walter Prescott Webb has said that the riparian rights doctrine was abandoned in the Southwest by necessity, rather than through any conscious borrowings from the civil law of Mexico, other students of the problem have shown that Mexican precedents were frequently cited in the decisions of Western courts and must, therefore, have had some influence on the formation of the present-day Doctrine of Appropriation.

Under the Spanish scheme of colonization, the pueblos were invested with certain special "pueblo rights" in respect to water. Usually four square leagues of land were set aside as communal lands belonging to the pueblo. Title to the water in streams flowing through these common lands, including the right to the underground flow, was reserved to the pueblo and its inhabitants, not only for domestic use, but for parks, trees, and non-agricultural purposes. Safeguarded by the Treaty of Guadalupe Hidalgo, these "pueblo rights" proved to be of inestimable value to the City of Los Angeles which succeeded to the rights of the former pueblo. In a famous lawsuit between the City of Los Angeles and the landowners of the San Fernando Valley, the Supreme Court of the United States finally ruled that the "pueblo rights" of the city took precedence over the common law rights of the landowners. Thus the city was given a prior claim to all waters originating within the watershed of the Los Angeles River, a claim paramount to that of all appropriators subsequent to 1781 when the pueblo was founded. One could not, therefore, estimate what the City of Los Angeles owes to the lucky circumstance that it was founded by Spanish colonists.

In general, the land-use systems developed by the Spaniards and Mexicans were much better adapted to an arid environment than were those long traditional with the Anglo-Americans. A Mexican homestead consisted of 4,470 acres: twenty-eight times the size of a homestead in the Ohio Valley. The land unit which Anglo-Americans found in the Southwest had no counterpart in the East or Middle West. It was a contribution, as Dr. Webb has said, "from Latin-America, and it came by way of Texas into the Great Plains: it was the cattle ranch." A cattle ranch might comprise two thousand or twenty thousand acres, depending on the circumstances. The Mexican idea was to give the settler some good land along a stream, for farming and considerably more land, back from the stream and not necessarily contiguous, for stock-grazing. Sometimes a three hundred-foot strip along a stream or *acequia-madre* extended fifteen miles back from the stream. Grants were never made without an adequate *porción* or portion of water. This land-use system was of major importance in the rapid development of the sheep and cattle industries in the Southwest. In 1839 Texas enacted a homestead law which was directly patterned upon the Mexican homestead. In fact, "the Texas land system," writes Dr. Webb, "had for its foundation the Mexican and Spanish system."

Property rights as between husband and wife are regulated today in California, Arizona, New Mexico, and Texas, in accordance with the Spanish *ganancial* system of community property. "Our whole system," wrote one California jurist, "by which the rights of property between husband and wife are regulated and determined is borrowed from the civil and Spanish law." When the first state constitution was adopted in California, specific provision was made for the retention of the Spanish law of community property. Of great incidental benefit to the residents of the Southwest, this system has been called "one of the most important landmarks of Spanish civilization in America." It was certainly a much more equitable system, so far as the wife was concerned, than the Anglo-Spanish common law doctrine which conferred an almost unrestricted control over the wife's property on the husband and recognized virtually no right, on her part, to property accumulated during marriage. Here, again, the needs of the West created a predisposition to accept the Spanish practice. For it has been suggested that the unequal ratio between men and women in California, when the first constitution was adopted, was an important factor in the decision to adopt the Spanish law of community property.

Any study of cultural borrowings and mutations in the Southwest must recognize that necessity has been as influential as conscious imitation. In the long run, the basic industries of the region, including mining, sheep- and cattle-raising, and irrigated farming, would have developed much as they have developed without the aid of Spanish precept and example. Peoples change their habits and customs in response to the challenge of a new environment; the question, in this instance, is one of the speed and facility with which these changes were made. On this score there can be little doubt but that the Spanish example greatly accelerated the process of cultural adaptation. For instance, studies which have been made of the California system of irrigation districts, widely imitated throughout the West, have traced the beginnings of this system to the mission establishments and their communal utilization of a limited water supply. It is also true that other cases can be cited in which the lineage of present-day institutions is uncertain and can, perhaps, never be determined. But one does not need to accept the "diffusionist" interpretation of cultural history to accord Spanish-Mexican influences due recognition in the heritage of the Southwest.

IX

The Borderlands Are Invaded

Captain Luis de Velasco, who accompanied De Oñate on the *entrada* of 1598, had a most remarkable wardrobe. It consisted, according to Bolton, of one suit of blue Italian velvet trimmed with wide gold passementerie, with green silk stockings, blue garters, and points of gold lace; a suit of rose satin; one of straw-colored satin; another of purple Castilian cloth; another of chestnut-colored cloth; a sixth, and daintier, suit of Chinese flowered silk; two doublets of Castilian dressed kid and one of royal lion skin gold-trimmed; two linen shirts; six linen handkerchiefs; fourteen pairs of Rouen linen breeches; forty pairs of boots, shoes, and gaiters; a raincoat; three hats including one of purple taffeta trimmed with blue, purple, and yellow feathers and a band of gold and silver passementerie. His equipment naturally matched the splendor of his wardrobe: four saddles; three suits of armor, three suits of horse-armor, a silver-handled lance with gold and purple tassels, a sword and gilded dagger, a broadsword, two shields; a bedstead, two mattresses, numerous sheets, pillows and pillowcases; a bevy of servants; thirty horses and mules, and a silken banner. Indeed, the first Spaniards to invade the borderlands did so with plumes waving, banners flying, and armor gleaming.

But when Spanish-speaking people re-invaded the borderlands three hundred years later, their leaders were landless peons who forded across the Rio Grande in the dead of night. Their wardrobe—indeed their worldly possessions—consisted of the clothes they wore. No taffeta-trimmed hats for them; no blue, purple, and yellow feathers; no gold and silver ornaments; no mattresses, sheets, and pillowcases. For these latter-day conquistadores were Mexican *cholos* who came to chop brush, to build railroads, to work in copper mines, and to pick cotton in lands which De Oñate and Juan Bautista de Anza had mapped and charted, explored and colonized. The first *entrada* was made up of Spanish hidalgos and caballeros; the second of Mexican peons. The first invaders came in search of gold and silver; the second in search of bread and a job. What the second invasion lacked in color, splendor, and majesty, was more than offset by the capacity of the peons for hard work and endurance.

Those colorful murals that one can see nowadays throughout the Southwest in which figures like Captain Luis de Velasco are depicted in all their finery might well be balanced by a few murals showing Mexican migratory workers sweating in desert cement plants, in the copper mines of Morenci, the smelters of El Paso, and the great farm-factories of the San Joaquin Valley. Captain de Velasco and his colleagues may have discovered the borderlands but Spanish-speaking immigrants from Mexico have built the economic empire which exists in the Southwest today.

No one knows precisely how many Mexican immigrants came to the United States in the period from 1900 to 1930 but it is generally agreed that the number was in excess of a million. Prior to 1900 there had been a trickle of Mexican immigration to the borderlands: Texas had an immigrant population of 71,062 in 1900; Arizona 14,172; California, 8,096; New Mexico, 6,649. The bulk of these earlier immigrants, of course, were concentrated in the Southwest; and, of the post-1900 immigrants, nine-tenths settled in the borderlands. At first the immigration was largely restricted to Texas, for the use of oriental labor, particularly the Chinese, barred the way to Mexican immigration in California until about 1917. The rapid increase of Mexican immigrants in the border states after 1900, however, can be seen in the following table:

	1900	*1910*	*1920*	*1930*
Arizona	14,171	29,987	61,580	114,173
California	8,086	33,694	88,881	368,013
New Mexico	6,649	11,918	20,272	59,340
Texas	71,062	125,016	251,827	683,681

Three facts should be noted about the great wave of Mexican immigration which brought to the Southwest after 1900 nearly ten per cent of the total population of Mexico: it was overwhelmingly concentrated in the old Spanish borderlands; in point of time it coincided with the birth of the Southwest as an economic empire; and, in each instance, Mexican immigrants labored in the building of industries in which there had been an earlier Spanish-Mexican cultural contribution. The industries in which Mexicans were concentrated, moreover, were those vital to the economic development of the Southwest. In all essentials, therefore, the story of the invasion of the borderlands can be told in terms of railroads, cotton, sugar beets, and truck or produce farming.

1. Spanish Trails, American Rails

> *The Spanish introduction of the horse, mule, burro, and ox to America marked the longest stride that so many people, in so short a time, have ever taken in the arts of transportation.*
> CHARLES FLETCHER LUMMIS

The terrain of the Southwest is rugged, mountainous and semi-desert; waterholes are few and far between; and great reaches have remained wholly uninhabited for centuries. To establish a system of transportation in such a region was infinitely more difficult than to build a flatboat at Pittsburgh and float down the Ohio and the Mississippi to New Orleans. Spain is also a country of elevated mountain ranges, of narrow, winding defiles, of rocky trails, and stretches of torrid plain. From the eighth century, when the Spaniards had acquired the *aparejo* or packsaddle from the Moors, mules and burros had been used as transport. Washington Irving records that in 1486 Isabella organized, equipped and maintained pack-trains consisting of fourteen thousand mules and burros which were used to supply an army of fifty thousand in the conquest of Granada. This efficient system of transport the Spanish brought to the Americas, where, for three hundred years, the pack-train was the life line of their colonies.

The trails that later became rail lines and highways in the Southwest were first discovered, charted, and travelled by Spaniards and Mexicans. The historic trail that De Anza blazed from Tubac to San Gabriel might well be regarded as the initial survey for the present-day Southern Pacific line. Long before the rail lines were built, the Spaniards and Mexicans had organized an elaborate system of pack-trains which operated over the endless trails blazed by the conquistadores. In the early days, the "King's Wagons,"—the famous *Carros del Rey,*—made the long journey from Mexico City to Santa Fe, from Santa Fe to Veracruz, carting merchandise, supplies, and silver from the mines.

THE BORDERLANDS ARE INVADED 165

Crisscrossing the deserts and mountain ranges, these pack-trains were the principal means of transportation as late as the 1880's, transporting merchandise to the towns, supplying the army posts, carrying the mail. The tinkling of the pack-train bell was heard throughout the West until the whistle of the locomotive began to echo in the mountain passes and canyons.

Mule and burro transport, so well adapted to desert conditions, was a Spanish invention and Southwestern pioneers were in complete agreement that no one could handle burros or mules as skilfully as Mexicans. For efficient service, pack-trains had to be thoroughly organized. The form of organization and the type of equipment were well established when Columbus discovered America. A typical pack-train consisted of the pack-master or *patrón;* the head-loader or *cargador;* a blacksmith; a cook; and eight or ten packers or *arrieros.* The duties of each man in the pack-train were defined by custom in the most precise detail. Operating from Tucson to San Diego, from Santa Fe to El Paso, from Tucson to Guaymas, pack-trains constituted an extremely efficient and economical mode of transportation for the time and place.

Santiago Hubbel, a famous pack-master of New Mexico, freighted heavy mining equipment overland from Lavaca, Texas, to the Heintzelman mine in Arizona—a distance of 1,200 miles—and his pack-trains carried ore to the Missouri River in rawhide bags. Freight rates ranged from thirty to seventy-cents per ton per mile and the mules, carrying an average load of 250 pounds, often made thirty miles a day. It was not uncommon for desert pack-trains to travel three hundred miles in four days and, in 1881, a pack-train, loaded two hundred pounds to the pack mule, travelled eighty-five miles in twelve hours. Pack-trains carried supplies to mining camps throughout the West and New Mexico *arrieros* made their appearance as far north as the Salmon and Frazer rivers.

The operation of these pack-trains was based on the most elaborate and intricate lore. In Spain the pack mules had housings, similar to those of the cavalry, of rich cloth embroidered with gold; halters brocaded with silk; and bridles, headpieces, and harnesses that glittered with silver. The *arrieros* of the Southwest kept this great tradition alive. In odd moments they decorated their equipment with figures of animals and birds, insignia and legend, woven with silken threads of various colors. A pack saddle, stock and all, often cost $100 and was beautifully stamped and engraved by hand, trimmed with Mexican silver dollars, cut and chased in various designs; while the bridles were inlaid with silver and gold. The *arrieros* dressed like their grandfathers in Spain: with high-heeled top boots and tiny spurs, silken *banda* or sash wrapped around the waist two or three times, embroidered shirt front, and conical sombrero with a silver snake around the crown, the underside of the brim being trimmed with silver braid.

"Such was the holiday costume of the packer of thirty-five or forty years ago," wrote H. W. Daly in 1910, "when, mounted on his favorite mule, he would sing some Spanish ditty when visiting friends in some nearby hamlet; a man who never turned his back on a foe or forsook a friend in moments of peril, honest and honorable in all his dealings with his fellow men, kind to animals in his care, with a love for his calling and thoroughly imbued with an 'esprit de corps' for the pack service." "I cannot recall," wrote Charles Fletcher Lummis, "hearing of any *arriero* that ever robbed his employer."

Used by General Crook in the 'sixties in campaigns against the Shoshones in Nevada, pack-trains played an important part in his later campaigns against the Apaches in the Southwest; in fact, some historians believe they were the decisive factor. Among the famous muleteers who operated these supply trains for the army were such names as Chileno John, José de Leon, and Lauriano Gómez. Later the army used this same pack-train system in the Spanish-American War, both in Cuba and in the Philippines, and it became a standardized unit in army transport. Just how intricately organized and delicately articulated the whole system was can be seen by reference to a manual of pack transportation which the army issued in 1910. The technique of roping packsaddles, for example, was highly intricate and the most elaborate lore existed about hitches, knots, and splices. Prepared by Chief Packer H. W. Daly, the manual points out that the whole system, in its every detail, was taken over from the Mexicans intact, including its vocabulary.

The load was, of course, the cargo, from the Spanish *cargar,* to load. The pack-train was the *atajo;* the pack-cushion, or saddle, the *aparejo;* the sweat-cloth, the *suadera;* the crupper, the *grupera;* the saddle cloth, the *corona;* the cover for the harness was the *sobre-en-jalma* or *sobrejalma;* the bell, the *cencerro;* the canteen, the *gerafe;* the saddlebags, the *alforjas;* the bell-mare, the *acémila;* the eye-blind, the *tapaojo;* the currycomb, the *almohaza.* Much of the vocabulary of the pack-train was Arabic in origin; but its organization was Andalusian.

Estevan Ochoa, whose family had come from Spain to Mexico in the days of Cortez, was born in the cathedral city of Chihuahua in 1831. As a young man, he had journeyed to Independence, Missouri, where he lived for a time, learning the English language. Returning to the Southwest in 1859, by way of the Santa Fe Trail, he established a chain of stores and a well-organized pack-train system that supplied them. When troops of the Confederacy under Captain Hunter seized Tucson during the Civil War, Ochoa was given the alternative of taking an oath of allegiance to the Confederacy or of leaving Tucson. He answered this ultimatum by climbing on his horse and riding out alone through the Apache territory to Mesilla. A partner in the famous early-day freighting firm of Tully and Ochoa, his pack-trains freighted throughout the Southwest and deep into Mexican territory. As a pioneer resident of Tucson, he led the fight that finally resulted in the establishment of the first public school system in the territory.

Member of the territorial legislature and mayor of Tucson, Estevan Ochoa was perhaps the first citizen of Tucson in the 1870's. At his beautiful home in Tucson, scores of friends annually assembled from points as distant as El Paso and Guaymas for the ten-day celebration of the festival of Saint Augustine. When the railroad finally reached Tucson on March 25, 1880, Don Estevan Ochoa presented Charles Crocker with the silver spike used in the dedication ceremonies. As a pioneer freighter in the Southwest, Don Estevan was, in effect, presenting his competitor with a spike to be driven into his own coffin. For the coming of the railroads spelled the end of the pack-trains and proved to be the undoing of Ochoa, who died, a few years later, a ruined man.

2. Life in a Boxcar

Mexican labor was extensively used in the construction of the Southern Pacific and Santa Fe lines in the Southwest in the 'eighties, particularly on the desert sections built by the Southern Pacific. From that day to this, Mexicans have repaired and maintained Western rail lines. As watchmen of the rails, section hands must live near their work, while the extra crews literally live on the rails in boxcars which are shunted about the divisions. "Their abode," as one railroad executive tersely phrased it, "is where these cars are placed." Hundreds of Mexican families have spent their entire sojourn in the United States bouncing around the Southwest in boxcar homes.

Since 1880 Mexicans have made up seventy per cent of the section crews and ninety per cent of the extra gangs on the principal western lines which regularly employ between 35,000 and 50,000 workmen in these categories. In 1930 the Santa Fe reported that it was then employing 14,000 Mexicans; the Rock Island 3,000; the Great Northern 1,500; and the Southern Pacific 10,000. According to the census of 1930, 70,799 Mexicans were engaged in "transportation and communication" mostly as common laborers on the western lines and as maintenance workers on the street-car systems of the Southwest. In Kansas and Nebraska, Mexican settlements will be found to extend along the rail lines while the colonies of Kansas City and Chicago are outgrowths of Mexican railroad labor camps. As late as 1928 the boxcar labor camps of the railroads housed 469 Mexican men, 155 women, and 372 children in Chicago.

The principal large-scale importers of Mexican labor, the rail lines of the Southwest constantly fed workers to other industries since so much railroad labor is seasonal in character. Forever losing labor, the railroads kept recruiting additional workers in Mexico. This process was greatly accelerated as increased freight and passenger traffic paralleled the economic development of the region. Railroad employment naturally stimulated migration, since the companies provided transportation to various points along the line. Just how important the railroads were in setting the tide of Mexican immigration in motion can be seen from a statement made by an investigator for the Department of Labor in 1912. Most of the Mexicans then in the United States, he said, had at one time or another worked for the railroads. For years the prevailing wage for section hands in the Southwest was a dollar a day—considerably below the rate paid for similar labor on the middle western and eastern lines.

Recruited by labor agents and commissary companies, Mexicans were assembled in El Paso and from there sent out on six-month work-contracts with the Southern Pacific and Santa Fe. In 1908 some sixteen thousand Mexicans were recruited in El Paso for railroad employment. Two years later as many as two thousand Mexicans crossed the border into El Paso in a single month at the instigation of the commissary companies. Starting around 1900, railroad recruitment reached its peak in 1910 and 1912. Originally recruited by the Southwestern lines, Mexicans were used after 1905 in an ever-widening arc which gradually extended

THE BORDERLANDS ARE INVADED 169

through Colorado, Wyoming, Utah, Montana, Idaho, Oregon, and Washington.

As early as 1900 the Southern Pacific was regularly employing 4,500 Mexicans on its lines in California. By 1906 the Southern Pacific and the Santa Fe were importing as many as two and three carloads of *cholos* a week to Southern California. The rapid extension of the Pacific Electric interurban system in Southern California also greatly stimulated the demand for Mexican labor. Wherever a railroad labor camp was established, a Mexican *colonia* exists today. For example, the Mexican settlement in Watts—called *Tajauta* by the Mexicans—dates from the importation of a carload of *cholos* in 1906. While the lines were being built, the *cholos* lived in boxcars and tents. Later the company built row-houses on its property and rented these houses to the employees. Thirty or forty such camps are still to be found in Los Angeles County. Around the initial camp site, Mexicans began to buy lots at $1 down and $1 a week and to build the shacks in which their children live today.

In the sparsely settled semi-arid Southwest, the construction of the rail lines was well in advance of actual settlement. Elsewhere in the West and Middle West, settlers had promoted railroads; but here railroads promoted settlement. The first great land "boom" in Los Angeles, for example, was strictly a railroad promotion. In the economic development of the region, railroads have played an all-important role. Prior to the completion of the Southern Pacific and Santa Fe lines in the 'eighties, the Southwest was hardly a part of the United States. In every state in the region, the modern phase in its development dates from the arrival of the first passenger or freight train. Largely built by Mexican labor along routes first explored and mapped by Spanish-speaking people, the railroads of the Southwest have been maintained by Mexicans from 1880 to the present time. All the products of the region,—copper, cotton, lettuce, produce, wool, beef, and dairy products,—move to markets on desert lines dotted at regular intervals by small, isolated clusters of Mexican section-crew shacks lost in time and space.

3. COTTON IN TEXAS

As early as the 1890's, Mexican labor from both sides of the Rio Grande was following the cotton harvest on foot into the old cotton-producing sections of east Texas. East Texas was then devoted to cotton; south and west Texas to cattle. Since the Negroes were concentrated in the eastern section, Mexicans remained a secondary source of labor. But from 1890 to 1910 the cattle industry began to retreat before the forces of King Cotton, first in middle Texas and later (1910–1930) in west Texas. In these areas the plantation system had never been firmly established and large land units and inflated land values demanded a more "efficient" type of labor at lower costs. This was achieved largely through an increasing use of mechanized methods and the substitution of transient Mexican labor for Negro and "poor white" sharecroppers and tenants. Writing in *Current History* for February, 1930, Remsen Crawford observed that "in the unirrigated plains regions of Texas and Oklahoma millions of acres formerly used as ranges for cattle and sheep and goats are being cultivated in cotton, mainly for non-resident landlords, by Mexican tenants, or hired workers, living in miserable shacks. . . . New cotton gin plants have sprung up everywhere. Old towns have greatly increased in size, and new ones have been built. The bulk of the work of making and gathering this cotton is done by Mexicans imported from over the border."

With the coming of cotton, middle and west Texas were inundated with hordes of people who, in the words of one observer, "planted cotton, talked cotton, thought cotton, sold cotton, everything but ate cotton." It so happened that the expansion of cotton in these new areas coincided with the first rumblings of the social revolution which began in Mexico in 1910. Thus as cotton pushed its way into the Southwest, Mexicans from across the border came to meet it. "It was in Southwest Texas," writes Dr. Edward Everett Davis, "that fourteenth century feudalism met the southern plantation" and from this meeting came the large-scale cotton farming of Texas based on the use of migratory Mexican labor. As early as 1908, writes Dr. Davis, the Mexican invasion "had driven itself like a wedge into the heart of Texas beyond San Antonio, veering to the south of the Balcones Escarpment and the ranch country, and sticking close to the cotton fields of Comal, Hays, and Caldwell counties" (1). Coming through the ports of Laredo, Eagle Pass, and Brownsville, the Mexicans had concentrated at San Antonio, and that city, "like the small end of a funnel, poured them out into the cotton fields with such speed that by 1920, the greatest density of rural Mexican population in Texas was not along the Rio Grande but in Caldwell County in sight of the dome of the State Capitol."

THE BORDERLANDS ARE INVADED 171

In the story of Keglar Hill, Dr. Robert H. Montgomery has given a graphic account of what happened in one Texas community when this invasion began. Keglar Hill had moved from cattle to cotton in one generation. As cotton supplanted cattle, the first Mexicans began to arrive in 1887 and 1888. At first they returned to their homes across the Rio Grande after the cotton harvest. But each year a few stayed over at the end of the season and, as the number increased, they gradually began to displace the white tenants, not as tenants, however, but as day laborers. The white tenants were the first to leave, around 1900, but were soon followed to the towns by their former landlords. Since the Mexicans did not speak English and were not in the habit of sending their children to school, the rural schools vanished with the white tenants and landlords. Of some three hundred-odd white settlers who had made up this small rural community in 1895, writes Dr. Montgomery, not one remained on the land by 1910 (2).

Obviously it was the joint appearance of cotton *and* Mexicans that brought about this disintegration of rural life. But the white tenants and sharecroppers, resenting the new dispensation, tended to blame Mexican labor for the transition, whereas the Mexicans were as much victims of the transformation as the tenants they displaced. "Before the incoming hosts of Mexicans," writes Dr. Davis, "three rural institutions,—the home, the church, and the school,—fell like a trio of staggering tenpins at the end of a bowling race. White tenants could not compete with cheap Mexican labor. Prosperous owners moved to town, leaving the menial work for Mexicans to do. Rural dwellings, orchards, and yard fences went to wreck; deserted country churches made excellent hay barns and tool sheds for absentee landlords; and the large rural schools packed with happy white children dwindled into sickly institutions for a few indifferent Mexican muchachos, as a wilderness of rag-weeds and cockleburs grew on the school grounds. . . . The Mexican did not hit the interior cotton lands with the impact of a hurricane, but seeped in silently and undermined the rural social structures like termites eating out the sills of a wooden house." Needless to say, I quote this passage for its revealing explanation of the basis of much anti-Mexican sentiment in Texas rather than to describe the transformation that took place. Actually new modes of production and new social forces had "undermined the rural social structures" of Texas; the appearance of the Mexicans was a symptom, not a cause, of this process. Mexicans did not "seep" into Texas: they were recruited for employment. To charge them with responsibility for the disappearance of rural schools and churches, while exonerating their employers, was certainly to give a vulgar and misleading interpretation to a familiar economic process.

By 1940 nearly four hundred thousand workers, two-thirds of whom were Mexicans, were following "the big swing" through the cotton-growing regions of Texas. Starting in the southern part of the state in June, the migratory army sweeps eastward through the coastal counties and then turns west for the later harvest in the central section. It then splits into three units: one moves into east Texas; another proceeds to the Red River country; and a third treks westward to the San Angelo-Lubbock area. Organized in the south, the army gains recruits as it proceeds along the line of march. From the Lower Valley, where the season starts, comes the initial vanguard of about twenty-five thousand Mexican migratory workers. As the army marches through the Robstown-Corpus Christi area, an additional twenty-five thousand recruits join the procession. By the time the army has reached central Texas it has probably grown to two hundred thousand workers. During the depression, as many as four hundred thousand Mexicans made this great circle, travelling distances of from 1,800 to 2,000 miles. Over this long and wearisome route, Mexican families travel "like the starlings and the blackbirds."

The generals of this tatterdemalion army are the Mexican labor contractors and truckers. About sixty per cent of the cotton-picking, in fact, is contracted through these *jefes* or *papacitos*. The contractor, who usually speaks English, knows the routes, deals with the employer, and organizes the expedition. He is really a *capitán* or *jefe* because he happens to own a truck. Paid to transport workers, he is also hired to weigh the cotton, take charge of the commissary, and oversee the work. The trucks are often loaded with fifty or sixty workers as well as quantities of bedding and equipment. Thoroughly mechanized, the cotton-picking army moves on wheels in open or stake trucks. In an accident at McAllen, Texas, in 1940, forty-four Mexicans riding in one of these trucks were injured: twenty-nine were killed and of these, eleven were children under sixteen years of age—a tragedy memorialized in a famous border *corrido*. In depression years the army, of course, is inflated to fantastic proportions. The growers are anxious to have their crops harvested as rapidly as possible and, with the pay on a piecework basis, total labor costs remain the same regardless of the size of the crew.

THE BORDERLANDS ARE INVADED

Here is a picture of what happens, and has been happening for years, on this great circle (from a report by Pauline Kibbe to the coordinator of Inter-American Affairs, December 29, 1944):

> On one Saturday afternoon in October, 496 migratory labor trucks were counted on the streets of Lubbock. Lubbock is a city of between 40,000 and 50,000. Each truck carries an average of 15 migrants, of all ages, which means an estimated total of 7,440 migrants who had come to Lubbock to spend the weekend, seek new employment, purchase their groceries, and other supplies, find a little recreation, etc. . . . Suppose each of the 496 trucks in Lubbock spent an average of $25.00. . . . That is a total of $12,400.00 income to the business places of all kinds for one weekend. Yet Lubbock had made no provision whatever for taking care of this influx of people which occurs regularly every fall, and every weekend during each fall. There is no place provided where they may park their trucks, take a bath, change their clothes, even go to the toilet. In Lamesa it was stated . . . that toilet facilities in the City Hall, which the migrants could use most conveniently, were locked up at noon on Saturdays, and filling station facilities were used except where the owners prohibited it because of the objections of customers.

Of 117 complaints of discrimination against Mexicans in public places filed with the Texas Good Neighbor Commission in 1944, two-thirds of the total involved mistreatment in towns of less than five thousand population. These towns were scattered over the general area through which the migratory labor movement passes. It would seem to be obvious, therefore, that a degree of correlation exists between migration and discrimination.

4. Cotton Moves West

With the first World War creating a sharp demand for long-staple cotton, the cotton kingdom jumped from west Texas to the Salt River Valley in Arizona. Agents of the Arizona Cotton Growers Association recruited thousands of workers in Mexico for employment on the large-scale irrigated cotton farms. In most cases, the costs of transportation and of subsistence en route were later deducted from earnings. Up to June 30, 1919, 5,824 Mexicans had been imported into Arizona and 7,269 were specifically recruited for cotton-picking, not including those who came without contracts or special inducements. When the cotton boom exploded after the war, thousands of these workers were stranded in Arizona. In the Salt River Valley alone, ten thousand Mexicans were destitute in the winter of 1921 and the Mexican consul had to seek an appropriation of $17,000 to provide temporary relief. When four thousand imported Mexicans went on strike in the cotton fields in 1920, the growers had their leaders deported and arrested scores of the strikers. At about the same time, the development of irrigated cotton in the Mesilla Valley of New Mexico also began to attract Mexican workers from across the border (3).

In 1910 the first cotton was planted in the Imperial Valley in California. As the cotton acreage expanded in response to wartime demands, the Imperial Valley growers began to bring in truckloads of Mexicans, in units of 1,500 and 2,000, from such communities as San Felipe and Guaymas. After the war, cotton production declined for a time and then soared to new heights as the center of production shifted to the huge farm-factories of the San Joaquin Valley. With 5,500 acres planted in cotton in 1919, the acreage in the San Joaquin increased to 172,400 acres in 1931. As the cotton acreage expanded, more and more Mexicans were imported, with the year 1920 being referred to in the farm journals as the first "Mexican harvest." From 1924 to 1930, an average of 58,000 Mexicans trekked into the San Joaquin Valley each year, principally for the cotton harvest. In the middle 'twenties, over a hundred trucks loaded with Mexicans were counted crossing the Ridge Route in a single day. The townspeople would provide the Mexicans stranded in the valley towns at the end of the season, from public funds, with just enough gasoline to make the trip back over the Ridge Route to Los Angeles, where welfare and charitable agencies took care of them during the winter months.

Commanding a premium price, with a yield-per-acre nearly twice the national average, cotton soon became a $40,000,000 crop in California. Largely produced on high-priced irrigated lands which had been capitalized on the basis of five decades of cheap labor, the expansion of cotton in California was premised upon the availability of a large supply of low-cost labor exclusively earmarked for the cotton growers. Consistently opposed to Mexican immigration, the labor unions failed to note that the cotton fields of the Imperial and San Joaquin valleys were a major factor in the location of large automobile tire factories in Los Angeles which, in turn, stimulated the demand for industrial labor.

5. VITAMINS AND MEXICANS

Irrigation equals Mexicans.
DR. PAUL S. TAYLOR

Twice the size of Germany and larger in area than the thirteen original states, the Southwest had a population in 1902 about half the size of the City of Chicago in the same year. Irrigation was the magic key that unlocked the resources of the region. Irrigated farming is intensive farming: with high yields per acre, heavy labor requirements, year-round production, and crop specialization. Small in area, the "winter gardens" of the Southwest have off-set, by their exceptional productivity, many of the disadvantages of an arid environment. Throughout the region, the distribution of Mexicans in rural areas is largely determined by the location of irrigated crops. As an economic empire, the Southwest dates from the passage of the Reclamation Act in 1902 which outlined a development policy for the arid West and made possible the use of federal funds in the construction of large-scale irrigation and reclamation projects. Irrigation has had more to do with the economic growth of the Southwest than any single factor.

Today a visitor from the North, driving into the Lower Rio Grande Valley in midwinter, would have the illusion, writes Hart Stilwell, "of moving into a modern version of the Garden of Eden. As he drove along the Valley's 'Main Street,' a 65-mile highway, he would see stately palms and green citrus-fruit trees laden with golden orange fruit; bougainvillea vines in full bloom; bright green papaya plants. . . . And when he came to the level, rich fields he would see bronze-skinned people by the thousands harvesting vegetables—red beets with their green tops, white and purple turnips with their green tops, golden carrots with their green tops—everything green. He might see other laborers harvesting cabbage, broccoli, endive, peppers, beans, tomatoes, new potatoes, peas, anise, cauliflower or squash." In the valley today Mexican laborers —forty thousand of them illegal entrants or "wetbacks"—plant, cultivate, and harvest fruit and vegetable crops worth $100,000,000 a year. Virtually none of this development existed in 1904 when the St. Louis, Brownsville, and Mexico Railway finally completed its line to Brownsville (4). A miraculous transformation, indeed; but just how was it brought about?

"The hand of the Mexican laborer," wrote Dr. Paul S. Taylor in 1927, "is grubbing out the chaparral of south Texas." Before the lands could be levelled, planted, and irrigated, the brush had to be cut away for this was the *brasada* or brush country of Texas. While an occasional tractor was used to pull out small trees, Mexicans grubbed most of the brush by hand with the use of grubbing hoes. "Grubbing brush," the Texans said, "is a Mexican job." And properly so, perhaps, for the Mexicans alone knew and understood the brush country. To the Anglo-Americans, writes J. Frank Dobie, the *brasada* vegetation was just "brush," an all-encompassing term; but generations of Mexicans had learned to distinguish, and had named, the endless varieties of shrubs and plants to be found in this section. When these varieties are distinguished today, it is by their Spanish-Mexican names: *mogotes,* or thick patches of evergreen; *coma,* with its dirk-like thorns; the *cejas* or thickets; the wand-like *retama* with its yellow flowers called *lluvia de oro* ("showers of gold"); *grandjero* with its yellow berries; the *agarita* or wild currant; the bitter *amargosa;* the black chaparral or *chaparro prieto;* and the *tasajillo* or rat-tail cactus. Thousands of acres of this densely thicketed brush had to be grubbed out by hand to make way for the fabulously rich "winter garden" that exists today in the Lower Valley.

After 1900 the increasing urbanization of population, the disappearance of the backyard garden, the development of new canning processes, and the introduction of refrigerator cars, brought about an enormous increase in the production of fruits and vegetables on large-scale commercial farms in the irrigated portions of the Southwest. "Citrus fruit output," writes Dr. Harry Schwartz, "jumped more than five fold in the first decades of this century, while grape tonnage increased four times. Between 1919 and 1939 production of fresh market spinach, lettuce, cauliflower, snap beans, and carrots increased five times or more, while celery output tripled. In 1900 most fruits and vegetables were not considered sufficiently important to justify extensive collection of statistics regarding them. By 1940 they contributed more than a billion dollars to cash farm income, roughly 30% of the total *from all crops"* (5). (Emphasis added.) It should be emphasized that this increased production represented a net addition to the total American agricultural income (6).

Virtually all of this phenomenal increase occurred in the Southwest and was made possible by the use of Mexican labor. In the growth of commercial fruit and vegetable production in the Southwest between 1900 and 1940, there is not a single crop in the production and harvesting of which Mexicans have not played a major role. This fabulous increase in production—which set the Southwest on its feet financially—could never have taken place so rapidly without the use of Mexican labor. To grow and harvest an acre of wheat, during the 1930's, required on the average only about 13 man-hours of labor; but an acre of lettuce required 125 man-hours and an acre of strawberries 500 man-hours. Unorganized Mexican labor in inexhaustible quantities made this production possible (7).

It should be noted that the increased production took place on irrigated acreages within the confines of the old Spanish borderlands. It was here that the Spanish and the Mexicans had first demonstrated the value of irrigation and had developed an understanding of irrigation techniques. Prior to the development of the Southwest, as Ray Stannard Baker pointed out, Anglo-Saxons had never attempted irrigation on a large scale and irrigation "means a complete change of many racial institutions and customs." Thus the contribution of Mexican laborers related back to a much earlier cultural contribution which had been made by the Spanish and Mexican settlers. Reclaimed and irrigated at enormous costs, much of this land was overcapitalized. Overcapitalization, in turn, had created a terrific pressure for cheap labor. But the years during which the Southwest became an economic empire saw a great increase in living standards for the American working class brought about by the use of more efficient machines. It was precisely in the production of truck crops, fruit, cotton, and sugar beets that the least progress had been made in the introduction of machines. Thus the use of Mexican labor fitted into the economic cogs of the Southwest in perfect fashion (8).

To appreciate what Mexican labor meant to the economy of the Southwest, one simple, obvious fact needs to be stressed, namely, the desert or semi-desert character of the region. In the San Joaquin, Imperial, Salt River, Mesilla, and Lower Rio Grande valleys, temperatures of 100, 110, and 112 degrees are not uncommon. Those who have never visited the copper mines of Morenci in July or the cotton fields of the San Joaquin Valley in September or the cantaloupe fields of Imperial Valley in June are hardly in a position even to imagine what Mexican workers have endured in these areas. It should be remembered that the development of the Southwest occurred at a time when the living and working conditions of American workmen were undergoing rapid improvement. It was not easy to find in these years a large supply of labor that would brave the desert heat and perform the monotonous stoop-labor, hand-labor tasks which the agriculture of the Southwest demanded. Under the circumstances, the use of Mexican labor was largely non-competitive and nearly indispensable.

6. Coyotes and Man-Snatchers

Spearheaded by the completion of the rail lines, the westward movement of cotton, the spread of "winter garden" fruit and vegetable production, and the phenomenally rapid economic expansion of the Southwest after 1900 created an enormous demand for unskilled labor. Mexicans poured into Texas by the thousands. "Farming is not a profitable industry" said John Nance Garner the Uvalde millionaire, "and in order to make money you have to have cheap labor." From 70,981 in 1900 the number of Mexicans in Texas shot up to 683,681 in 1930. With enforcement of the contract-labor law being suspended from 1918 to 1921, over 50,000 workers were directly recruited in Mexico for employment in the United States. By the time the border patrol was established in 1924, and administrative restriction adopted as a policy in March, 1929, the great labor pool of Texas had been filled to overflowing with Mexican immigrants. From this reservoir Mexican labor was siphoned off in all directions as the war and the Immigration Act of 1924 drastically reduced the volume of European immigration. The tip of the wave of Mexican immigration reached as far north as Detroit and as far east as Pittsburgh. "Mexicans," said a California grower in 1927, "scatter like clouds. They are all over America." From Texas, Mexicans were recruited, in small numbers, for employment on the plantations in the Mississippi Delta; thousands were recruited for employment in the Northern and Western sugar-beet fields; and an entire trainload was, at one time, shipped from Texas to Seattle for employment in the Alaska canneries.

Throughout the borderlands prior to 1924 the contract-labor law of 1885 was more often honored in the breach than in its observance. For a quarter of a century, Texas growers had recruited labor in Mexico whenever they needed it. In large measure this traffic had been made possible by the activities of labor smugglers who developed a lucrative racket in Mexicans. The labor smuggler or "coyote" crossed the border, not only to round up crews, but to get workers across the line in violation of the immigration regulations. For a fee of ten or fifteen dollars, the coyote would arrange to get Mexicans across the line, by having them "jump the fence" at La Colorado; or come across concealed in automobiles, carts, or trucks; or by fording the Rio Grande at night. In many cases, forged passports and head-tax receipts were provided. Once across the line, the Mexican was turned over by the coyote to a labor contractor (*enganchista*), who sold him for a fee of fifty cents to one dollar a head to some agricultural, railroad, or mining employer. Labor agents operating out of Laredo and El Paso had forwarding agents elsewhere in Texas, notably in San Antonio. Charging the employers a fee for supplying the labor, the contractors charged the workers for transportation and subsistence en route. The profits in this racket were really enormous and the smugglers and coyotes and labor-contractors constituted an intimate and powerful alliance from Calexico to Brownsville.

Another type of agent, the man-snatcher, also figured in this dubious traffic. The man-snatchers made a business of stealing Mexican labor and selling the same crew to several different employers. Delivering a crew to an employer, they would steal the crew at night and resell it to still another employer. In this manner, the same crew would often be sold to four or five employers in the course of a few days. Frequently the man-snatchers raided crews imported by the labor contractors and made off with them by force of arms. Shipments of workers en route to employers were often kept locked up at night, in barns, warehouses, and corrals, with armed guards posted to prevent their theft. Crews of imported Mexicans were marched through the streets of San Antonio under armed guard in broad daylight and, in Gonzales County, workers who attempted to breach their contracts were chained to posts and guarded by men with shotguns (9). "Large planters," wrote James L. Slayden, "welcome the Mexican immigrant as they would welcome fresh arrivals from the Congo, without a thought of the social and political embarrassment to their country."

7. Los Betabeleros

Mexicans have been identified with the sugar-beet industry since its inception; the phrase "Mexican sugar-beet worker" is as common as "Mexican sheepherder." Prior to the tariff of 1897, the sugar-beet acreage in this country was insignificant; but, by taxing foreign sugar seventy-five per cent of its value, the Dingley Tariff immediately created a great demand for sugar beets. States paid bounties, offered tax exemption, and otherwise encouraged the growing of sugar beets as a matter of official policy. From 135,000 acres in 1899, the sugar-beet acreage increased to 376,000 acres in 1906 and, for the last decade, has averaged about 750,000 acres. With each increase in the sugar-beet acreage, of course, the demand for Mexican labor has been stepped up.

The production of a large acreage in sugar beets has consistently required, until the last few years, a large amount of labor, for blocking and thinning in the spring and for harvesting in the fall. To induce labor to stay over in the area, so as to be available for the harvest, the sugar-beet companies have always used the device of contract-labor in which workers, more often families, contract to block, thin, and harvest beets for a stipulated sum per acre. For many years, the major companies included in the contract a "hold-back" provision to insure that the workers would be present in the fall for the harvest. The growing of sugar beets is unique in that it represents "a curious union of family farms and million dollar corporations." The sugar-beet refineries, rather than the individual farmers, have long assumed responsibility for the recruitment, distribution, and control of the labor supply.

The principal growing areas are to be found in California, Michigan, and Colorado. From the beginning of the industry, Mexican workers were used in California. Elsewhere the sugar-beet companies at first experimented with other types of labor: Japanese in Colorado; the so-called "Volga-Germans" in Nebraska and other areas; and Belgians and Poles in Michigan. But these non-Mexican groups showed a tendency to aspire to farm ownership and, in some areas, by dint of unbelievably hard effort, succeeded in achieving their goal. It was to curb this tendency that the companies shifted to Mexican labor, particularly after the first World War and the passage of the Immigration

Act of 1924. In fact, it was at the insistence of the sugar-beet companies that the contract-labor law was suspended from 1918 to 1920 to permit direct recruitment in Mexico. By 1927 it was estimated that, of 58,000 sugar-beet workers, 30,000 were Mexicans. Today sixty-six per cent of the 100,000 workers in the industry are Mexicans. In states such as Ohio, Michigan, Minnesota, and North Dakota, Mexicans constitute from seventy-five to ninety per cent of the labor supply.

In Colorado the Great Western Sugar Beet Company began to recruit Mexican labor in 1916, at first from southern Colorado and New Mexico, and, later, from Mexico. In 1920 the company spent $360,000 in the recruitment of Mexican labor. In one year alone, 1921, some ten thousand Mexican workers were imported, most of them from Texas; and, between 1910 and 1930 a total of at least thirty thousand Mexicans were brought to the Colorado sugar-beet areas. Throughout its history, the company has shown a marked preference for the "unspoiled" Mexican, "fresh from Mexico clad in the sombrero, light cotton clothing, and even sandals of the Mexican peon." Even during the depression years, the company attempted to recruit Mexican labor from outside the state. In an effort to prevent this practice, the governor of Colorado on April 20, 1936, proclaimed a state of martial law and stationed Colorado National Guardsmen along the Colorado-New Mexico border to turn back Mexican workers from New Mexico.

At the outset, the sugar-beet companies sought to anchor the imported labor in the sugar-beet areas: first, by some feeble efforts at colonization; then by offering a bonus to those families who agreed to waive the payment of transportation back to the point of recruitment; and, more frequently, by simply stalling on final settlement under the contract at the end of the season. The earnings of the Mexican beet workers were, in not a few cases, so low that they were compelled to stay over during the winter months. Thus wherever Mexican labor has been imported for sugar-beet employment, small Mexican colonies have developed. In the South Platte area of Colorado, the number of stay-overs rose in a six year period from 537 to 2,084. El Paso was the principal place of recruitment for Mexican sugar-beet workers in the Rocky Mountain states, with San Antonio being the center from which they were recruited for the principal Middle Western areas. Over the years, however, Denver has come to occupy, in relation to the sugar-beet areas in Utah, Wyoming, and Montana, much the same relationship that El Paso and San Antonio occupied at an earlier period. There are today some 14,631 Spanish-speaking residents in Denver.

Needless to say, the Texas growers became extremely annoyed when the agents for the sugar-beet companies began to tap their great reservoir of Mexican labor. Noting that more and more Mexican labor tended to stay over in the sugar-beet areas, the cotton growers took matters into their own hands. Holes were shot in the tires on the trucks of the sugar-beet agents and Mexicans, in any number of cases, were prevented by force from keeping their rendezvous with the sugar-beet agents. In a final effort to stop this out-of-state recruitment, the cotton growers secured the passage of the Texas Emigrant Agent Law of 1929 which, in effect, barred outside agents from recruiting labor in Texas. The principal consequence of this law was to make of out-of-state recruitment a kind of illegal, underground conspiracy. For, despite the law, thousands of Mexicans continued to leave every year for out-of-state employment. For example, it has been estimated that nearly sixty thousand Texas-Mexicans leave the state every year. Originally this movement was organized by the sugar-beet companies through the use of special trains; but, for the last decade, it has been handled by Mexican truckers and contractors.

Most of the trucks are open, stake trucks, never intended for passenger transportation. Planks or benches are placed on the truck, which is then loaded with passengers and equipment. Frequently fifty or sixty Mexicans are huddled, like sheep, in these trucks. Once the Mexicans have crowded into the back of the truck, a heavy tarpaulin is thrown over them and fastened down around the edges so that the passengers are concealed. The reason for this conspiratorial atmosphere is, of course, that perhaps two-thirds of the Mexicans who leave the state have been recruited in violation of the Emigrant Agent Law. Outwardly the truck looks as though it were loaded with a cargo of potatoes. Before climbing into the driver's seat, the trucker tosses a couple of coffee cans into the back of the truck which are used as urinals during the long journey north. Then, usually around midnight, the truck rolls out of San Antonio and heads north.

With a relief driver in the cab, the truckers drive straight through to Michigan, and other equally remote destinations, stopping only for gas and oil. By driving night and day, they can make the trip in forty-five to fifty hours. Paid $10 a head to deliver Mexicans in Michigan, which is ultimately charged up by the sugar-beet companies against earnings, the average trucker can make about $3,000 a season. Naturally the truckers are in a hurry; they want to make, if possible, two or three trips. Instead of travelling the main highways, they pursue a crazily zigzag course, making many detours, zooming along country roads and minor highways, in an effort to avoid highway patrolmen. Almost every season since this traffic developed serious accidents have occurred along the line of march.

Wherever sugar beets are grown,—in Michigan and Minnesota, in Colorado and Montana,—the same pattern can be traced. In the sugar-beet area around Findlay, Ohio—dominated by the Great Lakes Sugar Company—nearly three thousand Mexican workers are imported each year from Texas. Telesforo Mandujano, and his six sons, made the trip to Ohio from San Antonio in a truck that carried forty Mexican workers. Here is his abbreviated statement before the Tolan Committee: "The truck did stop a few times for bowel evacuations and eating, when the truck needed gas or oil; but on most occasions cans were used as urinals and dumped out of the truck. Passengers had to stand all the way and one man tied himself upright to a stake so he could not fall out if he should happen to fall asleep." After deducting all expenses, Telesforo and his six sons made $200.10 for the season. Catarino Ramirez also made the trip from San Antonio to Findlay—in a truck that carried thirty-seven adults and eight children, making the trip in two days and three nights. "No stops were made unless the truckers were forced to," he testified, "and when such stops were made we ate if we had time."

No aspect of Mexican immigration has been more frequently or more thoroughly investigated than the history of their employment in sugar beets. The documentation is voluminous and covers every aspect of their employment in every sugar-beet area in the United States. It would serve no purpose, here, to attempt a summarization of this data, with its appalling revelation of low earnings, miserable health and housing conditions, child labor, sickness and disease. The data, for those who are interested, is summarized in Part 19 of the Tolan Committee Hearings (the "Detroit Hearings," September 23, 24, 25, 1941). Suffice it to say, that from 1916 to the present time, between thirty thousand and sixty thousand Mexican workers have been directly dependent upon sugar-beet employment with average annual earnings of from $500 to $600 *per family*.

8. IN MIDWEST INDUSTRIES

Beginning around 1916, Mexican laborers began to appear in the Chicago industrial area, in Gary, Indiana Harbor, and Calumet. Most of these workers were from such states as Jalisco, Michoacan, and Guanajuato, having "leap-frogged" from the interior of Mexico to the Midwest industrial centers, "literally passing through and beyond," writes Dr. Paul S. Taylor, "their compatriots of the Mexican northern border states who have made the shorter migration to the adjacent southwestern United States." Appearing first as track laborers, they were later employed in the steel mills, the packing plants, and the tanneries. From 1920 to 1930 the Mexican population of Chicago increased from 3,854 to 19,362 and is today generally estimated at about 25,000.

The small Mexican colony in Detroit had its beginnings in 1918, when several hundred Mexican workers were brought to work in the automobile industry as student-workers. From eight thousand in 1920, the Mexican colony in Detroit rose to a peak of fifteen thousand in 1928, and then declined during the depression years, when many workers returned to the Texas communities from which they had been recruited or were repatriated by welfare agencies to Mexico. Today the colony is estimated to number about 6,515 residents. Throughout the Midwest there are similar colonies, usually quite small, in most of the industrial centers, totalling perhaps seventy thousand for the region. In 1923 the National Tube Company, an affiliate of U.S. Steel, brought 1,300 Mexicans from Texas to work in its plant at Lorain, Ohio. And, in the same year, the Bethlehem Steel Company imported about one thousand to work in its plant at Bethlehem, Pennsylvania. When the first trainload arrived from San Antonio, police were on hand to escort the workers to their barracks as the "Mexicans in their broad plain sombreros" marched stoically through the streets.

The movement to import Mexican labor for industrial employment would have reached large proportions after 1923 had it not been for two factors. Both the sugar-beet companies and the Southwestern agricultural interests were strenuously opposed to any attempt to establish a pattern of Mexican employment in industry and also feared that, if Mexicans spread into new territory, the agitation for a quota on Mexican immigration would immediately assume serious proportions. Hence the passage of the Texas Emigrant Agent Law in 1929, and the depression of that year, brought the movement to a halt. The second factor had to do with immigration policy. The first bill aimed at placing Mexican immigration on a quota basis was introduced in 1926 and was supported by a rapidly growing exclusionist sentiment. Largely for diplomatic reasons, the federal government in March, 1929, adopted a policy of "administrative restriction" by simply tightening up the enforcement of existing immigration regulations with the aid and cooperation of the Mexican government. Thus the northbound movement of Mexican immigrants had virtually ceased by 1930; and, in the depression years, some sixty-five thousand Mexican immigrants were repatriated, some voluntarily, some with the aid of the Mexican government, some being summarily shipped back to Mexico by welfare agencies in this country.

This pattern of events has a twofold bearing on the so-called "Mexican Problem" in this country. It explains, to some extent, the concentration of Mexicans in the old borderlands region; and it also explains why so many immigrants have been involved in cul-de-sac types of employment. For the doors of Middle Western industrial employment were closed almost as soon as they were opened; and, in the Southwest, employment opportunities were restricted, by custom, by discrimination, and by other factors, to a few limited types of employment. It is not surprising, therefore, that the 1930 census should show that of Mexicans gainfully employed, ten years of age or over, 189,005 should have been employed in agriculture, 150,604 as common laborers.

9. The Balance Sheet

Testifying before congressional committees in the 'twenties, the principal employers of Mexican labor in the Southwest presented facts and figures showing that Mexicans had been a vital factor in the development of agricultural and industrial enterprises valued at $5,000,000,000. Starting with a scant production in 1900, the Southwest was by 1929 producing between 300,000 and 500,000 carloads of vegetables, fruit, and truck crops,—forty per cent of the nation's supply of these products. Most of this development took place in less than two decades and was directly based on the use of Mexican labor which constituted from sixty-five to eighty-five per cent of the common labor used in the production of these crops. All the gold and silver that have ever been taken from the mountains of Colorado or that may still be awaiting the touch of pick and drill, cannot compare in value to the wealth already produced by sugar beets (10). From 1900 to 1940, Mexican labor constituted sixty per cent of the common labor in the mines of the Southwest and from sixty to ninety per cent of the section and extra gangs employed on eighteen western railroads. Obviously the transformation of the Southwest which has occurred in the last forty years was largely made possible by the use of Mexican labor. Conversely, the employment of Mexicans in the Southwest has been of enormous importance to Mexico in this same period. Some gauge of this importance may be found in the fact that from 1917 to 1927, Mexican immigrants sent a yearly average of $10,173,719.31 in remittances to families in Mexico.

It was not only the availability of Mexican labor for this period that meant so much to the economy of the Southwest, but its exceptional adaptability to the types of work and to the environmental conditions which prevailed throughout the region. Mexicans were inured to the heat, the aridity, the dust, the isolation that prevailed in most of the areas in which they worked. With Oriental immigration barred and European immigration placed on a rigid quota basis, it is, indeed, questionable if employers could have found other available labor sources. While these employers undoubtedly exaggerated the "indispensability" of the Mexican, it is nevertheless apparent that there was a measure of truth in what they said. For example, in 1920, the Department of Labor appointed a committee to investigate the consequences of Mexican immigration. Two of the members of this committee were old-time officials of the American Federation of Labor. Yet this committee reported that the Mexicans who had been imported during the war years had not come into competition with or displaced "white" labor.

In part, the special adaptability of Mexican labor was related to the presence in the Southwest of a large resident Mexican-American population. This circumstance greatly facilitated the use of Mexican labor. From this element came many of the foremen, the straw-bosses, and the contractors who recruited, transported, and supervised Mexican labor. Wherever Mexican immigrants moved in the Southwest, they found colonies of Mexican residents, with Mexican rooming houses, restaurants, barber shops, and stores; and, of course, throughout the

THE BORDERLANDS ARE INVADED

entire area they found Spanish-speaking people. Always a buffer group, the native-born Mexican-Americans were the go-betweens, the conduits, which made possible the rapid, large-scale utilization of Mexican labor.

Nowadays the migratory phase of Mexican immigration is drawing to a close. By 1937 machines had taken over about ninety per cent of the work involved in preparing, bedding, and cultivating the land in produce or truck crops; and the practice of crating produce in the fields, rather than in the sheds, had brought about a noticeable reduction in the number of workers. Utilizing mobile, mechanized packing sheds in the fields, the shipper-growers of Texas, Arizona, and California are nowadays drastically reducing the number of workers required. Mechanical cotton-pickers are reducing the number of pickers in California at the rate of one machine where forty workers were formerly used and at a picking cost of $5 per bale; and the first successful experiment in the mechanization of the sugar-beet industry occurred in 1936 (11).

The use of segmented seed, first introduced in 1943, has already greatly reduced the number of workers needed to thin sugar beets. Blocking and thinning machines have been in use since 1940. Experiments have shown that the use of these machines reduces the man-hours of labor required to thin sugar beets from 27.2 man-hours per acre to 2.5 man-hours per acre. The final step in mechanization in sugar beets is, of course, the introduction of the new mechanical harvester which picks, tops, and sorts the beets. One such machine will replace from six to eight men at harvest time. First placed in general use in 1946, this new harvester is destined to have a revolutionary effect on sugar-beet production. Generally speaking, much of the seasonal farm-labor problem of the past two or three decades has resulted from the much more rapid development of machines and techniques for handling the preparation of the soil, the sowing of crops and their cultivation, than of machines for the harvesting of crops. With the perfection of harvesting machines, the rate of technological displacement in agriculture is certain to increase.

In social terms this means that the isolation of the Mexican is drawing to a close. Large employers of Mexican labor have consistently pursued a policy of isolating Mexicans as a means of holding them to certain limited categories of work. Systematically discouraging all "outside contacts," they have kept Mexicans segregated by occupation and by residence. The effect of this policy has been to create several different labor markets, co-existing in time and space, with each group being relatively insulated from the competition of the others by the different attitudes which employers have cultivated toward particular jobs. This policy has directly fostered antagonism against the Mexican and has severely limited his opportunities for acculturation. Technological change, however, is not solely responsible for the gradual abandonment of this policy. The truth is that the Mexicans have forced its abandonment, as the next chapter will explain.

X

The Second Defeat

Having been defeated in their first encounter with Anglo-Americans in the Southwest, the Spanish-speaking people were naturally somewhat reluctant to seek a new accord. Like other minorities under similar circumstances, they sought to minimize contacts with the dominant group by withdrawing into their own world. As time passed, it seemed as though relations between the two groups might be stabilized on the basis of a bicultural accommodation. But the partial accommodation which had been achieved by 1900 was completely disrupted by the avalanche of immigration. As thousands of immigrants streamed across the border at a dozen points, the old conflict of cultures was renewed. The new immigrants were, of course, fitted into the mold of subordination which had previously crystallized in the borderlands. Once they had become conscious, however, of the way in which they were being subordinated in the social structure, the immigrants attempted to rebel. Dating from the late 'twenties, this rebellion was most decisively crushed.

It is this defeat—the second which Spanish-speaking people have suffered in the borderlands—that explains the present-day tendency of the immigrants to retire within the confines of the Mexican *colonia* and to seek, as their predecessors had sought, a bicultural accommodation. The rebellion of the immigrants found expression in the form of militant trade-unionism; in more than one field, Mexican immigrants have been the pioneers of the trade-union movement in the Southwest.

1. THE MYTH OF DOCILITY

When the tide of immigration reached California (the number of immigrants trebled between 1920 and 1930), the growers were at first most eloquent in their praise of Mexican labor and every attempt to restrict Mexican immigration was strenuously resisted. "No labor that has ever come to the United States," said Dr. George P. Clements of the Los Angeles Chamber of Commerce, "is more satisfactory under righteous treatment. The Mexican as the result of years of servitude, has always looked upon his employer as his *patrón,* and upon himself as part of the establishment." "The Mexican," wrote Ralph Taylor, editorial spokesman for the large shipper-grower interests, "has no political ambitions; he does not aspire to dominate the political affairs of the community in which he lives." Testifying before a congressional committee, a lobbyist for the California growers explained that "the Mexican likes the sunshine against an adobe wall with a few tortillas and in the off time he drifts across the border where he may have these things."

In a speech in 1927, Simon J. Lubin had said that California growers were treating the Mexicans like peons, corralling them in barbed-wire stockades on the ranches. To this charge, the influential *Pacific Rural Press* replied: "Peon? Isn't the word peon a little out of character when applied to a Mexican family which buzzes around in its own battered flivver, going from crop to crop, seeing Beautiful California, breathing its air, eating its food, and finally doing the homing pigeon stunt back to Mexico with more money than their neighbors dreamed existed?"

It is true that the immigrants were at first pleased with the new opportunities which they found in the border states. But as they came to realize that the occupations assigned them and the conditions under which they worked were regarded by American urban labor as undesirable and substandard, they began to show signs of restiveness. Not only were they set apart as a caste,—stereotyped, segregated, and regarded as an inferior "race,"—but the discrimination which they encountered in most California communities had the effect of stimulating them to organize in self-protection. When several hundred cowboys had gone on strike in the Panhandle in 1883—the first attempt to form a union of "agricultural" workers in the United States—the strike call was signed by one Juan Gómez. As early as 1903, over a thousand Mexican and Japanese sugar-beet workers went on strike at Ventura, California. The wave of strikes which culminated in the dynamiting of the Los Angeles *Times* in 1910 was initiated by a strike of Mexican workers on the local street railway. In 1922 Mexican field-workers had sought to establish a union of grape-pickers at Fresno. Most of these early efforts, however, proved to be abortive.

The first stable organization of Mexican workers was established in Southern California in 1927, when the CUOM was formed: the *Confederación de Uniones Obreras Mexicanas,* with three thousand workers organized in twenty locals throughout the region. The first strike called by the union, in Imperial Valley in 1928, was broken by wholesale arrests and deportations. Two years later five thousand Mexican field-workers struck in Imperial Valley for the second time. Caught by surprise, the growers were forced to settle the strike. But a few months later, when the cantaloupe harvest began, the union was viciously attacked before it could call a strike. Over 103 arrests were made and a local newspaper reported that "the county has purchased more tear-gas guns, shells, and bombs than ever before."

In June, 1933, seven thousand Mexicans walked out of the berry, onion, and celery fields of Los Angeles County in the largest strike of agricultural workers that had occurred in California up to that time. It was this strike which first aroused acute apprehensions on the part of the growers that the Mexicans might not be quite as docile as they had imagined. "In my opinion," said Dr. Clements, "this is the most serious outbreak of the Mexican workers here." Later, in the fall of 1933, the left-wing Cannery and Agricultural Workers Industrial Union called a series of great farm strikes in California. Three-fourths of the strikers in the southern San Joaquin Valley were Mexicans who had been drawn to the union, writes Dr. Paul S. Taylor, "by race discrimination, poor housing, and low pay."

Reported at great length and with elaborate documentation in the LaFollette Committee hearings, these strikes were broken by the use of wholesale violence. "We protect our farmers here in Kern County," said a deputy sheriff. "They are our best people. . . . They keep the county going. . . . But the Mexicans are trash. They have no standard of living. We herd them like pigs." Later in the year Mexicans struck for the third time in Imperial Valley. On this occasion, they provoked a whirlwind of violence: union meetings were broken up by tear gas and clubs; several labor lawyers and "outside" spectators were kidnapped by the growers and escorted to the county line; and over eighty-six arrests were made.

In 1936 Mexican field-workers were involved in two strikes in Southern

California which forever ended the infatuation of the growers with Mexican labor and left a heritage of ill-will which still survives in the region. The first of these strikes occurred in the celery fields located, so to speak, in the backyards of Los Angeles County. With two thousand workers on strike, the police marshalled a force of approximately 1,500 armed men to break the strike. When the strikers attempted to march from their headquarters to the fields, Captain William ("Red") Hynes and his men broke up the procession on three successive days. Strikers were pursued by the police to their homes and, in a number of cases, tear-gas bombs were tossed into shacks where children were playing. One striker was seriously wounded and another badly burned when police fired tear-gas bombs from a distance of five or six feet. In the Domingues hills near San Pedro,—on the doorstep of the beautiful Palos Verdes estates,—a miniature battle was staged when police converged on an old barn in which the strikers had barricaded themselves. So many arrests were made that neither the police nor the union could keep a tally. Injured strikers had difficulty in securing medical aid at the county hospital and public funds were used to employ field agents who visited the growers and urged them not to settle. The growers alone spent thousands of dollars in the employment of armed guards recruited from a local strikebreaking detective agency.

In midsummer 1936 a strike of 2,500 Mexicans tied up for several weeks a $20,000,000 citrus crop in Orange County. During this strike, Orange County was in a state of virtual siege; even highway traffic was under close police surveillance. Over four hundred special armed guards were recruited. Two hundred arrested strikers were formally arraigned in an outdoor bull-pen or stockade which served as a courtroom. Guards with rifles and shotguns patrolled the citrus belt and the sheriff issued "shoot-to-kill" orders. I was in court one day when fifty or more strikers were brought in by guards armed with sub-machine guns, rifles, and shotguns. The Los Angeles *Examiner* spoke feelingly of the "quieting effects of the wholesale arrests," while the Los Angeles *Times* gave a graphic account of one raid: "suddenly, late in the night, three or four automobiles loaded with grim faced men, appeared out of the darkness surrounding the little settlement. In a few seconds, tear gas bombs hissed into the small building where the *asserted* strikers were in conclave, the conferees with smarting eyes broke and ran out under cover of darkness and the meeting was at an end." (My emphasis.) In a front-page story on July seventh, the *Times* gleefully announced that "old vigilante days were revived in the orchards of Orange County yesterday as one man lay near death and scores nursed injuries."

2. THE HONEYMOON IS OVER

By 1930 the myth of the docility of Mexican labor had been thoroughly exploded and the Mexicans had fallen in grace in the eyes of the Associated Farmers. "The Mexican on relief," wrote the irrepressible Dr. Clements, "is being unionized and is being used to foment strikes among the few still loyal Mexican workers. The Mexican casual labor is lost to the California farmer unless immediate action is taken to get him off relief."

"Getting the Mexican off relief" involved large-scale forced repatriations to Mexico. I watched the first shipment of "repatriated" Mexicans leave Los Angeles in February, 1931. The loading process began at six o'clock in the morning. *Repatriados* arrived by the truckload,—men, women, and children,—with dogs, cats, and goats; half-open suitcases, rolls of bedding, and lunchbaskets. It cost the County of Los Angeles $77,249.29 to repatriate one trainload, but the savings in relief amounted to $347,468.41 for this one shipment. In 1932 alone over eleven thousand Mexicans were repatriated from Los Angeles. A few years later Dr. Clements was writing that "of the 175,000 Mexicans who from 1917 to 1930 met the agricultural labor requirements of the whole state, moving from place to place to meet seasonal demands, there were possibly not more than 10% available in 1936."

This background is of major importance to an understanding of "attitudes" in Southern California. For it shows, first of all, that Mexicans were quick to rebel against the subordinate status which had been imposed upon them. "The most effective agricultural labor unions during 1935 and 1936," writes Dr. Stuart Jamieson (1), "were those organized among Mexicans." Long charged with a lack of "leadership" and talent for organization, they proved all too effectively that neither talent was lacking.

The strikes in California in the 'thirties, moreover, were duplicated wherever Mexicans were employed in agriculture. Mexican fieldworkers struck in Arizona; in Idaho and Washington; in Colorado; in

Michigan; and in the Lower Rio Grande Valley in Texas. When Mexican sheep-shearers went on strike in west Texas in 1934, one of the sheepmen made a speech in which he said: "We are a pretty poor bunch of white men if we are going to sit here and let a bunch of Mexicans tell us what to do." In 1933 a fifty-car caravan of Mexican workers, members of the *Asociación de Jornaleros,* paraded the length of the Lower Rio Grande Valley in protest against anti-union activity. In 1934 the Mexican pecan-shellers, employed in the sweatshops of San Antonio, struck against piece-rates of 2¢ and 3¢ a pound for shelling pecans. Over six thousand workers were involved in this protracted strike. Later the introduction of shelling machines deprived most of these workers of their jobs, as the number of pecan-shellers was cut from twelve thousand to two thousand (2).

With scarcely an exception, every strike in which Mexicans participated in the borderlands in the 'thirties was broken by the use of violence and was followed by deportations. In most of these strikes, Mexican workers stood alone, that is, they were not supported by organized labor, for their organizations, for the most part, were affiliated neither with the CIO nor the AFL.

"Logic," writes Dr. R. W. Rosskelly, of the Colorado State Agricultural College, "suggests the impossibility of scoffing at the Mexican culture patterns, of indoctrinating them with those of the Nordics and still expecting them to perform a type of labor and live under conditions which Nordic standards taboo. Neither can it be expected that they will willingly relegate themselves to the status of second-class citizens in a country where equal opportunity, regardless of race, is the symbol of freedom." Yet this inconsistency in the treatment of Mexican immigrants continues to be the most conspicuous aspect of Anglo-Hispano relations in the United States.

Nothing illustrates more clearly the degree to which Mexican immigrants have shown a capacity for "assimilation" than the rebellion which they attempted in the 'thirties. In two decades, they had learned to protest, in a typically American fashion, against an annual family wage of $600; against poor housing; and above all, against discrimination. In analyzing these strikes, Dr. Stuart Jamieson points out that Mexicans had become dissatisfied with their "distinct status as a lower caste, which they held because of their poverty, color, and cultural attributes. Their position . . . in many ways came to parallel that of Negroes in the

Southern States. 'White Trade Only' signs appeared in business establishments in some towns, segregation in seating arrangements was imposed in moving picture houses, residential restrictions were applied to real estate, and a sentiment for segregation in the schools was widespread. Mexicans and Spanish-Americans also faced discrimination before the law." Once their commendable efforts toward self-organization were crushed—with violence and gross brutality, with mass arrests, deportations, and "repatriations"—the immigrants became demoralized and momentarily abandoned any attempt to establish a *rapprochement* with the Anglo-Americans. For the suppression of these strikes represented, in effect, a second defeat, a second rebuff.

3. The Gallup Incident

In the middle 'thirties, several thousand Mexican coal miners, employed by the Gallup-American Company in New Mexico (a subsidiary of Kennecott Copper Company), went on strike. Although no violence was reported, the area was placed under martial law for six months. During the strike, three hundred of the miners, most of them immigrants from Chihuahua, settled on a piece of company property which they named Chihuahuaita. Here they built seventy-five or eighty shacks and determined to sit out the strike. Without notifying the occupants, the company sold the property in 1935 to a New Mexico politician. Unable to buy the lots at the prices demanded or to pay the rents which were fixed, they then faced a series of eviction suits. When the first of these eviction suits was brought on for hearing in the local court, a bloody riot ensued. Over a hundred miners were arrested and charged with a variety of offenses. For weeks Gallup was in a state of great excitement as writers and artists flocked in from Santa Fe and Taos to lend the miners a hand (3). During the excitement, Jesús Pallares, a miner from Chihuahua, organized the *Liga Obrera de Habla Española* which soon claimed eight thousand members. Pressure from this organization forced the authorities to abandon criminal syndicalism proceedings which were then pending against the rioters and finally won relief rights for the strikers. But Jesús Pallares met the fate of many Mexican immigrant labor leaders in the borderlands: he was arrested and deported to Mexico.

4. IN THE COPPER MINES

Prior to 1896, the copper miners of Arizona lacked organization. Resembling feudal baronies, the mining camps were an outgrowth of company towns some of which had existed prior to the American conquest. The copper-mining companies had inherited a pre-1846 system of peonage in Arizona which they showed little inclination to change or to abolish. In the early 'seventies, when most of the great copper mines were discovered, common labor was paid 37½¢ a day in the Sonora mines, while furnace-workers received from 50¢ to 75¢ a day. On the American side of the border, according to Sylvester Mowry, the going-rate for Mexican labor was $1 a day, "paid in large part in merchandise at large profits." With a plentiful supply of Mexican labor so near at hand, the American mineowners naturally used Mexican immigrants as common laborers and, in an effort to avert unionization, pitted Mexicans against non-Mexicans. From 1875 to the present time, the copper companies have carried Mexican employees on their payrolls under a special heading of "Mexican Labor" and have paid them at lower rates than those commanded by non-Mexican labor for the same job classifications (4). Uniformly the Mexicans have been segregated in a separate section of the camp known to the Anglo-Americans as "frogtown" or "jim-town."

Needless to say, the non-Mexican miners in the skilled labor classifications have always resented the encroachment of peonage which the appearance of Mexican immigrants has symbolized. In their eyes, the Mexicans have been potential scabs and strikebreakers whose employment at substandard wage rates has served as a constant threat to their jobs and wage standards. It was largely for this reason that certain copper-mining districts, particularly those at Bisbee and Prescott, were for many years "white men's camps" with a tradition that Mexicans were not allowed to stay overnight. Because of this antagonism, the number of Mexicans employed has ranged from twenty per cent in the Bisbee mines to fifty-three per cent at Douglas, fifty per cent at Morenci, and ninety-three per cent at Nacozari. In fact, the first strike in the copper mines occurred in 1896, when the Western Federation of Labor struck at the Old Dominion mine against the employment of Mexican labor.

Trade-union organization in the copper mines dates from the formation of the first trusts and consolidations. "As the copper mining activities grew in magnitude," writes Will H. Robinson, "the close relationship between employer and employee that had obtained in the early days largely disappeared." Troops were called out to suppress one of the first major organizational drives in 1903. In October, 1915, three unions of Mexican miners, numbering about five thousand men, went on strike at the Clifton, Morenci, and Metcalf mines. This strike was largely called over the issue of the "Mexican rate" and against the tyrannous conduct of foremen who sold jobs to Mexicans and forced them to buy tickets in raffles as a condition to holding their jobs. The company sealed up the mouth of the mine with cement and told the strikers "to go back to Mexico." Hundreds of miners were arrested and the National Guard was finally sent in to break the nineteen-week strike (5).

On June 27, 1917, the Arizona copper miners, Mexican and non-Mexican, went on strike. After being out for a month, a vigilante mob rounded up 1,186 of the strikers and shipped them, in boxcars, to Columbus, New Mexico. The Columbus officials would not permit them to detrain so they were taken out and dumped in the desert. Investigating the strike some months later for the federal government, Felix Frankfurter reported that "too often there is a glaring inconsistency between our democratic purposes in this war abroad and the autocratic conduct of some at home." In the aftermath of the famous "Bisbee deportations," Walter Douglas, president of the Phelps-Dodge Company, was indicted in the federal court for his part in the deportations; but the charges were later dismissed.

In 1944, the International Union of Mine, Mill and Smelter Workers, CIO, hailed three companies,—the Miami Copper Company, the Inspiration Consolidated Copper Company, and the International Smelting and Refining Company,—before the National War Labor Board on charges of discriminating against Mexican employees. The board found that these companies classified employees as "Anglo-American Males" and "Other Employees." Included in the latter classification were all females, "Latin-Americans," Negroes, Filipinos, and Indians. If a Mexican with no experience was hired, he was classified as a "common laborer" and paid $5.21 for a shift; but, if an Anglo-American with no experience was hired, he was classified as a "helper" and paid $6.36 per shift. The board also found that "there was no apparent relationship between the length of service of an employee and his wage rate." Workers classified in the "Other Employees" group who had been employed for ten years rarely received more than the starting rate for Mexican labor. "The problem with which the commission is confronted in these cases," to quote from its decision, "is one which is *woven into the fabric of the entire community,* indeed of the entire Southwest. Unions and employers alike have had a part, and a significant part, in its creation and continuation. All the forms in which contemporary society is organized are in varying degrees affected." In its decision, the board ordered the elimination of the discriminatory rates (6).

Somewhat later, in a proceeding involving certain refineries of the Shell Oil Company in Texas, the President's Fair Employment Practice Commission found that the company had two rates of pay for the same work: a "white" rate for Anglo-Americans, and a "non-white" rate, for Negroes and Mexicans. The differential was ten cents an hour. In Region X of the FEPC, embracing New Mexico, Texas, and Louisiana, thirty-seven per cent of the complaints received involved discrimination against Mexicans; and in Region XII, comprising California, Nevada, and Arizona, 22.6 per cent of the cases involved Mexicans.

Following the history-making decision of the National War Labor Board, the copper miners struck throughout the Southwest in March, 1946, largely because the companies had been stalling on compliance with the order of the board. "Before the war," said one of the strikers, Manuel Fraijo, "all good jobs,—hoistman, mechanic, pumpman, and time-keeper,—were held by Anglo-Americans. The low-bracket, common jobs were held by Mexicans. . . . When the war came, millions of men were drafted and sent overseas . . . the majority of those drafted from our town were 'Mexicans.' Curiously enough, a good percentage of these supposedly stupid Mexicans became pilots, radio operators, and radarmen and many became sergeants and lieutenants. . . . Now that we are together again, if only some of these Aryan-minded 'Anglos' would discard their white supremacy theories, they would realize that we are just workers kept divided to be used against each other."

One of the leaders of this strike—he had organized Local No. 509 of the International Union of Mine, Mill and Smelter Workers in El Paso in 1940—was Humberto Silex. Entering the United States in 1921, Silex had served a term of enlistment in the army. Married, the father of seven children, he had resided in El Paso since 1931. Employed by the American Smelting and Refining Company, Silex had organized Local 509, which is largely made up of Mexican-Americans, and had been elected its first secretary; later its president. Discharged for union activity in 1945, he had a fist fight with his foreman and was arrested and fined $35. Like most immigrants in El Paso, Silex held a valid resident alien's border-crossing card and frequently crossed the largely mythical border between El Paso and Juárez. After the strike was called in March, 1946, he was arrested on a warrant of deportation based on the charge that he had committed a crime involving "moral turpitude,"—namely the $35 fist fight,—prior to his last entry into the United States—namely his last pleasure trip to Juárez. One of the outstanding Mexican labor leaders in the Southwest, Silex recently won his fight against deportation in the courts.

5. La Niña de Cabora

Teresa de Cabora, as she was later known, was born in Sinaloa in 1872. An illegitimate child, her father was a wealthy Mexican rancher; her mother a Yaqui Indian. At the age of sixteen she went to live with her father, where a servant-woman, whose name was María, taught her to read. One day she went into a trance which, according to local legend, lasted three months and eighteen days. While in this state of trance, she is also supposed to have "cured" María of paralysis by a gentle laying on of hands. Later she effected many similar "cures" and her fame spread throughout Sinaloa and Sonora, where she went to live in the village of Cabora. Saint Teresa did not claim that she possessed the healing power; she merely said that she was willing to pray for the poor and the sick out of her love for them. This strange girl—"the Saint of Cabora" or "La Niña de Cabora" as she was called—was strongly anti-clerical and preached against the Catholic Church which she said took money from the poor under false pretenses. With hundreds of Mexicans flocking to Cabora from points as distant as Hermisillo and Tomachic just to see and gaze upon La Niña, the hierarchy in Mexico City issued orders to the priests of Sonora to denounce her from the pulpit as a heretic.

Later, at the prompting of the Church, Díaz dispatched a troop of soldiers to arrest La Niña de Cabora. Determined to protect their saint, the Yaqui Indians ambushed the expedition near Cabora. Thus started what was called the "Tomachic War" or the Revolt of the Yaquis. In the course of this "war," Teresa was finally arrested and taken to Guaymas where she was imprisoned. To pacify the Yaquis, however, the governor was finally forced to release her. But constant bickering between La Niña and the priests resulted in the issuance of an order in 1893 for her deportation. Hounded out of Tomacacori and El Paso by the malicious denunciations of the Church, she moved to Clifton, Arizona, in 1897. In the eyes of the Mexican copper miners of Clifton, La Niña was a saint whose prayers and intercessions could heal the sick and restore sight to the blind. By them she was loved and worshipped as a miraculous border-counterpart of the Virgin of Guadalupe. When La Niña married a Yaqui Indian, she was separated from her husband by a mob of irate miners who looked upon the marriage as a sacrilege. Good Catholics that they were—and as this action proved—they ignored the interdictions of the priests and never ceased to worship the anticlerical Saint of Cabora.

It was in Clifton that Teresa cured the daughter of a local Anglo-American banker who, in wonderment and gratitude, took her to Los Angeles that her healing powers might be more widely known. In the magical atmosphere of Our City the Queen of the Angels her fame, needless to say, was instantaneous and a purse was raised to send her on a tour of the United States and Europe. In 1904 she returned to Clifton and, with the money which she had earned on the tour, built a large two-story building which was used as a hospital. And in Clifton she died, eighteen months after her return, "with a smile on her lips." Although the doctors said that she had died of tuberculosis, the Mexicans of Clifton insisted that she had worn out her spirit in the service of their people; to them she is still the Saint of Cabora.

6. The Forty Blonde Babies

It was in Clifton, also, that the famous affair of the forty blonde babies occurred. The same year that La Niña de Cabora had built a hospital for the Mexicans of Clifton, a new priest, whose name was Father Mandin, came to the local Catholic church. One day the new priest received a routine letter from a New York foundling home, asking if there were any good Catholics in Clifton who might want to adopt children. New to Clifton and unfamiliar with his Mexican parishioners, Father Mandin naively read the letter at the next Sunday service. When asked if any of them desired to adopt children, almost the entire congregation, with audible enthusiasm, lifted their hands. Greatly pleased by this generous response, Father Mandin immediately wrote the hospital to send the children along but specified that only those of fair complexion should be sent since the Mexicans had insisted that they wanted "blonde babies."

On October first, forty children from eighteen months to five years of age arrived in Clifton accompanied by Sister Anna Michella. Each child carried a tag which gave its name and birthday and the name of the adopting family. The entire Mexican population of Clifton went with Father Mandin to the station to greet Sister Anna Michella and the forty blonde children. Quite unprepared to cope with the situation, Sister Anna Michella vainly protested that the foster homes would first have to be inspected before she would release the children from her care. But the Mexicans, in a passion of enthusiasm, would not be put off with such technicalities and insisted on immediate delivery of their wonderful blonde wards. After a great deal of argument, Father Mandin upheld the position of his parishioners. Before a child was delivered to its foster parents, however, the parents had first to reimburse Sister Anna Michella for the cost of the clothes in which the children had made the journey and for their rail fare to Clifton. The families immediately paid over the sums stipulated and great enthusiasm prevailed in South Clifton that night as the Mexican community celebrated the arrival of the children.

When word got around that the Mexicans had "bought forty blonde babies" a mob of three hundred angry Anglo-Americans assembled in downtown Clifton. Everyone agreed that the iniquity of the situation cried for redress and so a posse was formed which made the round of the Mexican homes collecting the children. When one Mexican miner suggested that a court order would be necessary before the custody of the children could be changed, a leader of the posse shoved a gun in his ribs and said: "Here's your court order." Once collected the forty children were taken to the local hotel. "It was raining," writes the historian of Clifton, "and the crowd had swollen and they were in an angry mood. There was even talk of hanging the priest." Some of the children were sick, probably from the excitement and the feasts of chili, beans, and tortillas which had been prepared for them. A few, the irate Anglo-Americans noted, even had the odor of beer on their breath. Before the night was over, the children had been parceled out to various residents of Clifton. Later the New York foundling home, bewildered by this strange mix-up in faraway Arizona, brought suit to recapture possession of the children but, in the meantime, adoption proceedings had been perfected, and the Supreme Court of Arizona upheld the adoptions in a decision which was affirmed by the United States Supreme Court. Great was the sorrow of the Mexican copper miners of Clifton when the beautiful blonde children, in their handsomely embroidered hand-stitched garments, were taken from them (7).

7. The Battle of Cananea

In the early years of the century, Ricardo Flores Magon and his brother Enrique, published a newspaper in Mexico City called *Liberación*. Sons of an Indian who had held office under Benito Juárez, they were outspoken critics of the Díaz regime. It was as a result of their activities that the First Liberal Congress was called in Mexico. At this meeting, the liberals declared themselves in favor of land distribution, the eight-hour day, the right to strike, and social insurance, all things for which, presumably, the people had fought a successful revolution. Díaz ignored the first liberal congress, but when the second was called in 1906, federal troops raided the meeting, the Magons were sent into exile, and their newspaper was suppressed.

In exile the Magons established their headquarters in St. Louis where they published a newspaper called *Regeneración,* which called for a revolution against the Díaz regime, and where, on September 28, 1906, they organized the Mexican Liberal Party. From St. Louis copies of the newspaper were smuggled across the border and widely distributed in Mexico. Early in 1906, one of their lieutenants, Enrique Bermúdez, started a newspaper in Douglas, Arizona, which he called *El Centenario.* From Douglas, copies of both newspapers, and other propaganda issued by the Magons, was circulated among the copper miners in La Cananea, Sonora, where a liberal club was formed.

In an effort to keep the *peones* on the haciendas, Díaz had fixed a maximum rate of pay for all non-agricultural employment. This policy fitted in perfectly, of course, with the policies of the Cananea Consolidated Copper Company which, like the companies with which it was affiliated on the American side of the border, consistently paid a lower wage to Mexican employees. That Mexicans should be subject to this type of discrimination in their own country naturally created a situation which the Magons could exploit to advantage. The American-owned Cananea mines employed between eight and nine thousand workers. On June 1, 1906, the company raised the wages of its Anglo-American employees but refused to raise those of its Mexican employees. The Mexican employees—two thousand in number—promptly struck in protest and before the three-day "Battle of Cananea" was over five Americans and thirty Mexicans were dead and property damage of $250,000 had resulted. Buildings were burned and stores were sacked, as armed Mexican strikers carried on a rifle duel with the company guards. Several hundred Anglo-Americans in Bisbee formed a volunteer company and marched across the border to relieve the beleaguered mine officials while Díaz rushed federal troops up from the south. The strike, of course, was broken and the employees were forced to return to work under the same conditions which had prevailed when the conflict began. The leaders of the strike who survived the battle were promptly sent to San Juan de Ulua, a prison fortress on a tiny island in the harbor of Veracruz. Some of them were still confined in the prison when the Díaz regime was finally overthrown.

Until the Cananea strike nothing much in the way of a labor movement had existed in Mexico, for the country was still overwhelmingly agricultural and Díaz had suppressed whatever resistances labor had shown. The present-day Mexican labor movement, therefore, dates from the Battle of Cananea which has been called the first major labor strike in the history of Mexico (8). As a matter of fact, the labor movement in Mexico was largely initiated by returning immigrants from the United States who had observed the ways of organized labor in this country (9).

8. "The Wearers of the Red"

When the Madero revolution was launched in Mexico, the Magons appeared in Chihuahua at the head of a band of a hundred armed men. However they were soon disillusioned with Madero who, as they stated in one of their manifestos, was "a millioniare who has seen his fabulous fortune grow with the sweat and tears of the peons of his hacienda." On their refusal to accept Madero as the leader of the revolution, Orozco, Madero's lieutenant, ordered them to leave Chihuahua. On this exile, they came to Los Angeles where they established their headquarters at 519½ East Fourth Street, now the center of a Mexican neighborhood.

From this headquarters, they sent out an appeal from the "Organizing Junta of the Mexican Liberal Party of Los Angeles" for funds with which they could equip an army to pursue a truly Socialist revolution in Mexico. Los Angeles was "seething with social discontent," as Emma Goldman put it, in these years; and a strong Socialist movement existed in the city. Local chapters of the Socialist Party and the I.W.W. helped the Magons raise money, sponsored the Mexican Liberal Party, and sent speakers to their meetings. In fact, the contributions are said to have averaged more than $1,000 a month.

While they were raising money, the Magons were also recruiting an army for the invasion of Lower California. For commander-in-chief they selected Rhys Pryce, a British soldier of fortune. Admittedly the recruitment was amateurish. Single rifles were borrowed from their owners with the promise to return them, in good order, "when the revolution is over." When the invasion was actually launched, the Magon Army had precisely one machine gun.

Converging from New Mexico, Texas, Arizona, and California, the Magon forces, made up of Mexican immigrants, met at Calexico, on the American side of the border. Under the command of Pryce and three Mexicans named Leyva, Berthold, and Salinas, they crossed the border on May 8, 1910, took Mexicali without much fighting and then captured Tijuana. By the time they had captured these two towns, however, they had run out of ammunition. Once having possession of the customs fees at Mexicali, they thought they would be able to buy whatever arms were needed. But, alas! they collected only $850. All that Ricardo Magon could buy in the way of arms in Los Angeles, with this meager sum, were fifty rifles and some ammunition, which he rushed to the Magonistas in Tijuana. It wasn't until the rifles were unloaded that Magon discovered that they were old, condemned U.S. Army Springfields which had been sold as souvenirs. The ammunition which he had purchased, moreover, would not fit the guns. After a few days, Tijuana was abandoned and the Magonistas began to drift back to Los Angeles and San Diego in small groups. In July of the same year they made another attempt to invade Lower California, but by then Madero had dispatched federal troops to the border and they were easily repulsed.

Shortly after the second battle of Tijuana, the United States government stepped in. The Magons, together with the rest of the Organizing Junta, were arrested and placed in jail on charges of conspiring to violate the neutrality laws. Being in jail, however, did not dampen their revolutionary enthusiasm. They proceeded to name one Tirza de la Toba as general of the Magonistas and delegated him to carry on the revolution until their release. It was Tirza's idea to buy arms in the United States and cache them in Mexico. Raising a force of two hundred men, he began to smuggle arms across the border. In the meantime, however, Congress passed an act in March, 1912, making it illegal to export arms to Mexico and this gave the authorities a chance to go after De la Toba. Although he was never captured, his force was broken up and a large number of rifles and a large store of ammunition were seized.

The trial of the Magons in Los Angeles lasted, in all its phases, from July, 1910, to June, 1912. At the end of the long trial, the brothers were convicted of breaching the neutrality laws of the United States and were sentenced, along with their co-conspirators, to twenty-three months in a federal prison. The trial was a constant source of interest and intense excitement to the Mexican residents of Los Angeles who had known and loyally supported the Magon brothers. Later the prosecuting attorney told a Senate committee that "the courtroom was constantly filled by the followers of the Mexican Liberal Party . . . all Mexicans, the men and the women alike wearing the red badge of the Mexican Liberal Party in the courtroom. Every morning as we began the trial, we would turn around and face a solid phalanx of the wearers of the red."

Ricardo Flores Magon died in Leavenworth Prison. When his body was brought back to Mexico for burial, the Mexican Chamber of Deputies declared a recess in honor of his efforts on behalf of the Mexican labor movement and Mexicans along the border, from San Diego to Brownsville, mourned his passing. According to Walter Prescott Webb, the Texas-Mexicans had also contributed to his revolutionary efforts. Although Mexican immigrants had suffered a second defeat from Anglo-Americans in the borderlands, they had helped launch the movement that was to liberate Mexico.

XI

"The Mexican Problem"

In the vast library of books and documents about ethnic and minority problems in the United States, one of the largest sections is devoted to "the Mexican Problem." There is a curious consistency about the documents in this section. For one thing, the singular is always used. Presumably, also, no problem existed, singular or plural, prior to 1920. *Readers' Guide* lists fifty-one articles on "the Mexican Problem" from 1920 to 1930 by comparison with nineteen articles on the same subject for the previous decade. When these articles are examined, it will be found that "the problem" apparently consists in the sum total of the voluminous statistics on Mexican delinquency, poor housing, low wages, illiteracy, and rates of disease. In other words, "the Mexican Problem" has been defined in terms of the social consequences of Mexican immigration.

It will also be found that the documents devoted to the problem have been deeply colored by the "social work" approach. With the passage of the 1924 Immigration Act, the immigrant social agencies and Americanization institutes simply had to discover a new "problem" and it was the Mexican's misfortune to appear on the scene, sombrero and all, concurrently with the impending liquidation of these agencies. As a consequence, he was promptly adopted as America's No. 1 immigrant problem. The whole apparatus of immigrant-aid social work, with its morose preoccupation with consequences rather than causes, was thereupon transferred to Mexican immigration with little realization that this immigration might not be, in all respects, identical with European immigration.

Once assembled and classified, this depressing mass of social data was consistently interpreted in terms of what it revealed about the inadequacies and the weaknesses of the Mexican character. The data "proved" that Mexicans lacked leadership, discipline, and organization; that they segregated themselves; that they were lacking in thrift and enterprise, and so forth. A mountainous collection of masters' theses "proved" conclusively that Spanish-speaking children were "retarded" because, on the basis of various so-called intelligence tests, they did not measure up to the intellectual calibre of Anglo-American students. Most of this theorizing was heavily weighted with gratuitous assumptions about Mexicans and Indians. Paradoxically, the more sympathetic the writer, the greater seems to have been the implied condescension. All in all, the conclusion is unavoidable that Mexicans have been regarded as the essence of "the Mexican Problem."

The use of this deceptive, catchall phrase has consistently beclouded the real issues by focusing attention on consequences rather than on causes. Actually the basic issues have always had to do with Anglo-Hispano relations in a particular historical setting as influenced by a specific set of cultural, economic, geographical, and social forces. Once these factors are seen in proper perspective, if only in outline form, the elusive character of "the Mexican Problem" vanishes into thin air.

1. The Structure of the Problem

In unravelling the real issues the first question to be raised is: what kind of a minority is the Mexican minority? Here, at the risk of being repetitious, I want to summarize several points. Unlike most European minorities in America, Mexicans have been rooted in space,—in a particular region,—over a long period of years. One of the important factors in "the problem" has always been their relation to, and their feeling about the region in which they are concentrated. As Dr. Carolyn Zeleny has pointed out, they are more like the typical minority in Europe than like the typical European minority in the United States. Mexicans were *annexed by conquest,* along with the territory they occupied, and, in effect, their cultural autonomy was guaranteed by a treaty.

About the closest parallel that can be found in this hemisphere for the Mexican minority is that of the French-Canadians in Quebec. The parallel would be closer, of course, if the Province of Quebec were part of the United States. Then New Mexico could be regarded as the Quebec of the Mexicans and the million or so French-Canadians in the United States might be compared with the Mexican immigrants outside New Mexico. Like the Mexicans, the French-Canadians were "here first"; hence they have shown much the same tenacity about *notre langue, notre foi, nos traditions* that Mexicans have shown. With French-Canadians in the United States the question of *la survivance* is as important as the future of *la raza* is to most Mexicans. Like the French-Canadians in New England, the Spanish-speaking people know that they are Americans. Yet, as Dr. Campa points out, they never speak of themselves in Spanish as *nosotros los americanos* any more than they say *nosotros los españoles*.

What a minority is called by others or how it likes to think of itself is less important than the way members of the minority actually speak of themselves in moments of "unbuttoned frankness." In such moments, Mexican-Americans are likely to say *nosotros, nuestra gente, la raza,* or *nosotros los mexicanos*. But, as Dr. Campa carefully emphasizes, by *mexicanos* they do not mean Mexicans; nor can it be translated as such. Like the French-Canadians, and, I suppose, like all annexed or conquered peoples, the Mexicans have been deeply influenced by discrimination. French culture is indigenous to Quebec in much the same sense that Spanish culture is indigenous in New Mexico. Thus there is a time-factor and a space-factor involved in both situations which is not to be found in the usual European immigrant "problem" in America (1).

The spatial relation of Mexico to the Southwest, the proximity of the border, the closeness of the parent group, are all important factors in "the Mexican Problem." It should also be noted that relations between Anglos and Hispanos have been constantly influenced by the state of relations between the United States and Mexico. The assimilation of Italian immigrants might have assumed a different form, for example, if the United States and Italy had been involved in conflict for a hundred years. In the past, the attitude of Mexican consuls in the Southwest has been much more possessive and paternal than that of Italian consuls toward Italian immigrants. Historically the Southwest was once a part of Mexico—an obvious but all-important factor. Geographically the Southwest is one with the northern portions of Mexico and wars do not alter the facts of geography. Thus a specific set of historical and geographical factors are also very much a part of "the Mexican problem."

Furthermore, a unique set of cultural factors has been involved. Three cultures, not two, have fought for supremacy in the Southwest: Anglo, Hispano, *and* Indian. In fact, the three-sided relationship is so complex, interrelated, and historically interwoven as to defy analysis. Indians were a conquered race despised by Anglo-Americans. Mexicans are related to

Indians by race and culture with the Indian part of their cultural and racial inheritance being more important than the Spanish. Mexicans were consistently equated with Indians by the race-conscious Anglo-Americans. Quite apart from the question of how much Indian blood flows in the veins of the Mexican minority, Mexicans are regarded as a racial minority in the Southwest.

In the past, Indians exploited every tension between Anglos and Hispanos and each of the latter groups attempted to use the Indians against the other. This conflict has not died out. Native New Mexicans have continued to accuse the federal government of showing more concern for its treaty obligations with the Pueblo Indians than for its obligations under the Treaty of Guadalupe Hidalgo—and candor compels the admission that these complaints have been justified. Indians have recovered lost lands or been compensated for their loss and have received heavy financial subsidies from the federal government not granted Spanish-speaking people. But there is still another facet which distinguishes *the* Mexican problem from what have appeared to be similar issues.

2. The Buffer Group

In the United States a minority has long existed within the Mexican minority: the native-born of native-born parents. The census of 1930 estimated the size of this group as 264,338, although it is easily twice this size or larger. The attitude of the buffer group toward the immigrants and of the immigrants toward them has always been highly ambivalent. To the native-born, the immigrant is a *cholo* or *chicamo;* to the immigrant, the native-born is a *pocho*. The immigrant is likely to be "darker," more Indian, than the native-born. The immigrant stresses his Mexican-Indian background; the native-born boasts of his "Spanish" inheritance in blood and culture. The immigrant is, also, more likely to be illiterate and to know less English. Despite the division between the two groups, however, Anglo-Americans regard them as one,—as Mexican,—except for ceremonial occasions when elements of the native-born become "Spanish." On the other hand, the native-born seek to distinguish their status, in the eyes of the Anglo-Americans, by referring to themselves as Spanish-Colonials, Latin-Americans, Spanish-Americans, "native Californians," and similar terms.

While some of the native-born have "passed" completely into the Anglo-American world, the majority have not been able to do so nor have they always wished to do so. Constant discrimination, which became more pronounced with the arrival of the immigrants, has complicated their existence and stiffened their resistance to absorption. The Anglo-Americans, in fact, have made it impossible for them to dissociate themselves, as a group, from the immigrants. Noting this fact, the immigrants have taunted the native-born with the mockery of their citizenship. Criticizing the native-born as renegades, they have derided their customs, morals, and affections. Dr. Gamio quotes a popular *corrido* of the immigrants called *"El Renegado"*—"The Renegade," which he translates as follows:

> You go along showing off
> In a big automobile.
> You call me a pauper
> And dead with hunger
> And what you don't remember is
> That on my farm
> You went around almost naked
> And without sandals.
> This happens to many
> That I know here
> When they learn a little
> American
> And dress up like dudes,
> And go to the dance.
> But he who denies his race
> Is the most miserable creature.
> There is nothing in the world
> So vile as he
> The mean figure of the renegade.
> And although far from you,
> Dear Fatherland,
> Continual revolutions
> Have cast me out—
> A good Mexican
> Never disowns
> The dear fatherland
> Of his affections.

(This *corrido,* incidentally, originated in Los Angeles.)

Paradoxically, however, both groups regard themselves as members of *la raza.* They often live in the same districts; speak the same language; attend the same church; and frequently intermarry. Yet the distinction,—the cleavage,—remains. In some respects, the native-born occupy somewhat the same relation to the immigrants that "light" middle-class Negroes occupy to the masses of "dark" Negroes. The relationship between the two groups is, also, somewhat similar to that between German Jews and Russian Jews.

It is a truism that the expectations which a dominant group hold forth influence the behavior and attitude of a minority. In this respect, the position of the native-born has been ambiguous. In some circles, they are expected to behave "like Mexicans"; elsewhere this expectation is reversed and the tactful assumption is made that they are "Spanish" or "American." This ambiguity explains the conflicting attitudes which the native-born have toward "assimiliation." I know a successful young Mexican-American lawyer in Southern California—one of the few in the region—who takes a most extreme view toward "Americanization." He believes that Mexicans should cut loose entirely from their Mexican background; that they should "mix" more with Anglo-Americans; and that they should, as he says, "quit beefing" about discrimination. But this individual has been highly favored by circumstances, background, and upbringing. It is probably true, as he contends, that he has encountered little discrimination (although he makes this point a little *too* emphatically); but other Mexican-Americans, "darker" than he is, less favored by circumstance, have encountered consistent discrimination and are much less anxious to "mix" with Anglo-Americans.

To some extent the two groups are separated by a "third" culture—that of the native-born. "The cultural contacts of the Mexican immigrants in the United States," writes Dr. Gamio, "are complicated by the fact that besides the modern American civilization there is another and different Mexican-American culture, that of the Americans of Mexican origin. This civilization is American nominally, and exhibits the principal material aspects of modern American civilization, but intellectually and emotionally it lives in local Mexican traditions. This element [the American-born] can be said to constitute a peculiar nationality, within the United States. To the immigrant it is a sort of go-between, since these

Mexican-Americans do not feel racial prejudice against them. Though a struggle occurs between the purely Mexican culture and this semi-Mexican, in the end it often absorbs the Mexican immigrant. With it there can occur a closer fusion than with the purely American culture, for with the latter it already shares many traits, while the great difference between the purely American and the purely Mexican, together with the fact of race prejudice, makes an intellectual, emotional, and traditional disparity too great to be bridged rapidly and perhaps never completely."

3. The Conflict in Cultures

The central plateau region of Mexico has fed immigrants to Texas; the northern mesa and northwestern coastal sections to California. Immigrants from these sections have had certain distinct handicaps. Most of them have been illiterate; a great many were peons in Mexico; and they have been extremely poor (actually undernourished, according to Dr. Gamio). In the main, also, they have come from a society which, prior to 1910, was calculated to rob individuals of a sense of enterprise, thrift, and initiative.

Most Mexican immigrants have come to the United States from a folk culture. A folk culture, writes Dr. Robert Redfield (2), is a small, isolated, non-literate, homogeneous society. Intimate communication among the members of the society is matched by a lack of communication with the exterior world. It is a society in which people have little access to the thought and experience of the past and in which "oral tradition has no check or competitor." The people are much alike and have a strong sense of belonging together and the ways by which recurrent problems are solved have been conventionalized. Economically the folk society is independent of other societies: the people produce what they consume and consume what they produce. There is not much division of labor—one person doing what another does. The tools of production are few and simple. There are no tools to make tools; no rapid, multiple machine manufacture; little use of natural power. "Life," writes Dr. Redfield, "for the member of the folk society, is not one activity and then another and different one; it is one large activity out of which one part may not be separated without affecting the rest." Since behavior is strongly influenced by convention, there is little disposition to reflect upon traditional

"THE MEXICAN PROBLEM"

acts or to consider them objectively and critically. Behavior is personal, with even nature, the animals, and the environment being personalized and invested with human attributes. Obviously the members of such a society are not prepared for a rapid transition to a society which, at nearly every point, negates the values of their folk culture.

In many areas of Mexico, the folk culture centered in the feudalistic hacienda which provided no opportunity for change in status. Ideas of justice were personalized, based on the whims and fancies of the haciendado. Money was meaningless; trade was limited; and the division of labor was simple. Superimposed on this folk society, the ceremonial aspect of the Catholic Church was emphasized somewhat to the detriment of its ethical teachings. Native folk practices were interwoven with church ritual and a "magical mentality" attributed illnesses to *los aires* or evil spirits. Dr. Gamio gives a long list of herbs which he found on sale in a Chicago drug-store that catered to Mexican immigrants; and one can still see a weird variety of herbs, leeches, and patent medicines on sale in the Mexican drug-stores in Los Angeles. Slight wonder, then, that the Mexican peon faltered and became confused and often demoralized when he came in close contact with a highly industrialized, urban society.

Uniformly his culturally conditioned traits have been interpreted in the Southwest as racial or biological. The Mexican was "lawless" and "violent" because he had Indian blood; he was "shiftless and improvident" because such was his nature; his excellence as a stoop-laborer consisted precisely in the fact that he did not aspire to landownership. Point by point, his cultural traits re-enforced the earlier stereotype of "the Mexican."

In the Southwest, the immigrant faced a set of formidable handicaps. A strong prejudice had existed in the region against Mexicans for many years; the tradition of dominance was interwoven into the fabric of the community; generations had been steeped in the Mexican stereotype. Almost by instinct, Anglo-Americans equated Mexicans with Indians. The language handicap would have been much less formidable had the immigrant been literate; but learning to read and write in English involved first learning to read and write in Spanish. Unskilled, in the American sense, the immigrant had little acquaintance with trade-unionism. Even his religion, in such muscularly Protestant states as Texas, served to set him apart.

But his greatest handicap consisted in the migratory character of his employment. "One assimiliates a new culture," writes Dr. Norman Humphrey, "as one did the old one, largely through perception and imitation of examples." Travelling over a wide territory, usually in the company of other Spanish-speaking workers, bossed by a Mexican foreman, living in a Mexican labor camp or shacktown, the immigrant had few chances to learn Anglo-American ways by example or imitation. The presence of a large buffer group of native-born Mexicans also retarded assimilation. The Mexican, moreover, was a late immigrant; "the last man in."

"Near the center of a culture," writes Dr. Humphrey, "are the layers of meaning identified as values"; while, at the periphery, are the utilitarian symbols. When two sharply contrasting cultures come in contact the utilitarian symbols of each are brought into immediate juxtaposition: "utilitarian meaning competes with utilitarian meaning and, in the long run, the meaning having the greater utility supplants that which has the less." Universally, Mexican immigrants, supposedly "incapable of assimilation," have rapidly assimilated the utilitarian phases of Anglo-American culture. High on the list of items which 2,104 immigrants brought back to Mexico from the United States, according to Dr. Gamio, were such items as bathtubs; wooden and metal toilets; refrigerators; metal kitchen utensils; washing machines; metal stoves; sewing machines; and automobiles (thirty-seven per cent returned with cars).

But where the values of the two cultures have been in juxtaposition, the immigrant has been less willing to abandon or to modify the imported cultural pattern. "Spanish speech is retained," writes Dr. Humphrey, "and *la raza* is esteemed." Similarly Dr. Gamio has found that the intellectual culture of Mexico has continued to exert a great influence among Mexican-Americans; that, where values are concerned, they prefer to remain Mexicans. It should be noted, however, that these conclusions were based on studies made in the Southwest. Throughout the Southwest immigrants have been drawn within the folds of existing colonies and opportunities to learn "by perception and imitation," on an individual basis, have been minimized. Immigrants are more limited in their choice of residence, employment, and associations than in the northern industrial communities where a different pattern of acculturation prevails. Persistent discrimination has repelled the immigrant from the value-side of Anglo-American culture.

4. The Pattern of Employment

The basic factor retarding the assimilation of the Mexican immigrant, at all levels, has been the pattern of his employment. A very large proportion of Mexican immigrants were imported, often under contract, by particular employers, for employment in particular industries at particular tasks. With few exceptions, only a *particular class* of employers has employed Mexican labor in the Southwest: large-scale industrial enterprises; railroads; smelters; copper mines; sugar-beet refineries; farm-factories; large fruit and vegetable exchanges. These concerns have employed *many* Mexicans, in gangs, crews, and by families as in the sugar-beet industry. It is not the individual who has been employed but the group. If a concern employs Mexicans, it will usually be found that they dominate or are used exclusively in specific types of employment rather than being scattered through the plant. The universality of this pattern was clearly established in a study made in California in 1930.

In this same study it was found that the jobs for which Mexicans were employed en masse had certain basic characteristics: they were undesirable by location (as section-hand jobs on the desert sections of the rail lines or unskilled labor in desert mines and cement plants); they were often dead-end types of employment; and the employment was often seasonal or casual. Between 1914 and 1919 the number of Mexicans in the citrus industry in California increased from 2,317 to 7,004 (thirty per cent of the total); today some 22,000 Mexicans are employed. In effect, Mexicans work, not for individual citrus growers, but for the California Fruit Growers Exchange. The exchange bears about the same relationship to "farming" that the typical industrial plant in which Mexicans are employed bears to "business": it is highly organized; it represents an enormous capital investment; and it is an enterprise which provides no ladder of advancement for field and packing-house employees. One could count on the fingers of one hand the number of Mexicans who have become owners of citrus groves or who have risen to managerial positions in the exchange.

To keep Mexicans earmarked for exclusive employment in a few large-scale industries in the lowest brackets of employment, their employers have set them apart from other employees in separate camps, in company towns, and in segregated *colonias*. Traditionally, Mexicans have been paid less than Anglo-Americans for the same jobs. These invidious distinctions have re-enforced the Mexican stereotype and placed a premium on prejudice. By employing *large* numbers of Mexicans for *particular* types of work, employers have arbitrarily limited the immigrants' chance for the type of acculturation that comes from association with other workers on the job. The pattern of employment has, in turn, dictated the type and location of residence. Segregated residential areas have resulted in segregated schools; segregated schools have re-enforced the stereotype and limited opportunities for acculturation. In setting this merry-go-round in motion, the pattern of employment has been of crucial importance for it has stamped the Mexican as "inferior" and invested the stereotype with an appearance of reality. "There are people," writes Bogardus, "who insist on thinking that the Mexican is unable to rise above an unskilled labor level. They cannot visualize a Mexican immigrant on any other plane."

The pattern of employment has consistently fostered prejudice by jeopardizing or appearing to threaten, the standards of the trade-unions. Always opposed to Mexican immigration, the American Federation of Labor has permitted many of its affiliates to bar Mexicans from membership. Exclusion from trade-unions has, of course, closed another avenue of escape from the merry-go-round and provided a further sanction for the stereotype. By keeping Mexicans segregated occupationally, employers have created a situation in which the skilled labor groups have naturally regarded Mexicans as *group* competitors rather than as individual employees. The nature of the situation has thus inclined such groups as the AFL to take a narrow, particularistic view of Mexican immigration and to regard Mexican labor as "cheap labor."

In some areas, as in west Texas, it is also apparent that the use which has been made of Mexican labor has tended to drive out Anglo-American small farmers and tenants. With the labor of the small farmer and tenant being necessarily in competition with the paid labor of the large-scale farm, cheap agricultural wage rates have been a powerful factor working toward concentration in farm ownership and production. In the various congressional hearings on Mexican immigration, small farmers were invariably lined up with organized labor in opposition to Mexican immigration. While the conflict has always been economic, it has consistently been rationalized as racial or cultural in character.

The far-reaching ramifications of the pattern of employment can scarcely be overemphasized. In the citrus belt communities, the California Fruit Growers Exchange has long exercised a decisive influence on local affairs. It has been in a position to influence—and has not hesitated to influence—local school-board policies and to affect the attitude of the police, the courts, and the townspeople. When Mexican workers have gone on strike, the townspeople have generally been arrayed against them. Therefore it is patently nonsensical to regard segregated schools for Mexicans as a more or less "natural" outgrowth of "differences," racial or cultural in character, between Anglos and Hispanos. A copper town is dominated by the mine ownership and management; a sugar-beet town reflects the attitude and policies of the sugar-beet refineries, etc.

5. THE *Colonia* COMPLEX

Scattered throughout Southern California outside Los Angeles are, perhaps, 150,000 or 200,000 Mexicans and Mexican-Americans, for the most part immigrants or the sons and daughters of immigrants. Approximately thirty per cent of the total is made up of "aliens" but the alien element is rapidly diminishing. Most of these people—perhaps eighty per cent of them—live in "colonies" or *colonias* which vary in size from a cluster of small homes or shacks to communities of four, five, six, eight, and ten thousand people (3).

The history of these settlements is almost uniformly the same. They came into existence some twenty or thirty years ago when the first immigrants began to arrive. Most of them are located in unincorporated areas adjacent to a town or city but invariably on "the other side" of something: a railroad track, a bridge, a river, or a highway. Site location has been determined by a combination of factors: low wages, cheap rents, low land values, prejudice, closeness to employment, undesirability of the site, etc. None of the colonies was laid out or planned as a community, although a few are located on the sites of abandoned "boom towns." Some are outgrowths of labor camps; others have been grafted on a pre-1900 *barrio;* while a few have come into existence more or less accidentally. For example, the settlement known as Hick's Camp came into existence thirty-three years ago when a river-bottom camp was washed out by a flood. The health authorities and the Red Cross moved the families to the river bank where a squatter camp grew up because the land was cheap. Nowadays completely surrounded, the *colonia* in San Gabriel is located near the old Mission—one of the few cases where a Mexican settlement is to be found at the center of an Anglo-American community.

North Town, a community near Upland, is a fairly typical *colonia*. Located on the site of an abandoned subdivision, it is within fifteen minutes' driving radius of the wineries, packing houses, truck farms, and citrus groves where most of the residents are employed. Here a few Mexican families lived before the great wave of migration began and to these residents the immigrants attached themselves. Today some 1,500 Mexicans live in the six square blocks of North Town surrounded, on all sides, by agricultural land. North Town has a small grocery store; a pool hall; and a motion picture theater. Most of the residents, however, make their purchases in Upland. Two or three blocks from the village is an elementary school in which the enrollment is ninety-five per cent Mexican.

With as many as three shacks to a lot, the structures are unpainted, weatherbeaten, and dilapidated. The average house consists of two or three rooms and was built of scrap lumber, boxes, and discarded odds-and-ends of material. Ten, twenty, and thirty years old, the houses are extremely clean and neat on the inside and much effort has obviously gone into an effort to give them an attractive appearance. Virtually all the homes lack inside toilets and baths and a large number are without electricity. Almost every family owns an automobile, a radio, and any number of American-made household gadgets of one kind or another. Being unincorporated, almost all forms of municipal service are lacking. Water is purchased from a private owner at rates higher than those paid by the conspicuously successful residents of Upland. North Town is one of dozens of similar *colonias* scattered all the way from Santa Barbara to San Diego. Occasionally the *colonia* is part of an incorporated town or city with the Mexican population comprising from twelve to twenty-five per cent or more of the total population.

It would be misleading, however, to convey the impression that the location of the *colonias* was accidental or that it has been determined by the natural play of social forces. On the contrary, there is a sense in which it would be accurate to say that the location of the *colonias* has been carefully planned. Located *at just sufficiently* inconvenient distances from the parent community, it naturally became most convenient to establish separate schools and to minimize civic conveniences in the satellite *colonia*. "Plainly," writes Fred W. Ross, "it was never intended that the *colonias* were to be a part of the wider community; rather, it was meant that they were to be apart from it in every way; *colonia* residents were to live apart, work apart, play apart, worship apart, and unfortunately trade, in some cases, apart."

The physical isolation of the *colonias* has naturally bred a social and psychological isolation. As more and more barriers were erected, the walls began to grow higher, to thicken, and finally to coalesce on all sides. The building of the walls, as Mr. Ross puts it, "went on concomitantly from without and from within the *colonia,* layer by layer, tier by tier." While the walls may have the appearance of being natural growths, they are really man-made. For the relationship that finally emerged between parent and satellite community is the civic counterpart of the relationship between the California Fruit Growers Exchange and its Mexican employees.

Living in ramshackle homes in cluttered-up, run-down shacktowns, set apart from their neighbors, denied even the minimum civic services, the residents of the *colonia* have come to resent the fenced-in character of their existence. They are perfectly well aware of the fact that they are not wanted, for their segregation is enforced by law as well as by custom and opinion. That the *colonias* lack swimming pools might be explained in terms of the ignorance or indifference of the Anglo-Americans were it not for the revealing circumstance that Mexicans are also denied access to municipal plunges in the parent community. Hence the ostracism of the Mexicans cannot be accounted for in the facile terms in which it is ordinarily rationalized.

When public-spirited citizens in the parent community have sought "to do something about the Mexican Problem," they have generally sought to impose a pattern on the *colonia* from without. Establishing a clinic or reading-room or social center in the *colonia* has no doubt been helpful; but it has not changed, in the slightest degree, the relationship between parent and satellite community. In the face of this reality, it is indeed annoying to hear Anglo-Americans expatiate about the Mexicans' "inferiority complex" and to charge them with being clannish and withdrawn. Friendly, warm-hearted, and generous to a fault, it would be difficult to find a people more readily disposed to mingle with other groups than the Spanish-speaking people of the Southwest. Their "inferiority complex" is really a misnomer for a defeatist attitude arising from their frustration at being unable to break out of the *colonia*.

Resenting the implication of inferiority that attaches to segregated schools and being well aware of economic discrimination, a majority of the youngsters have not bothered to transfer from the segregated elementary school to the usually non-segregated high school. Dropping out of school at the eighth grade level, they have been unable to compete successfully with Anglo-Americans for the more desirable jobs and have fallen back on those for which their fathers were imported. According to the census of 1930, only 5,400 Mexicans were to be found in clerical jobs; 1,092 were teachers; 93 were lawyers and judges; and 165 were physicians and surgeons—this in a population of close to three million people. Once the cycle of employment has been repeated in the second and third generation, writes Mr. Ross, "the insidious process, which began so long ago with low wages and relatively low, dominant group hostility, almost swings full circle." By the time this has happened, the hostility of the dominant group is fully reciprocated" (4).

Hedged in by group hostility, the immigrants long ago lost interest in citizenship. Lack of funds, the language difficulty, and illiteracy were important factors but not nearly as influential as segregation and discrimination. Mexicans have never been encouraged, by prevailing community attitudes, to become citizens. Bogardus, who studied the problem years ago, concluded that in both rural and urban areas segregation was primarily responsible for the lack of interest in citizenship. For the last twenty years, the number of Mexicans who have been naturalized has averaged about a hundred a year. In a Mexican community of fifty thousand in California, Bogardus found only 250 registered voters in 1928, not all of whom were of Mexican descent. In the same year, Charles A. Thompson reported that only two or three naturalization petitions a year were filed in El Paso with a Mexican population of fifty thousand. To some extent, of course, this reluctance to seek naturalization may be traced to the fact that so many Mexican immigrants are in the United States illegally; but this, too, has been a secondary factor. Voluntary disenfranchisement, whatever the cause, has perpetuated the caste-like social structure in which Mexicans are encased.

The second generation, however, has begun to show a lively interest in the ballot. Residents of a few citrus belt settlements have, in recent years, elected Mexican-Americans to school boards and city councils and have begun to exercise a measure of their great potential political strength. Wherever they have "come of age" politically, an immediate change has been noted in the attitude of the Anglo-Americans. Anglo-American politicians cannot afford to ignore the needs of Mexican-American communities if the residents will assert their political rights. Acting in liaison with the well-organized Negro community in Los Angeles, Mexicans could easily become a balance-of-power group.

While a few political victories have been won, it requires no special insight to foresee that a point will soon be reached when a serious struggle will develop between Anglos and Hispanos. The average Anglo-American community will accept, if somewhat reluctantly, one Mexican-American on the city council or the school board; but there are communities in which Mexican-Americans could elect a majority of the officeholders. In these communities, resistances will stiffen for the stakes are high. Once this has happened, Mexican-Americans will have to seek out allies in those segments of the Anglo-American community which are now disposed to cooperate with them, namely, in the liberal-labor-progressive groups. By comparison with Negroes, Mexicans are still novices in the tactics and strategy of minority-group action and politics.

6. THE NORTHERN SETTLEMENTS

In the Middle Western industrial centers, Mexicans have been brought into much sharper and fuller contact with Anglo-American culture than in the Southwest. Here the colony is strikingly similar to that of the typical "foreign" settlement. Much less mobile than their compatriots in the Southwest, Mexicans in Chicago and Detroit work with members of other nationality groups in highly mechanized industries. The boundaries of the *colonia* are not sharply defined and, in some cases, have already disappeared. Since nearly one-third of the "northern" Mexicans have been *solos* or single men, the rate of intermarriage has been higher than in the Southwest. Originally concentrated in packing plants, tanneries, steel mills, foundries, and railroad yards, Mexican labor is today more widely and more typically distributed. Generally speaking, Mexicans are less sharply set apart in the Midwest industrial centers than in the Southwest. In Chicago and Detroit, Mexicans are merely another immigrant group; in the Southwest they are an indigenous people.

The tendency to regard Mexicans as a "racial minority" is much less pronounced in the Midwest and there is less discrimination. As might be expected, therefore, a much higher proportion have applied for citizenship and English tends to be substituted for Spanish as the language of the home. The lack of cohesion and unity in these colonies is reflected in many ways. For example, Archbishop Mooney in Detroit has strongly discouraged the development of group-consciousness among his Mexican parishioners. Priests have been forbidden to give any encouragement to the idea of a church especially for Mexicans and have been warned that no racial or nationality distinctions, so far as Mexicans are concerned, will be tolerated. Perhaps no one detail points up the contrast between these communities and those in the Southwest more sharply than Dr. Humphrey's comment that in Detroit Mexicans refer to themselves simply as "Mexicans" and show little sensitivity to the term.

The story of the Lorain, Ohio, colony is quite typical of the Midwest settlements which nowadays total around 75,000 Mexicans. In 1923 the National Tube Company, an affiliate of United States Steel Corporation, imported 1,500 Mexicans from Texas to replace an equal number of Negroes (throughout the Midwest, Mexicans have been used to "dilute" or "thin out" Negro labor). From time to time, the colony was augmented by new recruits and by replacements drawn to Lorain from the beet fields of the Midwest. At first most of the Mexicans lived in the boxcars in which they had travelled north but most of them have since moved into small homes and apartments. Originally employed by National Tube or the Baltimore and Ohio Railroad, many of them have now secured jobs in restaurants, dry-cleaning shops, trucking firms, and other miscellaneous occupations.

The homes in Lorain reflect a striking mixture of the two cultures. "American radios," writes Robert O. O'Brien, "are covered with zarapes and bits of Indian pottery. Stone *metates* grind out corn which is cooked on gas and even on electric stoves. American phonographs play South American tangos and Mexican marches. Mexican trunks contain a mixture of objects from Gringo Sunday clothes to old country sombreros. Corona typewriters in vivid colors compete for space with bits of cactus from the Southwest. Bottles of medicine from Lorain doctors

"THE MEXICAN PROBLEM"   223

vie with patent medicines or Mexican 'teas' for position on the bathroom shelf. . . . American 'canned' food is supplemented by *enchiladas, chili verde,* and *tamales.*" A Lorain merchant sold thirty-six typewriters to Mexican residents in a year, all but two of them being equipped with a Spanish language keyboard. Here the second generation is already far removed from the first and the parents are vainly seeking to arrest the process by attempting to "Mexicanize" their children. It is a foregone conclusion that the northern Mexican settlements will have largely vanished in another generation.

7. *Qué Maravilla!*

The oldest settlers in Los Angeles, Mexicans were pushed aside and swept under by the extraordinary velocity and volume of Anglo-American migration after the first great "land booms" in the 'eighties. Isabel Sherrick, a Middle Western journalist, reported in the 1880's that the Mexicans "little by little are being crowded out and one by one the adobes are falling into ruins or giving way to the thrifty homes of Americans." Some of the sections in which Mexicans formerly lived are today occupied by factories, terminal facilities, and office buildings.

The typical residence of Mexicans in early-day Los Angeles was the "house court" derived from the Mexican *vecindad:* a sort of tenement made up of a number of one- and two-room dwellings built around a court with a common water supply and outdoor toilets. This same type of settlement, similar to the *plaza,* is still quite common in Los Angeles, San Antonio, and El Paso. House-courts multiplied in Los Angeles as the demand for Mexican housing became acute with high land costs and rising rents. In 1916 the city had 1,202 house-courts, occupied by 16,000 people with 298 house-courts being occupied exclusively by Mexicans (5). In some respects, the house-court was not unlike the "bungalow courts" of a later period. The house-court areas quickly became slums as the city pushed westward from its original center in the old Plaza section. One of the first studies of Mexican housing conditions indicated that some twenty or thirty thousand Mexicans were living in the courts of Old Sonoratown, near the Plaza, in the shacks and houses of Chavez Ravine, and similar areas, and in the railroad labor camps. The houses and courts had dirt floors; wood was used for fuel; there were no bathing facilities; and the outdoor hydrant and toilet, used by a group of families, were universal. Made in 1912, this survey is still up-to-the-minute so far as Mexican housing is concerned, for little improvement has occurred in the last thirty-five years.

When the great wave of Mexican immigration reached Los Angeles, an unincorporated section on the "east side" known as Belvedere became the principal area of "first settlement" for most of the immigrant families. *"Qué Maravilla!"* the immigrants exclaimed when they first arrived in Los Angeles: what a marvel! what a wonderful city! Maravilla was their name for Belvedere and Maravilla it still is to thousands of Mexicans. With a Mexican population of fifty thousand in the middle 'twenties, the Belvedere section has a population today, mostly Mexican, of around 180,000. A city in size, it is still governed by remote control as an unincorporated area.

Aside from Maravilla, Mexicans are nowadays scattered in "pockets" of settlement in Los Angeles. While they are not segregated as rigidly as Negroes, the various pocket-settlements are almost exclusively Mexican and are, if anything, more severely isolated than the *colonias* of the outlying sections. The "pockets" are all similar in character,—Chavez Ravine, Happy Valley, *El Hoyo* (The Hollow), and the rest. Chavez Ravine, located in the hills between Elysian Park and North Broadway, is an old Mexican settlement. Shacks cling precariously to the hillsides and are bunched in clusters in the bottom of the ravine. For forty years or more, the section has been without most of the ordinary municipal services. At various points in the ravine, one can still see large boards on which are tacked the rural mail-boxes of the residents—as though they were living, not in the heart of a great city, but in some small rural village in the Southwest. Goats, staked out on picket lines, can be seen on the hillsides; and most of the homes have chicken pens and fences. The streets are unpaved; really trails packed hard by years of travel. Garbage is usually collected from a central point, when it is collected, and the service is not equal to that which can be obtained in Anglo districts bordering the ravine. The houses are old shacks, unpainted and weather-beaten. Ancient automobile bodies clutter up the landscape and various "dumps" are scattered about. The atmosphere of the ravine, as of *El Hoyo* and the other pocket-settlements, is ancient, antiquated, a survival,—something pushed backward in time and subordinated.

One can make a swift turn off the heavy traffic of North Figueroa or

North Broadway and be in Chavez Ravine in a minute's time. In this socially regressive dead-end, goats bleat and roosters crow and children play in the dirt roads. Were it not for the faraway hum of traffic, a visitor might well imagine that he was in some remote village in New Mexico or Arizona. From the City Hall to Chavez Ravine is a five-minute drive by modern traffic-time; sociologically, the two points are separated by a time-span of between fifty and seventy-five years. Today a great modern highway span is being built over the Hollow. Bulldozers have moved in and houses have been jacked-up and lifted out of the way. The shacks not directly in the way of the juggernaut mechanical progress of the city are now left perched on the sides of the Hollow, thirty years old, still bady in need of paint, gradually falling apart. Thousands of motorists will rush over the new span every hour, travelling so fast that they will probably not even notice that they are passing over the remains of what was once a small Mexican village.

At 720 San Vicente Boulevard, near the intersection of San Vicente and Santa Monica—on the "west side" of Los Angeles—is an ironic little island of Mexicans completely surrounded by middle-class residences many of which have been built in the so-called "Spanish-Colonial" style with white stucco walls, patios, and red-tiled roofs. This "island" is a thirty-year-old Pacific Electric labor camp where forty Mexican families live as they might live in a village in Jalisco. The company has generously provided four "outside" showers for 120 residents. It has even provided them with "hot water"—on Mondays, Wednesdays, and Saturdays! The only facilities for washing clothes or dishes consist of outside sinks, detached from the shacks in the court, and used by all the families. Probably not one per cent of the people who live in the surrounding areas know or have ever heard of the camp's existence.

What the Mexican immigrants probably think of Maravilla today is suggested by one of their best-known *corridos*—*El Enganchado* * (literally, "the hooked-one"—the labor contractor):

> I came under contract from Morelia
> To earn dollars was my dream,
> I bought shoes and I bought a hat
> And even put on trousers.
>
> For they told me that here the dollars
> Were scattered about in heaps;

* Quoted from *Mexican Labor in the United States* by Dr. Paul S. Taylor.

That there were girls and theaters
And there here everything was good fun.

And now I'm overwhelmed—
I am a shoemaker by trade
But here they say I'm a camel
And good only for pick and shovel.

What good is it to know my trade
If there are manufacturers by the score,
And while I make two little shoes
They turn out more than a million.

Many Mexicans don't care to speak
The language their mothers taught them
And go about saying they are Spanish
And deny their country's flag.

Some are darker than *chapote* *
But they pretend to be Saxon;
They go about powdered to the back of the neck
And wear skirts for trousers.

The girls go about almost naked
And call *la tienda* "estor"
They go around with dirt-streaked legs
But with those stockings of chiffon.

Even my old woman has changed on me—
She wears a bob-tailed dress of silk,
Goes about painted like a *piñata* **
And goes at night to the dancing hall.

My kids speak perfect English
And have no use for our Spanish
They call me "fader" and don't work
And are crazy about the Charleston.

I'm tired of all this nonsense
I'm going back to Michoacan;
As a parting memory I leave the old woman
To see if someone else wants to burden himself.

* *chapote*—black tar.
** *piñata*—a gaily-colored container.

XII

The Pattern of Violence

In March, 1942, the Japanese were excluded from the West Coast and the remaining citizens found, rather to their surprise, that this drastic wartime measure had not solved all their social and economic problems as the more rampant West Coast newspapers had led them to believe. Problems which had existed before the Japanese exclusion still existed, intensified by the war activities which involved most of Southern California. In Los Angeles, where fantasy is a way of life, it was a foregone conclusion that Mexicans would be substituted as the major scapegoat group once the Japanese were removed. Thus within a few days after the last Japanese had left, the Los Angeles newspapers, led by the Hearst press, began to play up "Mexican" crime and "Mexican" juvenile delinquency, as though the Mexican element in crime and delinquency could be considered apart from the ordinary crime experienced by a large, congested metropolitan area in wartime.

A number of minor incidents in the spring of 1942 enabled the newspapers and the police to build up, within the short period of six months, sufficient anti-Mexican sentiment to prepare the community for a full-scale offensive against the Mexican minority. Once prepared, of course, this sentiment could be expected to assume violent expression with the first major incident. A young Mexican who had been arrested and sentenced to forty-five days in jail for having accosted a woman was, upon his release, taken before the Grand Jury and, if you please, re-indicted for rape, on the same offense, and promptly sentenced to prison for twelve years! The case was quickly appealed and, of course, the conviction was reversed. A short time later, a group of Mexican men, celebrating a wedding, were arrested for playing a penny crap game, an offense usually ignored by the police as being inconsequential. But, in this instance, a "conspiracy" indictment was secured from the Grand Jury, thereby neatly converting a petty misdemeanor into a felony charge.

On July 13, 1942, the press gave great prominence to a story involving a fight between two groups of Mexican boys, the Belvedere "gang" and the Palo Verde "gang." In all these preliminary "incidents" pointed mention was made of the "Mexican" character of the people involved. By these techniques, the groundwork was carefully prepared for the "big incident."

1. The Case of Sleepy Lagoon

On the afternoon of August 1, 1942, Henry Leyvas, a young Mexican-American, had taken his girl for a drive near a little pond in a gravel pit near what was called the Williams Ranch on the east side of Los Angeles. In lieu of other recreational facilities, this abandoned gravel pit had long been used by Mexican youngsters in the neighborhood as a swimming pool. Early that evening, a Saturday night, Leyvas and his girl had been set upon by members of a rival "gang" and a fight had occurred. (Leyvas himself was a member of a group known as the 38th Street "gang.")

Later, the same evening, Leyvas returned to the gravel pit with members of his own gang, in several cars, to look for the troublemakers. Some of the members of this sortie knew that Leyvas intended "to get even," but others merely went along for the ride and a swim and a general good time. Finding the gravel pit deserted, they discovered that a party was in progress at a nearby house belonging to the Delgadillo family and decided "to crash the gate." Some fighting and scuffling occurred at the Delgadillo home and the invaders, after a time, left the scene of the party.

Early on the morning of August second, the body of young José Díaz was picked up from a dirt road near the Delgadillo house and taken to the General Hospital where Díaz died without ever regaining consciousness. The autoposy showed that he had met his death as the result of a fracture at the base of the skull. He had apparently been in a fight for his hands and face were bruised but there were neither knife nor gun wounds on the body. The road where his body was found was well travelled and the autopsy showed that he was probably drunk at the time of his death. Díaz had left the Delgadillo home with two friends—presumably the last persons to have been with him prior to his death.

Never called as witnesses, their version of what happened to Díaz is not known. The autopsy surgeon, it should be noted, testified that Díaz could have met his death by repeated hard falls on the rocky ground of the road and admitted that the injuries at the base of his skull were similar to those seen on the victims of automobile accidents. Such are the facts of the case.

With the prior background in mind, it is not surprising that the Los Angeles press welcomed the death of Díaz like manna from the skies. Around the essentially bare facts of the case, they promptly proceeded to weave an enormous web of melodramatic fancy. The old gravel pit was dubbed "The Sleepy Lagoon" by a bright young reporter and the whole case was given an air of sordid mystery. Quick to cooperate, the police rounded up twenty-four youngsters, all alleged to be members of the 38th Street "gang," and charged them with the murder of Díaz. Two of them had the wit to demand separate trials and the charges against them were later dropped. But to a fantastic orchestration of "crime" and "mystery" provided by the Los Angeles press, seventeen of the youngsters were convicted in what was, up to that time, the largest mass trial for murder ever held in the county.

In the process of "investigating" the case, the police severely beat up two of the boys. While testifying that he had been beaten by the police, one of the boys was shown a photograph by the prosecution. This photograph had been taken of him, purportedly, just prior to his entering the Grand Jury room, and indicated that, at that time, he was unmarked and unbeaten. The boy then pulled from his pocket a photograph which had been taken by a newspaper photographer just as he was leaving the Grand Jury room. This untouched photograph showed him with severe bruises about the head and face. Anna Zacsek, attorney for Leyvas, testified that she had walked into a room at the police station where her client, handcuffed to a chair, was being beaten by the police, and that she found him barely conscious, smeared with his own blood. Held incommunicado while they were being "worked over" by the police, the defendants were then marched, en masse, to the Grand Jury which proceeded to indict the lot of them for first-degree murder. When they appeared before the Grand Jury they were dirty, haggard, bruised—a thoroughly disreputable-appearing group of youngsters completely terrified by the treatment they had just received. Who were these "criminals,"—these hardened "gangsters"?

Henry Leyvas, twenty, worked on his father's ranch. Chepe Ruiz, eighteen, a fine amateur athlete, wanted to play big league baseball. In May, 1942, his head had been cracked open by the butt of a policeman's gun when he had been arrested on "suspicion of robbery," although he was later found not guilty of the charge. In San Quentin Prison, where he and the others were sent after their conviction in the Sleepy Lagoon case, Ruiz won the admiration of the warden, the prison staff, and the inmates when he continued on in a boxing match, after several of his ribs had been broken. Robert Telles, eighteen, was working in a defense plant at the time of his arrest. Like many Mexican youngsters on the east side, he had remarkable skill as a caricaturist and amused his co-defendants during the trial by drawing caricatures of the judge, the jury, and the prosecutor. Manuel Reyes, seventeen, had joined the navy in July, 1942, and was waiting induction when arrested. Angel Padilla, one of the defendants most severely beaten by the police, was a furniture-worker. Henry Ynostrosa, eighteen, was married and the father of a year-old girl. He had supported his mother and two sisters since he was fifteen. Manuel Delgado, nineteen, also a woodworker, was married and the father of two children, one born on the day he entered San Quentin Prison. Gus Zamora, twenty-one, was also a furniture-worker. Victor Rodman Thompson, twenty-one, was an Anglo youngster who, by long association with the Mexican boys in his neighborhood, had become completely Mexicanized. Jack Melendez, twenty-one, had been sworn into the navy before he was arrested. When a dishonorable discharge came through after his conviction, he said it was "like kicking a guy when he's down." John Matuz, twenty, had worked in Alaska with the U.S. Engineers.

These, then, were the "criminals," the "baby gangsters," the "murderers" who provided Los Angeles with a Roman holiday of sensationalism, crime-mongering, and Mexican-baiting. From the very outset, a "gang" was on trial. For years, Mexicans had been pushed around by the Los Angeles police and given a very rough time in the courts, but the Sleepy Lagoon prosecution capped the climax. It took place before a biased and prejudiced judge (found to be such by an appellate court); it was conducted by a prosecutor who pointed to the clothes and the style of haircut of the defendants as evidence of guilt; and was staged in an atmosphere of intense community-wide prejudice which had been whipped up and artfully sustained by the entire press of Los Angeles.

From the beginning the proceedings savored more of a ceremonial lynching than a trial in a court of justice. The defendants were not allowed to sit with their counsel—there were seven defense attorneys—and were only permitted to communicate with them during recesses and after adjournment. For the first weeks of the trial, the defendants were not permitted to get haircuts and packages of clean clothes were intercepted by the jailer on orders of the prosecutor. As a consequence of this prejudicial order, the defendants came trouping into the courtroom every day looking like so many unkempt vagabonds. Following a trial that lasted several months and filled six thousand pages of transcript, they were convicted on January 13, 1943: nine were convicted of second-degree murder plus two counts of assault and were sentenced to San Quentin Prison; others were convicted of lesser offenses; and five were convicted of assault and sentenced to the county jail.

Following the conviction, the Sleepy Lagoon Defense Committee was formed which raised a large fund to provide new counsel and to appeal the case. I served as chairman of this committee and Harry Braverman, a member of the Grand Jury who had tried to stop the indictment, served as its treasurer. On October 4, 1944, the District Court of Appeals, in a unanimous decision, reversed the conviction of all the defendants and the case was later dismissed "for lack of evidence." In its decision, the court sustained all but two of the contentions which our defense committee had raised, castigated the trial judge for his conduct of the trial, and scored the methods by which the prosecution had secured a conviction. On October twenty-fourth, when the charges were finally dismissed after the defendants had served nearly two years in San Quentin Prison (we had been unable to provide bonds during the appeal), hundreds of Mexicans crowded the corridors of the Hall of Justice to greet the boys. "Hysterical screams and shrieks," reported the Los Angeles *Times,* "laughter and cries of jubilation welled from the crowd. The atmosphere was electric with excitement as the liberated men were beseiged by well-wishers who enthusiastically pumped their hands and slapped their backs. Tears flowed unashamedly." For the first time in the history of Los Angeles, Mexicans had won an organized victory in the courts and, on this day, bailiffs and deputy sheriffs and court attachés were looking rather embarrassed in the presence of Mexicans.

The work of the Sleepy Lagoon Defense Committee received nation-wide attention and was hailed as an important contribution to the war effort by ex-President Cárdenas of Mexico and by the Mexican consul-general. In Mexico City, the magazine *Hoy,* devoted a three-page spread in its issue of September 30, 1944, to the work of the defense committee. During the time the committee was in existence, we received hundreds of letters from GI's, from posts in Guam, New Guinea, Hawaii, the Fiji Islands, the Aleutians; in fact, from all over the world. Soldiers with names like Livenson, Hart, Shanahan, Hecht, Chavez, Scott, Bristol, Cavouti, and Burnham, enclosed dimes, quarters, and dollars for the work of the committee. Marine Corps Captain M. A. Cavouti wrote us from New Guinea: "This war is being fought for the maintenance and broadening of our democratic beliefs and I am heartily in accord with any effort to apply these principles by assisting in obtaining a review of this case. Please accept my modest contribution." From Hawaii, Corporal Samuel J. Foreman, a Negro, wrote: "I saw in the Pittsburgh *Courier* that you were leading the fight for victims of aggression. We members of the colored race are sympathetic to your worthwhile and moral fight to free these Mexican boys." Dozens of letters came from Mexican-Americans in the service.

Everyone liked what we had done except, of course, the dominant cliques in Los Angeles. Since the initial suggestion for the formation of the committee had come from LaRue McCormick, a member of the Communist Party, we were systematically red-baited. The press accused us of "inciting racial prejudice," scoffed at the charge of bias during the trial, and lauded the trial judge and the prosecutor. Even the unanimous decision of the District Court of Appeals, sustaining the charges we had made, failed to bring so much as a mumbled retraction of the accusations that had been made against the boys or so much as a grudging acknowledgment that we had been right.

While the case was pending on appeal, several members of the committee, including myself, were subpoenaed by the Committee on Un-American Activities in California, headed by Senator Jack Tenney, and grilled at great length. Naturally these various grillings were reported in the press in a manner calculated to make it most difficult for us to raise money for the appeal. The assistant district attorney, who conducted the prosecution, threatened the First Unitarian Church of Los Angeles with the removal of its tax-exempt status if it permitted the committee to hold a meeting on its premises. In fact, permission to hold the meeting, was, at the last minute, revoked by the church in response to this pressure. That I had expressed opposition to segregation and had testified that I was opposed on principle to miscegenation statutes was actually cited by the Tenney Committee on page 232 of its report as *proof* (!) of Communistic inclinations!

As a postscript to this section, I should add that not long after his release from prison Henry Leyvas was convicted of a criminal offense after receiving a fair trial. So far as Leyvas was concerned, he had been convicted of being a Mexican long years ago and the damage was done. Needless to say, his general morale and attitude were not improved by his experiences in the Sleepy Lagoon case.

2. Captain Ayres: Anthropologist

To appreciate the social significance of the Sleepy Lagoon case, it is necessary to have a picture of the concurrent events. The Anti-Mexican press campaign which had been whipped up through the spring and early summer of 1942 finally brought recognition, from the officials, of the existence of an "awful" situation in reference to "Mexican juvenile delinquency." A special committee of the Grand Jury, shortly after the death of José Díaz, was appointed to investigate "the problem." It was before this committee, within two weeks after the arrest of the defendants in the Sleepy Lagoon case, that Captain E. Duran Ayres, chief of the *"Foreign* Relations Bureau" of the Los Angeles sheriff's office, presented a report presumably prepared under the instructions of his superiors.

"Mexicans as a whole, in this county," reads the report, "are restricted in the main only to certain kinds of labor, and that being the lowest paid. It must be admitted that they are discriminated against and have been heretofore practically barred from learning trades. . . . This has been very much in evidence in our defense plants, in spite of President Roosevelt's instructions to the contrary. . . . Discrimination and segregation, as evidenced by public signs and rules, such as appear in certain restaurants, public swimming plunges, public parks, theaters, and even in schools, cause resentment among the Mexican people. . . . There are certain parks in this state in which a Mexican may not appear, or else only on a certain day of the week. There are certain plunges where they are not allowed to swim, or else only on one day of the week, and it is made evident by signs reading to that effect, for instance, 'Tuesdays reserved for Negroes and Mexicans.' . . . Certain theaters in certain towns either do not allow Mexicans to enter, or else segregate them in a certain section. Some restaurants absolutely refuse to serve them a meal and so state by public signs. . . . All this applies to both the foreign and American-born Mexicans."

So far, in the report, Captain Ayres was simply drawing a true picture of conditions in Los Angeles County. But, since his real purpose was "to explain" the causes of Mexican juvenile delinquency, he soon began to draw some extraordinary conclusions. "The Caucasian," he went on to report, "especially the Anglo-Saxon, when engaged in fighting, particularly among youths, resort to fisticuffs and may at times kick each other, which is considered unsportive: but this Mexican element considers all that to be a sign of weakness, and all he knows and feels is a desire to use a knife or some lethal weapon. In other words, his desire is to kill, or at least let blood. That is why it is difficult for the Anglo-Saxon to understand the psychology of the Indian or even the Latin, and it is just as difficult for the Indian or the Latin to understand the psychology of the Anglo-Saxon or those from northern Europe. When there is added to *this inborn characteristic* that has come down through the ages, the use of liquor, then we certainly have crimes of violence." (Emphasis added.)

This passage should, perhaps, be compared with similar conclusions drawn by another amateur anthropologist. "Race," wrote Adolf Hitler, "does not lie in the language but exclusively in the blood. A man may change his language without any trouble but . . . his inner nature is not changed." The close agreement between these two experts was shown after the publication of the Ayres' Report when Radio Berlin, Radio Tokyo, and Radio Madrid quoted passages from the report to show that Americans actually shared the same doctrines as those advocated by Hitler. The Los Angeles sheriff, who had previously made much fuss over his "Latin blood" and his "early California background," was sufficiently embarrassed by these broadcasts to suggest to a reporter from the New York *Daily News* that the Japanese, upon being evacuated, had incited the Mexican population of Los Angeles to violence. Thus the sheriff, who had always identified himself with the Mexican population on Cinco de Mayo and the Sixteenth of September, inferentially charged that the Mexicans, his own people, had become agents of the Japanese government!

In considering the subsequent pattern of events, it is important to remember that the Ayres Report had been formally presented to the Grand Jury by the sheriff and had presumably represented the official views, candidly expressed, of law enforcement officers in Los Angeles. Thus the chief law enforcement agency in the county had given voice to the view that the Mexican minority possessed an inborn tendency to criminal behavior and to crimes of violence. Being primarily men of action, the law enforcement officials proceeded to act in accordance with this belief. Essentially, therefore, there is nothing incredible about their subsequent behavior and conduct.

3. Plotting a Riot

If one spreads out the span of one's right hand and puts the palm down on the center of a map of Los Angeles County with the thumb pointing north, at the tip of each finger will be found a community where the population is predominantly Mexican. In each of these neighborhoods, moreover, a majority of the juveniles living in the area will be found to be first-generation Mexican-Americans, sons and daughters of the Mexican immigrants who came to Southern California during the 1920's.

Now, if one believes that Mexicans have an inherent desire to commit crimes of violence, the logical first step, in a crime prevention program, is to arrest all the people living in these areas. Unfortunately for the practice of this cosy little theory, there are well over a hundred thousand people living in these areas who are of Mexican descent. The maximum capacity of the Los Angeles jails being somewhat under this figure, it therefore becomes necessary to proceed on a more selective basis. If one group of Mexicans, say, the young people, could be selected for token treatment, and if sufficient arrests could be made from this group, perhaps this would serve as an example to all Mexicans to restrain their inborn criminal desires. . . .

If this sounds a bit fantastic, consider the following letter which Captain Joseph Reed sent to his superior on August 12, 1942:

C. B. Horrall,
Chief of Police.
Sir:
    The Los Angeles Police Department in conjunction with the Sheriff, California Highway Patrol, the Monterey, Montebello, and Alhambra

Police Departments, conducted a drive on Mexican gangs throughout Los Angeles County on the nights of August 10th and 11th. All persons suspected of gang activities were stopped. Approximately 600 persons were brought in. There were approximately 175 arrested for having knives, guns, chains, dirks, daggers, or *any other implement that might have been used in assault* cases. . . .

Present plans call for drastic action. . . .

Respectfully,
JOSEPH F. REED
Administrative Assistant

(Emphasis added.)

On the nights in question, August 10 and 11, 1942, the police selected the neighborhoods which lay at our fingertips on the maps and then blockaded the main streets running through these neighborhoods. All cars containing Mexican occupants, entering or leaving the neighborhoods, were stopped. The occupants were then ordered to the sidewalks where they were searched. With the occupants removed, other officers searched the cars for weapons or other illicit goods.

On the face of it, the great raid was successful, for six hundred people were arrested. The charges? Suspicion of assault, suspicion of robbery, suspicion of auto thefts, suspicion of this, suspicion of that. Of the six hundred taken into custody, about 175 were held on various charges, principally for the possession of "knives, guns, chains, dirks, daggers, or any other implement that hight have been used in assault cases." This is a broad statement, indeed, but it is thoroughly in keeping with the rest of this deadly serious farce. For these "other" implements consisted, of course, of hammers, tire irons, jack handles, wrenches, and other tools found in the cars. In fact, the arrests seem to have been predicated on the assumption that all law-abiding citizens belong to one or another of the various automobile clubs and, therefore, do not need to carry their own tools and accessories.

As for those arrested, taking the names in order, we have, among those first listed, Tovar, Marquez, Perez, Villegas, Tovar, Querrero, Holguín, Rochas, Aguilera, Ornelas, Atilano, Estrella, Saldana, and so on. Every name on the long list was obviously either Mexican or Spanish and therefore, according to the Ayres Report, the name of a potential criminal. The whole procedure, in fact, was entirely logical and consistent once the assumptions in the report were taken as true.

THE PATTERN OF VIOLENCE

Harry Braverman, a member of the Grand Jury who had opposed returning the indictment in the Sleepy Lagoon case, was greatly disturbed by these mass dragnet raids and by the manner in which the Grand Jury was being used as a sounding board to air the curious views of Captain Ayres. Accordingly, he arranged for an open Grand Jury hearing on October 8, 1942, at which some of the damage caused by the Ayres Report might, if possible, be corrected. At this hearing, Dr. Harry Hoijer of the University of California; Guy T. Nunn of the War Manpower Commission (who later wrote, on his return from a German prison camp, a fine novel about Mexican-Americans called *White Shadows*); Manuel Aguilar of the Mexican consulate; Oscar R. Fuss of the CIO; Walter H. Laves of the Office of the Coordinator of Inter-American Affairs and myself all endeavored to create in the minds of the Grand Jurors at least a doubt that everything that Captain Ayres had said was true. To appreciate the incomparable irony of this situation, suffice it to say that here we were having to defend "the biological character" of the Mexican people months after Mexico had declared war on Germany, Italy, and Japan on May 22, 1942; after the first shipment of 1,500 Mexican workers—the vanguard of an army of 100,000 workers that Mexico sent to this country during the war—had arrived in California on September 29, 1942; and after Henry Wallace, then vice-president of the United States, had declared to a great Sixteenth of September celebration in Los Angeles that "California has become a fusion ground for the two cultures of the Americas. . . ."

On the occasion of this hearing, representatives of the coordinator of Inter-American Affairs made the rounds of the newspapers, calling attention to the serious harm being done the war effort and the Good Neighbor Policy by the newspaper campaign against resident Mexicans. In the interest of winning the war, these officials had suggested, there might well be some abatement in this campaign: we were fighting the Germans and the Japanese, not the Mexicans. With stated reluctance, and obvious misgivings, the newspapers promised to behave and, from October to December, 1942, the great hue and cry either disappeared from the press or was conducted *sotto voce*. That the campaign had seriously interfered with the war effort, there can be no doubt. When the Sleepy Lagoon defendants were convicted, for example, the Axis radio beamed the following message in Spanish to the people of Latin America:

In Los Angeles, California, the so-called City of the Angels, twelve Mexican boys were found guilty today of a single murder and five others were convicted of assault growing out of the same case. The 360,000 Mexicans of Los Angeles are reported up in arms over this Yankee persecution. The concentration camps of Los Angeles are said to be overflowing with members of this persecuted minority. This is justice for you, as practiced by the "Good Neighbor," Uncle Sam, a justice that demands seventeen victims for one crime. (Axis broadcast, January 13, 1943).

The representatives of the Coordinator's Office urged the newspapers in particular to cease featuring the word "Mexican" in stories of crime. The press agreed, but, true to form, quickly devised a still better technique for baiting Mexicans. "Zoot-suit" and "Pachuco" began to appear in the newspapers with such regularity that, within a few months, they had completely replaced the word "Mexican." Any doubts the public may have harbored concerning the meaning and application of these terms were removed after January 13, 1943, for they were consistently applied, and only applied, to Mexicans. Every Mexican youngster arrested, no matter how trivial the offense and regardless of his ultimate guilt or innocence, was photographed with some such caption as "Pachuco Gangster" or "Zoot-suit Hoodlum." At the Grand Jury hearing on October 8, 1942, some of us had warned the community that, if this press campaign continued, it would ultimately lead to mass violence. But these warnings were ignored. After the jury had returned its verdict in the Sleepy Lagoon case and Mr. Rockefeller's emissaries had left Los Angeles, the campaign, once again, began to be stepped up.

On the eve of the zoot-suit riots in Los Angeles, therefore, the following elements were involved: first, the much-publicized "gangs," composed of youths of Mexican descent, rarely over eighteen years of age; second, the police, overwhelmingly non-Mexican in descent, acting in reliance on the theories of Captain Ayres; third, the newspapers, caught in a dull period when there was only a major war going on, hell-bent to find a local scapegoat, "an internal enemy," on which the accumulated frustrations of a population in wartime could be vented; fourth, the people of Los Angeles, Mexican and non-Mexican, largely unaware that they were sponsoring, by their credulity and indifference, a private war; and, fifth, the men of the armed services stationed in or about the city, strangers to Los Angeles, bored, getting the attitudes of the city from its flamboyant press. They entered the plot, however, only at the climax. Knowing already of the attitude of the police and of the press, let's examine the Mexican "gang."

4. The Origin of *Pachuquismo*

In Los Angeles, in 1942, if a boy wished to become known as a "gangster" he had a choice of two methods. The first, and by far the more difficult, was to commit a crime and be convicted. The second method was easier, although it was largely restricted to a particular group. If you were born of Mexican parents financially unable to move out of certain specific slum areas, you could be a gangster from birth without having to go to all the trouble of committing a crime. For Los Angeles had revised the old saying that "boys will be boys" to read "boys, if Mexican, will be gangsters." The only reservation to be noted, of course, consists in the definition of a "gang."

Adolescent boys in the United States are among the most gregarious groups in our society. American boys traditionally "hang out with the gang." Their association is based, of course, on common interests. The boys in the "gang" may go to the same school, live in the same neighborhood or have the same hobbies. There is, however, a difference in the degree to which the members of various "gangs" feel a sense of solidarity. A boy who belongs to a club for those who make model airplanes may have little loyalty toward the club. It serves a particular interest and beyond this interest he must have other associations. But a "gang" of Mexican boys in Los Angeles is held together by a set of associations so strong that they outweigh, or often outweigh, such influences as the home, the school, and the church.

The various teen-age clubs in the better parts of Los Angeles often get together and spend an evening dancing in Hollywood. But the respectable places of entertainment will often refuse to admit Mexicans. The boys and girls who belong to the "Y" often make up theater parties. But the "best" theaters in Los Angeles have been known to refuse admission to Mexicans. Many youngsters like to go rollerskating or iceskating; but the skating rink is likely to have a sign reading "Wednesdays reserved for Negroes and Mexicans." Wherever the Mexicans go, outside their own districts, there are signs, prohibitions, taboos, restrictions. Learning of this "iron curtain" is part of the education of every Mexican-American boy in Los Angeles. Naturally it hits them hardest at the time when they are trying to cope with the already tremendous problems of normal adolescence. The first chapters are learned almost on the day they enter school, and, as time passes and the world enlarges, they learn other chapters in this bitter and peremptory lesson.

Most of the boys are born and grow up in neighborhoods which are almost entirely Mexican in composition and so it is not until they reach school age that they become aware of the social status of Mexicans. Prior to entering school, they are aware, to a limited extent, of differences in background. They know that there are other groups who speak English and that they will some day have to learn it, too. But it is at school that they first learn the differences in social rank and discover that they are at the bottom of the scale. Teachers in the "Mexican" schools are often unhappy about their personal situation. They would much rather be teaching in the sacrosanct halls of some Beverly Hills or Hollywood school. Assignment to a school in a Mexican district is commonly regarded, in Los Angeles, as the equivalent of exile. Plagued by teachers who present "personality problems," school administrators have been known to "solve" the problem by assigning the teacher to "Siberia." Neither in personnel nor equipment are these schools what they should be, although a definite attempt to improve them is now under way.

Discovering that his status approximates the second-rate school has the effect of instilling in the Mexican boy a resentment directed against the school, and all it stands for. At the same time, it robs him of a desire to turn back to his home. For the home which he knew prior to entering school no longer exists. All of the attitudes he has learned at school now poison his attitude toward the home. Turning away from home and school, the Mexican boy has only one place where he can find security and status. This is the gang made up of boys exactly like himself, who live in the same neighborhood, and who are going through precisely the same distressing process at precisely the same time.

Such is the origin of the juvenile gangs about which the police and the press of Los Angeles were so frenetically concerned. Gangs of this character are familiar phenomena in any large city. In Los Angeles, twenty years ago, similar gangs were made up of the sons of Russian Molokan immigrants. They have existed in Los Angeles since the city really began to grow, around 1900, and they will continue to exist as long as society creates them. Thus "the genesis of pachuquismo," as Dr. George Sanchez has pointed out, "is an open book to those who care to look into the situations facing Spanish-speaking people" in the Southwest. In fact, they were pointed out over a decade ago in an article which Dr. Sanchez wrote for the *Journal of Applied Psychology* (1).

The *pachuco* gang differs from some other city gangs only in the degree to which it constitutes a more tightly knit group. There is more to the *pachuco* gang than just having a good time together. The *pachucos* suffer discrimination together and nothing makes for cohesiveness more effectively than a commonly shared hostility. Knowing that both as individuals and as a group they are not welcome in many parts of the city, they create their own world and try to make it as self-sufficient as possible.

While the fancier "palladiums" have been known to refuse them, even when they have had the price of admission, there are other dance halls, not nearly so fancy, that make a business of catering to their needs. It should be noted, however, that Mexican boys have never willingly accepted these inferior accommodations and the inferior status they connote. Before they have visited the "joints" on Skid Row, they have first tried to pass through the palatial foyers on Sunset Boulevard. When they finally give up, they have few illusions left about their native land.

It should also be remembered that *pachuquismo* followed a decade of important social change for Mexicans in Los Angeles. During the depression years, thousands of Mexicans had been repatriated and those remaining began to adjust to a new mode of existence. The residence of those who had been migratory workers tended to become stabilized, for residence was a condition to obtaining relief. Thousands of Mexicans were replaced, during these same years, by so-called Okies and Arkies in the migratory labor movement. A greater stability of residence implied more regular schooling, better opportunities to explore the intricacies of urban life, and, above all, it created a situation in which the Mexican communities began to impinge on the larger Anglo-American community.

During the depression years, one could watch the gradual encroachment of Mexicans upon downtown Los Angeles. Stores and shops catering to Mexican trade crossed First Street, moving out from the old Plaza district and gradually infiltrated as far south as Third or Fourth streets. The motion picture theaters in this neighborhood, by far the oldest in the city, began to "go Mexican" as did the ten-cent stores, the shops, and the small retail stores. Nowadays the old Mason Opera House, in this district, has become a Mexican theater. Being strangers to an urban environment, the first generation had tended to respect the boundaries of the Mexican communities. But the second generation was lured far beyond these boundaries into the downtown shopping districts, to the beaches, and above all, to the "glamor" of Hollywood. It was this generation of Mexicans, the *pachuco* generation, that first came to the general notice and attention of the Anglo-American population.

Thus concurrently with the growth of the gangs there developed a new stereotype of the Mexican as the *"pachuco* gangster" the "zoot-suiter." Many theories have been advanced and reams of paper wasted in an attempt to define the origin of the word *"pachuco."* Some say that the expression originally came from Mexico and denoted resemblance to the gaily costumed people living in a town of this name; others have said that it was first applied to border bandits in the vicinity of El Paso. Regardless of the origin of the word, the *pachuco* stereotype was born in Los Angeles. It was essentially an easy task to fix this stereotype on Mexican youngsters. Their skin was enough darker to set them apart from the average *Angeleno*. Basically bilingual, they spoke both Spanish and English with an accent that could be mimicked by either or both groups. Also there was an age-old heritage of ill-will to be exploited and a social atmosphere in which Mexicans, as Mexicans, had long been stereotyped. The *pachuco* also had a uniform—the zoot-suit—which served to make him conspicuous.

Mexican-American boys never use the term "zoot-suit," preferring the word "drapes" in speaking of their clothes. "Drapes" began to appear in the late thirties and early forties. In general appearance, "drapes" resemble the zoot-suits worn by Negro youngsters in Harlem, although the initiated point out differences in detail and design. Called "drapes" or "zoot-suit," the costume is certainly one of the most functional ever designed. It is worn by boys who engage in a specific type of activity, namely, a style of dancing which means disaster to the average suit. The trouser cuffs are tight around the ankles in order not to catch on the heels of the boy's quickly moving feet. The shoulders of the coat are wide, giving plenty of room for strenuous arm movements; and the shoes are heavy, serving to anchor the boy to the dance floor as he spins his partner around. There is nothing esoteric about these "sharp" sartorial get-ups in underprivileged groups, quite apart from their functional aspect. They are often used as a badge of defiance by the rejected against the outside world and, at the same time, as a symbol of belonging to the inner group. It is at once a sign of rebellion and a mark of belonging. It carries prestige (2).

For the boys, peg-topped pants with pleats, high waists up under the armpits, the long loose-backed coat, thick-soled bluchers, and the ducktailed haircut; for the girls, black huaraches, short black skirt, long black stockings, sweater, and high pompadour. Many of the boys saved their money for months to buy one of these get-ups. The length of the coat and the width of the shoulders became as much a mark of prestige as the merit badges of the Boy Scout. But, it should be noted, that the zoot-suit was not universal among Mexican boys. Some never adopted it, while others never adopted it completely. There were all varieties of acceptance. The newspapers, of course, promptly seized upon the zoot-suit as "a badge of crime." But as one zoot-suited boy said to me, with infallible logic, "If I were a gangster, would I wear a zoot-suit so that everyone would know I was a gangster? No, I'd maybe dress like a priest or like everyone else; but no zoot-suit."

With the backdrops all in place, the curtain now rolls up on an interesting tableau in Our City the Queen of the Angels which was founded in the year 1781 by Mexican *pobladores* under the direction of Spanish officers who wore costumes far more outlandish than those worn by the most flamboyant *pachucos*.

XIII

Blood on the Pavements

On Thursday evening, June 3, 1943, the Alpine Club—made up of youngsters of Mexican descent—held a meeting in a police substation in Los Angeles. Usually these meetings were held in a nearby public school but, since the school was closed, the boys had accepted the invitation of a police captain to meet in the substation. The principal business of the meeting, conducted in the presence of the police captain, consisted in a discussion of how gang-strife could best be avoided in the neighborhood. After the meeting had adjourned, the boys were taken in squad cars to the street corner nearest the neighborhood in which most of them lived. The squad cars were scarcely out of sight, when the boys were assaulted, not by a rival "gang" or "club," but by hoodlum elements in the neighborhood. Of one thing the boys were sure: their assailants were not of Mexican descent.

Earlier the same evening a group of eleven sailors, on leave from their station in Los Angeles, were walking along the 1700 block on North Main Street in the center of one of the city's worst slum areas. The surrounding neighborhood is predominantly Mexican. On one side of the street the dirty brick front of a large brewery hides from view a collection of ramshackle Mexican homes. The other side of the street consists of a series of small bars, boarded-up store fronts, and small shops. The area is well off the beaten paths and few servicemen found their way this far north on Main Street. As they were walking along the street, so they later stated, the sailors were set upon by a gang of Mexican boys. One of the sailors was badly hurt; the others suffered minor cuts and bruises. According to their story, the sailors were outnumbered about three to one.

When the attack was reported to the nearest substation, the police adopted a curious attitude. Instead of attempting to find and arrest the assailants, fourteen policemen remained at the station after their regular duty was over for the night. Then, under the command of a detective lieutenant, the "Vengeance Squad," as they called themselves, set out "to clean up" the gang that had attacked the sailors. But—miracle of miracles!—when they arrived at the scene of the attack they could find no one to arrest—not a single Mexican—on their favorite charge of "suspicion of assault." In itself this curious inability to find anyone to arrest—so strikingly at variance with what usually happened on raids of this sort—raises an inference that a larger strategy was involved. For the raid accomplished nothing except to get the names of the raiding officers in the newspapers and to whip up the anger of the community against the Mexican population, which may, perhaps, have been the reason for the raid. . . .

Thus began the so-called "Zoot-Suit Race Riots" which were to last, in one form or another, for a week in Los Angeles.

1. THE TAXICAB BRIGADE

Taking the police raid as an official cue,—a signal for action,—about two hundred sailors decided to take the law into their own hands on the following night. Coming down into the center of Los Angeles from the Naval Armory in Chavez Ravine (near the "Chinatown" area), they hired a fleet of twenty taxicabs. Once assembled, the "task force" proceeded to cruise straight through the center of town en route to the east side of Los Angeles where the bulk of the Mexicans reside. Soon the sailors in the lead-car sighted a Mexican boy in a zoot-suit walking along the street. The "task force" immediately stopped and, in a few moments, the boy was lying on the pavement, badly beaten and bleeding. The sailors then piled back into the cabs and the caravan resumed its way until the next zoot-suiter was sighted, whereupon the same procedure was repeated. In these attacks, of course, the odds were pretty uneven: two hundred sailors to one Mexican boy. Four times this same treatment was meted out and four "gangsters,"—two seventeen-year-old youngsters, one nineteen, and one twenty-three,—were left lying on the pavements for the ambulances to pick up.

It is indeed curious that in a city like Los Angeles, which boasts that it has more police cars equipped with two-way radio than any other city in the world (Los Angeles *Times,* September 2, 1947), the police were apparently unable to intercept a caravan of twenty taxicabs, loaded with two hundred uniformed, yelling, bawdy sailors, as it cruised through the downtown and east-side sections of the city. At one point the police did happen to cross the trail of the caravan and the officers were apparently somewhat embarrassed over the meeting. For only nine of the sailors were taken into custody and the rest were permitted to continue on their merry way. No charges, however, were ever preferred against the nine.

Their evening's entertainment over, the sailors returned to the foot of Chavez Ravine. There they were met by the police and the Shore Patrol. The Shore Patrol took seventeen of the sailors into custody and sent the rest up to the ravine to the Naval Armory. The petty officer who had led the expedition, and who was not among those arrested, gave the police a frank statement of things to come. "We're out to do what the police have failed to do," he said; "we're going to clean up this situation. . . . Tonight [by then it was the morning of June fifth] the sailors may have the marines along" (1).

The next day the Los Angeles press pushed the war news from the front page as it proceeded to play up the pavement war in Los Angeles in screaming headlines. "Wild Night in L.A.—Sailor Zooter Clash" was the headline in the *Daily News*. "Sailor Task Force Hits L.A. Zooters" bellowed the *Herald-Express*. A suburban newspaper gleefully reported that "zoot-suited roughnecks fled to cover before a task force of twenty taxicabs." None of these stories, however, reported the slightest resistance, up to this point, on the part of the Mexicans.

True to their promise, the sailors were joined that night, June fifth, by scores of soldiers and marines. Squads of servicemen, arms linked, paraded through downtown Los Angeles four abreast, stopping anyone wearing zoot-suits and ordering these individuals to put away their "drapes" by the following night or suffer the consequences. Aside from a few half-hearted admonitions, the police made no effort whatever to interfere with these heralds of disorder. However, twenty-seven Mexican boys, gathered on a street corner, were arrested and jailed that evening. While these boys were being booked "on suspicion" of various offenses, a mob of several hundred servicemen roamed the downtown section of a great city threatening members of the Mexican minority without hindrance or interference from the police, the Shore Patrol, or the Military Police.

On this same evening, a squad of sailors invaded a bar on the east side and carefully examined the clothes of the patrons. Two zoot-suit customers, drinking beer at a table, were peremptorily ordered to remove their clothes. One of them was beaten and his clothes were torn from his back when he refused to comply with the order. The other—they were both Mexicans—doffed his "drapes" which were promptly ripped to shreds. Similar occurrences in several parts of the city that evening were sufficiently alarming to have warranted some precautionary measures or to have justified an "out-of-bounds" order. All that the police officials did, however, was to call up some additional reserves and announce that any Mexicans involved in the rioting would be promptly arrested. That there had been no counterattacks by the Mexicans up to this point apparently did not enter into the police officers' appraisal of the situation. One thing must be said for the Los Angeles police: it is above all consistent. When it is wrong, it is consistently wrong; when it makes a mistake, it will be repeated.

By the night of June sixth the police had worked out a simple formula for action. Knowing that wherever the sailors went there would be trouble, the police simply followed the sailors at a conveniently spaced interval. Six carloads of sailors cruised down Brooklyn Avenue that evening. At Ramona Boulevard, they stopped and beat up eight teenage Mexicans. Failing to find any Mexican zoot-suiters in a bar on Indiana Street, they were so annoyed that they proceeded to wreck the establishment. In due course, the police made a leisurely appearance at the scene of the wreckage but could find no one to arrest. Carefully following the sailors, the police arrested eleven boys who had been beaten up on Carmelita Street; six more victims were arrested a few blocks further on, seven at Ford Boulevard, six at Gifford Street—and so on straight through the Mexican east-side settlements. Behind them came the police, stopping at the same street corners "to mop up" by arresting the injured victims of the mob. By morning, some forty-four Mexican boys, all severely beaten, were under arrest.

2. Operation "Dixie"

The stage was now set for the really serious rioting of June seventh and eighth. Having featured the preliminary rioting as an offensive launched by sailors, soldiers, and marines, the press now whipped public opinion into a frenzy by dire warnings that Mexican zoot-suiters planned mass retaliations. To insure a riot, the precise street corners were named at which retaliatory action was expected and the time of the anticipated action was carefully specified. In effect these stories announced a riot and invited public participation. "Zooters Planning to Attack More Servicemen," headlined the *Daily News;* "Would jab broken bottlenecks in the faces of their victims. . . . Beating sailors' brains out with hammers also on the program." Concerned for the safety of the Army, the Navy, and the Marine Corps, the *Herald-Express* warned that "Zooters . . . would mass 500 strong."

By way of explaining the action of the police throughout the subsequent rioting, it should be pointed out that, in June, 1943, the police were on a bad spot. A man by the name of Beebe, arrested on a drunk charge, had been kicked to death in the Central Jail by police officers. Through the excellent work of an alert police commissioner, the case had finally been broken and, at the time of the riots, a police officer by the name of Compton Dixon was on trial in the courts. While charges of police brutality had been bandied about for years, this was the first time that a seemingly airtight case had been prepared. Shortly after the riots, a Hollywood police captain told a motion picture director that the police had touched off the riots "in order to give Dixie (Dixon) a break." By staging a fake demonstration of the alleged necessity for harsh police methods, it was hoped that the jury would acquit Dixon. As a matter of fact, the jury did disagree and on July 2, 1943, the charges against Dixon were dismissed.

On Monday evening, June seventh, thousands of *Angelenos,* in response to twelve hours' advance notice in the press, turned out for a mass lynching. Marching through the streets of downtown Los Angeles, a mob of several thousand soldiers, sailors, and civilians, proceeded to beat up every zoot-suiter they could find. Pushing its way into the important motion picture theaters, the mob ordered the management to turn on the house lights and then ranged up and down the aisles dragging Mexicans out of their seats. Street cars were halted while Mexicans, and some Filipinos and Negroes, were jerked out of their seats, pushed into the streets, and beaten with sadistic frenzy. If the victims wore zoot-suits, they were stripped of their clothing and left naked or half-naked on the streets, bleeding and bruised. Proceeding down Main Street from

BLOOD ON THE PAVEMENTS

First to Twelfth, the mob stopped on the edge of the Negro district. Learning that the Negroes planned a warm reception for them, the mobsters turned back and marched through the Mexican east side spreading panic and terror.

Here is one of numerous eye-witness accounts written by Al Waxman, editor of *The Eastside Journal:*

> At Twelfth and Central I came upon a scene that will long live in my memory. Police were swinging clubs and servicemen were fighting with civilians. Wholesale arrests were being made by the officers.
>
> Four boys came out of a pool hall. They were wearing the zoot-suits that have become the symbol of a fighting flag. Police ordered them into arrest cars. One refused. He asked: "Why am I being arrested?" The police officer answered with three swift blows of the night-stick across the boy's head and he went down. As he sprawled, he was kicked in the face. Police had difficulty loading his body into the vehicle because he was one-legged and wore a wooden limb. Maybe the officer didn't know he was attacking a cripple.
>
> At the next corner a Mexican mother cried out, "Don't take my boy, he did nothing. He's only fifteen years old. Don't take him." She was struck across the jaw with a night-stick and almost dropped the two and a half year old baby that was clinging in her arms. . . .
>
> Rushing back to the east side to make sure that things were quiet here, I came upon a band of servicemen making a systematic tour of East First Street. They had just come out of a cocktail bar where four men were nursing bruises. Three autos loaded with Los Angeles policemen were on the scene but the soldiers were not molested. Farther down the street the men stopped a streetcar, forcing the motorman to open the door and proceeded to inspect the clothing of the male passengers. "We're looking for zoot-suits to burn," they shouted. Again the police did not interfere. . . . Half a block away . . . I pleaded with the men of the local police substation to put a stop to these activities. "It is a matter for the military police," they said.

Throughout the night the Mexican communities were in the wildest possible turmoil. Scores of Mexican mothers were trying to locate their youngsters and several hundred Mexicans milled around each of the police substations and the Central Jail trying to get word of missing members of their families. Boys came into the police stations saying: "Charge me with vagrancy or anything, but don't send me out there!" pointing to the streets where other boys, as young as twelve and thirteen years of age, were being beaten and stripped of their clothes. From affidavits which I helped prepare at the time, I should say that not more than half of the victims were actually wearing zoot-suits. A Negro defense worker, wearing a defense-plant identification badge on his workclothes, was taken from a street car and one of his eyes was gouged out with a knife. Huge half-page photographs, showing Mexican boys stripped of their clothes, cowering on the pavements, often bleeding profusely, surrounded by jeering mobs of men and women, appeared in all the Los Angeles newspapers. As Al Waxman most truthfully reported, blood had been "spilled on the streets of the city."

At midnight on June seventh, the military authorities decided that the local police were completely unable or unwilling to handle the situation, despite the fact that a thousand reserve officers had been called up. The entire downtown area of Los Angeles was then declared "out of bounds" for military personnel. This order immediately slowed down the pace of the rioting. The moment the Military Police and Shore Patrol went into action, the rioting quieted down. On June eighth the city officials brought their heads up out of the sand, took a look around, and began issuing statements. The district attorney, Fred N. Howser, announced that the "situation is getting entirely out of hand," while Mayor Fletcher Bowron thought that "sooner or later it will blow over." The chief of police, taking a count of the Mexicans in jail, cheerfully proclaimed that "the situation has now cleared up." All agreed, however, that it was quite "a situation."

Unfortunately "the situation" had not cleared up; nor did it blow over. It began to spread to the suburbs where the rioting continued for two more days. When it finally stopped, the Eagle Rock *Advertiser* mournfully editorialized: "It is too bad the servicemen were called off before they were able to complete the job. . . . Most of the citizens of the city have been delighted with what has been going on." County Supervisor Roger Jessup told the newsmen: "All that is needed to end lawlessness is more of the same action as is being exercised by the servicemen!" While the district attorney of Ventura, an outlying county, jumped on the bandwagon with a statement to the effect that "zoot suits are an open indication of subversive character." This was also the opinion of the Los Angeles City Council which adopted a resolution making the wearing of zoot-suits a misdemeanor! On June eleventh, hundreds of handbills were distributed to students and posted on bulletin boards in a high school attended by many Negroes and Mexicans which read: "Big Sale. Second-Hand Zoot Suits. Slightly Damaged. Apply at Nearest U.S. Naval Station. While they last we have your Size."

3. When the Devil Is Sick . . .

Egging on the mob to attack Mexicans in the most indiscriminate manner, the press developed a fine technique in reporting the riots. "44 Zooters Jailed in Attacks on Sailors" was the chief headline in the *Daily News* of June seventh; "Zoot Suit Chiefs Girding for War on Navy" was the headline in the same paper on the following day. The moralistic tone of this reporting is illustrated by a smug headline in the Los Angeles *Times* of June seventh: "Zoot Suiters Learn Lesson in Fight with Servicemen." The riots, according to the same paper, were having "a cleansing effect." An editorial in the *Herald-Express* said that the riots "promise to rid the community of . . . those zoot-suited miscreants." While Mr. Manchester Boddy, in a signed editorial in the *Daily News* of June ninth excitedly announced that "the time for temporizing is past. . . . The time has come to serve notice that the City of Los Angeles will no longer be terrorized by a relatively small handful of morons parading as zoot suit hoodlums. To delay action *now* means to court disaster later on." As though there had been any "temporizing," in this sense, for the prior two years!

But once the Navy had declared the downtown section of Los Angeles "out of bounds," once the Mexican ambassador in Washington had addressed a formal inquiry to Secretary of State Hull, and once official Washington began to advise the local minions of the press of the utterly disastrous international effects of the riots, in short when the local press realized the consequences of its own lawless action, a great thunderous cry for "unity," and "peace," and "order" went forth. One after the other, the editors began to disclaim all responsibility for the riots which, two days before, had been hailed for their "salutary" and "cleansing" effect.

Thus on June eleventh the Los Angeles *Times,* in a pious mood, wrote that,

> at the outset, zoot-suiters were limited to no specific race; they were Anglo-Saxon, Latin and Negro. The fact that later on their numbers seemed to be predominantly Latin was in itself no indictment of that race

at all. No responsible person at any time condemned Latin-Americans as such.

Feeling a twinge of conscience, Mr. Boddy wrote that "only a ridiculously small percentage of the local Mexican population is involved in the so-called gang demonstrations. Every true Californian has an affection for his fellow citizens of Mexican ancestry that is as deep rooted as the Mexican culture that influences our way of living, our architecture, our music, our language, and even our food." This belated discovery of the Spanish-Mexican cultural heritage of California was, needless to say, rather ironic in view of the fact that the ink was not yet dry on Mr. Boddy's earlier editorial in which he had castigated the Mexican minority as "morons." To appreciate the ironic aspects of "the situation," the same newspapers that had been baiting Mexicans for nearly two years now began to extol them (2).

As might have been expected, this post-mortem mood of penitence and contrition survived just long enough for some of the international repercussions of the riots to quiet down. Within a year, the press and the police were back in the same old groove. On July 16, 1944, the Los Angeles *Times* gave front-page prominence to a curious story under the heading: "Youthful Gang Secrets Exposed." Indicating no source, identifying no spokesman, the story went on to say that "authorities of the Superior Court" had unearthed a dreadful "situation" among juvenile delinquents. Juveniles were using narcotics, marihuana, and smoking "reefers." Compelled to accept drug addiction, "unwilling neophytes" were dragooned into committing robberies and other crimes. Young girls were tatooed with various "secret cabalistic symbols" of gang membership. The high pompadours affected by the *cholitas,* it was said, were used to conceal knives and other "weapons." Two theories were advanced in the story by way of "explaining" the existence of these dangerous gangs: first, that "subversive groups" in Los Angeles had organized them; and, second, that "the gangs are the result of mollycoddling of racial groups." In view of the record, one is moved to inquire, what mollycoddling? by the police? by the juvenile authorities? by the courts? Backing up the news story, an editorial appeared in the *Times* on July eighteenth entitled: "It's Not a Nice Job But It Has To Be Done." Lashing out at "any maudlin and misguided sympathy for the 'poor juveniles,'" the editorial went on to say that "stern punishment is what is needed; stern and sure punishment. The police and the Sheriff's men *should be given every encouragement* to go after these young gangsters" (emphasis mine).

Coincident with the appearance of the foregoing news story and editorial, the Juvenile Court of Los Angeles entered a most remarkable order in its minutes on July 31, 1944. The order outlined a plan by which Mexican wards of the Juvenile Court, over sixteen years of age, might be turned over to the Atchison, Topeka, and Santa Fe Railroad for a type of contract-employment. A form of contract, between the parents of the youngsters and the railroad, was attached to the order. The contract provided that the ward was to work "as a track laborer" at $58\frac{1}{2}$¢ per hour; that $1.03 per day was to be deducted for board, $2.50 per month for dues in a hospital association, and 10¢ a day for laundry. It was also provided that one-half of the pay was to be turned over to the probation officers to be held in trust for the ward. That this order was specifically aimed at *Mexican* juveniles is clearly shown by the circumstance that the court, prior to approving the arrangement, had first secured its approval by a committee of "representative" leaders of the Mexican-American community.

4. The Strange Case of the Silk Panties

All of this, one will say,—the Sleepy Lagoon case, the riots, etc.,—belongs to the past. But does it? On the morning of July 21, 1946, a thirteen-year-old Mexican boy, Eugene Chavez Montenegro, Jr., was shot and killed by a deputy sheriff in Montebello Park on the east side of Los Angeles. The deputy sheriff later testified that he had been called to the area by reports of a prowler. On arriving at the scene, he had stationed himself near a window of the house in question and had played his flashlight on the window. A little later, he testified, "a man" lifted the screen on the window, crawled out, and ran past him. When the "man" failed to halt on order, he had shot him in the back. At the coroner's inquest, the same deputy also testified that he had seen another officer remove a pair of "silk panties" from the dead boy's pocket and that the boy was armed with "a Boy Scout's knife."

While incidents of this kind have been common occurrences in Los Angeles for twenty years, in this case the officers had shot the wrong boy. For it turned out that young Montenegro was an honor student at St.

Alphonsus parochial school; that his parents were a highly respectable middle-class couple; and that the neighbors, Anglo-Americans as well as Mexicans, all testified that the boy had an excellent reputation. Accepting the officers' version of the facts, it was still difficult to explain why they had made no effort to halt the boy, who was five feet three inches tall, when he ran directly past them within arms' reach. Before the hearings were over, the "silk panties" story was exposed as a complete fake. Despite a gallant fight waged by Mr. and Mrs. Montenegro to vindicate the reputation of their son, nothing came of the investigation. "Raging Mother Attacks Deputy Who Slew Son" was the *Daily News* headline on the story of the investigation.

. . . On January 23, 1947 the attorney general of California ordered the removal of two police officers for the brutal beating of four Mexican nationals who, with eight hundred of their countrymen, had been brought to Oxnard to harvest the crops. . . . On March 30, 1946, a private detective killed Tiofilo Pelagio, a Mexican national, in a café argument. . . . On the same day affidavits were presented to the authorities that confessions from four Mexican boys, all minors, had been obtained by force and violence. . . . Esther Armenta, sixteen years of age, complained to her mother that she was being mistreated by Anglo-American classmates in a Los Angeles junior high school. "They would spit on her," said Mrs. Catalina Armenta, the mother, "and call her a 'dirty Mex.' Esther would come home in tears and beg me to get her transferred." A few weeks later the girl was in juvenile court charged with the use of "bad language." She was then sent to the Ventura School for Girls, a so-called "correctional" institution. When Mrs. Armenta finally got permission to visit her daughter, in the presence of a matron, the girl had "black and blue marks on her arm" and complained that she had been whipped by one of the matrons. . . . On April 10, 1946, Mrs. Michael Gonzales complained to the Federation of Spanish-American Voters that her daughter had been placed in the Ventura School without her knowledge or consent and that when she had protested this action she had been threatened with deportation by an official of the juvenile court. . . . On the basis of a stack of affidavits, the San Fernando Valley Council on Race Relations charged on May 16, 1947 that the police had broken into Mexican homes without search warrants; that they had beaten, threatened, and intimidated Mexican juveniles; and that they were in the habit of making "wholesale roundups and arrests of Mexican-American boys without previous inquiry as to the arrested boys' connection—if any—with the crime in question." ... In 1946 a prominent official of the Los Angeles schools told me that she had been horrified to discover that, in the Belvedere district, Mexican-American girls, stripped of their clothing, were forced to parade back and forth, in the presence of other girls in the "gym," as a disciplinary measure. . . .*

5. THE POLITICS OF PREJUDICE

I reported the zoot-suit riots in Los Angeles for *PM* and *The New Republic* and had a hand in some of the hectic events of that memorable week. Following the June seventh rioting, I chaired a meeting of a hundred or more citizens at which an emergency committee was formed to bring about, if possible, a return to sanity in Los Angeles. That same evening we communicated with Attorney General Robert W. Kenny in San Francisco by telephone and urged him to induce Governor Earl Warren to appoint an official committee of inquiry. The next day the governor appointed a committee of five which included four names from a panel which I had submitted. The fifth member was the governor's own selection: Mr. Leo Carrillo. Mr. Carrillo, like the sheriff of Los Angeles, is a descendant of "an early California family." The committee immediately assembled in Los Angeles where Mr. Kenny presented to them a proposed report, with findings and recommendations, which I had prepared at his request. With some modifications, this report was adopted by the committee and submitted to the governor. Out of the work of our emergency committee there finally emerged, after a year of negotiation, the present-day Council of Civic Unity.

Praising the report of the governor's committee—which I had prepared—the Los Angeles *Times* devoted several harsh editorials to certain "reckless" individuals, myself included, who had suggested that "racial prejudice" might have had something to do with the riots! "When trouble arose," said the *Times* in an editorial of June 15, 1943, "through the depredations of the young gangs attired in zoot-suits, it was their weird dress and not their race which resulted in difficulties. That is a simple truth which no amount of propaganda will change." In the same

---

* For a detailed account of still another "incident," see *Justice for Salcido* by Guy Endore, published by the Civil Rights Congress of Los Angeles, July, 1948.

editorial, the charges of unfairness which I had raised in connection with the Sleepy Lagoon case were branded as "distortions," "wild charges," and "inflammatory accusations" (charges later confirmed in minute detail by the District Court of Appeals).

When Mrs. Eleanor Roosevelt innocently remarked in her column that the zoot-suit riots were "in the nature of race riots," she was severely taken to task by the *Times* in an editorial of June eighteenth under the caption: "Mrs. Roosevelt Blindly Stirs Race Discord." Even the president of the Los Angeles Chamber of Commerce felt compelled to reply to Mrs. Roosevelt. "These so-called 'zoot-suit' riots," he said, "have never been and are not now in the nature of race riots. . . . At no time has the issue of race entered into consideration. . . . Instead of discriminating against Mexicans, California has always treated them with the utmost consideration" (3).

The zoot-suit riots in Los Angeles were the spark that touched off a chain-reaction of riots across the country in midsummer 1943. Similar "zoot-suit" disturbances were reported in San Diego on June ninth; in Philadelphia on June tenth; in Chicago on June fifteenth; and in Evansville, Indiana, on June twenty-seventh. Between June sixteenth and August first, large-scale race riots occurred in Beaumont, Texas, in Detroit, and in Harlem. The Detroit riots of June 20–21 were the most disastrous riots in a quarter of a century. The swift, crazy violence of the Harlem riot resulted, in a few hours' time, in property damage totalling nearly a million dollars. The rapid succession of these violent and destructive riots seriously interfered with the war effort and had the most adverse international repercussions. The spark that ignited these explosions occurred in *El Pueblo de Nuestra Señora La Reina de Los Angeles de Porciúncula,* founded by Felipe de Neve in 1781, settled by Mexican *pobladores.*

None of these disturbances had more serious international consequences than the zoot-suit riots. On April 20, 1943, President Roosevelt had held his historic meeting with President Camacho on the soil of Mexico. At the time the riots occurred, Mexico was our ally in the war against Germany, Italy, and Japan. Large-scale shipments of Mexican nationals had just begun to arrive in the United States to relieve the critical manpower shortage. "Our two countries," President Roosevelt had said, "owe their independence to the fact that your ancestors and mine held the same truths to be worth fighting for and dying for. Hidalgo and

Juárez were men of the same stamp as Washington and Jefferson." President Camacho, replying to this toast, had said that "the negative memories" of the past were forgotten in the accord of today. And then in the largest city in the old Spanish borderland had come this explosion of hatred and prejudice against Spanish-speaking people.

In response to a request from the Mexican ambassador, Secretary of State Hull had asked Mayor Fletcher Bowron for an official explanation. With a perfectly straight face, the mayor replied that the riots were devoid of any element of prejudice against persons of Mexican descent! The same edition of the newspapers that carried this statement also carried another statement by the mayor under a headline which read: "Mayor Pledges 2-Fisted Action, No Wrist Slap"—a reference to police action contemplated against the Mexican minority. On June ninth Mr. Churchill Murray, local representative of the coordinator of Inter-American Affairs, wired Mr. Rockefeller that the riots were "non-racial." "The frequency of Mexican names among the victims," he said, "was without actual significance." If all this were true, asked Dan G. Acosta in a letter to the Los Angeles press, "Why are we consistently called hoodlums? Why is mob action encouraged by the newspapers? Why did the city police stand around saying very nonchalantly that they could not intervene and even hurrahed the soldiers for their 'brave' action? Not until these questions are answered, will the Mexican population feel at ease."

What the riots did, of course, was to expose the rotten foundations upon which the City of Los Angeles had built a papier-mâché façade of "Inter-American Good Will" made up of fine-sounding Cinco de Mayo proclamations. During the riots, the press, the police, the officialdom, and the dominant control groups of Los Angeles were caught with the bombs of prejudice in their hands. One year before the riots occurred, they had been warned of the danger of an explosion. The riots were not an unexpected rupture in Anglo-Hispano relations but the logical end-product of a hundred years of neglect and discrimination.

The riots left a residue of resentment and hatred in the minds and hearts of thousands of young Mexican-Americans in Los Angeles. During the rioting, one Los Angeles newspaper had published a story to the effect that the *cholitas* and *pachucas* were merely cheap prostitutes, infected with venereal disease and addicted to the use of marihuana. Eighteen Mexican-American girls promptly replied in a letter which the metropolitan press refused to publish: "The girls in this meeting room consist of young girls who graduated from high school as honor students, of girls who are now working in defense plants because we want to help win the war, and of girls who have brothers, cousins, relatives and sweethearts in all branches of the American armed forces. We have not been able to have our side of the story told." The letter, with a picture of the girls, was published in Al Waxman's *Eastside Journal* on June 16, 1943. Still another group of Mexican-American girls,—real *pachucas* these,— bitterly protested the story in another letter which the metropolitan press did not publish. These girls insisted that they should be examined, as a group, by an officially appointed board of physicians so that they could prove that they were virgins. Long after the riots, I have seen Mexican-American boys pull creased and wrinkled newspaper clippings from their wallets and exhibit this slanderous story with the greatest indignation. Four years have now passed since the riots, but the blood has not yet been washed from the pavements of Los Angeles.

XIV

The War Years

World War II has had, of course, a profound effect on Anglo-Hispano relations in the Southwest. The Spanish-speaking people had demonstrated their loyalty and patriotism during the Spanish-American War and World War I, but the enthusiasm with which they participated in the second World War had a special motivation. Prior to Pearl Harbor, the 200th and 515th Coast Artillery units of the New Mexico National Guard had been sent to the Philippines, largely because the officers and troops in these units spoke Spanish. That so large a percentage of the American troops captured or killed at Bataan were Mexican-Americans merely served to stress the intensity with which the Spanish-speaking identified themselves with the Allied cause.

While the precise number of Mexican-Americans who served in the armed forces is not known, the available estimates range from 375,000 to 500,000. That the figure was actually somewhat disproportionate to the size of the Spanish-speaking minority can be assumed from the large number of Mexican-Americans of draft age and the fact that so few Mexican-Americans served on selective service boards. Throughout the war long lists of Mexican-American casualties appeared in the newspapers of the Southwest, usually accompanied by stories of Mexican-Americans who had won special citations for gallantry. Long before the war was over, the cumulative effect of the casuality lists and the stories of Mexican-American gallantry had left a noticeable impress on the Anglo-American conscience.

1. Joe Martínez and Company

One of the most impressive stories of Mexican-American gallantry in the war was that of Joe Martínez. Born in Taos, Martínez was working in the sugar-beet fields of Colorado when he enlisted in the army. For exceptional gallantry in the Aleutians, where he was killed, Martínez was posthumously awarded the Congressional Medal of Honor. A chapter of the American Veterans Committee in Colorado has been named in his honor. Five Texas-Mexicans also received the Congressional Medal of Honor, as did Sylvester Herreras, of Phoenix, who lost both legs in battle, and Pfc. Manuel Perez, of Oklahoma City, who was killed in the Battle of Luzon. Indeed the list of Mexican-American war heroes is a long one and includes names from every state in the Southwest.

"As I read the casualty lists from my own state," said Congressman Jerry Voorhis, "I find anywhere from one-fourth to one-third of those names are names such as Gónzales or Sanchez, names indicating that the very lifeblood of our citizens of Latin-American descent in the uniform of the armed forces of the United States is being poured out to win victory in the war. We ought not to forget that. We ought to resolve that in the future every single one of these citizens shall have the fullest and freest opportunity which this country is capable of giving him, to advance to such positions of influence and eminence as their own personal capacities make possible" (1).

Born on the rancho *Los Potreros* in the Lower Rio Grande Valley, Ricardo Noyola, like his father, could not speak English. Having worked as a farm hand since the age of thirteen, he had had little opportunity for schooling. There were fifty-five or sixty such boys at Camp Robinson, some from Texas, some from New Mexico, some from Colorado. Not knowing what to do with them, the post commander finally put them in a special platoon under the command of an officer who spoke Spanish. Within thirteen weeks, the members of the unit had not only mastered the technique of soldiering but had acquired a conversational knowledge of English sufficient to enable them to serve in mixed units. Several of these soldiers, including Noyola, won special citations for gallantry. For such men wartime service was a real opportunity for acculturation, perhaps the first such opportunity they had ever had.

In every phase of the war, including the defense plants and the training schools as well as the armed services, similar opportunities opened up for thousands of Mexican-Americans: to learn new skills, to acquire new experiences, to come in contact with entirely new currents of thought and opinion. In more than one community, joint service in various civilian defense agencies had a marked tendency to break down the barriers which had so long separated the Spanish-speaking from the rest of the population. Out of this wartime experience, as might have been expected, came a new pride in citizenship and a growing resentment of all forms of discrimination.

Sergeant Macario García was one of the five Texas-Mexicans who received the Congressional Medal of Honor. One day while home on furlough he dropped into the Oasis Café in Sugarland, Texas, for a cup of coffee. Informed that the Oasis Café did not serve Mexicans, he demanded service in no uncertain terms. Two sailors came to his aid in the fight which ensued when the proprietor attempted to eject him. A deputy sheriff, summoned to the café, broke up the fight and told the participants to "forget it." The story naturally aroused a great furor in Mexico and Walter Winchell brought the facts to the attention of his radio listeners. Once Sugarland had received this unwelcome notoriety, the county authorities felt compelled to vindicate the honor of the community: García was then arrested on a charge of "aggravated assault!"

Sergeant José Mendoza López, of Brownsville, another winner of the Congressional Medal of Honor, was denied service in a restaurant in a small town in the Rio Grande Valley, under similar circumstances, following his return from a goodwill tour of Mexico which had been arranged by the army (2). Needless to say, Sergeant López protested the incident with a vehemence which must have come as quite a surprise to the Anglo-American residents.

On February 25, 1946, Pfc. Daniel S. Elizalde, while on leave in Los Angeles, was killed by a special night watchman under circumstances that might easily have resulted in a murder prosecution had the victim not been a Mexican-American. The failure of the authorities to prosecute, despite the most insistent pressure from the Mexican community, resulted in the formation of the Elizalde Anti-Discrimination Committee made up of Mexican-American veterans.

"Mexican-American soldiers," said Marine Corps veteran Balton Llanes, "shed at least a quarter of the blood spilled at Bataan. . . . What they want now is a decent job, a decent home, and a chance to live peacefully in the community. They don't want to be shot at in the dark."

On the evening of April 23, 1947, Charles White, a Mexican-American war veteran who had been awarded the Silver Star, the Purple Heart, the Infantry Badge, and a Presidential Citation, demanded service at the Silver Slipper Nite Club near La Junta, Colorado, after two other

Mexican-Americans had been denied service. In a fight with the proprietor, Sergeant White was killed. Petitions signed by three thousand Mexican-Americans demanded the indictment of the night-club owner but the authorities ignored the petitions and even refused to revoke the liquor license for the club. Out of this incident came a committee which has been conducting a militant campaign in Colorado against all forms of discrimination. In fact, wherever incidents of this sort have occurred, similar committees have been formed, usually spearheaded by Mexican-American veterans.

2. A Tear for José Davilla

During the war an increasing number of Anglo-Americans began to protest acts of discrimination against Mexican-Americans. While working in the cherry orchards near Hart, Michigan, José Davilla, nineteen years of age, became acquainted with an Anglo-American girl. They played together; worked together; and, on several occasions, went out together. One day, as a silly prank, young Davilla took the girl's glasses and refused to return them. Hearing of this affront to Anglo-American womanhood, the sheriff of Oceana County sought out Davilla in the main street of Hart and attempted to arrest him without a warrant. For half an hour the man and the boy fought in the street. When the sheriff was unable to subdue the boy, even with the aid of an eighteen-inch blackjack, he shot and killed him.

Swift Lathers, editor of the local *Mears News,*—"the smallest newspaper in the world,"—promptly wrote an editorial accusing the sheriff of murder. When the sheriff had Lathers arrested for criminal libel, he replied:

> Do I stand alone facing the sullen crowd? I have stood there before. I am that way. I would rather stand up against the whole world to defend the underdog than to sit on the plush chairs of the aggressors.
>
> I know that somewhere there is a tear for José Davilla. Short days ago he worked and sang among us, felt dawn and saw sunsets glow. A few more days and his lingering countrymen will go back to the Border. But that pool of blood on the sidewalk of Hart will not wash away.

With such newspapers as the Detroit *Free Press* rushing to his defense, Lathers was finally acquitted. "The streets of Hart are wet today," wrote James S. Pooler in the *Free Press* (November 1, 1944), "and golden leaves are plastered over the spot where José Davilla died. José hasn't been dead a month. In fact it was only a week ago that his family took their son's body home to Texas. José has no tomb or tombstone here but he has an epitaph, written by Swift Lathers."

Nor was Swift Lathers the only editor who wrote an epitaph for a Mexican-American during the war. Led by the St. Louis *Star-Times,* the newspapers of St. Louis devoted five hundred thousand words of copy to their contention, finally vindicated, that Edward Melendes, a Mexican-American, had been kicked to death by policemen in a St. Louis jail on July 2, 1942. "If Melendes can die in a St. Louis police cell," wrote the *Star-Times,* "as the result of an inhuman beating, and the perpetrators go unpunished, the painfully established liberties of all men have been whittled away. Human beings in a democracy cannot be divided into two classes, those who may safely be beaten and left to die in police stations and those who may not. That is why the *Star-Times* will continue to fight to learn and print the truth, and continue to ask, 'Who Killed Edward Melendes?'"

3. Across the Border

During the war, also, Mexican-Americans began to receive some extremely effective assistance from their brothers across the border. Anxious to see the Good Neighbor Policy realized, many groups, individuals, and organizations in Mexico began to give a new emphasis to the treatment of Spanish-speaking people in the United States. One of the most effective of these groups was the *Comité Mexicano Contra el Racismo,* formed in August, 1944. In its publication *Fraternidad* appeared a regular column entitled "Texas, *Buen Vecino?*" ("Texas, Good Neighbor?"). In issue after issue, the column kept listing acts of discrimination against Mexicans in Texas. Giving names of establishments, and the dates of "incidents," *Fraternidad* documented a long list of discriminatory practices which had occurred in approximately 150 Texas communities. This constant needling soon began to have its effects on both sides of the border. Mexican officials were compelled to bring pressure on both the State Department and the Texas authorities to correct these conditions, while, on this side of the border, Texans began to make "goodwill" tours in Mexico and to play up the Good Neighbor Policy.

At the same time, the issue of discrimination was raised at a series of official or semi-official meetings in Mexico City: at the meeting of the Inter-American Bar Association in August, 1944; at the conference of the International Labor Organization in April, 1945; and at the Inter-American Conference on Problems of War and Peace at which the Act of Chapultepec was adopted on March 6, 1946. In a resolution adopted at this conference all of the nations of the Western Hemisphere entered into a pledge "to make every effort to prevent in their respective countries all acts which may provoke discrimination among individuals because of race or religion." These international pronouncements, coupled with the insistent pressure of Mexican officials, brought about a new recognition of the importance of equal treatment of Mexicans, aliens and citizens, in this country.

At the same time, social tensions in the borderlands were consistently aggravated, during the war years, by agents of the *Sinarquista* movement, founded in Leon, Mexico, in 1937, by Oskar Hellmuth Schreiter, a German Nazi, José Antonio Urquiza, and Trueba Olivares, both with close Falangist connections. Adopting a Fascist ideology, Point 13 in the movement's "16 Principles" stated that Mexico's true sons must be "worthy of their fatherland and *reclaim* as well as honor and respect its lands," a clear reference to the recapture of the borderlands taken from Mexico in 1848 (3).

The first regional *Sinarquista* Committee was organized in Los Angeles on November 1, 1937, shortly after the movement was founded in Mexico. By 1942 the movement boasted of two thousand members in the United States and "cells" were known to exist in such Southern California communities as Pacoima, San Fernando, San Bernardino, La Verne, Ontario, Watts, El Monte, Oxnard, Pomona, and Azusa; and, in Texas, at El Paso, McAllen, Mission, and Laredo. The first meeting of *Sinarquista* chiefs in the United States took place in El Paso on September 27, 1942. Stories in *El Sinarquista* tell, in elaborate detail, of how local committees were formed in the Belvedere section of Los Angeles. In April, 1943—and the date is important both in relation to the meeting of President Roosevelt and President Camacho in Mexico and to the zoot-suit riots in Los Angeles—four Mexican "students"—all men over thirty years of age—toured the United States lecturing on the principles of *Sinarquismo* to Mexican-American audiences. Two of these men were high-ranking officials of the *Sinarquista* movement in Mexico.

In the latter part of 1942 and throughout 1943 local *Sinarquista* committees were seeking to capitalize upon discrimination against Mexican-Americans in the borderlands to interfere, if possible, with the war effort. The Mexican government regarded the agitation with sufficient seriousness to send Ernesto Felix Díaz to Los Angeles, as its official representative, to alert the Mexican residents to the dangers of *Sinarquista* propaganda (4). Testifying before a legislative committee, Pedro Villasenor, president of the Southern California branch of the movement, said that the local branches had five hundred members; but the Department of Justice reported that the membership was nearer two thousand. With the local press charging that the zoot-suit riots had been fomented by subversive left-wing elements, it is ironic to note that the *Sinarquista* movement was completely whitewashed in this investigation which ended up by being yet another investigation of "Communism" (5). While it would be highly inaccurate to say that the *Sinarquista* movement had a direct responsibility for the zoot-suit riots, it is true that its propaganda had a most disquieting effect on Mexican opinion and, to this extent, was a factor in the riots. By harping on the theme that the United States was fighting another war of "Yankee imperialism" and aggression, *Sinarquista* had inflamed a small section of Mexican opinion and had treated the issue of discrimination in the most demagogic manner (6).

4. Los Braceros

With World War II the same clamorous demand for Mexican labor of 1918 was repeated. Concerned over the Good Neighbor Policy, however, the government did not capitulate quite so easily to these demands as it had in World War I. For one thing, the Mexican government looked with some considerable disfavor upon the proposal. But following Mexico's declaration of war on Germany, Italy, and Japan, on May 22, 1942, negotiations were renewed, and, in August, an agreement was entered into between the two nations setting forth the conditions on which Mexican labor might be recruited for wartime employment.

This agreement stipulated that imported workers were to be assured of free transportation to and from their homes; that they were to be provided subsistence en route; that they were not to be used to displace other workers or to reduce wage rates; and that certain minimum guarantees, governing wages and working conditions, would have to be observed. Both the idea of such an agreement and its form can be traced back to proposals which Dr. Manuel Gamio and Mr. Ernesto Galarza, of the Pan-American Union, had previously advanced.

On September 29, 1942, the first shipment of 1,500 Mexican *braceros* arrived in Stockton, California, with the slogan "De Las Democracias Será La Victoria" scribbled in chalk on the Pullman cars. Previously the Farm Security Administration had worked out the various forms and had defined the various relationships to be used in carrying the agreement into effect. Individual agreements were entered into with each worker recruited, which embodied the guarantees of the master agreement. The FSA then entered into agreements with various farm organizations which contained similar guarantees. To police the agreements, Mexican consuls and a limited number of Mexican labor officials were authorized to make inspections and to investigate complaints and grievances. The FSA officials were also careful to provide a friendly reception for the workers. Reception committees were on hand at the station, flags waved, bands played, and many speeches were made. Excellent recreational and educational programs had been worked out with the thought in mind of using the *braceros* as future ambassadors of goodwill in Mexico. As long as the FSA was in charge of the program, the agreement was carried out to the letter; but, on July 1, 1943, the War Food Administration was substituted for the FSA as the enforcing agency—a change which was tantamount to turning the whole program over to the farm associations.

Once they were in control of the program, the new arrangement could not have been improved upon from the growers' point of view. With the government paying all transportation and administration expenses, they were spared even the trouble of recruiting labor. Assured an unlimited market and a high level of prices, the large-scale employers of farm labor made fabulous wartime profits. From 1943 through 1947, the federal government appropriated $120,000,000 for the labor importation program—every penny of which should be regarded as a direct subsidy to the large-scale employers of farm labor in a period of unprecedented prosperity. While the War Food Administration did insist upon livable camps, the wage guarantees were farcical: *braceros* were assured $33 for each two weeks of employment. In an effort to insure payment of prevailing wage rates, hearings were held for each major crop in advance of the season. But these "hearings" were ludicrous. For example, on January 27, 1946, officials of the War Food Administration refused to hear the testimony of Isabel Gónzales, David Braco, and Vincent G. Vigil who had come to Salt Lake from Denver to present evidence that Mexican-American sugar-beet workers were earning, on an average, not more than $550 per year.

To appreciate what a bonanza this program was to the large farm-factories, it should be pointed out that the *braceros* were limited to agricultural employment. If any worker accepted a job in industry, he was subject to immediate deportation. The effect of this provision was to remove the farm-labor market from competition with industrial wage rates. Theoretically the employment of the *braceros* was not supposed to reduce wage rates; actually, with no fault on their part, it had this effect.

Nevertheless the agreement represented a notable advance over the 1918 experience and it also demonstrated that a migratory labor movement can be planned and rationalized. Workers were paid transportation and subsistence en route; they were provided with better camps, medical care, accident insurance, and minimum earnings were guaranteed. Ten per cent of these earnings were deducted by the government and transmitted to Mexico City for the account of the workers: in the nature of a compulsory savings fund. From 1943 to 1947, the *braceros* transmitted a huge sum to their families and dependents in Mexico. Thousands of Mexican workers were eager to enlist and even paid sizable sums, in the way of bribes, to be enrolled. Three members of the Chamber of Deputies in Mexico City, as well as a number of minor officials, were indicted for having solicited these bribes.

The number of workers recruited for agricultural employment were as follows: 1942—4,203; 1943—52,098; 1944—62,170; 1945—120,000; 1946—82,000; 1947—55,000. These are the totals for "foreign labor" and include a few thousand Puerto Ricans and other workers from the West Indies; but most of those imported were from Mexico. Each year, of course, workers returned to Mexico at the end of the season, with the number employed throughout the year not being in excess of twenty-two thousand. Hence it is impossible to give the actual total of workers recruited for agriculture during the war but it would be in excess of one hundred thousand.

These workers helped produce and harvest practically every major crop: sugar beets, grapes, tomatoes, apricots, peaches, prunes, cotton, and many others. In the Rocky Mountain states, they constituted half the labor supply used in harvesting 354,000 acres of sugar beets. Throughout the Middle West, they helped cultivate and harvest sugar beets, vegetables, orchard crops, and hay and grain. Working in twenty-one states, they harvested crops the value of which was estimated in 1944 at $432,010,000.

In addition to those employed in agriculture, eighty thousand Mexicans were recruited and brought to this country for employment as section hands and maintenance workers on the railroads at a minimum hourly rate of 57¢ with no guarantee of minimum earnings. Employed by thirty-two rail lines, these workers performed an indispensable service in keeping the Western lines in repair during a period of exceptionally heavy freight and passenger traffic. It has been estimated that the railroad workers received $63,000,000 in wages in 1944, a large portion of which was remitted to Mexico in the form of money orders.

The farm-labor importation program came to an end on December 31, 1947, but the large growers have kept up an incessant clamor for its renewal. Should the agreement be renewed, it is apparent that the planned migration of the war years can serve as an extremely important precedent. Although the wartime agreement was frequently violated it did provide a measure of protection against the hazards and rigors of migratory employment. Over the years the use of Mexican labor to relieve acute manpower shortages in the United States has proved to be of benefit to both nations. The issue has always turned on the choice between planned migration and unplanned immigration. For it is extremely debatable whether, under any circumstances, Mexican workers can be kept from crossing the border. Given the attraction of industrial employment in the United States and the ease with which the border can be crossed, Mexicans will continue to follow the old, familiar paths which lead north from Mexico. At the present time hundreds of them are paying as much as $150 to be smuggled into the United States in trucks and airplanes and recently one Mexican was so anxious to return to California that he rode a log upstream on the Colorado and then walked a hundred miles through the desert to a ranch in Imperial

Valley. In 1946, alone, sixty-six thousand "wetbacks" were apprehended by the Immigration Service along the far western section of the border (7).

5. THE COUNTERPOINT OF MIGRATION

One of the conspicuous advantages of the farm-labor importation agreement of 1942 was that it gave the Mexican government a firm basis on which to protest acts of discrimination against Mexicans in the borderlands and also provided a means by which these protests could be backed up. After the Farm Security Administration had been relieved of responsibility for enforcing the agreement, complaints began to multiply and repeated charges were made that the growers were chiselling on guaranteed wages and working conditions. On July 30, 1945, Ernesto Galarza prepared a fourteen-page memorandum setting forth in detail the various ways by which American employers in the Southwest were undermining the agreement. More important than any specific violations of the agreement, however, were the incidents of discrimination involving both Mexican nationals and Mexican-Americans, particularly in Texas.

In Snyder, Texas, an Anglo-American dentist refused to treat an American soldier of Mexican descent and in Melvin permission was refused a Mexican-American PTA group to use a community center built by the National Youth Administration. On October 15, 1943, the Mexican government formally protested against the segregation of children of Mexican descent in certain Texas schools. This protest was filed after a large number of Mexican-American families in Bolling and Goose Creek, Texas, had refused to send their children to the jim crow school. Visiting New Gulf, Texas, to participate in the celebration of the Sixteenth of September, Adolfo G. Gominguez, Mexican consul at Houston, was denied service in the Blue Moon Café. Alejandro Carillo, a member of the Chamber of Deputies, immediately brought the facts of this incident to the attention of President Ávila Camacho. Three days before Governor Coke Stevenson proclaimed the Sixteenth of September an official holiday in Texas, Sergeant Macario García had been arrested in Sugarland.

In October, 1943, a Mexican boy, seventeen years of age, entered a café in Levelland, Texas, to buy a package of cigarettes. The usual altercation developed in the course of which the owner of the café hit the boy over the head with a coke bottle. Within a few moments, a thousand or more Mexicans gathered outside the café and the sheriff arrived just in time to prevent a riot. In December, 1944, some three hundred AFL members went on strike at Huron, South Dakota, against the employment of Mexican *braceros*. A storm of protest immediately appeared in the Mexican press and the State Department received a call from the Mexican ambassador. Incidents of this sort had been occurring for a hundred years but never, prior to the war, had such significance attached to them.

Conditions reached such a point in Texas that Roberto Medellin of the Mexican Ministry of Labor announced in 1943 that no more *braceros* would be sent to work in the state "because of the number of cases of extreme, intolerable racial discrimination." In an effort to induce the Mexican government to lift this ban, Governor Stevenson made a "goodwill" tour of Mexico and on his return appointed a Good Neighbor Commission. On June 25, 1943, the governor issued a formal proclamation calling upon all tried-and-true Texans to adhere to the Good Neighbor Policy. A few days later, the Commissioners' Court in Cameron County adopted a resolution "condemning any discriminations against our fellow citizens of Latin-American extraction" and expressing regret that "embarrassing occurrences have injured the feelings of our said fellow citizens and neighbors." These feeble gestures of "goodwill," however, were largely offset by the tone of the press which proceeded to add insult to injury by explaining that the only reason Mexicans were discriminated against in Texas was because they were "dirty"! (8).

It is interesting to note, however, that Resolution No. 105, in which Governor Stevenson proclaimed the Good Neighbor Policy in Texas, merely called upon the citizens of the state to adopt a non-discriminatory policy as to "all persons of the Caucasian race," thereby attempting to deny long-resident Negro citizens a status sought to be conferred on Mexican nationals. It should also be noted that the three "Mexicans" named to the commission were upper-class, old-resident *Tejanos*. For these and other reasons, the Good Neighbor Commission has not been particularly effective although the mere appointment of such a commission, of course, is a significant gesture. Long after the proclamation creating the commission was issued, many Texas jails continued to exhibit signs which specified a special visiting day for "Negroes and Mexicans." Noting the reluctance of the Texans to abandon their folkways, the Mexican weekly *Mañana* said that "The Nazis of Texas are not political partners of the Fuhrer of Germany but indeed they are slaves to the same prejudices and superstitions."

During the visit of American dignitaries to Mexico City for the Independence Day celebration of 1943, Francisco de P. Jiménez, a member of the Chamber of Deputies, made a speech in which he bitterly denounced the mistreatment of Mexicans in the borderlands. A former member of the Mexican consular corps in Texas, he called attention to the case of one Antonio Rangel who had been murdered by an Anglo-American. The defendant was released, shortly after his arrest, on $25 bail! He also mentioned the case of one José Aguilar who, in the course of an assault, had been seriously injured by an Anglo-American. In this case, the aggressor was exonerated upon payment of a $50 fine. In the same speech, Deputy Jiménez quoted a pastoral letter in which Archbishop Lucey of San Antonio had denounced, by name, a certain Catholic church which had openly exhibited a sign reading: *"no se admite a Mexicanos."* Concluding a long recital of similar discriminatory acts, he demanded the appointment of a commission to meet with Governor Stevenson and to investigate conditions in Texas. A resolution to this effect was unanimously adopted by the Chamber of Deputies.

After appointing the Good Neighbor Commission, Governor Stevenson again appealed to Foreign Minister Padilla to lift the ban against sending *braceros* to Texas. The foreign minister replied that the appointment of the commission had not brought about a satisfactory correction of conditions in Texas. "In many parts of Texas," he said, "Mexicans cannot attend public gatherings without being subject to vexations, complaints and protests. There are towns where my fellow countrymen are forced to live in separate districts. Just a week ago the daughter of a Mexican consul was refused service in a public establishment." The ban would not be lifted, he went on to say, until Texas had passed a law prohibiting such practices. A bill to this effect was introduced in the 1945 session of the Texas legislature but, needless to say, it did not pass. As a consequence, Texas still remains on Mexico's blacklist. The boycott, however, has not seriously cramped the Texas growers for they still have a large pool of Mexican labor, including some forty thousand illegal entrants or "wetbacks."

6. GOOD NEIGHBORS AND BAND MUSIC

During the war years the circumstance that Mexico was our ally against an enemy that preached the doctrine of a master race, the magnificent record made by Mexican-Americans in the service, the emphasis on the Good Neighbor Policy, and our dependence on Mexican labor, all served to bring out and to emphasize the mistreatment of persons of Mexican descent in the United States. For the first time since 1848, the full pattern of this treatment was brought to light and glaringly exposed.

In a carefully documented article in *Common Ground* (9), Dr. George I. Sanchez, of the University of Texas, former president of the League of United Latin-American Citizens, called attention to the pattern of discrimination in employment, in the schools, and in civic life throughout the borderlands. In the course of a hike, a Scoutmaster and his troop of Boy Scouts, all in uniform, were ordered out of a public park, where they had stopped to rest, because they were "Mexicans." Texas churches posted signs reading "For Colored and Mexicans" and refused Mexicans permission to attend the "white churches" on Sundays. "In many cemeteries, whether owned by county authorities, by private individuals or corporations, or by religious organizations . . . the bodies of 'Mexicans' are denied the right of burial. . . . In those cemeteries where such bodies are received they are assigned a separate plot of land, far enough from the plot destined for the so-called 'whites' so as to be sure that the bodies of the 'whites' will not be contaminated by the presence of the bodies of the Mexicans." Toilets in many Texas courthouses have signs which read: "For Whites—Mexicans Keep Out."

Mexicans are segregated with Negroes in the balconies of many motion picture theaters in the Southwest. Certain subdivisions in Southern California are restricted against Mexican occupancy, although in at least one case such restrictions have been ruled illegal. Although the pattern of discrimination against Mexicans is "spotty" and less rigid than against Negroes, it is nevertheless true that Mexicans are generally assigned a second-class status throughout the borderlands today. A careful study of the status of minority groups in Los Angeles has shown that, by reference to a number of conventional indices of status, Mexicans occupy a lower position in the community than that occupied by Negroes.

In an article in *The Texas Spectator* for October 11, 1946, Hart Stilwell, the author of a fine novel about Mexicans in a Texas bordertown, placed his finger on the real crux of "The Mexican Problem" in the Southwest:

> An Anglo-American was tried in a criminal district court in a small Texas town recently on a charge of murder.
>
> The man who was killed was a Texas-Mexican, a Latin-American if you prefer that term.
>
> The Anglo-American was acquitted.
>
> The trial attracted small attention in Texas. It was not even reported fully in the newspapers printed in the town where it took place. If it made the wire services, I failed to see it in any of the larger Texas papers.
>
> I happened to be familiar with some of the details of this case. And from what I know of it, I make the following observations: if the man who was killed had been an Anglo-American and the man who did the killing had been a Latin-American, I believe the verdict would have been different. And if both men had been Latin-Americans, I believe the verdict would have been different.
>
> What happened in this case is typical of what has been happening in Texas courts for a hundred years or more—twenty-five years to my personal knowledge. I have been a newspaper man in Texas for twenty-five years and I have carefully watched criminal cases in which members of the two races were involved. And if an Anglo-American has served one day in the penitentiary for the killing of a Latin-American during that period of time, I have not heard of it. . . .
>
> We can bring ten thousand Tipica Orchestras to Texas and send five thousand Rotary Clubs and Kiwanis Clubs and other goodwill delegations into Mexico, yet so long as the Mexican knows that he may be killed with impunity by any American who chooses to kill him, then all our talk about being good neighbors is merely paying lip service to a friendship we both know is a joke.

In a broadcast on May 10, 1947, Antonio Espiñosa de los Monteros, Mexico's ambassador to the United States, called upon the people of the United States to make "a sincere, determined effort to do away with racial prejudices" against persons of Mexican descent. "The citizens of those sections," he said (referring to the borderlands), "should realize that the day has come when it is absolutely necessary to give the Mexican absolute equality of opportunity." There can be no doubt but that this issue is today the most sensitive test of good neighborly relations between Mexico and the United States. "Discriminations of this character," said Sumner Welles, "inevitably cut deep. They create lasting resentments, which no eloquent speeches by government officials, nor governmental policies, however wise, can ever hope to remove. . . . So long as they continue anywhere in the United States they are bound to undermine the foundations which the two governments have laid for those cooperative ties which are so greatly to the interests of both countries, and they will, in the wider sense, impair that inter-American relationship which is today more necessary than ever before. Unless these discriminations are obliterated, and obliterated soon, the term 'good neighbor policy' will lose much of its real meaning" (10).

XV

After A Hundred Years

During the century that has elapsed since the signing of the Treaty of Guadalupe Hidalgo, the borderlands have been twice invaded: by Anglo-Americans from the north and east; and, in our time, by Mexican immigrants from the south. The first invasion took place under the shadow of an approaching war between Mexico and the United States; the second invasion culminated at a time when a state of undeclared war existed between the two nations. Throughout this period of a hundred years, relations between Anglos and Hispanos in the Southwest have been affected by the state of relations between the United States and Mexico. In fact a prime condition to an improvement in Anglo-Hispano relations has always consisted in a clarification of relations between the two nations. After a hundred years, this clarification of relations has finally been achieved—in broad outline, in first principles. As relations between the United States and Mexico have been stabilized, on the basis of mutual dependency and respect, significant steps have been taken toward an improvement of Anglo-Hispano relations in the borderlands. It all began on a cold, raw day in March, 1933, when Franklin D. Roosevelt, in his first inaugural address, pledged the United States to the policy of the Good Neighbor.

1. A Beginning Is Made

While the Office of the Coordinator of Inter-American Affairs was apparently established without any thought of using it to improve Anglo-Hispano relations in the Southwest, Mr. Nelson Rockefeller was soon deluged with suggestions that it be used in this manner. To many people living in the Southwest it seemed obvious that here was the logical place to invest the Good Neighbor Policy with real meaning and content. On October 15, 1941, as commissioner of immigration and housing in California, I submitted to Mr. Rockefeller a plan for the improvement of Anglo-Hispano relations and similar suggestions were transmitted by Dr. Joaquín Ortega, of the University of New Mexico; by Dr. George Sanchez of the University of Texas; by Dr. W. Lewis Abbott, of Colorado College; by Dr. Ben Cherrington, of the University of Denver; and by Mr. C. J. Carreon, a Mexican-American member of the Arizona legislature.

After some initial hesitation, the coordinator sent Mr. David Saposs to make a survey of conditions in the Southwest. Upon receipt of his report on April 3, 1942, the Spanish-Speaking People's Division was established as part of the Office of Inter-American Affairs to stimulate and coordinate public and private rehabilitation programs aimed at preparing the Spanish-speaking to participate more actively in American life and to educate the English-speaking to the necessity of eliminating discriminatory practices injurious to the war effort and to our relations with Spanish America (1).

Unfortunately the coordinator had great difficulty in making up his mind about the real function of the new division. Limited funds were wasted in trifling ballyhoo campaigns of one kind or another and too often the division functioned as though its prime objective were to induce Anglo-American clubwomen to sponsor Latin-American "fiestas." In many ways, the division acted as though it wanted to frustrate any real efforts on the part of Spanish-speaking people to improve their lot. Some of the field representatives seemed to be actually afraid of Mexican-Americans, for they insisted on working with the least representative elements in the various Spanish-speaking communities.

On the board of the Southern California Council on Inter-American Affairs, subsidized by the CIAA, not a single Spanish-speaking person appeared although a local Mexican Affairs Coordinating Committee was set up to advise the council. This cleavage perpetuated, of course, the basic fault in Anglo-Hispano relations. A sample of items taken from the bulletin of the council will show how public funds were used to promote the Good Neighbor Policy: a cocktail party for Alfred Ramos Martínez, the Mexican painter, at the Hatfield Dalzell galleries; a breakfast for the Latin-American consular corps; a Pan-American "fiesta" at a local high school featuring José Arias and his Latin-American Troubadores; a cocktail party for the Latin-American consular corps at the Jonathan Club; an exhibit of New Mexico *santos* and *bultos* at the Southwest Museum; an institute on community relations which, the bulletin proudly notes, was reported "in a series of colorful and gossipy stories" by Princess Conchita Pignatelli in the Los Angeles *Examiner;* a series of lectures, illustrated "with many unusual colored slides" entitled "Travelling South Through Colombia, Ecuador, Peru, Bolivia, and Chile"; and an endless series of "goodwill" proclamations and radio programs stressing the necessity of Latin-American support in the war effort.

Feeble as these efforts were, the establishment of the Spanish-speaking section of the CIAA must be regarded as a landmark in Anglo-Hispano relations in the Southwest for it constituted a recognition, however belated, that the United States had not fulfilled its obligations under the Treaty of Guadalupe Hidalgo. Also, thanks largely to the work of Mrs. Jane W. Pijoan, not all of the division's funds were wasted on cocktail parties, receptions, and window displays of the flags of Latin-American countries. Field representatives were stationed in Los Angeles and Austin; grants-in-aid were made to a number of established institutions in California, Texas, New Mexico, Colorado, and Michigan; in cooperation with the Institute of International Education some ten or fifteen fellowships were provided for Spanish-speaking students; and a series of important and useful conferences were organized in the Southwest.

Patterned on the Northern Colorado Conference on the Problems of the Spanish-Speaking People held in Greeley on May 10, 1942, the Coordinator's Office organized a larger conference in Denver in June and July, 1943; in Santa Fe in August, 1943; and at the Arizona State Teachers College in Temple in June of the same year. Effectively organized and well-attended, these conferences initiated action programs which have had a wide influence throughout the region. At the University of New Mexico, four one-week institutes were organized for the training of Spanish-speaking rural leaders and teacher "work-shops" were promoted in many cities.

With funds provided by the Coordinator's Office, the National Catholic Welfare Conference organized its first seminar on "The Spanish-Speaking People of the Southwest and West," in San Antonio, in July, 1943, which was followed by similar conferences in Denver, Santa Fe, and Los Angeles. These conferences represent, to the best of my knowledge, the first region-wide effort by the Catholic Church to concern itself with the problems of the Spanish-speaking people. While individual Catholic leaders, like Archbishop Lucey in San Antonio, have long been concerned about the Spanish-speaking people, the same cannot be said of the Church as a whole. The principal institutional influence in the life of the Mexican-American, its main contribution to a solution of "the Mexican Problem" has been a policy of religious nationalism and exclusiveness which has further isolated the Mexican from the general community with which he must some day make his adjustment (2).

Several points should be noted about all these conferences and institutes. Beginning about 1943, that hardy perennial "the Mexican Problem" began to give way to a discussion of "The Spanish-Speaking People of the Southwest." Whereas communities had formerly been preoccupied with some situation in their backyards, they now began to realize, for the first time, that the phase of the problem with which they were concerned was related to a much larger situation throughout the Southwest. The particularistic view, in which the camera-eye was focussed on some specific Mexican shacktown, began to give way to the generic view, in which the camera swept the whole panorama of the Southwest. Public attention began to focus on Anglo-Hispano relations in the region, not as an intramural, domestic concern, but as an integral part of the much larger question of finding the basis for a new accord between the Anglo part of the hemisphere and the Spanish part.

Once events were seen in this perspective, thoughtful residents of the borderlands began to discuss, not "the Mexican Problem," but the Anglo-American problem. In the past, the isolation of the Spanish-speaking along a broken border had obscured the obvious fact that Mexicans were a large minority throughout the region and not merely "a local problem" in a few communities. Communities in Southern California, for example, still think of the Mexicans in their midst as though they were the only Mexicans in the United States. As more and more Mexicans began to participate in "Good Neighbor" conferences and institutes, the discussion shifted from a probing of conditions long deplored to a consideration of ways and means by which the Mexican people themselves might be given a chance to improve these conditions. Although the shift in attitude is difficult to describe in a phrase, one might say that the "social work" approach has gradually been replaced by the "social action" approach. What the "Good Neighbor" conferences and institutes reflected, of course, was the rise of a new and a more general interest in the Spanish-speaking people as an ethnic group (3). The interest, moreover, began to be extended in depth as well as in general range. The studies which Dr. Michael Pijoan made of nutritional factors in "the Mexican Problem" threw a glaring light on such questions as the ability of Spanish-speaking children to learn as rapidly as Anglo-American children (4).

2. Grass-Roots Democracy

Of the various projects sponsored by the coordinator, none was more significant than the formation of the "service clubs" in Colorado. With funds provided by the government, the Colorado Inter-American Field Service Commission was organized in the fall of 1944. By January of 1945, Mrs. Helen L. Peterson, the field director, had organized the first Latin-American service club in Rocky Ford. Before the year was over, eight additional clubs had been organized in Pueblo, Walsenburg, Trinidad, San Luis, Alamosa, Monte Vista, Greeley, and Taos. Fourteen of the clubs are now banded together in the Community Service Clubs, Inc., which publishes the *Pan-American News* in Denver. When the Coordinator's Office was liquidated in December, 1945, the program was taken over by the Institute of Ethnic Affairs.

The Colorado service clubs are an attempt to stimulate grass-roots democracy in Spanish-speaking communities. Unlike various left-wing efforts to organize the Spanish-speaking people,—such as the ill-fated Spanish-Speaking Congress of 1939,—the service clubs have their roots, not in international politics, but in the basic needs of the Spanish-speaking communities. Starting with some simple issue, the clubs have taken up, one at a time, the problems closest to the people. They have conducted campaigns to register voters; they have sponsored scholarships for Spanish-speaking students; financed community health surveys; brought about the elimination of discriminatory practices; fought for better recreational facilities; and secured their rights for Mexican-American veterans. One of the clubs has initiated a $60,000-medical-care program in the San Luis Valley. Tackling the problem of Mexican-

American truants, the Rocky Ford Club succeeded in returning ninety per cent of the youngsters to the schools in a week. In developing the service clubs, all that Mrs. Peterson has done has been to provide the initial leadership, direction, and guidance. Long eager for some such program, the people have quickly responded and have accomplished significant improvements in a remarkably brief space of time.

In Southern California a similar grass-roots, local type of organization has developed under the brilliant leadership of Ignacio López in the Pomona Valley. For all practical purposes, the Unity Leagues which he has organized are similar in purpose and function to the service clubs in Colorado. With Mexican-American veterans playing a leading role, the Unity Leagues have been consistently concerned with the most immediate and obvious needs of the Mexican communities. Indigenous and organic, they represent grass-roots democracy at its best, for it is their purpose to enlist the energies of the people. When this approach has been adopted, leaders have been found in Mexican communities without much trouble. In essence what the Unity Leagues have done, as Ruth Tuck puts it, is to "sprinkle the grass roots" (5). In 1946-1947, the American Council on Race Relations sent Fred W. Ross, an extremely talented grass-roots organizer, into the citrus belt communities in Southern California to expand the Unity League program. In a year's work, Mr. Ross set in motion tides of interest and activity which have had the widest ramifications. In Chicago, the Mexican Civic Committee, organized by Frank M. Paz, functions in much the same way. What these activities foreshadow, of course, is a great awakening of the Spanish-speaking people in the Southwest which I feel certain will mature within the next two decades.

3. The Westminster Case

Gonzalo Méndez, a citizen of the United States, had been a resident of the town of Westminster, in Orange County, California, for twenty-five years. Of immigrant background, he had come to be a moderately prosperous asparagus grower. There are two schools in Westminster: a handsomely equipped school with green lawns and shrubs for the Anglo-Americans; and a Mexican school whose meager equipment matches the inelegance of its surroundings. It was not the discrepancy between the two schools, however, that annoyed Gonzalo Méndez. Rather it was the fact, so he said, that he didn't like the idea of his Sylvia, Gonzalo, Jr. and Gerónimo, growing up with hatred in their hearts for the children who went to the beautiful school. In the nearby community of El Modeno, the two schools were side by side; but the Mexican youngsters were always served lunch at a different hour from the Anglo-American students. Concluding that this practice had gone on long enough, Méndez filed a suit in the federal courts on March 2, 1945, on behalf of some five thousand Mexican residents of the district, against the school officials of Orange County.

Oddly enough, this issue had never been squarely raised before in California. The School Code permits segregation of "Indian children or children of Chinese, Japanese, or Mongolian descent," but says nothing about Mexicans or Negroes. Without formal sanction, the practice of segregating Mexican children in the schools came about in California largely through default of any determined resistance on the part of Mexican-Americans. Once established, of course, the segregated schools were defended and rationalized. For example, the superintendent of one of the schools involved in the Méndez suit wrote a thesis in 1939 in which he defended segregation on the ground of "social differences" between the two groups; the higher percentage of "undesirable behavior patterns" among Mexican students (which one would assume it would be a function of the schools to correct); and the "lower moral standards" to be found in the Mexican group.

In some cases, segregation was accomplished by a fancy gerrymandering of school districts; but the more common practice was to use the arbitrary linguistic device of assigning all children with Spanish names to a separate school. Occasionally the school authorities would examine the appearance of youngsters so as to prevent the offspring of a Mexican mother whose married name might be O'Shaughnessey, from slipping into the wrong school. While the practice varied from district to district, the general scheme was to segregate Mexicans from the first through the sixth, and in some cases through the twelfth, grade.

In the trial of the Méndez case, the school authorities at first contended that Mexicans were a distinct and therefore an "inferior" race; but, confronted by the testimony of some world-famous anthropologists, they soon abandoned this position. As a matter of fact, it had been determined years ago—*In re Rodríguez,* 81 Fed. 337—that Mexicans of

Spanish descent and of mixed Spanish-Indian descent were "white persons" within the meaning of the naturalization laws. The superintendent of schools then testified that Mexican children were "dirty"; that they had lice and impetigo; that their hands, face, neck, and ears were often unwashed (presumably nothing of this sort had ever happened with Anglo-American youngsters); and that, generally speaking, they were "inferior" to the other students in point of personal hygiene.

In a memorable opinion handed down on March 21, 1945, Judge Paul J. McCormick ruled that segregation of Mexican youngsters found no sanction under the California laws and that it also violated the "equal protection" clause of the Fourteenth Amendment. Segregation, Judge McCormick suggested, might have something to do with the fact that Mexican youngsters were retarded in English speech. It also had the effect, he said, of "depriving them of a common cultural attitude . . . which is imperative for the perpetuation of American institutions and ideals" and of fostering antagonism. When the decision was appealed to the Ninth Circuit Court, *amicus curiae* briefs were filed on behalf of Méndez by the American Jewish Congress, the National Association for the Advancement of Colored People, the National Lawyers Guild, the American Civil Liberties Union, the Japanese-American Citizens League, and by Robert W. Kenny as attorney general of California. On April 14, 1947, the Ninth Circuit Court affirmed Judge McCormick's ruling.

In a brilliant concurring opinion, Justice William Denman exposed all the shabby rationalizations by which the school authorities had sought to justify their action. The segregation of Mexican students in the schools, he caustically noted, did not stand alone; on the contrary, it was part of a pattern of discrimination and could not be justified in pedagogic terms however facile. For, as he observed, the Rev. R. N. Núñez, a Catholic priest, Eugenio Nogueros, a college graduate, and Ignacio López, a newspaper publisher, had been forced to file a suit in the federal courts to enjoin the officials of nearby San Bernardino from barring "Latins" from the public swimming plunges. This discrimination had nothing whatever to do with educational theories; nor had it anything to do with hygiene. For *all* "Latins" had been barred: clean or dirty, healthy or diseased, black or white; in fact, as Justice Denman pointed out, the prohibition was so broad as to have embraced the nationals of twenty-one South American nations, Mexico, Italy, Spain and Portugal. In closing his opinion, Justice Denman suggested that the school authorities of Orange County should be punished for contempt of court in having failed to carry into effect the decision of the lower court.

The filing of this precedent-shattering case was in no sense "inspired." Outside organizations provided valuable assistance in handling the trial and the appeal, but the case had been filed simply because Gonzalo Méndez had "had enough." That the action was long overdue is shown by the manner in which one Mexican community after the other immediately raised the same issue. In a dozen or more communities similar suits were filed or movements launched to eliminate segregated schools; and in El Modeno the Mexicans followed up their victory in the courts by electing one of the group a member of the local school board.

Forty-five Mexican-American and thirty Negro families make up the little settlement of Bell Town near Riverside, California. The school in Bell Town is a four-room wooden structure built over twenty years ago. Two miles down the road is an attractive stucco "Spanish-style" modern school with excellent equipment and every teaching facility. Only Negroes and Mexicans attended the Bell Town school; while the other school was "lily white" with the exception of three Mexicans and one Negro student who lived so close to the school that they could not be excluded on any pretense. "White" children, regardless of where they lived, were invariably assigned to the better school.

Hearing about the Méndez case, the residents of Bell Town decided that they, too, had "had enough." Under the guidance of Fred Ross they founded the Bell Town Improvement League and petitioned the authorities to do away with segregation. In this instance, the school officials said nothing whatever about cleanliness or backwardness or godliness but frankly stated that the encroachment of Mexicans and Negroes would depreciate property values. . . . After a long fight, the residents of Bell Town won out. On September 16, 1946, the supervisor of schools told his staff: "If there is as much as one segregated Mexican-American pupil see to it that he gets unsegregated immediately."

Throughout Southern California, Mexican-Americans have been moving toward a new awareness, a new consciousness of their rights as citizens of the United States. Chavez Ravine, in the City of Los Angeles, has a large Mexican population. In June, 1946, the 4,500 residents announced that they had been "walking and walking for years and years and now we're very, very tired" and proceeded to form a civic organization and demand that the area be provided with the bus service which it had lacked for twenty-five years. Today busses are running in Chavez Ravine. When the Mexican-American veterans returned to Clearwater, where most of the Mexicans lived on Illinois Street, they decided that it was about time, after all these years, that the street was paved. Today Illinois Street is paved. This same process is at work all over Southern California: streets are being paved; lights are being turned on; busses are running; and Mexican children are beginning to attend general schools along with other children.

4. "Utilizable Cultural Residues"

Part of the change that is taking place in Anglo-Hispano relationships in the Southwest can be traced to the new interest and leadership that has developed at the colleges and universities. As early as 1912, Dr. E. D. Gray wanted to found a Spanish-American university in New Mexico, for he regarded the bilingual population as a national and international asset. Today, thanks to the leadership of Dr. Joaquín Ortega, the University of New Mexico has a School of Inter-American Affairs which is training students who want to work in Latin-American countries as teachers, businessmen, and technicians.

"New Mexico," writes Dr. Ortega, "still possesses utilizable cultural residues." It has the most homogeneous Spanish-speaking and the most cohesive Indian communities in the United States as well as a typical cross-section of Anglo-Americans and other immigrants. Here is the place, he has insisted, to study the process of acculturation in the Americas for nowhere else can one find the three major cultural groups,— Indians, Spanish, and Anglo-Americans,—living together in large numbers with a common national allegiance yet maintaining their traditional cultures.

"New Mexico," Dr. Ortega has also said, "is the shortest route to Mexican goodwill," and to the goodwill of all Latin-America. During the war, we had no more effective spokesman on our radio programs broadcast to South America than Senator Dennis Chavez of New Mexico. While we have not yet learned to utilize the cultural resources of the Southwest, some steps have been made in the right direction. We discovered during the war that Pueblo Indians from New Mexico made excellent spokesmen for the United States among the Indians of South America. And we have begun to use a few Spanish-speaking people in the diplomatic and consular services (Daniel Valdez, who did one of the first studies of the Spanish-speaking people in Colorado, was recently appointed attaché to the American embassy in Montevideo). In emphasizing the importance of understanding and developing these resources, the University of New Mexico has played a prominent part.

In 1936 the university came into possession of the Harwood Foundation through a gift from Mrs. Lucy C. Harwood and immediately set about using the foundation as the spearhead for an educational program designed to serve the needs of Spanish-American villagers. By way of preparing this program, Dr. George Sanchez made a study of Taos County which was published in 1940 under the title of *Forgotten People*. The publication of this extraordinarily fine, sensitive, and perceptive study of Spanish-American culture might be said to mark a new chapter in the history of the Spanish-speaking people of the Southwest. Based on this study, the university then launched the Taos Project of community and adult education which has attracted nation-wide attention. Essentially a self-help, cooperative, community organization project, the Taos Project has some impressive, if limited, accomplishments to its credit (6).

At about the same time, Mr. and Mrs. Cyrus McCormick made a grant to enable the University to revise the work of a small rural school in the village of Nambe. This school has since become an important "pilot" school in devising better teaching methods for Spanish-speaking children (7). All of these projects, as well as the founding of the San Jose Training School in Albuquerque in 1930—again to improve teaching methods—and the fine work being done at New Mexico Highlands University at Las Vegas by Quincy Guy Burris—indicate the kind of leadership the universities have shown in the last decade.

Similar developments have taken place at the University of Texas, particularly since the arrival there of Dr. George Sanchez. The Committee on Inter-American Relations in Texas has sponsored such excellent studies as Dr. Wilson Little's report on *Spanish-Speaking Children in Texas* (1944), which has been the basis for many improvements in the educational system. Under the guidance of the university, the State Department of Education is now making a serious effort to improve the teaching of Spanish in the public schools and free textbooks are furnished for teaching Spanish at every grade level. A summer school is now conducted by the university in Mexico City and an Institute of Latin-American Studies has been founded at Austin. Recently the First Regional Conference on the Education of Spanish-Speaking People in the Southwest was held at Austin (December 13-15, 1946)—one of the first attempts to consider the education of Spanish-speaking people as a region-wide problem in inter-American education. From this conference has come the Southwestern Council on the Education of the Spanish-Speaking Peoples whose recommendations have begun to have a wide influence in the Southwest. Some fifteen years ago, J. Frank Dobie said that there were only about twenty or thirty Mexican-American students at the university; today one hundred and fourteen are enrolled.*

All this activity of the last decade—the new role being played by the universities, the calling of conferences and institutes, the appointment of Good Neighbor commissions in Texas, and so forth—indicates that leaders of opinion in the Southwest have come to recognize that in discussing the education of Spanish-speaking people and related issues, they are dealing with aspects of a unitary region-wide problem which cannot be precisely correlated, say, with the assimilation of Italian-Americans in New Haven. For the Spanish-speaking minority in the Southwest, rather like the Negro issue in the Deep South, presents a problem in masses. Spanish-speaking people in the borderlands are the fringe of great masses of Spanish-speaking people in Mexico, Central America, and South America. To regard them as "merely another minority" is to gravely minimize the significance of the borderlands as a bridge to inter-American understanding.

5. From De Anza to Juan López

The movement traced in the foregoing section should be regarded as the latest chapter in the Anglo-Americans' belated discovery of the Southwest. The oldest settled portion of the United States, the Southwest is the newest in point of Anglo-American interest. In this sense, it was discovered by Hubert H. Bancroft and Bandelier in the 1880's. Bancroft's *History of the North Mexico States and Texas* appeared between 1884 and 1889; his *History of California* from 1885 to 1891; and his *His-*

* See *Texas-Born Spanish-Name Students in Texas Colleges and Universities: 1945-1946*, by Ruth Ann Fogartie, University of Texas Press (March, 1948).

tory of Arizona and New Mexico in 1889. Bancroft worked with documents; the man who really "discovered" the Southwest, as a cultural province, was Adolph F. A. Bandelier. Trained in geology at the University of Berne, Bandelier came to New Mexico in 1880 and in the course of a decade visited every nook and cranny of the Southwest. His *Final Report on The Southwestern United States,* Part II, appeared in 1892. These works by Bancroft and Bandelier, along with Frank W. Blackmar's *Spanish Institutions of the Southwest* (1891) and Charles Fletcher Lummis' *The Land of Poco Tiempo* (1893), represent the initial Anglo-American awareness of the cultural importance of the Southwest.

Those who first discovered the cultural riches of the Southwest emphasized, quite naturally, its archaeological and antiquarian interests. Largely as a result of Bandelier's work, the Archaeological Institute of America selected Santa Fe as the headquarters for its School of American Research in 1908. At about the same time, the influx of writers, artists, and intellectuals began, when Ernest Blumenschein and Oscar Berninghaus arrived in Taos in a covered wagon. Through the work of the Santa Fe and Taos artists, the nation became increasingly aware of the cultural importance of the Southwest. First discovering the Indians, the artists and writers gradually began to discover the Spanish-speaking. From 1920 to 1930 the native New Mexicans were "discovered" with a vengeance. Just as the somewhat earlier discovery of the Indians found expression in a movement primarily aimed at the reconstruction of Indian arts and crafts, so the discovery of the Hispanos coincided with a movement aimed at reconstituting the Spanish-Colonial handicraft arts. What both movements lacked was a social program by which the basic economy of the Indians and the Spanish-speaking might be reconstructed, for the arts and crafts could only flourish as the culture was vigorous and life sustaining.

This missing element,—the social program,—was supplied by the New Deal agencies in New Mexico in the 'thirties. Faced with heavy Spanish-speaking relief loads, these agencies were compelled to undertake, in conjunction with the Bureau of Indian Affairs, a thorough-going survey of natural and human resources in the Rio Grande Valley. The monumental Tewa Basin studies initiated by the Soil Conservation Service represent perhaps the first serious attempt to view the whole human scene in New Mexico and to ferret out the correlations between Anglo, Hispano, and Indian influences in the region. Much of the present-day interest in Spanish-speaking people in the Southwest can be traced to the work of federal agencies and federal officials in New Mexico in the period from 1933 to 1940. If the Indians received more attention than the Spanish-Americans, it was because they were somewhat better organized to demand attention for their problems. But both efforts—to rehabilitate Indian life and to reconstruct Spanish-American communities—were and still are closely interrelated.

What has happened in this process of discovery is that the focus of the Anglo-Americans has finally come to center in the contemporary scene. An interest in mission ruins and Indian relics has been known to lead to an interest in Mexicans and Indians. Hence the focus of interest has gradually shifted from the *entrada* of Juan de Oñate in 1598 to life in the village of Truchas in 1947; from Junípero Serra's first celebration of the mass in San Diego to a concern with the present-day Mexican-American *colonias*. Similarly an interest in Spanish-Colonial arts has gradually ripened into an interest in the handling of the chili crop and in tenant-herding in the Cuba Valley.

The nearer the focus has shifted to the contemporary scene, the more the Anglo-Americans have been surprised by their discoveries. Nowadays, a hundred years after the signing of the Treaty of Guadalupe Hidalgo, they have finally begun to study the actual social structure of the widely varying Mexican-American communities to be found between Brownsville and Los Angeles. From studies of this sort has come the realization, as Lee Casey puts it, that perhaps the Anglo-Americans should "do a little adjusting themselves." It is significant that the growing maturity of Mexican-American communities throughout the Southwest is closely related, in point of time, to the appearance of this new interest, not in Juan Bautista de Anza, but in Juan López.

XVI

"One And Together"

"No one who has grown up in California," wrote Josiah Royce, "can be under an illusion as to the small extent to which the American character, as here exemplified, has been really altered by foreign intercourse, large as the foreign population has always remained. The foreign influence has never been for the American community at large, in California, more than skin-deep. One has assumed a very few and unimportant California ways, one has freely used or abused the few (Spanish) words and phrases, one has grown well accustomed to the sight of foreigners and to business relations with them, and one's natural innocence about foreign matters has in California given place, even more frequently than elsewhere in our country, to a superficial familiarity with the appearance and the manners of numerous foreign communities. But all this in no wise renders the American life in California less distinctly native in tone. . . . You cannot call a community of Americans foreign in disposition merely because its amusements have a foreign look" (1).

To Royce,—the most perceptive and sensitive of California historians, —this summation seemed quite clear and obvious in 1886. But it was not quite accurate, even then, to say that "the California ways" which had survived were "few and unimportant." More deeply than Royce imagined, the customs, the laws, and the economic practices and institutions of the native Californians had exerted a definite influence on the culture which began to emerge after the American conquest. However it did appear in 1886 that the native Californians had suffered an irreparable defeat and that the initial contact between the two cultures had resulted in the eclipse of the one without any substantial modification in the basic pattern of the other.

But today the ineluctable facts of geography and history dictate a somewhat different conclusion. Mexico is not France or Italy or Poland: it is geographically a part of the Southwest. Residing in the Mexican states immediately south of the border are approximately 2,500,000 Spanish-speaking people; in the American border states approximately the same number of Spanish-speaking reside. Essentially these are one people, occupying a single cultural province, for the Spanish-speaking minority north of the border (a majority in some areas) has always drawn, and will continue to draw, support, sustenance, and re-enforcements from south of the border. Our Spanish-speaking minority is not, therefore, a detached fragment but an integral part of a much larger population unit to which it is bound by close geographic and historical ties. Furthermore, Hispanic influences in the United States have a strong anchor in New Mexico where these influences are actually older, and perhaps more deeply rooted, than in the Mexican border states.

The Spanish-speaking and the Indians of the Southwest have the highest birth rates of any ethnic groups in the region. Infant mortality rates are declining, for both groups, throughout the borderlands: between 1929 and 1944 the rate decreased in New Mexico from 145.5 infant deaths per 1,000 live births to 89.1. With high birth rates and rapidly declining infant mortality rates, the Spanish-speaking element will retain its position relative to Anglo-Americans for many years to come, barring unforeseeable contingencies.

These facts alone would indicate that the Hispanic minority cannot be regarded as merely another immigrant group in the United States destined for ultimate absorption. In this instance, however, demographical considerations are fortified by the facts of geography and the implications of history. While Spanish cultural influences have retreated in portions of the Southwest, they have never been eclipsed. "Whether they will or not," wrote J. P. Widney in the 1880's, "their future [that is, the future of Anglos and Hispanos] is one and together, and I think neither type of race will destroy the other. They will merge." With the Spanish-speaking element having been re-enforced by a million or more immigrants in the last forty years, virtually all of whom have remained in the Southwest, some type of cultural fusion or merger must result. In fact, a surprising degree of fusion has already taken place.

1. By Any Other Name

The development of speech and language patterns not only mirrors the relationships between Anglos and Hispanos in the Southwest but is the best gauge of the degree of cultural fusion that has occurred. Needless to say, I discuss this highly complex subject not as a linguist; nor in terms of its linguistic interest; but rather to indicate what has actually happened to the two cultures in the region and to trace a relationship. For the attitude of a minority toward language and speech has an important bearing on the direction that the process of acculturation is likely to take.

The language pattern in the Southwest has, of course, a number of variable factors. It varies in relation to the numerical proportion between the two groups in any one place; the age of the community; whether it is rural or urban; the degree of isolation; the history of social relations in the community and many other factors. Quite apart from these variations, however, there is a larger aspect to the language pattern which can be considered from three points of view: Spanish borrowings from American-English speech; Anglo-American borrowings from the Spanish; and the development in both groups of a kind of jargon which is more "Southwestern" than Spanish or English.

In 1917 Dr. Aurelion M. Espiñosa listed some three hundred words of Anglo-American origin which have been incorporated into the Spanish language as spoken in New Mexico after first being Hispanized. Most of these words had been borrowed from necessity rather than choice, for they related, in the main, to commodities, practices, things, and concepts for which there was no Spanish equivalent (at least not in the Spanish spoken in New Mexico). Many of them had to do with commercial, industrial, and political practices unknown to the Spanish population prior to the American conquest as shown by the fact that more than fifty per cent of the terms had been incorporated after 1880. In large measure the adopted words had to do with "work terms" related to the new jobs which New Mexicans had acquired; others related to slang expressions used in American sports. Obviously most of this borrowing was based on strictly utilitarian considerations (2).

In another study of word-borrowing, Dr. Manuel Gamio listed the following among many terms that had been hispanicized: picnic, laundry, ties (railroad ties), matches, stockyards (*estoque yardas*), groceries, lunch, tickets, depot, time-check, truck, truck-driver, biscuit, omelette, bootlegger, taxes, ice cream, board and boarder, boss, automobile, sweater, jumper, sheriff, etc. In still another list, Dr. Harold W. Bentley added: home run (*jonronero*); scraper (*escrepa*); plug (*ploga*); puncture (*ponchar*); jack (*llaqui*); and such expressions as *"vamos flat"*—to have a flat tire (literally, "we go flat"). Generally, the Spanish-speaking people have borrowed from necessity rather than choice and have shown either resistance or indifference to other types of borrowings. Still the number of such borrowings, from necessity or otherwise, has been substantial and would probably be much greater today than when these studies were made.

According to Alfred Bruce Gaarder, there are four types of Spanish spoken in the Southwest: the Spanish spoken by the "old folks," particularly in New Mexico, which contains many archaic forms known only to the sixteenth century; the language of the "middle generation" which keeps some of the archaic and obsolete forms but adds a large vocabulary of Anglicisms developed to meet the needs of trade or business; the speech of the "youngest group" which increases the confusion by the use of slang expressions current among their schoolmates; and, lastly, the jargon of the city gangs, identical with the third grouping above, except that expressions of a shady, sinister, or double meaning have been added; often this jargon is used as a secret language (3).

It is in the speech of the city gangs, "the *pachuco* patois," that the attempt to fuse the two languages is most clearly apparent. For these youngsters play wonderful variations on both languages, Anglicizing Spanish and Hispanicizing English as it suits their purpose and often coining an expression of their own. Here are some of their inventions or fusions as reported by Dr. Gaarder:

Pachuco	Spanish	English
bolar	dólar	dollar
borlo	baile	dance
calco	zapato	shoe
caldiarre	enojarse	to be angry
canton	casa	house
carlo	caló	cant
carnal	hermano	brother
carnala	hermana	sister
carrucha	automóvil	automobile
chero	policía	police
duro	dólar	dollar
frajo	cigarro	cigar-cigarette
grena	pelo	hair
greta	marihuana	marihuana
huisa	muchacha	girl
jando	dinero	money

jetiar	dormir	sleep
jura	policía	police
mostacho	bigote	mustache
pildora	policía	police
rolante	automóvil	automobile
simon	sí	yes
tonda	sombrero	hat
vesca	marihuana	marihuana

Other *pachuismos* are: *anteojos,* front window; *bote,* jail; *chante,* house (probably from shanty); *choque,* chalk; *chillar,* to cry; *escamado,* frightened; *jefa,* mother; *jefe,* father; *lira,* guitar; *tambo,* jail; *tambique,* jail; *tramo,* suit.

The second generation uses many slang expressions also found in the talk of the *pachucos: aleluyas,* converts to Protestantism; *birria,* beer; *bollío,* an American; *bolucha,* or *bolita,* picking oranges; *brecas,* brakes; *chapos,* Japanese; *cho,* a movie; *chutear,* to shoot; *cuivo,* hello; *datil,* a date; *diez y penny,* a five-and-ten store; *engascado,* in love; *esa,* hello (to a girl); *ficha,* money; *fila,* or *filero,* a razor; *gavacho,* an American; *ginar,* to commit robbery; *gua he,* a guitar; *guayn,* wine; *jalar,* to work; *lorcha,* a match; *lucas,* crazy; *manil,* money; *mono,* a movie; *nagualones,* imported worker from Mexico; *pistiar,* to drink liquor; *rolar,* to sleep; *ser maleta,* to see a movie; *sut,* suit; *tintos,* Negroes; and *trola,* a match (4).

2. Words That Fit

Anglo-American borrowings from Spanish have also been dictated by necessity, in many cases, but from other motives as well. One important grouping of borrowed words has to do with things and practices for which there was no English equivalent, as in the cattle industry, the mining industry, and in the pack-train business (as I have already shown). But, in addition to these borrowings-by-necessity, there is a long list of Spanish words which have apparently been taken over for local color, humorous effect, and, above all, for their appropriateness in an arid environment. In his *Dictionary of Spanish Terms in English* (1932), Dr. Bentley lists some four hundred words which have been incorporated in the English spoken in the Southwest. Actually the list is much longer than linguists such as H. L. Mencken and George Philip Krapp have indicated, for they have not been looking in the right quarter, namely, the Southwest.

Considering that we had just fought a war against Mexico, it is indeed remarkable that so few Spanish place-names were changed after 1846. In addition to the names of rivers and mountains, Dr. Bentley states that there are two thousand or more cities and towns in the United States with Spanish names: four hundred or more in California; two hundred and fifty in Texas and New Mexico; and a hundred or more in both Colorado and Arizona. In Colorado the name of the state and the names of nineteen counties are Spanish. Spanish place-names also appear, with less frequency, in such states as Nevada, Wyoming, Utah, Oregon, Montana, and Idaho; in fact, they appear in every state in the union. Often the original Spanish has been Anglicized, as in Waco, California (originally Hueco); and, in many cases, Spanish and English terms have combined, as in Buena Park, Altaville, and Minaview. There are eight "Mesas," four "Bonanzas," and thirteen "El Dorados" in the United States. Many of the Spanish place-names outside the Southwest refer to the names of battles or of events related to the Mexican-American War.

In the Southwest most of the Spanish place-names were preserved—in my opinion—because of their extraordinary appropriateness and beauty. The Spanish named places with the uncannily descriptive accuracy of poets. For example, who could improve on "Sangre de Cristo" for the name of the great range of mountains in northern New Mexico? The very persistence with which resident Spanish-speaking people kept calling mountains, rivers, and towns by their Spanish names must, also, have been a factor. In Southern California, virtually all the Spanish place-names were retained; but many of the street names, in places such as Santa Barbara, San Diego, and Los Angeles, were changed or Anglicized after 1846.

Long familiar with an arid environment, the Spanish gave vivid and accurate names to the novel features of the Southwestern landscape. "The *acequia madre* ("mother ditch") of every village," writes T. M. Pearce, "has almost a personality of its own. It becomes the most intimate friend of every inhabitant of the place. With dancing and ceremony, the *acequias* are opened in the spring . . . with scrupulous care the *acequias* are scraped and strengthened in the villages and towns." To call these life-giving main canals "ditches" would have been to minimize their importance in this environment.

"ONE AND TOGETHER"

And so it is with many similar expressions, relating to the natural environment of the Southwest, which were retained and incorporated into Anglo-American speech. The list is a long one indeed and includes such words as: *malpaís, mesa, vega, cumbre, bosque, sierra, pozo, hondo, loma, bajada, ciénaga, piloncillo, potrero, arroyo, laguna, barranca, cañon, llano, brasada, chaparral, canada,* and many others. "The Southwest," writes Pearce, "with its peculiar brilliance of day and quick shadows of nightfall, with its hard-baked earth and sudden water gushes, with its thirsty sands at the very edge of soggy river bottoms, cannot be described in terms of Shakespeare's Stratford." For example, an *arroyo* is *not* a gully. As Pearce points out, "it is a bare rent in the side of Mother Earth where only yellow jaws yawn until a cloudburst in the mountains miles away sends the lashing torrents hurtling through it to crush and engulf everything caught in its maw." The word *malpaís* means more than "badlands": it refers to the lava ridges or serrated volcanic ash "dumps" to be found in the Southwest. It is quite impossible to convey the peculiar significance of *ciénaga,* as used in the Southwest, by some such expression as "marshy place," for the latter does not carry the connotation of an encompassing aridity. Thus *vega* is not just "meadow"; *bosque* is more than "a clump or grove"; and *sierra* carries overtones of meaning not suggested by "saw-toothed range."

It is not by chance, furthermore, that so many Spanish names for trees, plants, and shrubs have been borrowed in the Southwest. Many of these items have never had a name other than that given them by the Spaniards: *grama, sacaton, aparejo, alfilaria* (grasses); *mesquite, chaparral, chamiso, sahuaro, palo verde, huisache, mogote, maguey, manzanito, bellotas, álamo, tule, amole, capulin, plumajillo,* and *piñones,* (for trees, shrubs, and plants). Similarly, the Anglo-Americans borrowed many terms related to the type of architecture they found in the Southwest: *portal, corbel, adobe, fogón* (three-cornered fireplace), *ramada* (shaded arbor), *azotea* (the flat, platform-like roof), *cabana, casa grande, hammock, presidio, hacienda, jacal, patio, placeta, plaza, viga, palacio, zaguán* (open passage way), *cañales* (roof gutters), *trostera* (large cubpboard), and many others. Many animals and insects—*tecolote* (owl), *coyote, cucaracha* (cockroach), *javalina, mosquito, cougar, lobos, jaguars, conejos* (rabbits), *venalos* (deer), are Spanish in origin or, in the Southwest, are known by their Spanish names. Names for items of dress have likewise been appropriated: *sombrero, tilma, rebozo, manta,* and *sarape*. From the Spanish-American War, came *rurale, machete, ley fuga, mañana,* hoosegow (*juzgado*), and a number of other words and expressions.

From the contact between the British and Spanish navies came such words as armada, cask, cork, and cargo. And then there is, of course, a long list of words, Spanish in origin, which have become fully "naturalized": vigilante, filibuster, avocado, barbecue, cockroach, corral, creole, tobacco, cannibal, vanilla, hammock, tornado, alfalfa, canary, cigar, maroon, Negro, palaver, paragon, parasol, sherry, soda, canoe, banana, alligator, cocoa, sassafras; as well as many words that came by way of South America: alpaca, armadillo, chinchilla, cocaine, condor, cougar, jaguar, llama, and tapioca.

Spanish borrowings from American speech have naturally been most numerous in the speech area along the Rio Grande and immediately south of the border; while American borrowings have been most common throughout the old Spanish borderlands area. Many southwestern words and idioms are Spanish in origin: jerky, hackamore, buckaroo, mustang, stampede, lariat, fandango, hoosegow, wrangler, desperado, vamoose, hombre, adios, agua, bandido. In this area, the corruption of Spanish has been paralleled by the cultivation of what J. Frank Dobie calls "sagebrush" or "bull-pen" Spanish. Most of the borrowings, on both sides, have been by ear for neither group has been a serious student of the language of the other. In the isolation of the region, each group borrowed from the other so that today part of the vocabulary of the Southwest is bilingual in origin. A kind of Spanish is still spoken in the range country along the border where, according to Doris K. Seibold, fully half the cowmen are bilingual (5). Most of the Mexicans born in the region since 1900 are, of course, bilingual. Cowboy talk is so thoroughly bilingual that, in a single issue of *Lariat,* a popular "western" or "cowboy" magazine, Dr. Bentley found 376 Spanish words or words of Spanish origin (6). Most authors who have written about the Southwest have felt compelled to include a glossary of Spanish terms in common use (7).

3. Neighbors in Isolation

Considering the degree of hostility which has prevailed between Anglos and Hispanos in the Southwest, the extent of cultural fusion which has already occurred is most surprising. The isolation of both groups has been a prime reason for this mutual borrowing and adaptation. In the absence of deeply rooted educational institutions, the borrowing has been unconscious, careless, and natural—a product of intimacy in isolation. However antagonistically each group may have regarded the other, the plain fact is that they have been in continuous, direct, and often intimate contact in the Southwest for over a century. There was a period, in all the borderland states, when the two groups existed, side by side, in the friendliest intimacy with mixed marriages being quite common. Dr. Espiñosa, and many other observers, have commented upon the fact that this intimacy was "much more frequent in the first years of the American occupation." Since most of the mixed marriages of this earlier period involved Anglo-American husbands and Spanish-speaking wives, it is impossible to estimate the degree of intermixture which has taken place but it is much greater than most people imagine.

This initial *rapprochement* came to an end when the railroads penetrated the Southwest. With the appearance of the railroads, wrote Dr. Espiñosa, "there has come a check in the race fusion and the mutual contact and good feeling between the two peoples." Obviously it was the sequence of economic changes which the railroads initiated, not the railroads per se, which produced this effect. Previously the motive for dominance was largely lacking, for, in the absence of markets, a barter rather than a profit economy prevailed. In the isolation of the frontier both groups felt compelled to seek a degree of cooperation to mitigate the rigors of a harsh and unfriendly environment; on the frontier, as someone has said, "all churches look alike." While this earlier intimacy came to an end, the relationships which came out of it could never be effaced. Thus there exists in the Southwest an antecedent pattern of fusion and merger which continues to exert an influence, however imperceptible, upon present-day relationships.

It must also be remembered that the process of acculturation is somewhat different in the Southwest than elsewhere in the United States. Here we adopted the Spanish-speaking minority; they did not adopt us. It is this difference which accounts for the tenacity with which the Spanish-speaking have clung to certain aspects of their native culture. As late as 1917, Dr. Espiñosa estimated that there was not one Spanish-American family out of a hundred in New Mexico that had entirely abandoned Spanish as the language of the home. Nowadays nine out of ten of the native-born New Mexicans speak English but Spanish is still the mother tongue for most of them. The persistence of Spanish speech, however, is due to many factors: the prevailing isolation; constant discrimination; the lack of educational facilities; the existence of segregated schools; the migratory pattern of employment, and so forth. Whatever the reasons may be, the point is that this persistence in Spanish speech has been most influential in forcing a degree of cultural fusion. To appreciate the importance of this factor all one has to do is to compare the rapidity with which the *Nisei* or native-born Japanese have abandoned or lost all familiarity with the Japanese language. Regardless of length of residence, only a small proportion of Mexicans in the United States have lost all knowledge of Spanish or have abandoned its use in the home, no matter how meager their training in the language may have been or how imperfectly they may speak it.

While Mencken and others have suggested that Southwestern Spanish is doomed to vanish, sooner or later, the facts would seem to cast grave doubts on this conclusion. This becomes more apparent when one considers the thorny issue of language instruction in the schools.

4. Who Is Being Stubborn?

In the bundle of issues that is called "the Mexican Problem" none has occasioned more discussion and controversy than the language issue in the schools. Both the history and latter-day ramifications of this issue are most complex. Prior to 1846 the borderlands were without schools, public or private; illiteracy was the rule, literacy the exception. The first school systems were dominated, in administration and personnel, by Anglo-Americans who knew little or no Spanish. While official concessions were made to Spanish speech in New Mexico, school officials in the Southwest have always insisted upon English as the language of instruction. They still invest their position, on this issue, with an emotional halo of moral and patriotic self-righteousness. To a generation of American teachers trained in the normal schools of the period from 1890 to 1910, it seemed both heretical and disloyal, despite the guarantees of the Treaty of Guadalupe Hidalgo, to tolerate any form of bilingualism. In some areas, the issue has even been colored by religious prejudices of one kind or another. According to Dr. Ortega,

Anglo teachers have actually changed the names of Spanish students, on the first day of school, to some English equivalent by way of emphasizing the "terrible handicap" that Spanish speech is supposed to be. In other cases, Hispano teachers in rural schools made up of Spanish-speaking children have used Spanish surreptitiously for fear of being called on the carpet by some irate Anglo administrator.

The natural consequence of this official attitude has been to foster a generation illiterate in both languages, for the teaching of Spanish has been as systematically neglected as instruction in English has been systematically stressed. Spanish-speaking children often come to the schools without a word of English and without the environmental experience upon which school life is based. In many cases, they are not even familiar with the concepts for which they are supposed to learn English names. The use of standard curricula, books, and instruction materials in such schools has been ludicrously inept.

Once Anglo-American teachers had "retarded" Spanish-speaking students, they sought to rationalize their incompetence as teachers by insisting on segregated schools which only aggravated the problem. Notoriously bad linguists, Anglo-American teachers have been known to show an unreasoning irritation over the mere sound of a Spanish word or phrase spoken in their presence. This irritation is often reflected in a hostile attitude toward Spanish-speaking students. Over a period of many years, I have heard Anglo-American teachers in the Southwest complain bitterly about the "stubbornness" of Mexican-American youngsters who just *will* persist in speaking Spanish on the playgrounds, etc.

Actually the language issue in the Southwest is part and parcel of a much larger set of socio-economic issues from which it cannot be separated. It is most absurd, therefore, to attempt to isolate this issue and to regard it as a special problem which might be solved, apart from the larger issues, by the development of special teaching techniques and especially trained personnel (important as these items would be). Obviously the issue is related to bad housing, lack of nutrition, migratoriness, social disorganization, segregation, dominant group hostility, and a dozen other factors. The language problem, in short, is a community problem; a problem involving the relationship of the school to the community and of the community to the school. Today the issue is widely recognized as the major educational problem in the Southwest.

Furthermore, the conclusions now being drawn are indirectly premised on the assumption that a type of cultural fusion actually exists. "The intermingling of different home languages in the Southwest," to quote from one report, *"is a relatively permanent* condition, for here the waters from two great reservoirs of language flow together, constantly renewed from sources back from the border" (8). (Emphasis added.)

In other words, the borderlands have consistently remained the borderland of the two cultures; neither has prevailed in toto and neither is likely to win a complete victory over the other. Each group has gained recruits; the number of bilinguals is steadily increasing; and the area of fusion is expanding south and, to some extent, north of the border. Dynamic factors are involved in the extension of the borderlands for experience has shown that Mexican immigrants cannot be kept out of this area. We stopped Mexican immigration but imported 180,000 Mexican workers in wartime; workers are still crossing the border illegally, as they have for years, and the number of "wetbacks" is currently estimated at around 80,000. Regardless of how it changes, the Southwest is "an ever-normal granary" so far as Mexicans are concerned.

Emphasis on the language issue as "relatively permanent" merely reveals the true cultural background of the region. There are more persons of Italian than of Mexican descent in the United States but no one has suggested that bilingual instruction is a major problem in the education of Italian-Americans.

By insisting on regarding "the Mexican Problem" as part of a familiar Americanization process, identical with European immigration, we have consistently missed the point. Failing to recognize the degree of cultural fusion which has actually occurred, we have steadily belabored the Mexican for his "stubbornness" in adhering to a culture which prevails in the very areas of the United States in which he resides. It is as though we were to accuse the Eskimos of Alaska for their "stubborn" adherence to the only culture they have ever known. In this instance, the "stubbornness" is ours in not recognizing the real character of the culture which prevails in the borderlands.

"Once I had a dream," writes Dr. Ortega, "that there was in Latin America a republic in the midst of which lived an English-speaking population just as a Spanish-speaking population lives in the midst of New Mexico. If that could be made a reality, we would have the right Pan-American setup for two complementary links, and then, perhaps, the delicate problems of adjustment might be solved with a measure of equity and mutual understanding. As it is today, the Spanish-speaking population of the Southwest represents a living example of disorientation, of American political and social failure as a colonizing metropolis. . . . How are we going to bid friendship to the Latin Americans, with what face are we to talk of democracy and equality to them, what are our titles, besides those of purely material power, to aspire to be the big brothers in the Pan-American empire, if we have made within our borders a mess of the relatively simple problem of dealing with an Hispanic group? How dare we, in all fairness, to call backward the Latin American republics and blame their lot on misgovernment, when we here have not managed in nearly a century to do a better job with the same human material?" (9)

5. The Indelible Imprint

Throughout the Southwest the imprint of Spain and Mexico is indelible; not as Spanish or Mexican influence per se but as modified by contact with Indian and Anglo-American culture. The three influences are woven into nearly every aspect of the economy, the speech, the architecture, the institutions, and the customs of the people. For the people of the Southwest share a mixed cultural heritage in which the mixtures, rather than the pure strains, have survived. In a Navajo rug, an adobe house, or an irrigated farm, one may find elements of the three cultures inextricably interwoven and fused. The rug may be of Indian design, woven by Indian hands, and colored by native dyes; but the loom may be Spanish or Mexican and the wool probably came from some New Mexican's herd or it may have been purchased from an American mail-order catalogue. The rug, however, is most likely to be owned by an Anglo-American. The irrigated farm may lie within a district irrigated by water from some huge dam or reservoir built by American engineers, but the fields will be tilled by Mexicans, using a knowledge of irrigation which, in part, was acquired from Indians.

"Three types of domestic architecture," writes Ruth Laughlin, "have come down to us in their chronological order—the Pueblo, the Mexican, and the American-Spanish. They are seldom found absolutely true to type for the needs of men have overlapped since the days of the first

Americans. In each we find resemblances to the others, like the faces of mothers and daughters." Where these elements have been mixed, as in the domestic architecture of New Mexico, they have attained the most enduring expression. Where the Indian element has been lacking, as in the so-called "Spanish-Colonial" architecture seen in Florida and Southern California, the fusion has been least successful. Even the public buildings of the Southwest tend more and more to derive from Indian and Spanish-Mexican sources with the Anglo-Americans showing great ingenuity in adapting these forms to modern uses. In short, this mixed heritage belongs to all the people of the Southwest; not to any one group or to the combination of any two.

Of paramount importance to the future of this culture is the role that the coming generation of Mexican-Americans will play. The region has yet to experience the impact of the first articulate generation of persons of Mexican descent. In another generation, Mexican-Americans will be found in all walks of life,—in the arts, the professions, in the colleges and universities,—and in significant numbers. In the past, Mexicans have been a more or less anonymous, voiceless, expressionless minority. There has yet to be written, for example, a novel of Southwestern experience by an American-born person of Mexican descent or a significant autobiography by a native-born Mexican. The moment the group begins to achieve this type of expression, a new chapter will be written in the history of the Southwest. For as the Spanish-speaking attain cultural maturity, as they achieve real self-expression, they will exert a profound influence on the culture of the region and Spanish-Mexican influences that have remained dormant these many years will be revived and infused with new meaning and vigor.

It is the borderlands, not the border, that is important in the Southwest. For the borderlands unite the Anglo-American and the Hispano-American worlds and the area in which this mixed culture exists is expanding north and south. As the possibilities of the Good Neighbor Policy are realized, the border will have even less meaning than it has had in the past. By simply exploring the neighboring state of Sonora, Arizona businessmen have been able to increase the total traffic through the port of Nogales from $50,000,000 in 1945–1946 to $76,000,000 in 1946–1947. Incredible as it may seem, these same Arizona businessmen had for years assumed that merchandise destined for Sonora had to be shipped to Mexico City and then re-routed north to Sonora. By investigating the situation at first hand, they discovered that trucks could transport merchandise from Arizona to any point in the province, just as the pack-trains had done two hundred years ago.

Today machinery, wire, pipe, cement, steel, farm implements, glass, crockery, paint, and plumbing fixtures are moving south across the border and Mexican minerals, shoes, fish, flax, bamboo, guano, tomatoes, chickpeas and other products are moving north. Furthermore the imbalance between imports and exports changed from $7,000,000 in favor of the United States to somewhat less than $1,000,000 in the space of one year and even this margin may soon disappear (10).

Just as Arizona is discovering that Nogales is the logical gateway to the west coast of Mexico, so Texas is discovering that its border-towns are the logical gateways to eastern Mexico. Over how large an area, therefore, is the cultural fusion of the borderlands likely to expand in the next quarter-century? As the borderlands expand, both the Anglo and the Hispano elements will receive numerical re-enforcements, so that the process of cultural fusion will be repeated; in fact, it is already apparent that this process is a constant factor in the life of the borderlands. Hence it is extremely difficult to imagine any working-out of this process that would involve the complete absorption of one culture by the other.

In a sense the settlement of the United States has always moved against the grain of geography, for the east-to-west movement of the American people has been *against* the flow, the natural movement, of the landscape. In moving westward, the American people have crossed mountain ranges, crossed the plains, crossed the rivers, crossed the deserts. Yet the geographical flow of the continent is not from east to west but from north to south; our major mountain ranges run along north-south lines as do most of our great river systems. Unwittingly we have been bucking geography, not cooperating with it. With the lodestar being ever in the West, we have simply failed to change our vision and to note the natural contours of the country.

Prior to the settlement of the eastern seaboard by European colonists, the continent was orientated on a north-south, rather than an east-west, axis and it may yet be orientated in this fashion. Since the westward movement of the American people "leapfrogged" over the intermountain states to the West Coast, we have failed to let our eyes follow the natural lines and contours which run in the opposite direction. Hence it involved an abrupt turnabout when the New Mexican frontier, with its face turned anxiously east, became a part of the last American frontier, with its face turned eagerly west. Not only is the movement "North from Mexico" older in point of time than the westward movement, but it has remained constant through 'the years; it is continuing now and is likely to continue indefinitely.

6. "The Sun Has Exploded"

On July 16, 1945, a rancher went to visit his sheep camp in the San Andres Mountains in New Mexico. "As usual his sheepherders," writes Ruth Laughlin, "had started out before dawn that morning in spite of a mountain rain storm. They had not gone far when they saw a terrific flash at the other side of the eighty-mile sweep of prairie. They ran back to the sheep camp, shaken and terrified, and cried to their *patrón,* 'The sun has exploded, señor. We saw it. It was so bright that we fell on our knees and our sheep stampeded. Take us back to our families and let us go into the church. It is the end of the world.'"

When the great mushroom-like cloud of smoke and dust cleared away from the testing ground beyond Almogordo—in this first release of atomic power in world history—the isolation of New Mexico—the isolation of all men everywhere—ended once and forever. Today New Mexico is the center of American research and experimentation in the use of atomic power and the corner where the states of New Mexico, Arizona, Colorado, and Utah meet is reported to be one of the richest centers of fissionable materials in the United States. Over the radio, as I write these lines, comes word of still another mysterious plant in New Mexico which is now employing sixty-five thousand people.

The explosion at Almogordo unlocked the latent richness of the mineral resources of the Southwest. What Emerson said many years ago has now come true: "To science there is no poison; to botany no weed; to chemistry no dirt." The science that released atomic power in the Southwest can now find new uses for resources long regarded as worthless and can reclaim large portions of its arid wastes. Here, in the heart of the old Spanish borderlands, the oldest settled portion of the United States, a new world has been born and the isolation of the region has been forever destroyed. Like the peoples of the world, the peoples of the borderlands will either face the future "one and together" or they are likely to find themselves siftings on siftings in oblivion.

ACKNOWLEDGMENTS

In preparing this volume I have received invaluable assistance from my greatly esteemed friend, Dr. Eshref Shevky, who served as director of the Tewa Basin Study in New Mexico and is now with the John R. Haynes Foundation in Los Angeles. I also wish to acknowledge my indebtedness to the following individuals: the late Arthur Shapiro, who helped me with some of the research; Fred Ross, formerly with the American Council on Race Relations and now directing the important work of the Industrial Areas Foundation among Spanish-speaking people in Los Angeles; Louise Evans and Charles Graham of the Colorado Civic Unity Council; Dr. Norman Humphreys of Wayne University; Dr. Ruth D. Tuck of the University of Redlands; and Alice Greenfield, who served as secretary of the Sleepy Lagoon Defense Committee. For help in preparing the manuscript, I am indebted to Ross B. Wills and Margaret O'Connor.

I wish to acknowledge my indebtedness to the Harvard University Press, Cambridge, Massachusetts, for permission to quote from *California Gold* by Rodman Wilson Paul (1947); to Ginn and Company, for permission to quote from *The Great Plains* by Walter Prescott Webb (1931); to Mr. J. Frank Dobie for permission to quote from *A Vaquero of the Brush Country;* to Duell, Sloan & Pearce, Inc., for permission to quote from *Piñon Country* by Haniel Long (1941) and *Palmetto Country* by Stetson Kennedy (1942); to Ross Calvin, for permission to quote from *Sky Determines* (copyright by The Macmillan Company, 1934; by The University of New Mexico Press, 1938); to Columbia University Press for permission to quote from *Seasonal Farm Labor in the United States* by Harry Schwartz (1945), *A Dictionary of Spanish Terms in English* by Harold W. Bentley (1932), and *Culture Conflict in Texas* by Dr. Samuel Harman Lowrie (1932); to Dr. Manuel Gamio and The University of Chicago Press for permission to quote from *Mexican*

Immigration to the United States (1930); to The University of New Mexico Press for permission to quote from *Latin Americans in Texas* by Pauline R. Kibbe (1946) and *Forgotten People* by Dr. George I. Sanchez; to Appleton-Century-Crofts, Inc., for permission to quote from *The United States and Mexico* by J. Fred Rippy (1926); to The University of North Carolina Press for permission to quote from *An American-Mexican Frontier* by Dr. Paul S. Taylor (copyright, 1934, by The University of North Carolina Press); to Coward-McCann, Inc., for permission to quote from *The Robin Hood of Eldorado* by Walter Noble Burns (1932); to Houghton Mifflin Company for permission to quote from *The Texas Rangers* by Walter Prescott Webb (1935) and *Texas: A Contest of Civilizations* by George P. Garrison (1903); to Ruth Laughlin for permission to quote from *Caballeros* (1931); to Appleton-Century-Crofts, Inc., for permission to quote from *Mexico and Its Heritage* by Ernest Gruening (1928); to Alfred A. Knopf, Inc., for permission to quote from *Rio Grande* by Harvey Fergusson (1933), *The Golden Hoof* by Winifred Kupper (1945), *Our Southwest* by Erna Fergusson (1940), *The Big Bonanza* by Dan De Quille, and *The Destiny of a Continent* by Manuel Ugarte (1925); to University of California Press for permission to quote from *The Civilization of the Americas* (1938) and to the same press and Dr. Paul S. Taylor for permission to quote from Dr. Taylor's monographs on Mexican labor in the United States; to Prentice-Hall, Inc., for permission to quote from *California* by John Walton Caughey (copyright, 1940, by Prentice-Hall, Inc.); to University of Oklahoma Press for permission to quote from *Shepherd's Empire* by Towne and Wentworth (1945). The quotation from *The Greater Southwest* by Rupert N. Richardson and Carl C. Rister is reprinted by permission of the publishers, The Arthur H. Clark Company, holders of the copyright.

NOTE ON SOURCES

For general bibliographic materials about cultural relations in the Southwest and the Spanish-speaking people, the best sources are: *Spanish-Speaking Americans in the United States: A Selected Bibliography* by Lyle Saunders (1944), and *A Guide to Materials Bearing on Cultural Relations in New Mexico* also by Lyle Saunders (University of New Mexico Press, 528 pp., 1944). Mr. Saunders has kept the last-mentioned guide current by bibliographic notes which have regularly appeared in the excellent *New Mexico Quarterly Review*. In view of the existence of these exhaustive, thoroughgoing bibliographies, I have deemed it unnecessary to include a bibliography in this volume. A word or two about the sources, however, may not be amiss.

On the general character of the Southwest as a region there are several valuable sources. Under this heading, the works of Dr. Walter Prescott Webb, particularly *The Great Plains* (1931) and *The Texas Rangers* (1935), are of major importance. Nor can I commend too highly *A Vaquero of the Brush Country* by J. Frank Dobie (1929), and, by the same author, *Coronado's Children* (1931) and *The Longhorns* (1941). Special mention should also be made of *The Greater Southwest* by Rupert Norval Richardson and Carl Coke Rister (1934), a first-rate general source; and, in this same category, *Our Southwest* (1940), by Erna Fergusson, and the well-known writings of Charles Fletcher Lummis and Mary Austin. The indispensable source, however, is Dr. Webb's *The Great Plains,* one of the finest volumes ever written about Western America.

There are many excellent books about New Mexico but my preferences, in this field, are the following: *Forgotten People: A Study of New Mexicans* by George I. Sanchez (1940), a most valuable source; *Old Santa Fe* by Ralph Emerson Twitchell (1925); *Piñon Country* by Haniel Long (1941); *Sky Determines* by Ross Calvin (1934); *Rio Grande* by Harvey Fergusson (1933); and *Caballeros* by Ruth Laughlin Barker (1931), the best discussion of the New Mexico arts and crafts. In the chapter on New Mexico, I have also drawn heavily upon two excellent unpublished dissertations: "Relations Between the Spanish-Americans and Anglo-Americans in New Mexico" by Dr. Carolyn Zeleny (Yale University, 1944); and "A Study of Isolation and Social

Change in Three Spanish-Speaking Villages in New Mexico" by Dr. Paul Walter (Stanford University, 1938).

On the Spanish-speaking in Texas, in addition to the sources indicated in the notes, I have drawn upon an unpublished dissertation by Jovita Gonzales entitled "Social Life in Cameron, Starr, and Zapata Counties," (University of Texas, 1930); *Cultural Conflict in Texas, 1821–1835* by Dr. Samuel Harman Lowrie (1932); and *Texas: A Contest of Civilizations* by Dr. George P. Garrison (1903). Mention should also be made, on this score, of *Latin Americans in Texas* by Pauline R. Kibbe (1946). Perhaps the most interesting material on the Spanish-speaking of Colorado is to be found in yet another unpublished dissertation: "The Spanish Heritage of the San Luis Valley" by Olibama López (University of Denver, 1942). Of the Spanish-speaking in California, the best single source is *Not With the Fist: Mexican-Americans in a Southwest City* by Ruth D. Tuck (1946), a fine, perceptive study, notable for its sympathetic understanding and interpretation of Mexican-American life and culture.

The outstanding authority on Mexicans in the United States, of course, is Dr. Paul S. Taylor of the University of California. Representing years of study, research, and field investigations, the series of monographs making up his study of Mexican labor in the United States are of the utmost importance. Included in the series are the following: Volume I: *Imperial Valley* (1928); Volume II: *Valley of the South Platte* (1929); Volume III: *Migration Statistics;* Volume IV: *Racial School Statistics California* (1927); Volume V: *Dimmit County, Winter Garden District, South Texas* (1930); Volume VI: *Bethlehem, Pennsylvania* (1931); and Volume VII: *Chicago and the Calumet Region* (1932). Dr. Taylor's volume, *An American-Mexican Frontier* (1934), is the finest single volume on Anglo-Hispano relations in print today. In 1939 the Soil Conservation Service in New Mexico released its famous *Tewa Basin Study* which, with the supplemental studies that accompanied the major two-volume report, constitutes an invaluable piece of research on the Indian pueblos and the Spanish-speaking villages of New Mexico.

CHAPTER NOTES

Chapter I
1. *New Mexico Historical Review,* Vol. 16, p. 1.
2. "Spanish Influences in the United States: Economic Aspects," *Hispanic American Historical Review,* February, 1938.
3. "The Spanish Contribution to American Agriculture" by Arthur P. Whitaker, *Agricultural History,* January, 1929.
4. *California Agriculture,* edited by Claude B. Hutchinson, University of California Press, 1946.
5. "The Spanish Heritage in America" by William R. Shepherd, *Modern Language Journal,* November, 1925.

Chapter II
1. *See* picture-spread Los Angeles *Daily News,* May 7, 1947.
2. *American Planning and Civic Manual* (1940), pp. 260–266.
3. *Spanish Folk-Poetry in New Mexico* (1946), by Dr. Arthur Campa, p. 13. See also "A New Mexican Village" by Helen Zunser, *Journal of American Folklore,* Vol. 48, p. 141.
4. New York *Times,* June 1, August 3, 4, 8, and September 4, 1947.
5. *Palmetto Country* by Stetson Kennedy (1942), pp. 269–296.
6. *The Civilization of the Americas* (1938), p. 116.
7. *Arizona Quarterly* (1946), Vol. 2, p. 34.

Chapter III
1. *The Greater Southwest* (1934), p. 26.
2. *The United States and Mexico* by J. Fred Rippy (1926), p. 382.

Chapter IV
1. *Caballeros* by Ruth Barker Laughlin; *see also* the article by Frank Applegate, *Survey-Graphic,* May 1, 1931.
2. Note the article by Juan B. Rael, *California Folklore Quarterly,* Vol. 1, p. 83.
3. *Man and Resources in the Middle Rio Grande Valley* (1943), in which

the process of deterioration in natural and human resources is discussed in great detail.
4. *Survey-Graphic,* May 1, 1931, p. 142.

Chapter V

1. *Arizona and Sonora: The Geography, History, and Resources of the Silver Region of North America* (1864).
2. *Harper's,* July, 1890.
3. *The Southwest Political and Social Science Quarterly,* December, 1929, p. 267.
4. *Spanish Institutions of the Southwest* (1891).
5. *Maverick Town: The Story of Old Tascosa* by John L. McCarty (1946).

Chapter VI

1. Rippy, *supra,* p. 296.
2. *Mexican Border Ballads,* edited by Mody C. Boatright (1946).
3. *Along the Rio Grande* by Tracy Hammond Lewis (1916).
4. *The Destiny of a Continent* (1925).
5. *A Journey Through Texas* (1857), p. 455.

Chapter VII

1. New Mexico *Guide,* p. 14.
2. *Sixty Years in Southern California,* p. 140.
3. *See* the article by Arthur E. Hyde, *Century,* March, 1902, Vol. 63, p. 690.
4. *Recollections of a Western Ranchman* (1884).
5. *New Mexico Historical Review,* Vol. 20, p. 202.
6. *See* article by C. P. Loomis, *Sociometry,* February, 1943; and "Race Relations in New Mexico," pp. 208–216, in *Mexican Immigration to the United States* by Manuel Gamio (1930).
7. *The Trampling Herd* (1939).
8. For an account of a lynching in Arizona, see *New Mexico Historical Review,* Vol. 18; and, for Colorado, *see* Gamio, *supra,* p. 213.
9. *Gold Days* (1929), p. 204.
10. *The Californians* (1876).

Chapter VIII

1. *California Gold* by Rodman W. Paul (1947), p. 36.
2. *Report on the Mineral Resources of the United States* by J. Ross Browne, 1867, p. 21. See also *A History of American Mining* by T. A. Rickard (1932).
3. *Arizona* by James H. McClintock (1916), Vol. I, p. 101.
4. *Harper's,* June, 1863; *see also* "Down in the Cinnabar Mines" by J. Ross Browne, *Harper's,* October, 1865.

5. *Gold Days* by Owen Cochran Coy (1929), p. 165.
6. *The Story of Arizona* by Will H. Robinson (1919).
7. McClintock, *supra*, Vol. II, p. 421.
8. *Shepherd's Empire* (1945).
9. *The Golden Hoof* by Winifred Kupper (1945).
10. *See* chapter on "New Mexican Folk Songs" by Charles Fletcher Lummis in *The Land of Poco Tiempo* (1897).
11. *Spanish Folk-Poetry in New Mexico* (1946), p. 97.
12. *Old California Cowboys* by Dane Coolidge (1939), Chapter X.
13. *Arizona Quarterly*, Summer, 1946, p. 24; *see also* "Mexican Color Terms for Horses" by W. H. Whatley, in *Mustangs and Cow Horses*, publication Texas Folklore Society (1940), p. 241.
14. *Journal of Political Economy*, Vol. 20, p. 807; *Journal of Economic History*, December, 1942, article by Sanford A. Mosk.
15. *The Desert and the Rose* by Edith Nicoll Ellison (1921), p. 37.
16. French, *supra*, p. 133.
17. *Journal of American Folklore*, Vol. IX, p. 81.

Chapter IX

1. *The White Scourge* by Edward Everett Davis (1940).
2. *Survey-Graphic*, May 1, 1931.
3. *Economic Geography*, January, 1931, p. 1.
4. *The New Republic*, April 7, 1947, p. 14.
5. *Seasonal Farm Labor in the United States* by Harry Schwartz (1945), p. 29.
6. *Commercial Survey of the Pacific Southwest*, Dept. of Commerce (1930), pp. 224–254.
7. "Transient Mexican Agricultural Labor" by Lawrence Leslie Walters, *Southwest Social and Political Science Quarterly*, June, 1941.
8. *See* article by Dr. Max Handman, *American Journal of Sociology*, January, 1930.
9. *See* testimony of Emelio Flores before the Industrial Relations Commission, 1915.
10. *History of Agriculture in Colorado* by Alvin T. Steinel and D. W. Working.
11. Hearings, Committee on Agriculture and Forestry, U.S. Senate, 80th Congress, March, 1947, p. 24.

Chapter X

1. *Labor Unionism in American Agriculture* by Dr. Stuart Jamieson (1945).
2. *The Pecan-Shellers of San Antonio* by Selden C. Menefee and Orin C. Cassmore (1940).

3. *The Nation*, May 1, 1935.
4. *Commercial Survey of the Pacific Southwest* (1930), p. 322.
5. *The Outlook*, February 2, 1916; *Survey*, October 27, 1917, p. 97.
6. *In the Matter of Miami Copper Company*, Non-Ferrous Metals Commission, National War Labor Board, February 5, 1944; also, *PM*, July 3, 1944, p. 3.
7. "The History of Clifton" by James Monroe Patton, unpublished thesis, University of Arizona, 1945.
8. *New Mexico Historical Review*, Vol. 13, p. 415; also *Organized Labor in Mexico* by Marjorie Ruth Clark (1934), p. 11.
9. Gamio, *supra*, p. 44.

Chapter XI

1. See *The Shadows of the Trees*, by Jacques Ducharme, 1943; many of his observations about French-Canadians in New England could be applied, without modification, to Mexicans in the Southwest.
2. "The Folk Society" by Robert Redfield, *American Journal of Sociology*, January, 1947, p. 293.
3. *Community Organization in Mexican-American Communities* by Fred W. Ross (1947), American Council on Race Relations.
4. "They Fenced Tolerance In" by Dallas Johnson, *Survey*, July, 1947, pp. 398–400.
5. *American Journal of Sociology*, Vol. 22, p. 391.

Chapter XII

1. *See* comments by Dr. George Sanchez, *Common Ground*, Autumn, 1943, pp. 13–20.
2. *See* comments by Albert Deutsch, *PM*, June 14, 1943; *Racial Digest*, July, 1943, pp. 3–7; New York *Times*, June 11, 1943.

Chapter XIII

1. Los Angeles *Herald-Express*, June 5, 1943.
2. "Imported Mexican Workers Save Millions in Citrus Crops," reads a headline, Los Angeles *Times*, June 30, 1943.
3. Los Angeles *Times*, June 18, 1943.

Chapter XIV

1. *Congressional Record*, April 24, 1945.
2. *The New Republic*, September 30, 1946, p. 412.
3. See "Mexico's Social Justice Party" by Betty Kirk, *The Nation*, June 12, 1943; *PM*, May 21, 1944, p. 3.
4. Los Angeles *Times*, October 15, 1942.

5. Los Angeles *Times*, December 20, 1942.
6. *See* article by Heinz H. F. Eulau, *The Inter-American*, March, 1944, pp. 25–28. Mr. Eulau, during the war, was chief of the Division of Propaganda Analysis, Department of Justice.
7. Los Angeles *Times*, Sept. 22, 1947, Part II, p. 1.
8. New Braunfels *Herald*, July 27, 1945.
9. *Common Ground*, Autumn, 1943, pp. 13–20.
10. New York *Herald Tribune*, February 16, 1944.

Chapter XV

1. *Interpreter Releases*, March 22, 1943.
2. *The Problem of Violence* by Lloyd H. Fisher, American Council on Race Relations (1945), p. 18.
3. *See* the series of articles by Agnes E. Meyer in the Washington *Post*, April 22–29, 1947.
4. *Nutrition and Certain Related Factors of the Spanish-American in Northern Colorado* (Denver, 1943); Inter-American Short Papers, No. VII (University of New Mexico, 1943).
5. *Common Ground*, Spring, 1947, pp. 80–83.
6. *It Happened in Taos*, by J. T. Reid (University of New Mexico Press, 1946).
7. *La Comunidad* (University of New Mexico Press, 1943).

Chapter XVI

1. *California* by Josiah Royce (1897), p. 226.
2. *The Pacific Ocean in History* (1917), the chapter on "Speech Mixture in New Mexico" by Aurelio M. Espiñosa.
3. *Hispania*, Vol. 28, pp. 505–507.
4. From a list given me by Ruth D. Tuck; see also "The Pachuco Patois" by Beatrice Griffith, *Common Ground*, Summer, 1947, pp. 77–84.
5. *Arizona Quarterly*, Summer, 1946, p. 24.
6. See also, *The Story of the Cowboy* by Emerson Hough p. 26; *Cowboy Lingo* by Ramón F. Adams, 1936.
7. *Starry Adventure* by Mary Austin, p. 62; *Coronado's Children*, by J. Frank Dobie, pp. 361–367; *Caballeros* by Ruth Laughlin, pp. 403–410.
8. Papers, Conference on Educational Problems in the Southwest, Santa Fe, August 19–24, 1943.
9. *The Compulsory Teaching of Spanish in the Grade Schools of New Mexico* by Joaquín Ortega (University of New Mexico Press, 1941), p. 9.
10. New York *Times*, August 10, 1947, article by Gladwin Hill.

Index

Abbott, Dr. W. Lewis, 276
Abeyta, Pablo, 34
Acosta, Dan G., 257
Adams, Dr. Frank, 33
Aguilar, José, 271
Aguilar, Manuel, 237
Alamitos, de los, Rancho, Calif., 91-92
Alamo slaughter, the, 100-101, 120
Almadén Silver Mine of Spain, 139-140
Alpine Club, Los Angeles, 244
Altamiro, El Colegio, 86
American Civil Liberties Union, 282
American Council on Race Relations, 280
American Federation of Labor, 194, 216, 270
American Jewish Congress, 282
American Smelting and Refining Company, 199
American Veterans Committee, 260
Anza, de, Juan Bautista, 25, 27, 41, 42, 82, 94, 135, 152, 162, 164, 288
Apache Indians, 29-30, 53, 66-67, 82-83, 125, 134, 142-143, 148, 166, 167
Applegate, Frank, 72
Arbadaos Indians, 22
Archaeological Institute of America, 287
Archevêque, l', Sostenes, 120-121
Arias, José, 276
Arid Region Doctrine, 159
Arizona
  cattle-raising in, 83, 120, 147
  cotton-growing in, 173-174
  Cotton Growers Association, 173
  Guide, 41
  Indians in, 80, 82-84, 125, 134
  Mexicans in, 41, 51-61, 81-84, 88, 125-127, 142-144, 163, 173-174, 187, 193, 196-198, 200-202, 260, 277
  mining in, 82, 83, 125, 134-135, 142-144, 196-198, 304
  Spanish exploration and settlement of, 25, 30, 81-82
  statehood, status of, 51-52, 83
  strikes in, 196-198
Arizona Mining Company, 142-143
Armenta, Esther, 254
Armijo, Manuel, 69, 117
Arnaz, Don José, 129
Asociación de Jornaleros, 194
Atchison, Topeka and Santa Fe Railroad, 253
Austin, Mary, 79
Austin, Stephen F., 156
Ayllón, de, Lucas Vásquez, 21
Ayres, E. Duran, 233-235, 236-238, 255

Baca, Bartolomé, 150
Baca, Elfego, 120
Baca, de, Ezequiel, 123
Baker, Ray Stannard, 177
Baltimore and Ohio Railroad, 222
Bancroft, Herbert H., 70, 117, 286-287
Bandelier, Adolph F. A., 286-287
Barela, Casimiro, 96
Bartlett, John R., 120
Bataan
  Mexican-Americans killed at, 259, 261
Bell, Horace, 130-131
Bell, Katherine M., 135
Bell Town Improvement League, 283
Belvedere, Los Angeles, 224-226, 255, 264
Benavides, Capt. Refugio, 102
Bent, Charles, 118
Bentley, Dr. Harold W., 291, 293-294, 296
Bermudez, Enrique, 202
Berninghaus, Oscar, 287
Bernstein, Harvey, 32
Bethlehem Steel Company, 184
Billy the Kid, 121
Bisbee Copper Mines, Arizona, 143, 196, 197, 203
Biscailuz, Eugene, 37
Blackmar, Frank W., 69, 77, 88-89, 287
Blanchard, Sarah E., 149

315

INDEX

Blumenschein, Ernest, 287
Boddy, Manchester, 251-252
Bolton, Herbert E., 23, 31, 67, 162
Borajo, Father, 111
Border Control, Immigration Service, 60, 269
Bork, Dr. A. W., 47
Bowron, Fletcher, 250, 257
Braco, David, 267
Brady, Peter H., 125
Braverman, Harry, 231, 237
Breakenridge, W. M., 125-126
Browne, J. Ross, 83, 137, 138, 140, 143
Bulvia, Louis, 130
Burlin, Natalie Curtis, 79
Burns, Walter Noble, 127
Burris, Quincy Guy, 285

Caballeros del Trabajo, Los, 46
Cabora, de, Teresa, 199-200
Cabrillo, Juan Rodríguez, 24, 37, 41
California
  agricultural development of, 32-33, 90, 93, 158-161, 175-178, 180, 187, 189-193, 215, 266-269
  Associated Farmers, 193, 266
  cattle- and sheep-raising in, 91-93, 130, 146-150, 152-153, 156
  Chinese in, 93, 163
  citrus-fruit groves of, 175, 176, 192-193, 215, 217, 218, 220-221, 280
  Committee on Un-American Activities in, 232-233
  cotton-growing in, 174, 187
  Fruit Growers Exchange, 215, 217, 219
  gold, discovery of, in, 50-51, 57, 82, 91, 102, 104, 127, 134-142, 151
  Mexicans in, 35-44, 51-61, 76, 81, 85-86, 88-94, 112, 115, 127-142, 158, 163, 169, 174, 175-178, 180, 187, 189-193, 198, 204-205, 212, 215, 217-221, 223-258, 261, 264-269, 272-273, 276-278, 280-284, 294
  ranches, large, 91-93, 152
  riots against Mexican people of, 127-128, 238-258, 264-265
  Spanish exploration and settlement of, 24-25, 30-33, 81, 88-89
  Spanish people and Puerto Ricans in, 44-45
  strikes in, 190-193
  Unity Leagues in, 280
Calvin, Ross, 71
Camacho, Ávila, 256-257, 264, 269
Camero, Manuel, 36
Cameron, Tom, 36-37

Campa, Dr. Arthur L., 43-44, 73-74, 208
Canales, Gen. Don Antonio, 101
Canales, J. T., 113
Cananea Consolidated Copper Company, 203
Cannery and Agricultural Workers Industrial Union, 191
Cárdenas, Lázaro, 232
Carillo, Alejandro, 269
Carr, Harry, 42
Carranza, Venustiano, 112, 113
Carrasco, José, 142
Carreon, C. J., 276
Carrillo, Leo, 38, 40, 255
Carson, Kit, 118
Cart War of 1857, 106
Carvajal, José M., 104
Casey, Lee, 288
Castillero, Capt. Andres, 139
Caughey, Dr. John W., 89
Centenario, El, 202
Cerda, de la, Albert, 111
Cerda, de la, Ramón, 111
Chaboya, Louis, 139
Chaves, Don Amado, 33
Chaves, Col. J. Francisco, 122-123
Chavez, Senator Dennis, 79, 124, 284
Chavéz, "El Guero," 150
Chavez, Col. Manuel, 148
Chavez Ravine, Calif., 223-225, 245-246, 283-284
Cherrington, Dr. Ben, 276
Chicago
  Mexican Civic Committee, 280
  Mexicans in, 55, 168, 184, 221-222, 256, 280
Chichorana, Francisco, 21
Chico, Anton, 78
Chiricahua Cattle Company, 126
"Cinco de Mayo" Celebration, 37-38, 41, 257
Civil War, American, 82-83, 103, 108, 122, 134, 145, 167
Clanton "gang," 125
Clements, Dr. George P., 190, 191, 193
Cleveland, Grover, 76
Clifton Copper Mines, 143-144, 197
Cobo, Bernabé, 29
Cochise, Apache Chief, 83
Colorado
  agricultural development of, 94, 96, 193
  cattle-raising in, 94, 147, 156
  conferences on the Problems of Spanish-Speaking People, 277
  Inter-American Field Service Commission, 279

INDEX

Mexicans in, 54-56, 61, 88, 94-96, 126, 127, 169, 180-183, 193, 260-262, 267, 277, 279-280, 285
  mining in, 144, 304
  service clubs and commissions established to aid Mexicans in, 279-280
  Spanish exploration and colonization of, 94
  sugar-beet industry in, 180-183, 267
Comanche Indians, 30, 66, 84, 98, 100
Comité Mexicano Contra el Racismo, 263
Community Service Clubs, Inc., 279
Comstock (Comstock Silver Mines), 138
Confederación de Uniones Obreras Mexicanas, 191
Congress of Industrial Organization, 194, 237
Contzen, Fritz, 125
Coolidge, Dane, 156
Cordoba, Leonardo, 127
Coronado, de, Francisco Vásquez, 20, 23-24, 34, 41, 42, 102, 144, 151
Cortez, Hernando, 20, 28, 156, 167
Cortina War, 106-108, 126
Cota, J. Y., 92
Cowboys, 119-121, 151-156, 296
Coy, Owen Cochran, 128
Crawford, Remsen, 170
Crocker, Charles, 167
Crockett, Davy, 120
Cubans, in the U.S., 45-46
Curry, William S., 125
Curtis, F. S., Jr., 28
Cutting, Bronson, 123-124

Daly, H. W., 166
Dana, Richard Henry, 131, 152
Daniel, Pancho, 130
Davilla, José, 262-263
Davis, Dr. Edward Everett, 170, 171
Davis, Henry Clay, 87
Delgado, Manuel, 230
Del Rey Palomino Club, 37
Denman, Justice William, 282-283
Department of Labor, 186
De Quille, Dan, 138
Detroit, Michigan
  Free Press, 262-263
  Mexicans in, 55, 178, 184, 221-222, 256
Díaz, Ernesto Felix, 265
Díaz, José, 228-229, 233
Díaz, Porfirio, 108, 111, 199, 202-203
Dingley Tariff, 180
Dixon, Compton, 248
Dobie, J. Frank, 109, 153-154, 176, 286, 296

Doctrine of Appropriation, 159
Douglas Copper Mine, 196
Douglas, Walter, 197
Dwyer, Senator, 110

Eagle Rock *Advertiser*, 250
Elizalde Anti-Discrimination Committee, 261
Elizalde, Daniel S., 261
Ellison, Edith Nicoll, 157
Emerson, Ralph Waldo, 304
Emery, Maj., 105
Espiñosa, Dr. Aurelio M., 73, 291, 297
Estevan, 22-23
Exchange Club, Santa Barbara, 37

Fair Employment Practice Commission, 198
Farm Security Administration, 266, 269
Federation of Spanish-American Voters, 254
Fergusson, Erna, 70, 77, 78, 101, 118
Fergusson, Harvey, 22, 69, 75, 119
Field, Stephen J., 128
Filipinos in U.S., 45, 197, 248
Fisher, King, 98
Fisher, Walter M., 129
Flores, Juan, 130
Florida
  colonization of by Spaniards, 21, 26, 29
  Spanish people in, 44-47
Ford, Col., 105
Fraijo, Manuel, 198
Frankfurter, Felix, 197
Fraternidad, 263
French, William, 119-120
Fuss, Oscar R., 237

Gaarder, Alfred Bruce, 292-293
Gadsen, James, 59-60, 134
Galarza, Ernesto, 266, 269
Gallegos, Father, 119
Gallup-American Company, 195
Gálvez, de, Bernardo, 44
Gamio, Dr. Manuel, 210-213, 214, 266, 291
García, Macario, 261, 269
García, Manuel, 130
Garner, John Nance, 178
Garrison, Dr. George P., 30, 84, 101
Garza, Albert, 108
Gerra, Manuel, 86
Gill, Irving, 73
Glavecke, Adolph, 107
Goldman, Emma, 204
Goliad Mission, 84
Gómez, Juan, 190
Gomez, Lauriano, 166
Gominguez, Adolfo G., 269

INDEX

Gonzales, Isabel, 267
Gonzales, Jovita, 41-42, 86, 87, 113
Gonzales, Manuel Pedro, 46
Gonzales, Mrs. Michael, 254
Good Neighbor Policy, 37, 237, 263-264, 265, 270, 272, 274-279, 284-285, 286, 301, 302-304
Gray, Dr. E. D., 284
Great Lakes Sugar Company, 183
Great Northern Railway, 168
Great Western Sugar Beet Company, 181
Gregg, Josiah, 66, 67-68, 131
Gruening, Ernest, 28, 112, 139
Guerra, de la, Anita, 37
Guerra, de la, Antonio María, 92
Guerra, de la, Pablo, 92
Guevavi Mission, 81-82
Guinn, J. M., 129-130

Harby, Lee C., 86
Harte, Bret, 115
Harwood Foundation, 285
Harwood, Lucy C., 285
Hayes, Rutherford B., 109
Henitzelman, Maj., 107
Heintzelman Mine, 142-143
Henry, Patrick, 29
Herreras, Sylvester, 260
Hick's Camp, Calif., 217-218
Hitler, Adolph, 234
Hoijer, Dr. Harry, 237
Horrall, C. B., 235-236
Horses, Spanish breed, 28-29, 154
Howser, Fred N., 250
Hubbel, Santiago, 165
Hughes, Charles Evans, 113
Hughes, Samuel, 125
Hull, Cordell, 251, 257
Humphrey, Dr. Norman, 214, 222
Hynes, Capt. William ("Red"), 192

Ibor, Vicente Martínez, 45
Immigration Act of 1924, 178, 180-181, 206
Imperial Valley, Calif., 174, 177, 191
Indians American
 culture of, 31-33, 49, 52, 65, 69, 71-74, 79, 147, 156, 157-158, 208-209, 284, 287, 288, 301-302
 discrimination against and exploitation of, 89, 90, 91, 131, 197, 207, 213, 234, 281
 encountered by Spanish explorers, 21-35, 52-53, 64, 82, 84, 88
 warfare in the Southwest, 52-53, 62, 63-64, 66-68, 70-71, 75, 82-85, 87, 94-95, 100, 102, 104, 125, 134, 142-143, 146, 148, 150, 152, 166, 209
Indian Bureau (Bureau of Indian Affairs), 122, 287-288
Inspiration Consolidated Copper Co., 197
Institute of Ethnic Affairs, 279
Institute of International Education, 277
Inter-American Bar Association, 264
Inter-American Conference on Problems of War and Peace, 264
International Labor Organization, 264
International Smelting and Refining Co., 197
International Union of Mine, Mill and Smelter Workers, 197, 198
International Workers of the World, 204
Irving, Washington, 164

Jaeger, L. J. F., 125
Jamieson, Dr. Stuart, 194-195
Japanese-American Citizens League, 282
Jennings, N. A., 109
Jessup, Roger, 250
Jiménez, de P., Francisco, 271
John, Chileno, 166
Juárez, Benito, 202, 257
Julian, George W., 76-77

Kansas
 Mexicans in, 168
Kendall, George, 117
Kennecott Copper Company, 195
Kennedy, Mifflin (Kennedy Ranch, Texas), 104, 155
Kenny, Robert W., 255, 282
Kibbe, Pauline, 173
King, Richard (King Ranch, Texas), 85, 104, 111, 155
Kino, Father Eusebio Francisco, 25, 81-82
Kiwanis Clubs of Southwest, 37, 273
Knights of Labor, 46
Krapp, George Philip, 293-294
Kupper, Winifred, 145, 150

La Bahia Mission, 84
LaFollette Committee, 191
Lamy, Bishop, 70, 119
Lara, de, José, 36
Larrazola, Octaviano A., 123
Lathers, Swift, 262-263
Laughlin, Ruth, 24, 72, 147, 301-302, 304
Laves, Walter H., 237
League of United Latin-American Citizens, 88, 272
Leon, de, José, 166
León, de, Ponce, 21

INDEX

Lesinsky, Henry, 143
Lewis, Lloyd, 103
Lewis, Tracy Hammond, 111, 113
Leyvas, Henry, 228-233
Liberación, 202
Liga Obrera de Habla Española, 195
Little, Dr. Wilson, 285
Llanes, Balton, 261
Lockwood, Dr. Frank C., 32, 125
Long, Haniel, 68, 70, 71
López, Clement, 127
López, Francisco, 134
López, Ignacio, 280, 282
López, José Mendoza, 261
López, Olibama, 95-96
Lorain, Ohio
   Mexicans in, 184, 222-223
Los Angeles, 35-42, 57, 98, 158, 159-160, 169, 174, 193, 204-205, 221, 223-258, 261, 264-265, 272-273, 277, 283-284, 294
   Council of Civic Unity, 255
   Daily News, 246, 248, 251, 254
   Eastside Journal, 249, 258
   Examiner, 192, 277
   First Unitarian Church of, 232-233
   Herald-Express, 246, 248, 251
   Juvenile Court, 253, 254
   Times, 36-37, 40-41, 190, 192-193, 231, 251, 252-253, 255-256
Louisiana
   Spanish people in, 44
Louisiana Purchase, 26
Lowrie, Dr. Samuel Harman, 99-100
Lubin, Simon J., 190
Lucey, Archbishop, 271, 278
Lulac Movement, 88
Lummis, Charles Fletcher, 49, 150, 166, 287

McClintock, James H., 138
McCormick, Mr. and Mrs. Cyrus, 285
McCormick, LaRue, 232
McCormick, Judge Paul J., 282
McGroarty, John Steven, 40
McNelly, Capt., 107

Magoffin, James W., 117
Magon, Enrique, 202-205
Magon, Ricardo Flores, 202-205
Mandin, Father, 200-201
Mandujano, Telesforo, 183
Maravilla, Los Angeles, 224-226, 255, 264
Marcos, Fray, 22-23, 24
Marmaduke, 131
Marshall, James W., 134

Martí, José, 45-46
Martínez, Alfred Ramos, 276
Martínez, Joe, 259-260
Martínez, Father José Antonio, 118-119
Marvin, George, 112
Matuz, John, 230
Meade, Lt. George C., 103
Medellin, Roberto, 270
Medina, de, Bartolomé, 139
Melendes, Edward, 263
Melendez, Jack, 230
Meline, Col. J. F., 75
Mencken, H. L., 74, 293-294, 298
Méndez, Gonzalo, 280-283
Mendoza, Viceroy, 22, 23
Mesa, Antonio, 36
Mesilla Riots, 123
Metcalfe Copper Mines, 197
Mexicans in the United States
   advancements, recent, made in Anglo relations with, 264, 275-288
   agricultural workers, as, 78, 157-158, 162-164, 175-183, 185-187, 190-193, 215, 218, 266-269
   assimilation of, 52, 99, 132, 188, 189, 194-195, 210-226, 260, 282, 290-304
   cattle- and sheep-hands, as, 69-70, 76-77, 85, 148-156, 170, 180, 194, 304
   citizenship of, 51, 87-88, 117, 220-222, 261, 283
   cotton-field hands, as, 169-174, 177-178
   culture of, 35-304
   depression, effects upon, 55, 78, 172, 184-185, 241-242
   discrimination against, and oppression of, 36-43, 47, 57, 79, 98-144, 168-174, 177-199, 201-202, 206-221, 223-258, 260-274, 276, 279, 280-284, 298-299, 301
   educational facilities for, 68, 79, 123, 124, 132, 167, 171-172, 195, 216-217, 219-221, 240, 255, 269, 272, 277, 279, 280-286, 298-299
   housing of, 167-168, 169, 170, 173, 191, 194, 216, 217-220, 222, 223-225, 299
   industry, exclusion from specialized, 184-185, 198, 215-216, 220, 233, 267
   "juvenile delinquency," so called, among, 227-258
   labor, exploitation of, 140, 143-144, 150-151, 168, 170-174, 177-199, 203, 215-217, 220, 233, 253, 267-268
   Midwest, in the, 55, 168, 178, 184-185, 221-223
   mining-hands, as, 42, 78, 83, 135-144, 162-164, 179, 186, 195-198, 203, 215

Mexicans in the United States (*continued*)
  police brutality to, 192-193, 229-230, 248-249, 253-255, 257, 262-263
  political significance of, 220-221, 279
  railroad-hands, as, 42, 75-76, 78, 83, 126, 162-164, 167-169, 178, 179, 186, 215, 222, 223, 253, 268
  relief rolls, on, 78, 174, 193, 241, 287
  religion of, 65-66, 71, 100, 103, 121, 298
  repatriation, forced, to Mexico, 55, 174, 184-185, 191, 193-195, 241
  slavery, opposition to, 100, 105-106
  smuggling of Mexican labor over border, 175, 179, 220, 268-269, 271, 300
  "Spaniards," so-called, set apart from, 37-43, 47, 78-79, 89, 124, 209-211, 234, 255
  trade-unionism of, 189-199, 213, 217
  World War II
    effect upon, 227-228, 259, 260-261
    importation of workers from Mexico, 237, 265-268, 272, 300
    participation in, 198, 232, 237, 258-262, 279, 280, 284
Mexico
  annexation of territories of, by U.S., 19, 51-62, 90, 102-103, 116-117, 207, 264, 294, 297
  First Liberal Congress, 202
  fraternity with Mexicans in U.S., 263-266, 269-271, 273
  immigration from, to U.S., 42, 55, 58-59, 60, 67, 79, 83, 85, 94, 162-163, 168-171, 173-174, 178-179, 181, 183, 184-187, 189-190, 206, 209-226, 235, 266-269, 271, 275, 290, 300, 303
  labor movement in, 203, 205
  League of Nations, and the, 113
  liberation from Spanish rule, 19, 69, 82, 84-85, 86, 151
  Madero Revolution, 203-205
  Mexican-American War of 1846, 59, 86-87, 98, 102-103, 110, 117, 127, 129, 130, 132, 134, 139, 275, 294
  Mexican Chamber of Deputies, 205
  Mexican Liberal Party, 202, 204-205
  Pershing Expedition in, 112
  revolution in, 100, 104, 111-112, 170, 202-205
  Sinarquista movement in, 264-265
  U.S. governmental relations with, 59-62, 99, 102-104, 108, 109, 112-114, 185, 205, 208, 251, 256-257, 261, 263-266, 269-275
  World War II, part played in, by, 237, 256, 265-266

Miami Copper Company, 197
Michella, Sister Anna, 201
Mining law and codes in the U.S., 141-142
Mirabal, Sylvestre, 150
Mitchell, J. J., 37, 40
Montano, Don Pedro, 126
Montenegro, Eugene Chavez, Jr., 253-254
Monteros, de los, Antonio Espiñosa, 273
Montgomery, Dr. Robert H., 171
Montoya, Pablo, 118
Mooney, Archbishop, 222
Morenci Copper Mine, 196, 197
Moreno, Antonio, 130
Moreno, José, 36
Morgan Hill Gold Mine, 137
Mowry, Sylvester, 83, 143, 196
Murieta, Joaquín, 128, 130
Murray, Churchill, 257

Nacogdoches, 84
Nacozari Copper Mine, 196
Narváez, de, Pánfilo, 21
National Association for the Advancement of Colored People, 282
National Catholic Welfare Conference, 277-278
National Lawyers Guild, 282
National Resources Committee, 56
National Tube Company (U.S. Steel), 184, 222
National War Labor Board, 197-198
Native American Party, 103
Native Sons of the Golden West, 39
Navajo Indians, 33, 67-69, 71, 147
Navarro, Antonio, 36
Negroes
  discrimination against, 47, 194-195, 197, 221, 222, 224, 248-250, 256, 270, 272-273, 283
  Harlem riots, 256
  slaves escaping into Mexico, 105
Neve, de, Felipe, 256
New Almaden Mine, 139-140
New Mexico
  agricultural development of, 69, 76, 157-159
  atomic research in, 304
  cattle-raising in, 69-70, 76, 119, 156
  cotton-growing in, 174
  Court of Private Land Claims, 77
  handicrafts of, 71-74, 287, 301
  Highlands University, 285
  Indians in, 63-74, 80, 83, 93, 94, 117
  Mexicans in, 43-44, 51-56, 59, 63-81, 83, 88, 91, 93, 94-97, 116-125, 142-144, 148-151, 158, 163, 174, 181, 195,

INDEX

198, 208-209, 259-260, 276-277, 284-285, 287-288, 290, 291-292, 294, 298, 300-302, 304
mining in, 142-144, 195, 198
National Guard, 200th and 515th Coast Artillery units of, 259
New Deal agencies in, 287-288
Revolt of 1846, 118-119
sheep-raising in, 68, 71, 76, 77-78, 91, 144-151, 152, 304
Spanish exploration and settlement of, 22, 24-31, 63-64, 67, 81, 94
statehood, status of, 51-52, 63, 83, 121-122
University of, 46, 79, 276, 277, 284-285
versus Texas, 59, 117, 119-121
Newmark, Harris, 115
Nogueros, Eugenio, 282
North Town, Calif., 218
Noyola, Ricardo, 260
Nuestra Señora de los Dolores Mission, 81
Núñez, Rev. R. N., 282
Nunn, Guy T., 237

O'Brien, Robert O., 222-223
Ochoa, Estevan, 167
Office of the Coordinator of Inter-American Affairs, 173, 237-238, 257, 275-279
Olivares, Trueba, 264
Olmstead, Frederick Law, 114, 131
Oñate, de, Juan, 24-26, 41, 42, 67, 102, 144, 162, 288
O'Neil, Owen, 92
Opata Indians, 22
Ord, Gen., 108
Orozco, 204
Ortega, Dr. Joaquín, 46, 63, 276, 284, 298-299, 300-301
Otero, Manuel, 120
Ovideo, 21

Pacheco, Romauldo, 92
Pacific Electric Co., 169, 225
Pacific Rural Press, 190
Padilla (foreign minister), 271
Padilla, Angel, 230
Padilla, de, Fray Juan, 23-24
Padua Institute, 40
Pallares, Jesús, 195
Pan-American Union, 266
Panhandle, Staked Plains of the, 96-97, 120-121, 190
Papago Indians, 82
Paredes, Ignacio, 137-138
Partido Revolucionario Cubano, 46
Paul, Dr. Rodman W., 134, 136, 140

Paz, Frank M., 280
Pearce, T. M., 294
Pelagio, Tiofilo, 254
Perea, Francisco, 119
Perea, Don José Leandro, 150
Perez, Manuel, 260
Perry, George Sessions, 155
Peterson, Mrs. Helen L., 279-280
Phelps-Dodge Company, 197
Pignatelli, Princess Conchita, 277
Pijoan, Jane W., 277
Pijoan, Dr. Michael, 279
Pima Indians, 22-23, 82
Pino, Don Pedro, 69
Pittsburgh
  Mexicans in, 178
Pooler, James S., 263
Prescott Copper Mines, 196
Press, effect of, upon riots in California, 227-231, 237-238, 243, 245-258
Pressley, Charles E., 37
Price, Col., 118
Procopio, 130
Pryce, Rhys, 204
Pueblo Indians, 25, 29-31, 49, 52-53, 64, 67-71, 93, 157, 209, 284-285, 301-302
Puerto Ricans, living in U.S., 45, 267

Ramirez, Catrarino, 183
Ramirez, de, Raoul, 36
Rangel, Antonio, 271
Reclamation Act of 1902, 76, 175
Redfield, Dr. Robert, 212
Reed, Joseph F., 235-236
Regeneración, 202
Reid, Hugo, 135
Resistencia, La, 46
Revolt of the Yaquis, 199-200
Reyes, Manuel, 230
Richardson, Rupert N., 49
Rio Grande River and Valley, 49, 56, 59-61, 64, 84-87, 100, 101, 104, 106-110, 119, 120, 157, 162, 169-171, 175-179, 194, 260, 261, 287, 296
Rippy, J. Fred, 61-62
Rister, Carl C., 49
Robert, Edward, 93
Robinson, Capt. Alfred, 37
Robinson, Will H., 143, 197
Rock Island Railway, 168
Rockefeller, Nelson, 238, 257, 275-276
Rocky Ford Service Club, 280
Rodríguez, Pablo, 36
Romero, Casimero, 97
Romero, José, 155
Roosevelt, Eleanor, 256

INDEX

Roosevelt, Franklin D., 256-257, 264, 275, 287-288
Rosas, Alejandro, 36
Rosas, Basilio, 36
Ross, Fred W., 219, 220, 280, 283
Rosskelly, Dr. R. W., 194
Rotarian Clubs of Southwest, 37, 40, 273
Royce, Josiah, 128, 129, 289
Ruiz, Chepe, 230
Russell, John, 65, 150
Ruxton, George F., 119

Saguaripa, Jesus, 127
St. Louis, Brownsville and Mexico Railway, 87, 175
St. Louis *Star-Times,* 263
Salinas, 204
Salt War, 1877, 111
San Antonio Mission, 84
San Fernando Valley Council on Race Relations, 254-255
San Gabriel Mission, 40, 88, 218
San Joaquin Valley, Calif., 174, 177, 191
San Jose Mission, 139, 152
San Jose Training School, 285
San Luis Valley, 56, 95-96
San Xavier del Bac Mission, 82
Sanchez, Dr. George I., 42-43, 54, 241, 272, 276, 285
Santa Anna, 101
Santa Barbara *Guide,* 39-40
Santa Fe Railway, 167-169
"Santa Fe Ring," 122-124
Santa Fe Trail, 50, 53, 72, 75, 83, 115-117, 132, 167
Santa Gertrudis Rancho, Calif., 92
Santa Rita Silver and Copper Mine, 142, 143
Saposs, David, 276
Schreiter, Oskar Hellmuth, 264
Schwartz, Dr. Harry, 176
Scott, Gen. Winfield, 102
Seibold, Doris K., 296
Semple, Ellen Churchill, 60
Serra, Father Junípero, 24, 41, 288
Shell Oil Company, 198
Sherrick, Isabel, 223
Shinn, Charles Howard, 156
Shoshone Indians, 166
Sierra Madre Republic, 104
Silex, Humberto, 198-199
Simpson, Lt. J. H., 149
Sinarquista movement, 264-265
Slayden, James L., 179
Sleepy Lagoon Case, 228-233, 237-238, 253, 256

Smith, Sarah Bixby, 149
Socialist Party, 204
Soil Conservation Service, 287
Southern California Council on Inter-American Affairs, 276-277
Southern Pacific Railway, 126, 164, 167-169
Southwest, the American
  agricultural development of, 32-35, 69, 76, 83, 87, 90, 93, 94, 96, 157-161, 162, 164, 175-183, 184-187, 189-194, 215, 266-269
  Anglo-American occupation and rule in, 36-44, 51-62, 69, 75-80, 83-88, 92-94, 97, 98-144, 153, 155, 157-160, 167-304
  architectural patterns of, 32, 69, 71, 73, 86, 94, 223, 252, 295, 301-302
  borders of, artificiality of, in view of ethnics of people, etc., 36-43, 47, 48-62, 75, 98, 110, 207-208, 222, 286, 289-290, 302-304
  cattle-raising in, 32, 69-70, 76, 83, 85, 91-93, 94, 97, 108-110, 111-112, 119, 125-126, 130, 151-156, 157, 160, 161, 170-171
  church, role of, in, 30, 32, 65-66, 68, 70, 81-84, 88, 90, 91, 118-119, 121, 124, 199-200, 213, 271-272, 277-278
  climate and natural environment of, 32, 48-50, 88, 145, 177-178, 186, 294-295, 297
  copper-mines of, 83, 142-144, 157, 161, 163, 195-198, 203, 215, 217
  cotton grown in, 33, 162, 164, 169-174, 177-178, 182, 187, 268
  culture of, 19-304
  education in, 41, 68-69, 71, 75, 79, 89, 123, 124, 132, 142, 167, 171-172, 195, 213, 216-217, 219-221, 240, 255, 269, 272, 277, 279, 280-286, 298-299
  ethnics of peoples of, 19-20, 36, 42-44, 47, 54-65, 67-68, 70-71, 75, 78-80, 84-87, 89-91, 94-95, 116, 121, 125, 208-209, 281-282, 290, 297
  feudalism and caste-system of, 38, 66-79, 85-87, 89-93, 96, 102, 121-125, 128-129, 131, 132, 146, 150-151, 155, 170-174, 190, 194, 196, 213, 220, 304
  fiesta-time in borderland cities of, 35-41, 127
  gold-mines of, 42, 50-51, 57, 91, 102, 127-130, 134-142, 144, 157, 161
  grass-roots democracy promoted by organizations to aid Mexicans in, 277-286

INDEX

handicrafts of, 33, 71-74, 147, 287, 301
intermarriage among Mexican, Indian, Spanish and Anglo-American peoples of, 36, 37, 42, 61, 65, 67-68, 75, 86-87, 90-91, 93, 116, 118, 125, 128, 281-282, 297
irrigation of lands of, 32, 64, 70, 87, 157-161, 174-177, 294, 301
land-grabbing by Anglo-Americans in, 76-78, 85, 93, 107, 110, 120, 122, 127, 130
land-use system of, 32, 76-77, 146, 159-160
language of, 19, 32, 41, 42, 71, 74, 86, 87, 93, 99-100, 115-116, 138, 153-156, 166, 176, 187, 207-208, 214, 242, 252, 282, 285, 290-301
lynchings in, 111-113, 126-128, 130-131
mission-system of, 25, 30, 42, 56, 70, 81-84, 88, 89, 91, 135, 152, 161, 288
music, folk-, of the, 148-149, 155, 252
pack-trains of, 106, 142, 143, 164-167, 303
political corruption of, 77, 86, 96, 110, 121-124, 127, 132, 150, 155, 190
poverty of peoples of, 65, 66, 68, 71-72, 75, 77-78, 79, 85, 124, 150-151, 162-163, 168, 183, 191, 194, 196, 212
property rights, between husband and wife, in, 160-161
quicksilver-mining in, 139-140
railroads, development of, in, 42, 51, 64, 75-76, 83, 87, 119, 126, 162, 164-165, 167-169, 178, 215, 223, 253, 268, 297
romanticism concerning origins of, 19, 35-43, 209, 234, 255
sheep-raising in, 44-45, 68, 76, 77-78, 91-93, 126, 144-151, 157, 160, 161, 180
silver-craft in, 33, 72
silver-mines of, 102, 138-140, 142, 144, 157, 161
sugar-beet industry of, 56, 147, 164, 177-178, 180-183, 184-185, 186, 187, 190, 215, 217, 222, 267, 268
weaving in, 33, 71, 72, 147, 301
Southwestern Council on the Education of the Spanish-Speaking Peoples, 286
Spain
culture of, brought to the Americas, 19-34, 49-54, 71-74, 80, 93-94, 95-96, 133-134, 138, 141-142, 144-147, 153-161, 164-166, 177, 243, 288, 301
exploration and colonization of Southwestern America, 19-35, 41, 42, 49-51, 52, 56, 63-64, 67, 73, 74-75, 76, 81-82, 84, 88-89, 94, 102, 133-134, 138, 139, 144-145, 151-152, 157, 162-163, 164, 243, 256, 288
immigration of Spaniards to U.S. (post-colonization), 20, 44-47, 74-75
Spanish-American War, 154, 166, 259, 296
Spanish-Speaking People's Division of the Office of Inter-American Affairs, 276-279
Steele, Gen., 109
Stevens, Hiram S., 125
Stevens, Thaddeus, 121
Stevenson, Coke, 269-271
Stilwell, Hart, 175, 273
Sunol, Antonio, 139

Taffola, José, 97
Taylor, Dr. Paul S., 105-106, 108, 109, 176, 184, 191, 225
Taylor, Ralph, 190
Telles, Robert, 230
Tenney, Senator Jack, 232-233
Texas
agricultural development of, 87, 176, 178-179, 187
cattle- and sheep-raising in, 85, 108-110, 125-126, 149, 152-156, 170-171, 194
Committee on Inter-American Relations, 285
cotton-growing in, 169-173, 182
Emigrant Agent Law of 1929, 182, 185
Good Neighbor Commission, 173, 270-271, 286
Institute of Latin-American Studies, 286
Mexicans in, 51-61, 76, 78, 81, 84-88, 94, 96-97, 98-114, 116-117, 155, 163, 169-173, 176, 178-179, 182-183, 184, 187, 194, 198, 205, 212, 216, 220, 256, 260-261, 263-264, 269-273, 276, 285-286
ranches, large, in, 85, 155
Rangers, 107, 108, 111-113
Republic, as a, 101-102, 117
revolution in, 100-102
Spanish exploration and settlement of, 24-26, 30, 81, 84, 94
University of, 272, 276, 285-286
versus New Mexico, 59, 117, 119-121
violence in, 100-114, 116-117, 127
Thompson, Charles A., 220
Thompson, Victor Rodman, 230
Tilden, Samuel, 109
Tisnado, Mariano, 127
Tlascalan Indians, 67
Toba, de la, Tirza, 205
Tolan Committee, 183

"Tomachic War," 199-200
Torres, Francisco, 131
Treaty of Guadalupe Hidalgo, 51-52, 59, 98, 102, 103-104, 113, 114, 117, 121, 123, 159, 207, 209, 275, 277, 288, 298
Trinchera Ranch, 96
Trujillo, Teofilo, 126
Tuck, Ruth, 280
Tumacacori Mission, 82
Turco, El, 23
Twitchell, R. E., 66, 69, 75, 76-77, 117, 122, 123, 124, 132, 150

Ugarte, Manuel, 113-114
United States Border Commission, 120
United States Steel Company, 184, 222
Unity Leagues, 280
Urquiza, José Antonio, 264
Ute Indians, 66

Vaca, de, Cabeza, 21, 24, 27
Valdez, Daniel, 285
Vargas, de, Diego, 25, 94
Variegas, José, 36
Vasconcellos, José, 101
Vásquez, Gen., 101
Vásquez, Tiburcio, 130
Velasco, de, Capt. Luis, 162-163
Ventura School for Girls, 254
Vigil, Domiciano, 118
Vigil, Vincent G., 267
Villa, Francisco, 112
Villalobos, de, Gregorio, 151
Villasenor, Pedro, 265
Villavicencio, Felix, 36
Viscáino, Sebastián, 24, 37
Vistadores, Los Rancheros, 37, 39-40

Vizetelly, 115
Voorhis, Jerry, 260
Vosburg, John C., 125

Wallace, Henry A., 237
Walter, Dr. Paul, 65
War Food Administration, 266-267
Warner, Solomon, 125
Warren, Earl, 255
Waxman, Al, 249-250, 258
Webb, Dr. Walter Prescott, 32, 61, 108, 110, 111, 155, 159, 160, 205
Welles, Sumner, 274
Wellman, Paul I., 125-126
Wells, Jim, 86
Western Federation of Labor, 196
White, Charles, 261-262
Widney, J. P., 290
Willard, Charles Dwight, 89
Williams Ranch, Calif., 228
Winchell, Walter, 261
Worcester, Donald E., 29
World War I, 42, 46, 79, 111, 180, 259, 265, 267
World War II, 198, 227-228, 232, 237, 258-268, 272, 279, 280, 284-285, 300

Ynostrosa, Henry, 230
Yudarte, 44

Zacsek, Anna, 229
Zamora, Gus, 230
Zarate, Elías, 113
Zeleny, Dr. Carolyn, 66, 67, 79, 124-125, 207
"Zoot-Suit Race Riots," 238-258, 264-265
Zuñi Indians, 23

ANDREW HILL HIGH SCHOOL